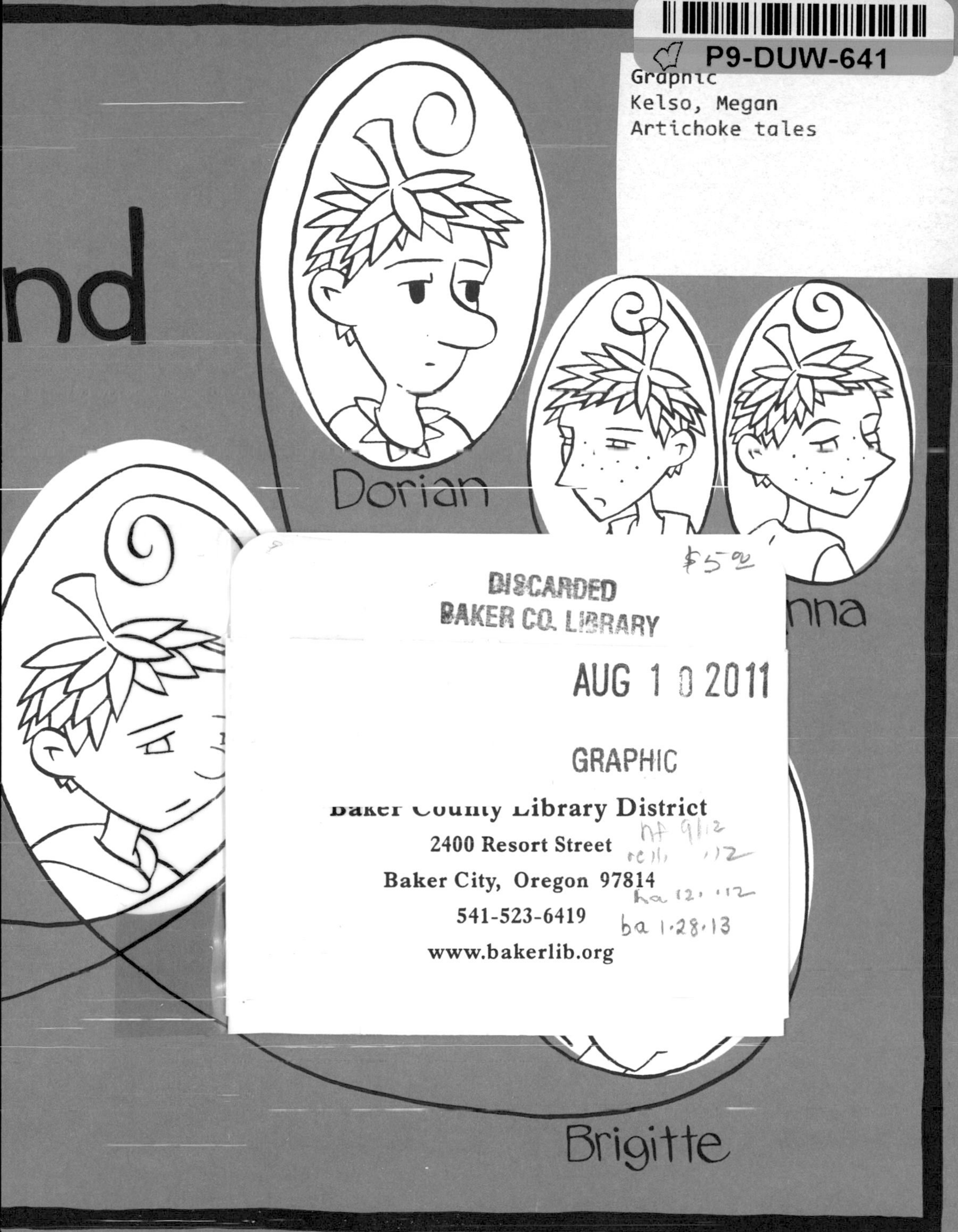
nd
Dorian
nna
Brigitte

Artichoke Tales

Also by Megan Kelso:
Queen of the Black Black (1998)
The Squirrel Mother (2006)

Fantagraphics Books
7563 Lake City Way NE
Seattle, WA 98115

Publishers: Gary Groth and Kim Thompson
Associate Publisher: Eric Reynolds
Editors: Virginia Haedt and Gary Groth
Design: Megan Kelso and Jacob Covey
Production: Paul Baresh
Publicist: Jacqueline Cohen

To receive a free full-color catalogue of comics, graphic novels, prose novels, and other fine works of artistry, call 1-800-657-1100, or visit www.fantagraphics.com. You may order books at our Web site or by phone.

Distributed in the U.S. by W.W. Norton and Co., Inc. (212-354-5500)
Distributed in Canada by the Canadian Manda Group (416-516-0911)
Distributed to comics stores by Diamond Comics Dist. (800-452-6642)
Distributed in the U.K. by Turnaround Distribution (108-829-3009)

First printing: May, 2010

ISBN: 978-1-60699-344-6

Printed in Singapore

Artichoke Tales

Megan Kelso

Fantagraphics Books
Seattle

for Virginia Carhart Haedt

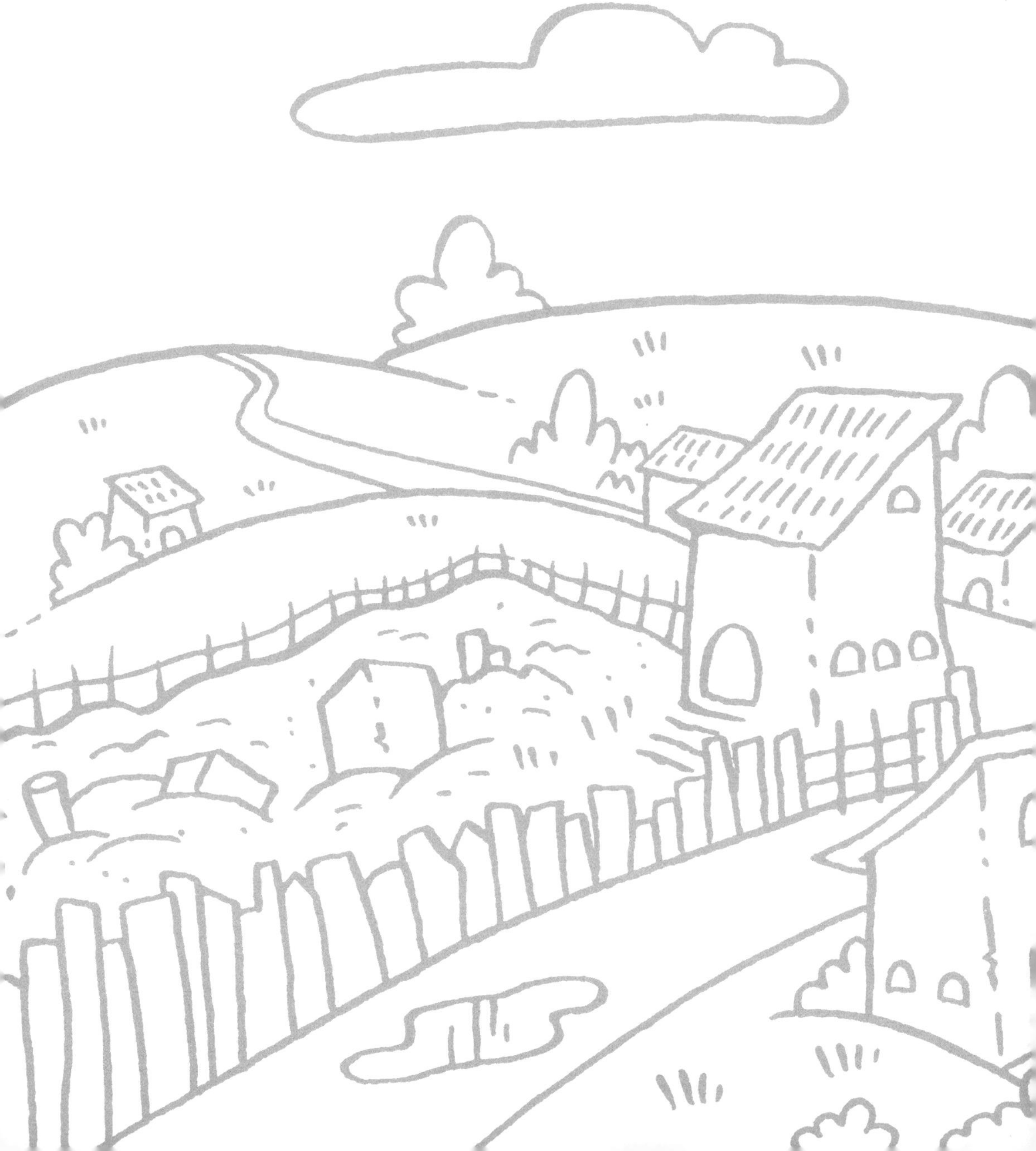

Chapter 1
RETREAT

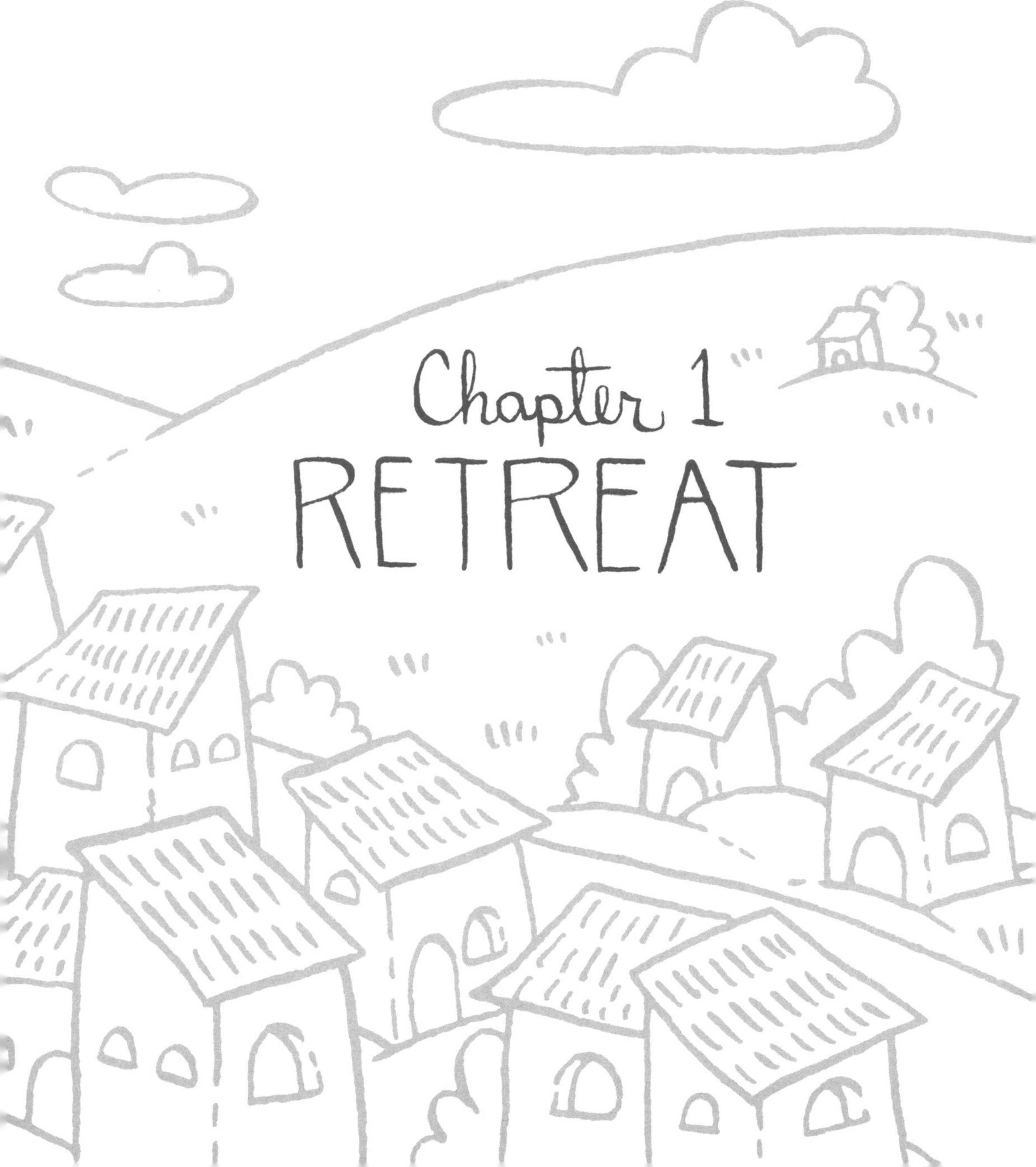

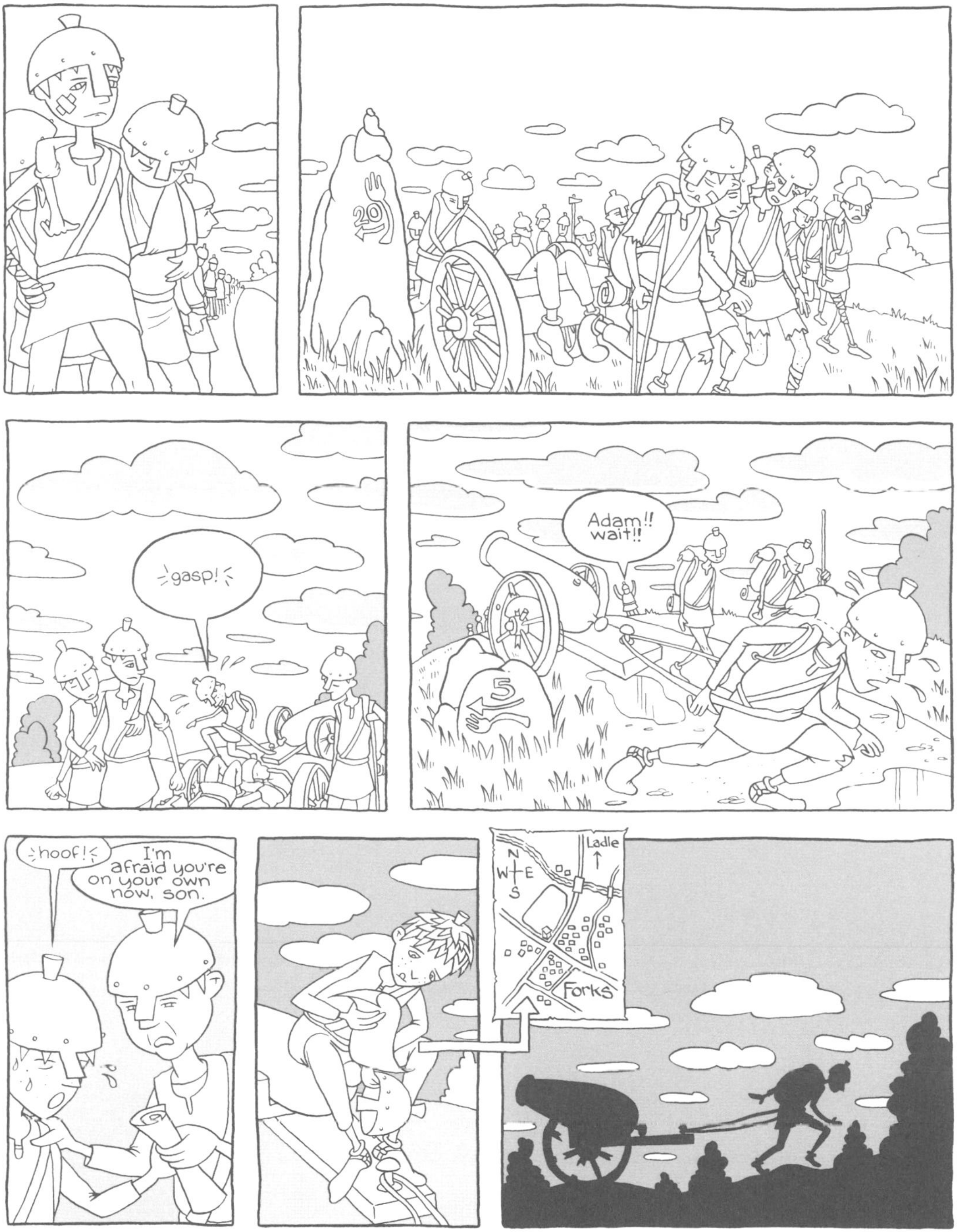
20
gasp!
Adam!!
wait!!
5
hoof!
I'm afraid you're on your own now, son.
N
W
E
S
Ladle
Forks

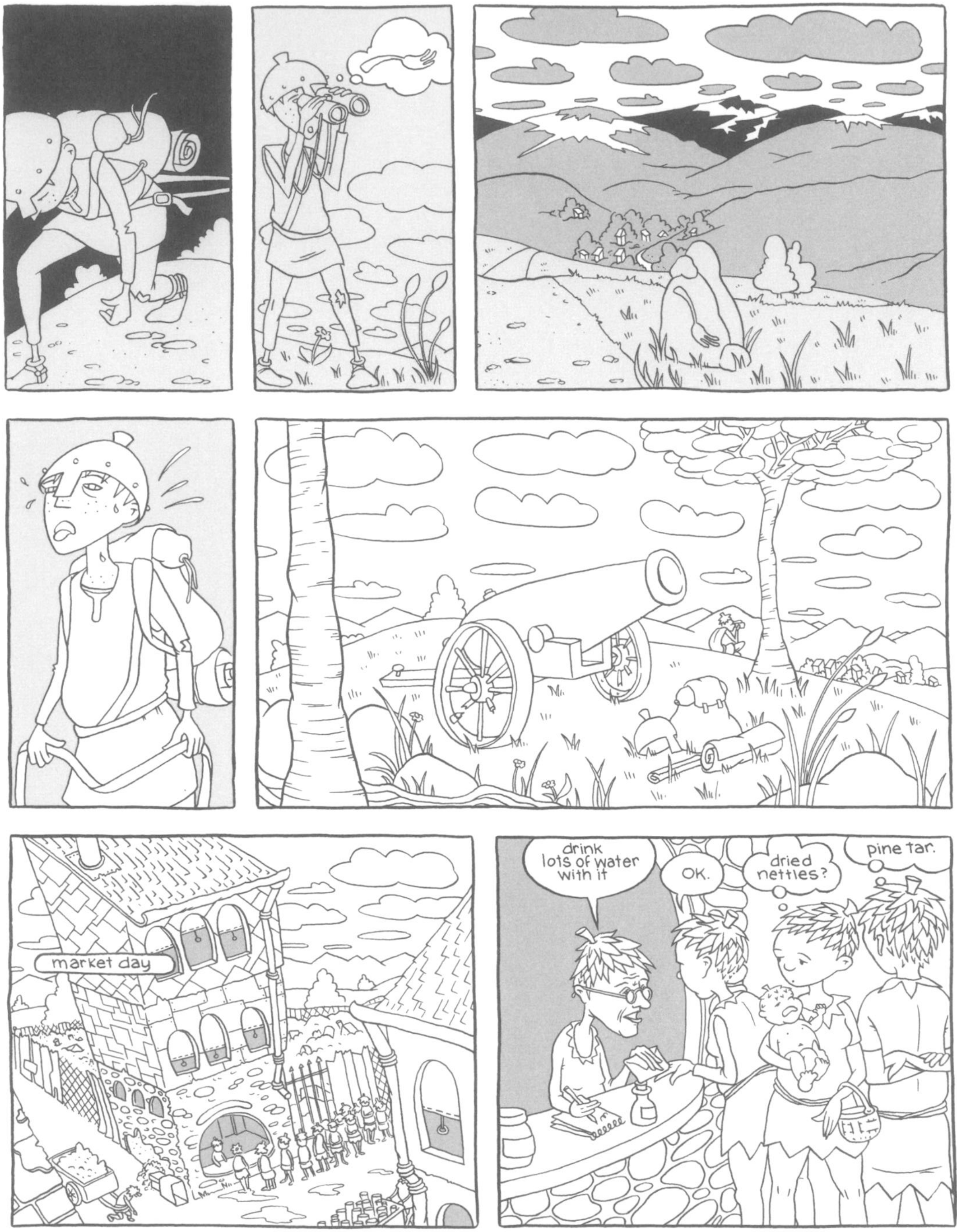
market day
drink lots of water with it
OK.
dried nettles?
pine tar.

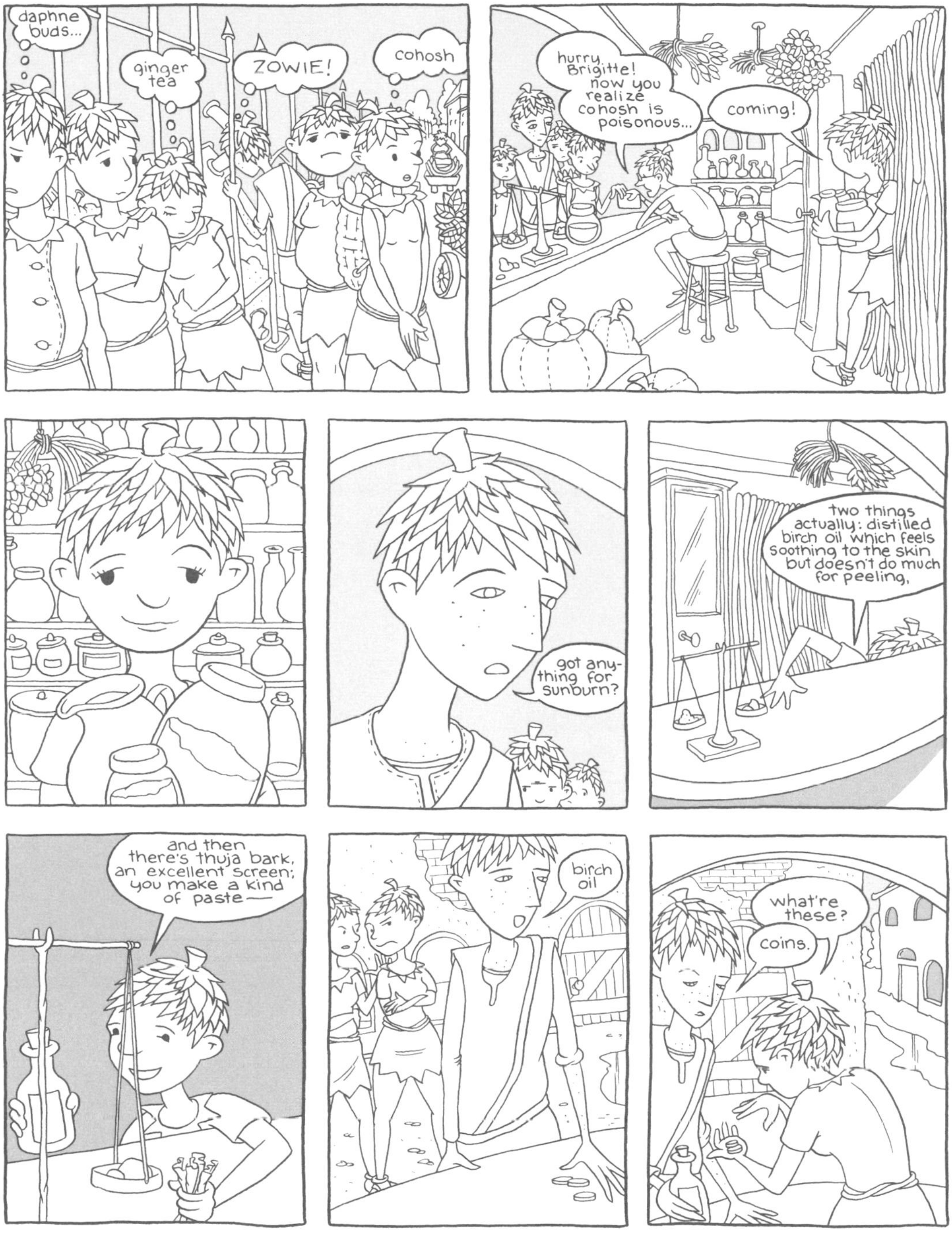
daphne buds...
ginger tea
ZOWIE!
cohosh
hurry, Brigitte! now you realize cohosh is poisonous...
coming!
got any-thing for sunburn?
two things actually: distilled birch oil which feels soothing to the skin but doesn't do much for peeling,
and then there's thuja bark, an excellent screen; you make a kind of paste—
birch oil
what're these?
coins.

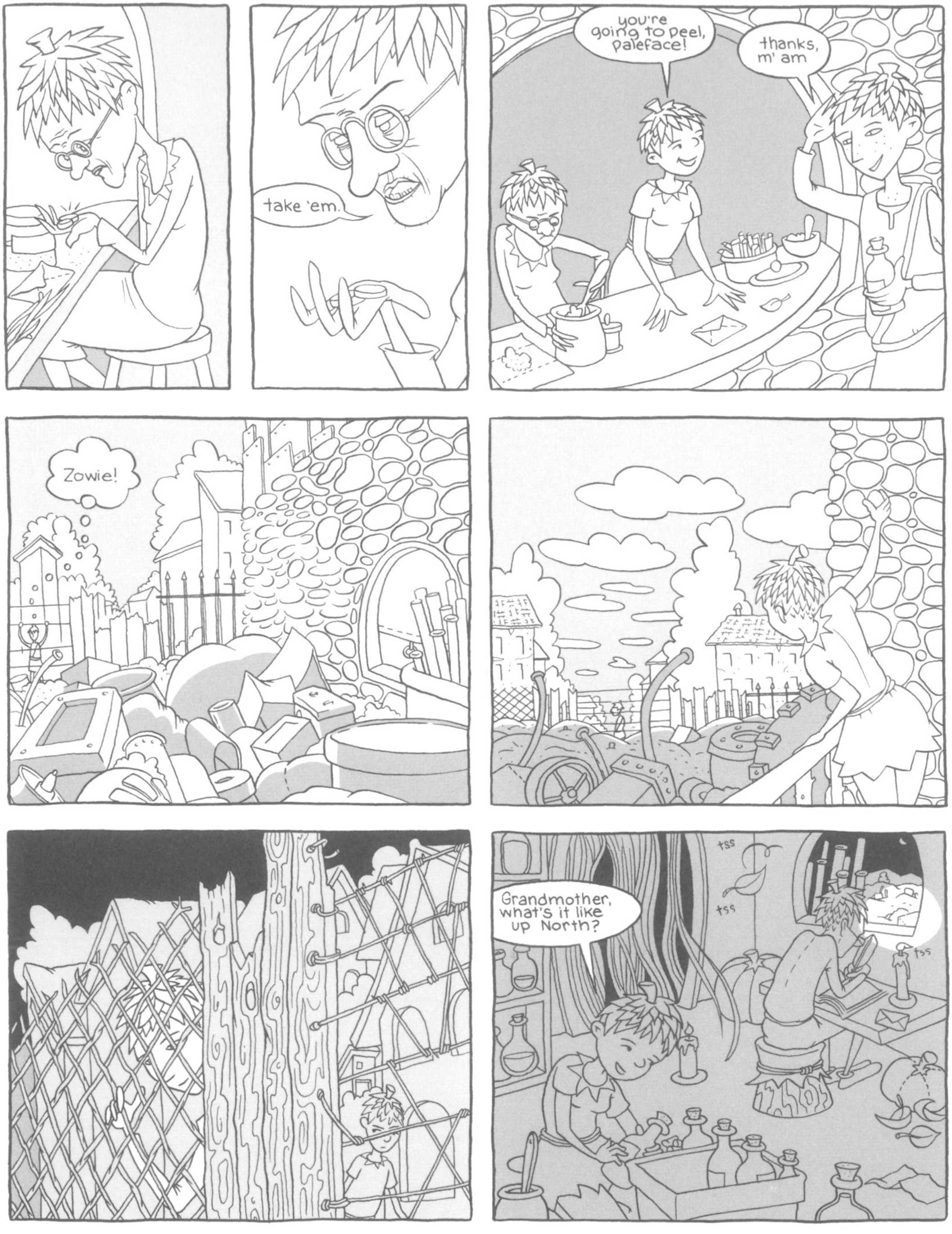
take 'em.
you're going to peel, paleface!
thanks, m' am
Zowie!
tss
tss
tss
Grandmother, what's it like up North?

fump!

cold. dirty and cold.

elsewhere.

The damp wind chills, darkness spreads as pale invaders with cold metal heads arrive to poison our land.

Our ancient dead cry, for how can warm rocks and perfumed green buds quell the mechanical ranks?

How long have we sung of our tender valleys? Our butterfly hearts, our Mother the sun?

In the small town of Ladle, we vanquished the Tyrants, forced them to flee and smashed their gun.

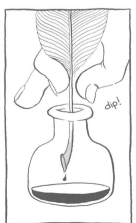

dip!

With spears and bows and torrential abandon, we defended our valleys against the cannon!

later.

foof!

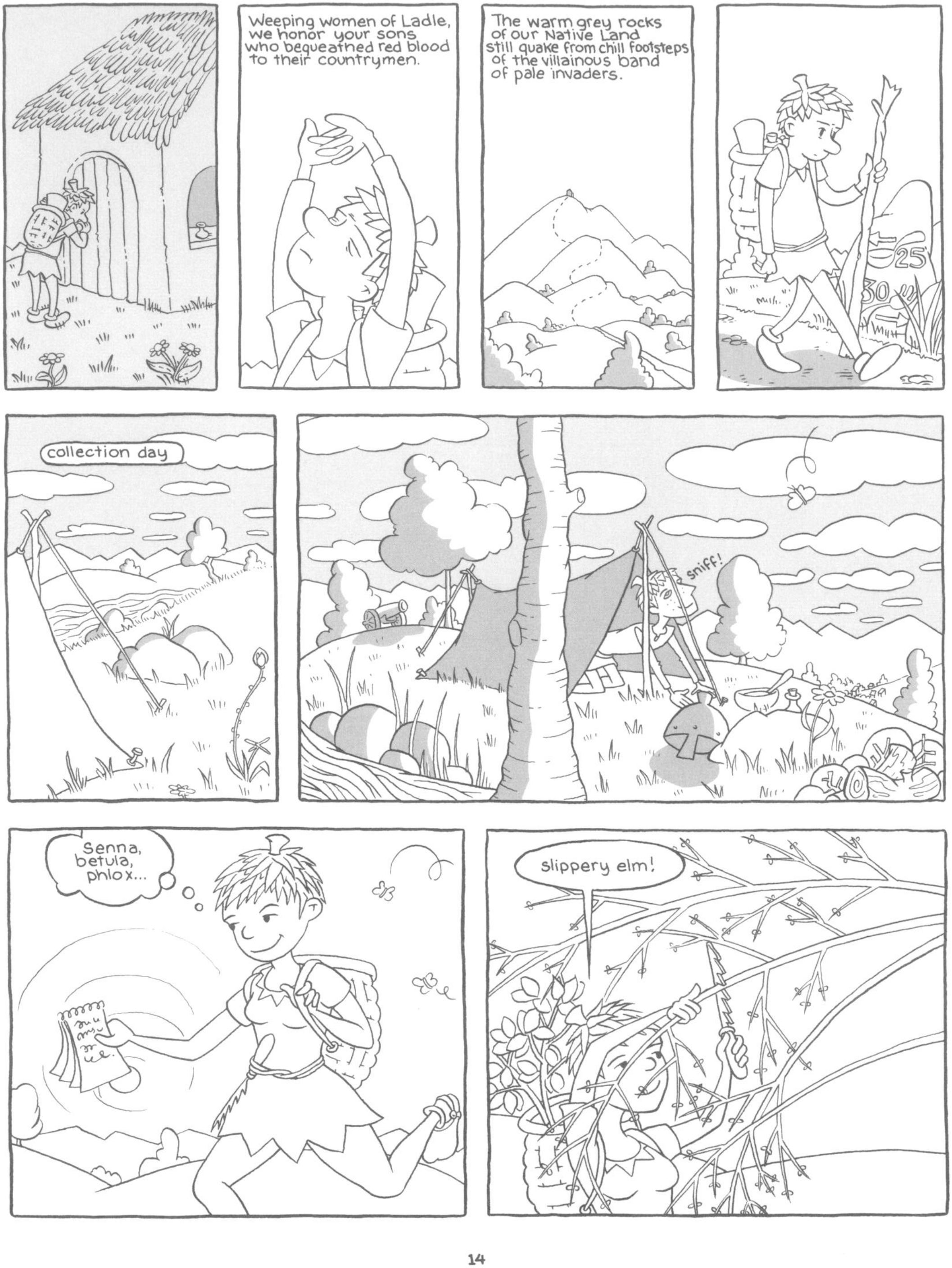
Weeping women of Ladle, we honor your sons who bequeathed red blood to their countrymen.
The warm grey rocks of our Native Land still quake from chill footsteps of the villainous band of pale invaders.
25
30
collection day
sniff!
Senna, betula, phlox...
slippery elm!

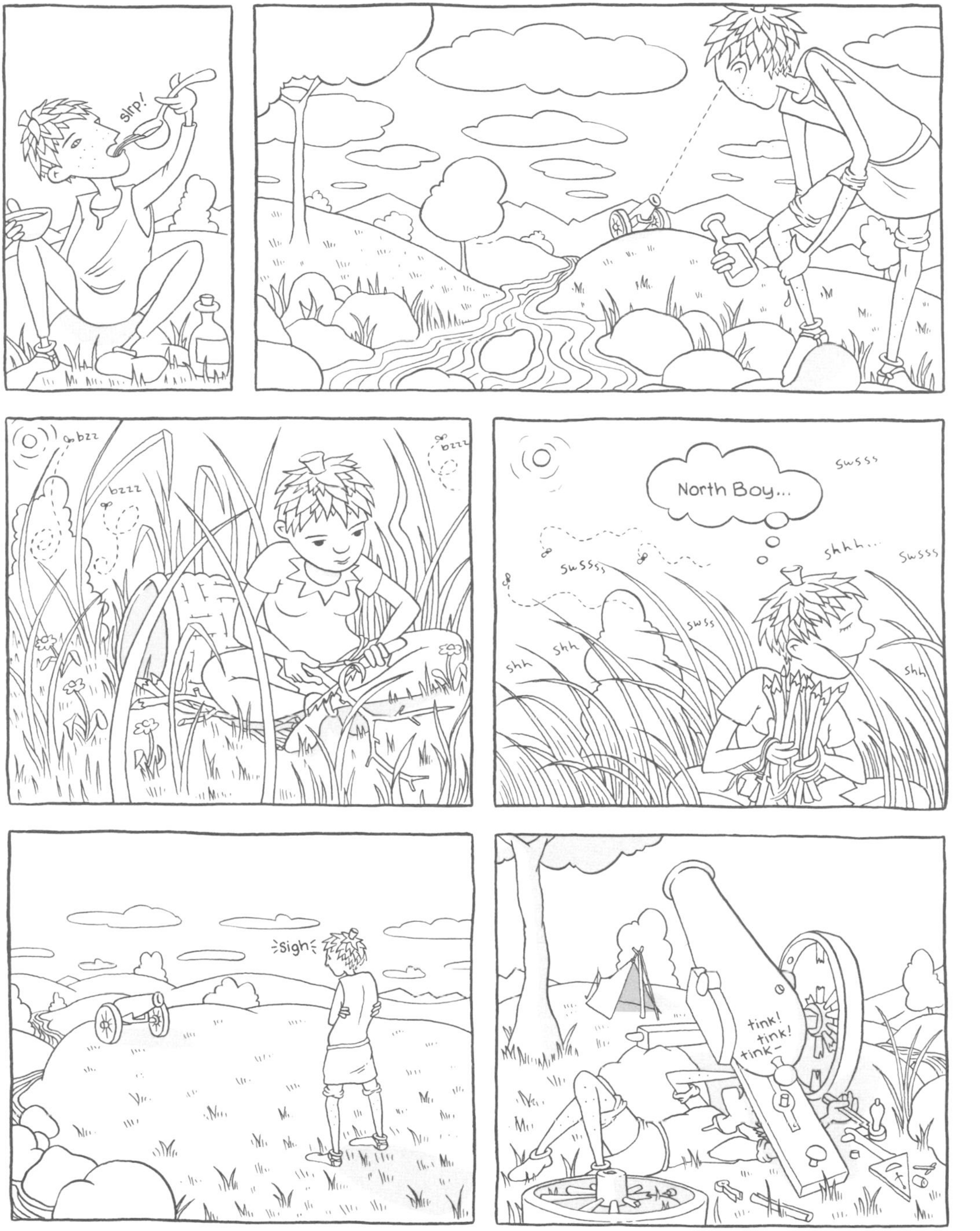
slrp!
bzz
bzzz
bzzz
North Boy...
swsss
shhh...
swsss
swsss
swss
shh
shh
shh
sigh
tink!
tink!
tink-

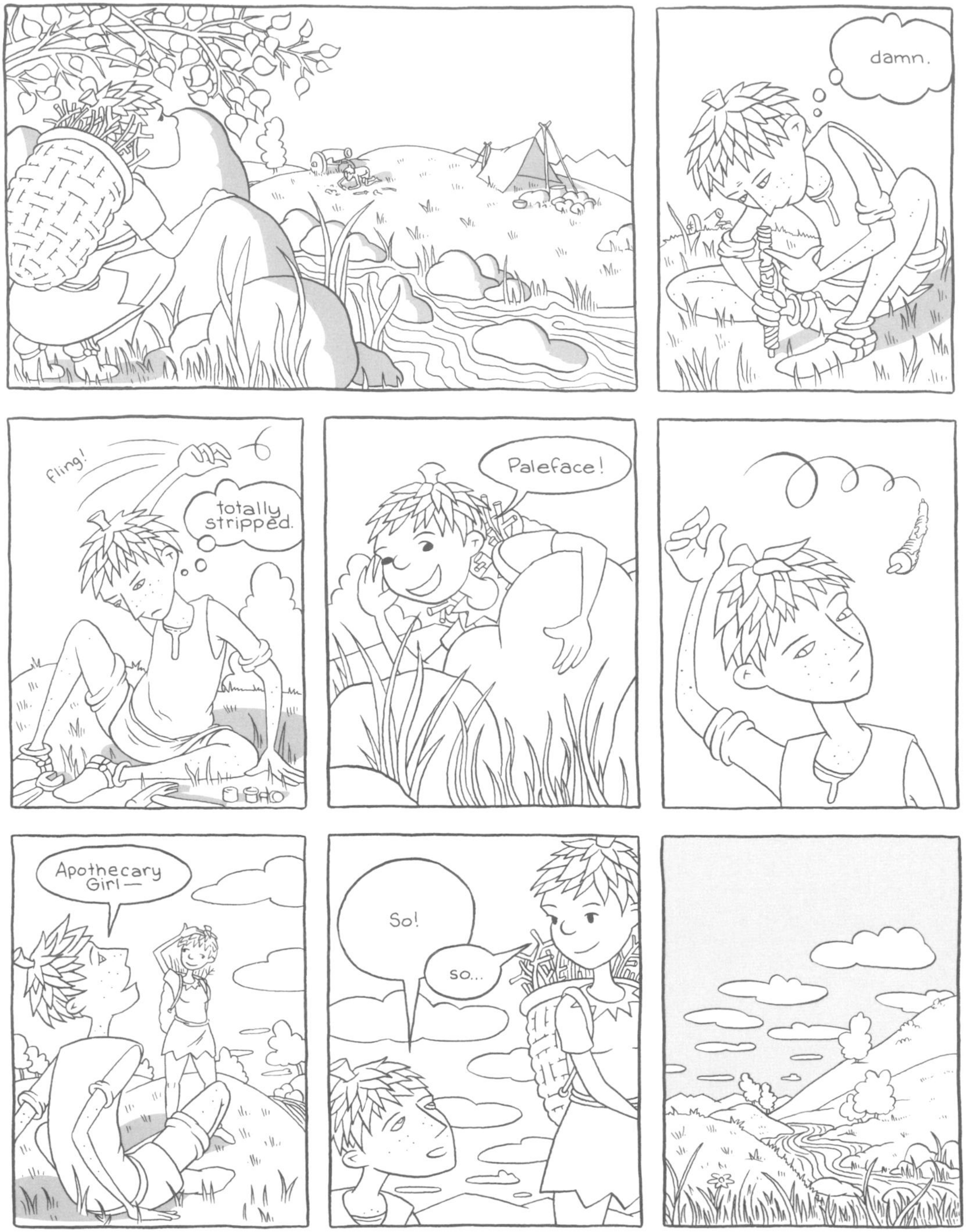
damn.
fling!
totally stripped.
Paleface!
Apothecary Girl—
So!
so...

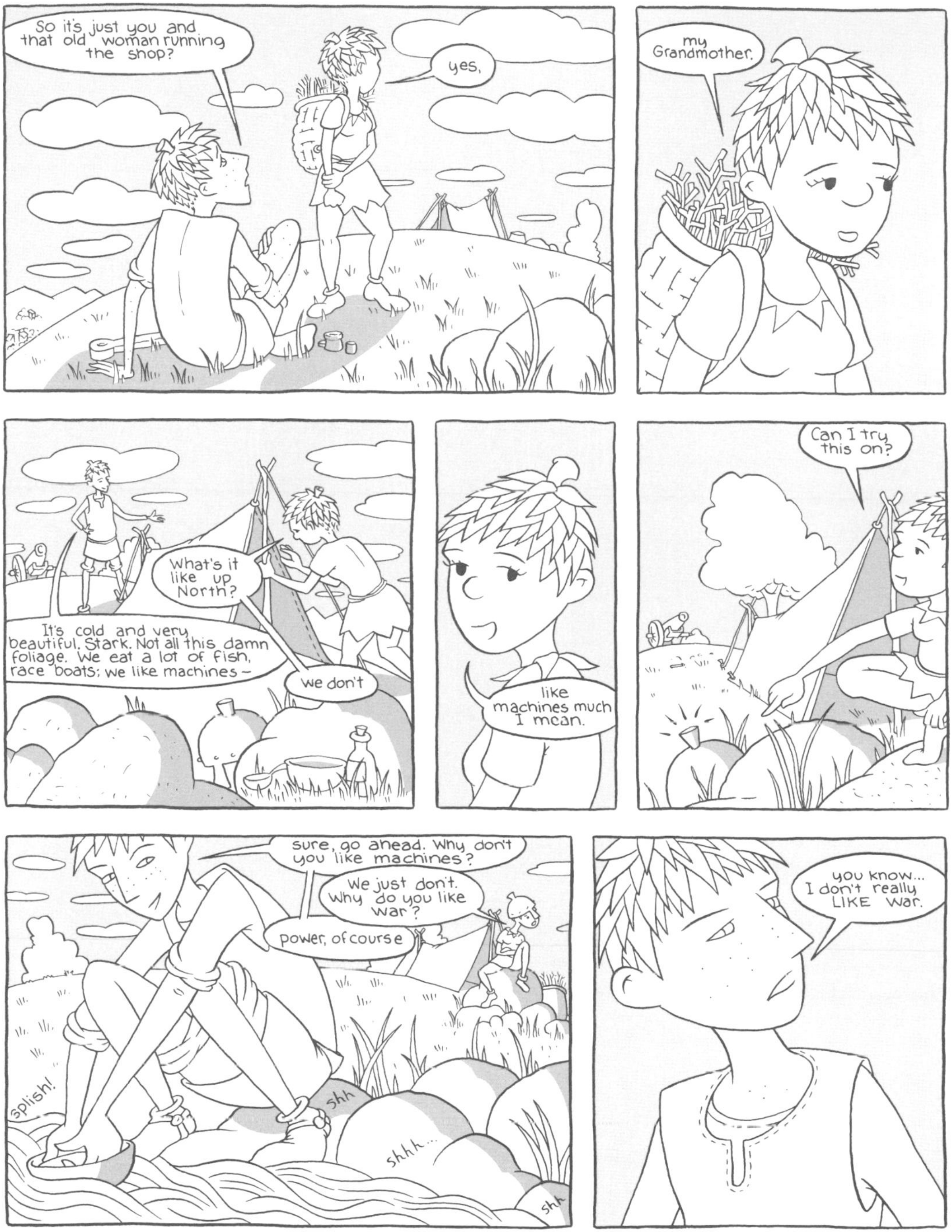
So it's just you and that old woman running the shop?
yes,
my Grandmother.
What's it like up North?
It's cold and very beautiful. Stark. Not all this damn foliage. We eat a lot of fish, race boats; we like machines~
we don't
like machines much I mean.
Can I try this on?
sure, go ahead. Why don't you like machines?
We just don't. Why do you like war?
power, of course
splish!
shh
shhh...
shh
you know... I don't really LIKE war.

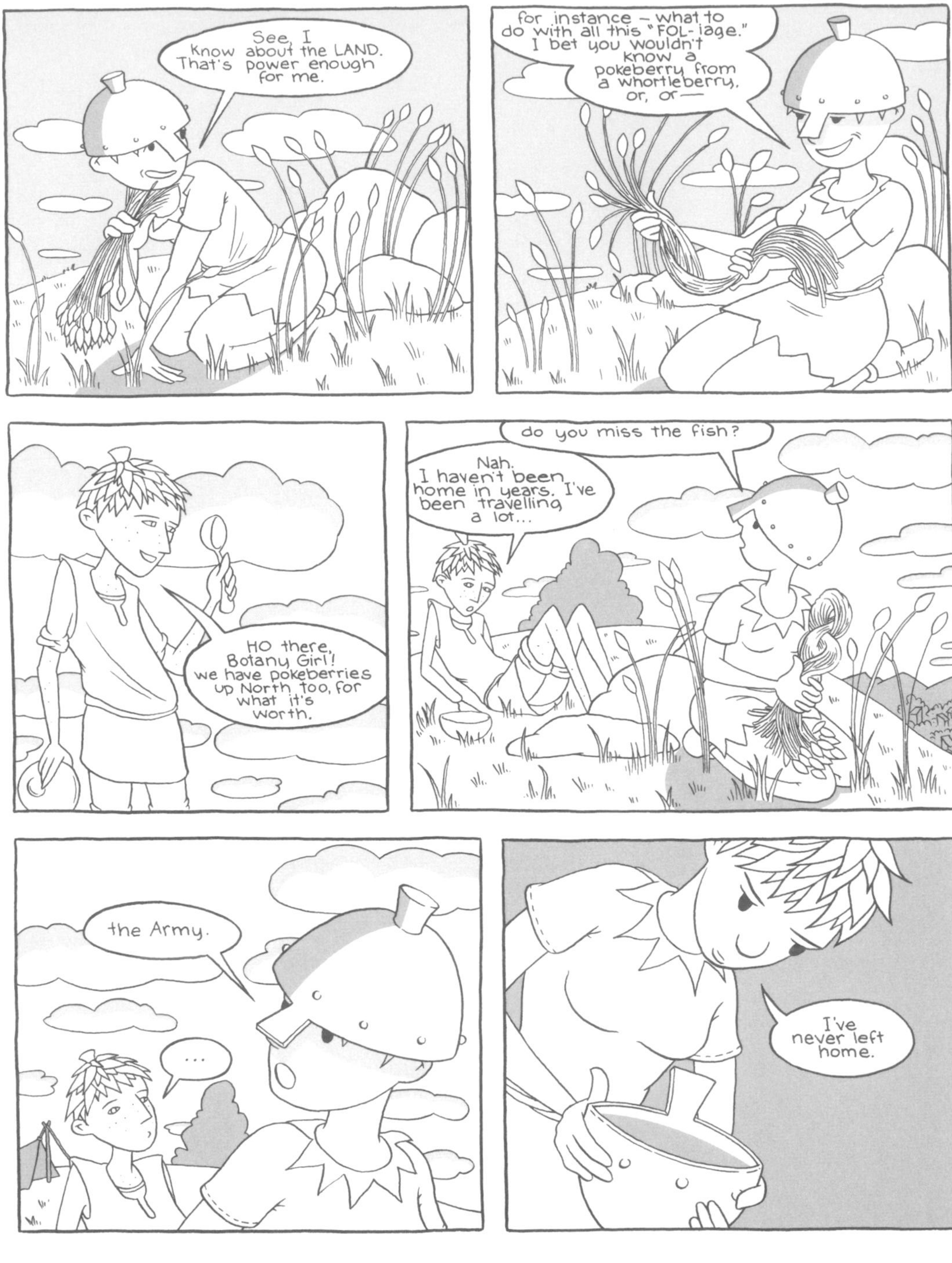
See, I know about the LAND. That's power enough for me.
for instance – what to do with all this "FOL-iage." I bet you wouldn't know a pokeberry from a whortleberry, or, or—
HO there, Botany Girl! we have pokeberries up North too, for what it's worth.
do you miss the fish?
Nah. I haven't been home in years. I've been travelling a lot...
the Army.
...
I've never left home.

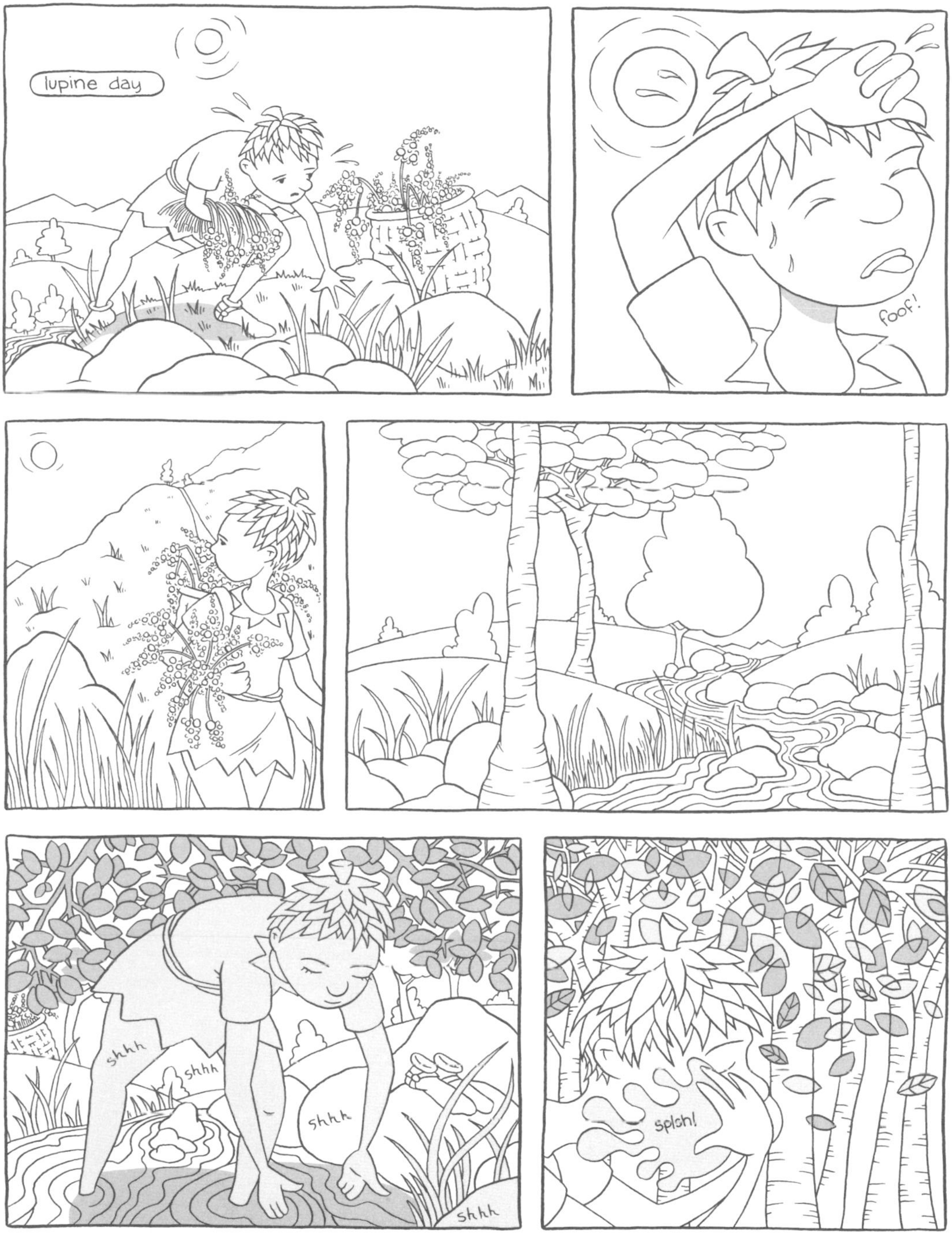
lupine day
foof!
shhh
shhh
shhh
shhh
splsh!

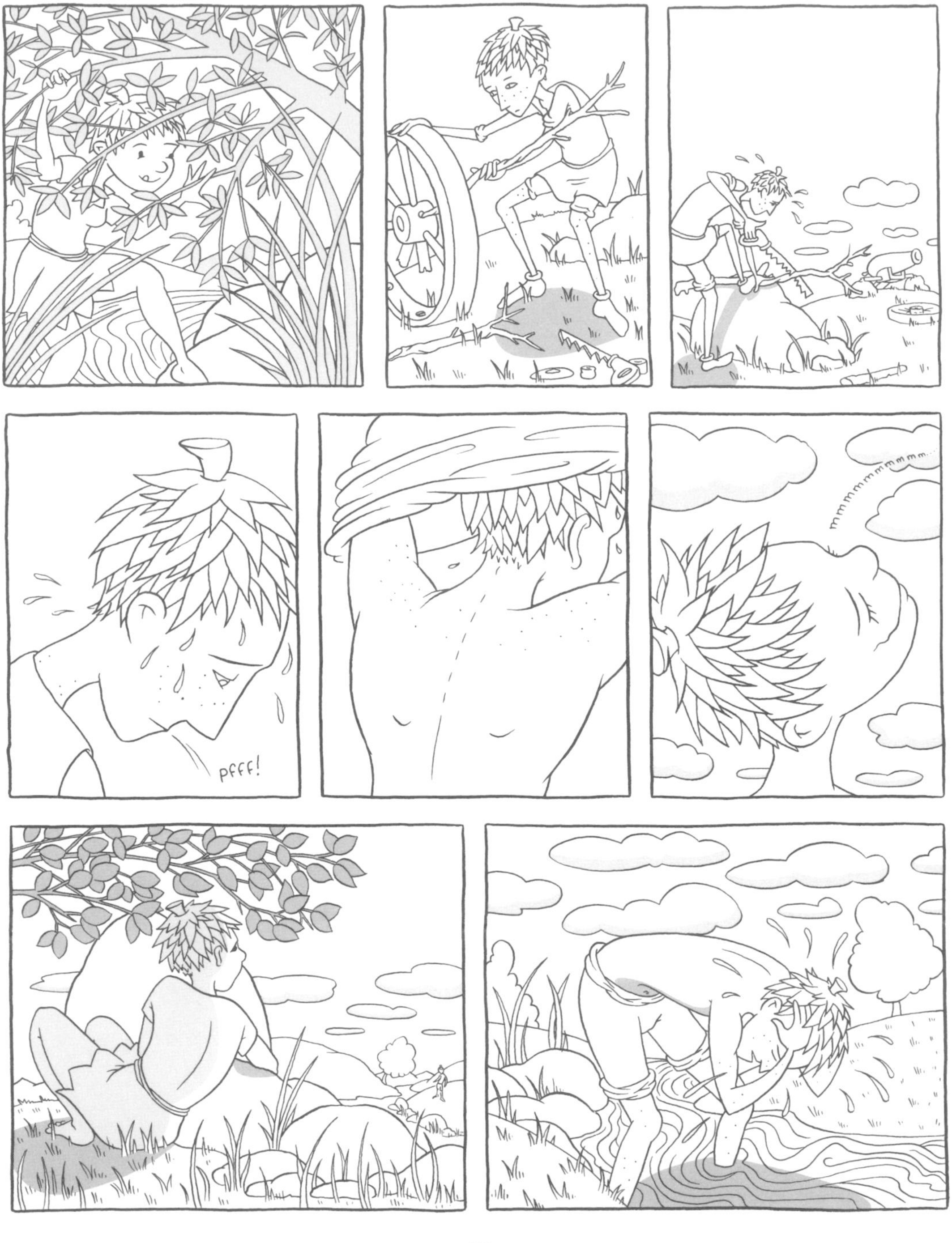
pfff!
mmmmmmmmmm...

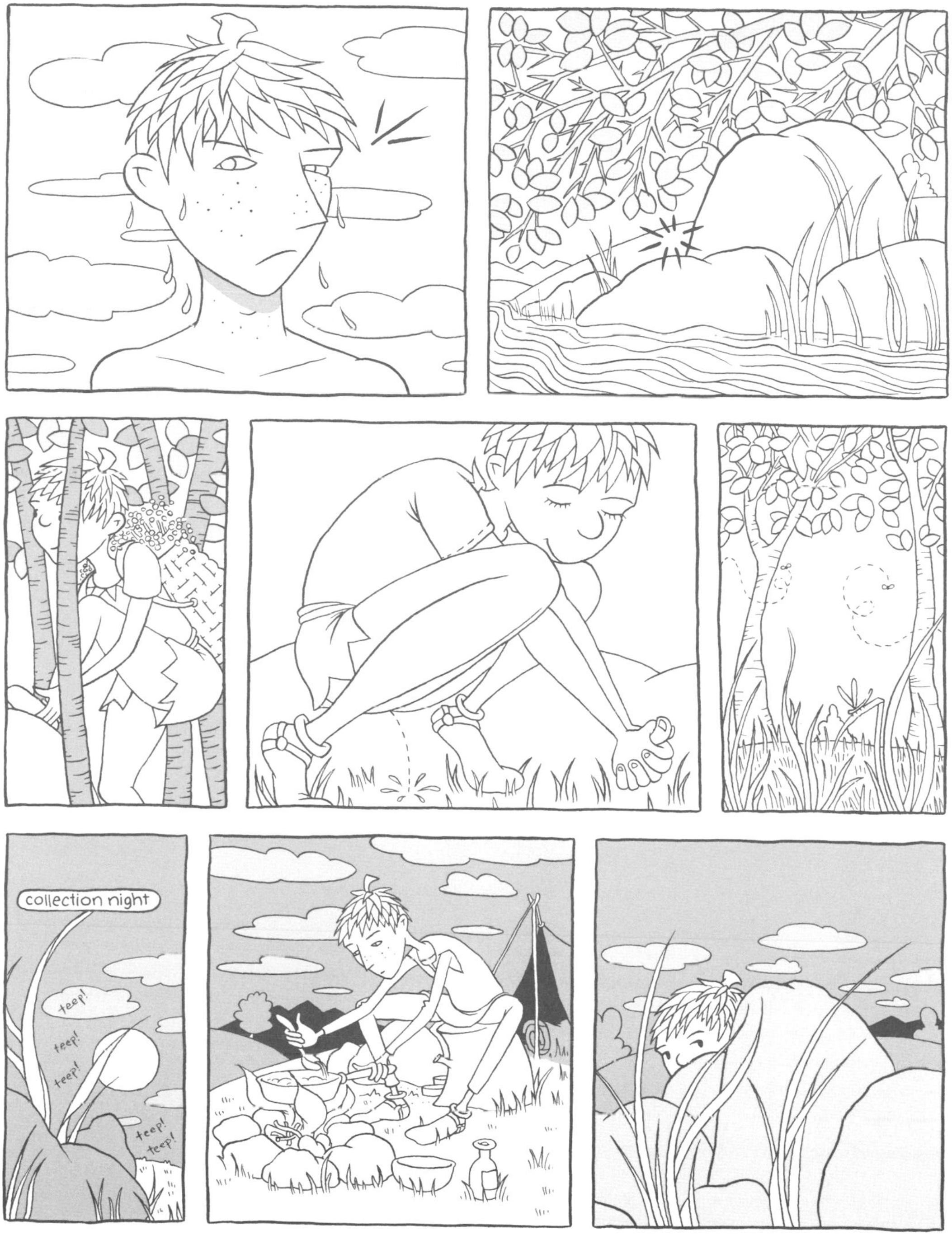
collection night
teep!
teep!
teep!
teep!
teep!

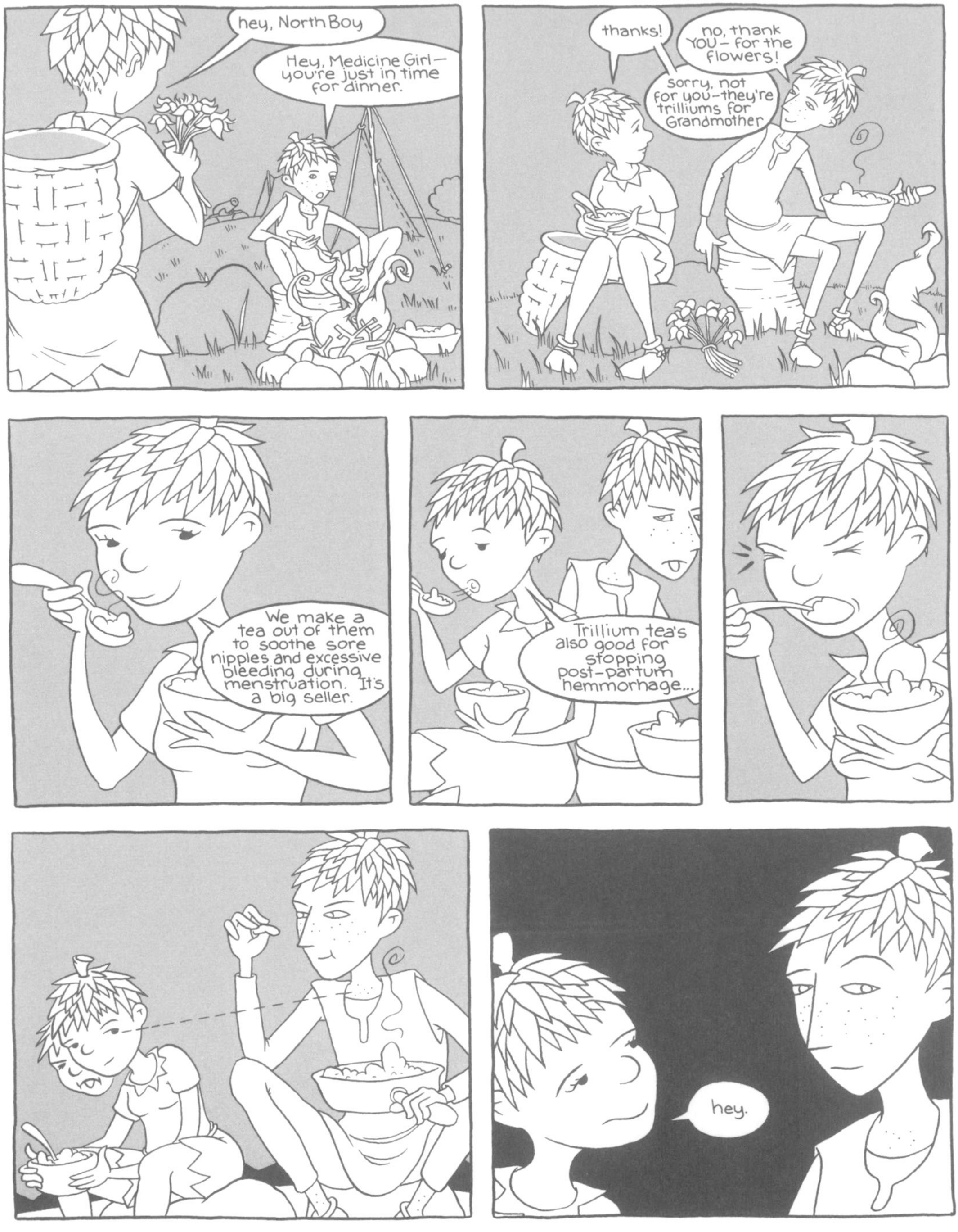
hey, North Boy
Hey, Medicine Girl— you're just in time for dinner.
thanks!
no, thank YOU— for the flowers!
sorry, not for you—they're trilliums for Grandmother
We make a tea out of them to soothe sore nipples and excessive bleeding during menstruation. It's a big seller.
Trillium tea's also good for stopping post-partum hemmorhage...
hey.

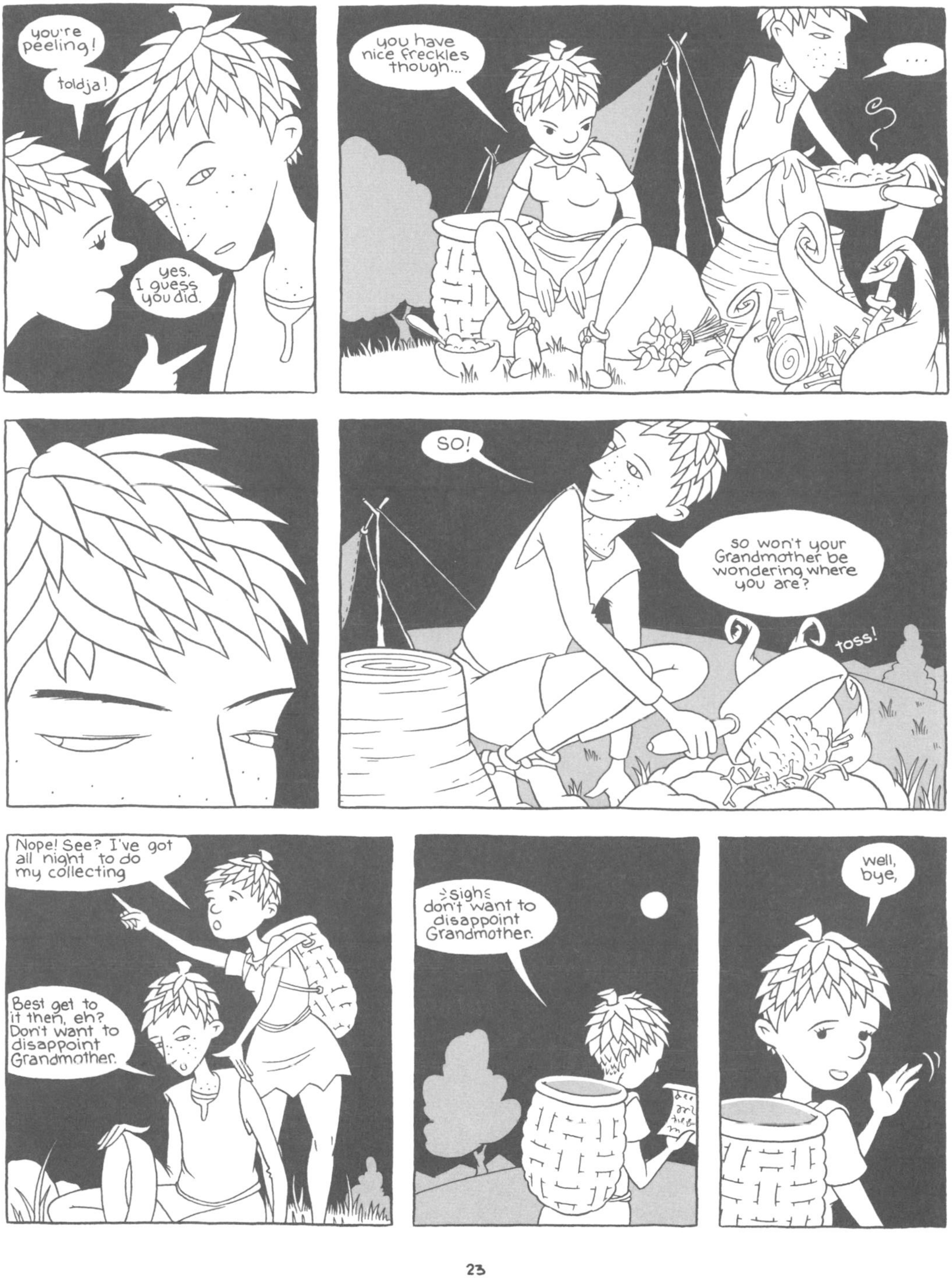
you're peeling!
toldja!
yes, I guess you did.
you have nice freckles though...
. . .
SO!
so won't your Grandmother be wondering where you are?
toss!
Nope! See? I've got all night to do my collecting
Best get to it then, eh? Don't want to disappoint Grandmother.
sigh don't want to disappoint Grandmother.
well, bye,

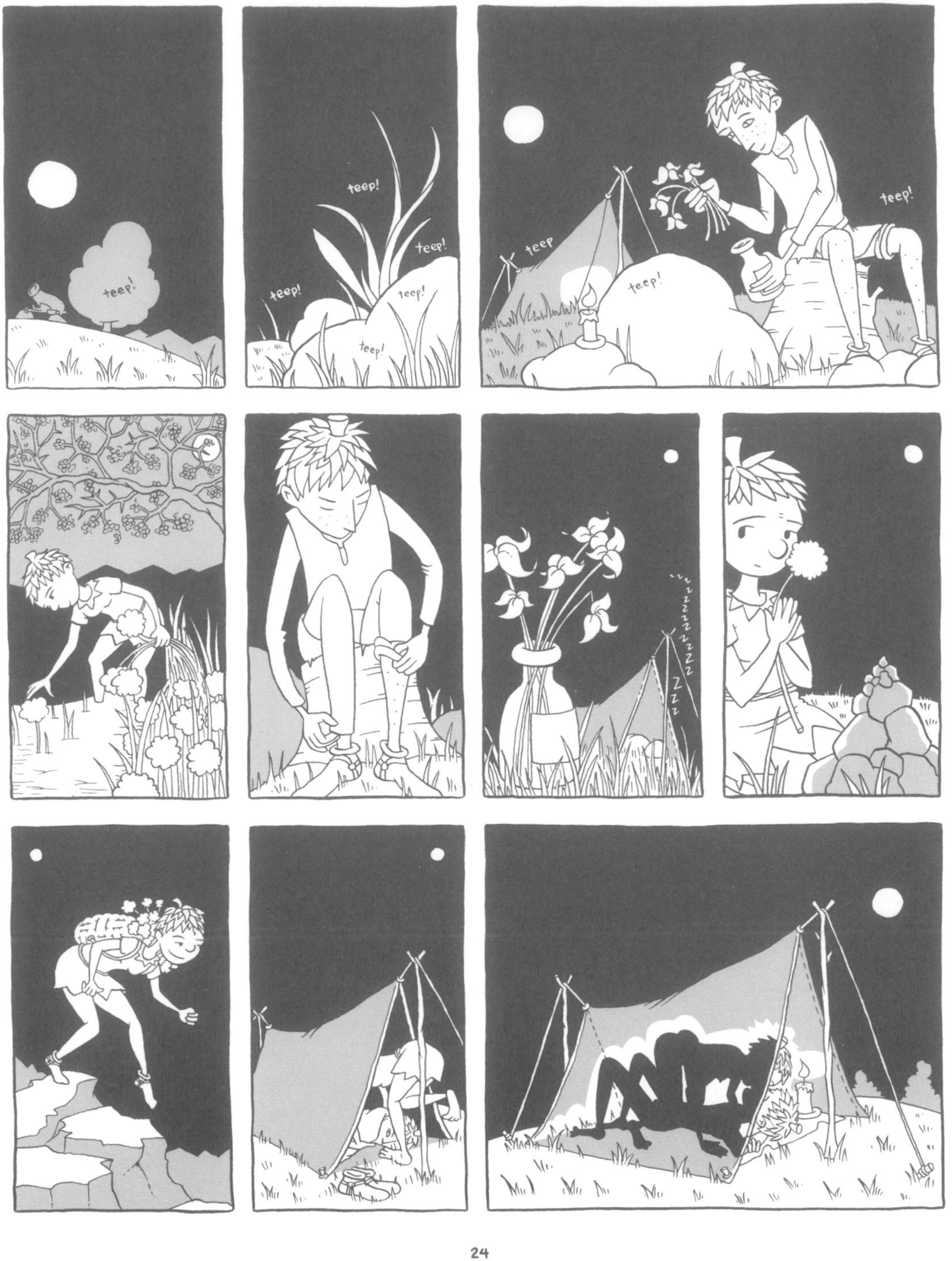
teep!
teep!
teep!
teep!
teep!
teep!
teep
teep!
teep!
z z z z z z z z Z Z Z

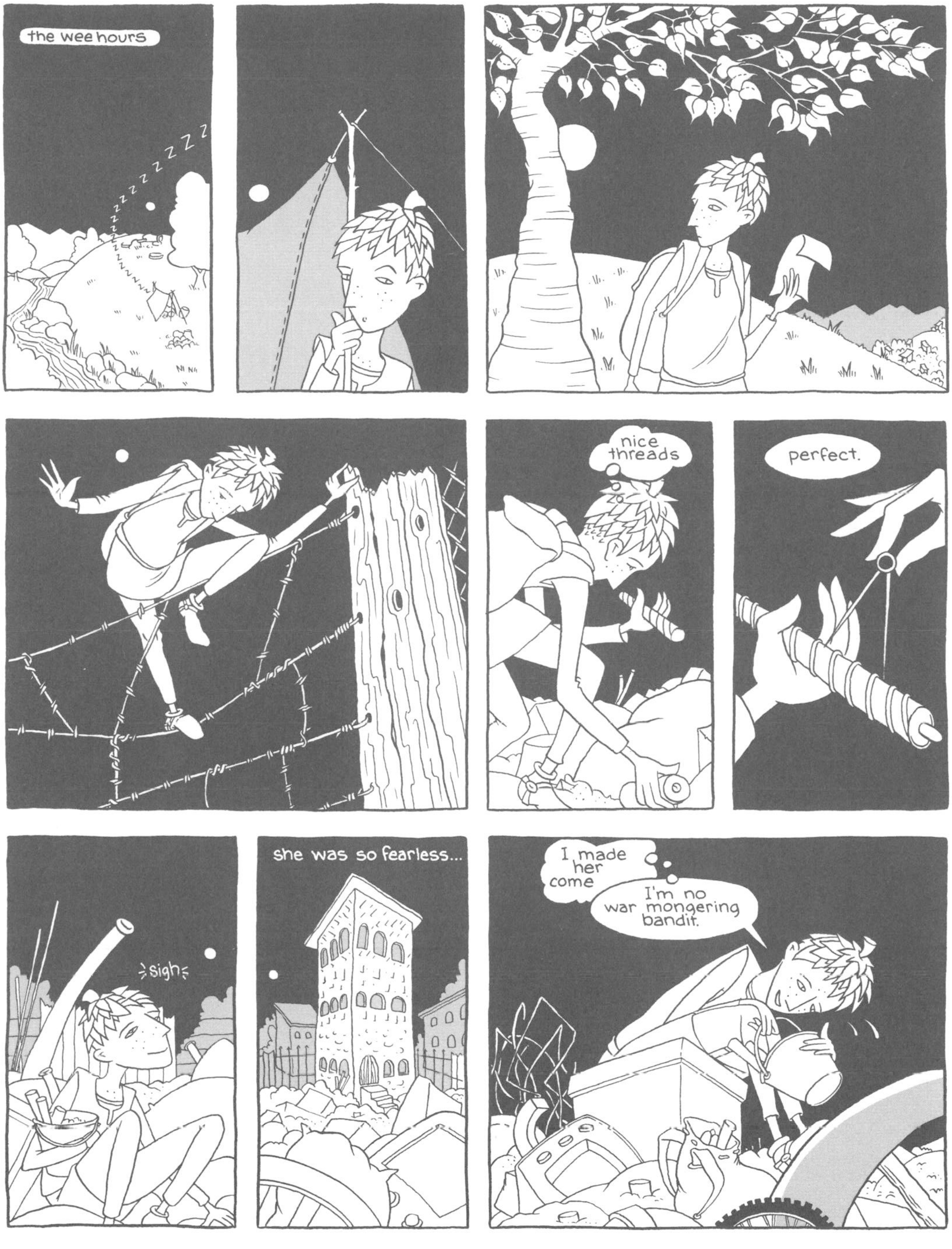
the wee hours
ZZZZZZZZZZZZZZ
nice threads
perfect.
sigh
she was so fearless...
I made her come
I'm no war mongering bandit.

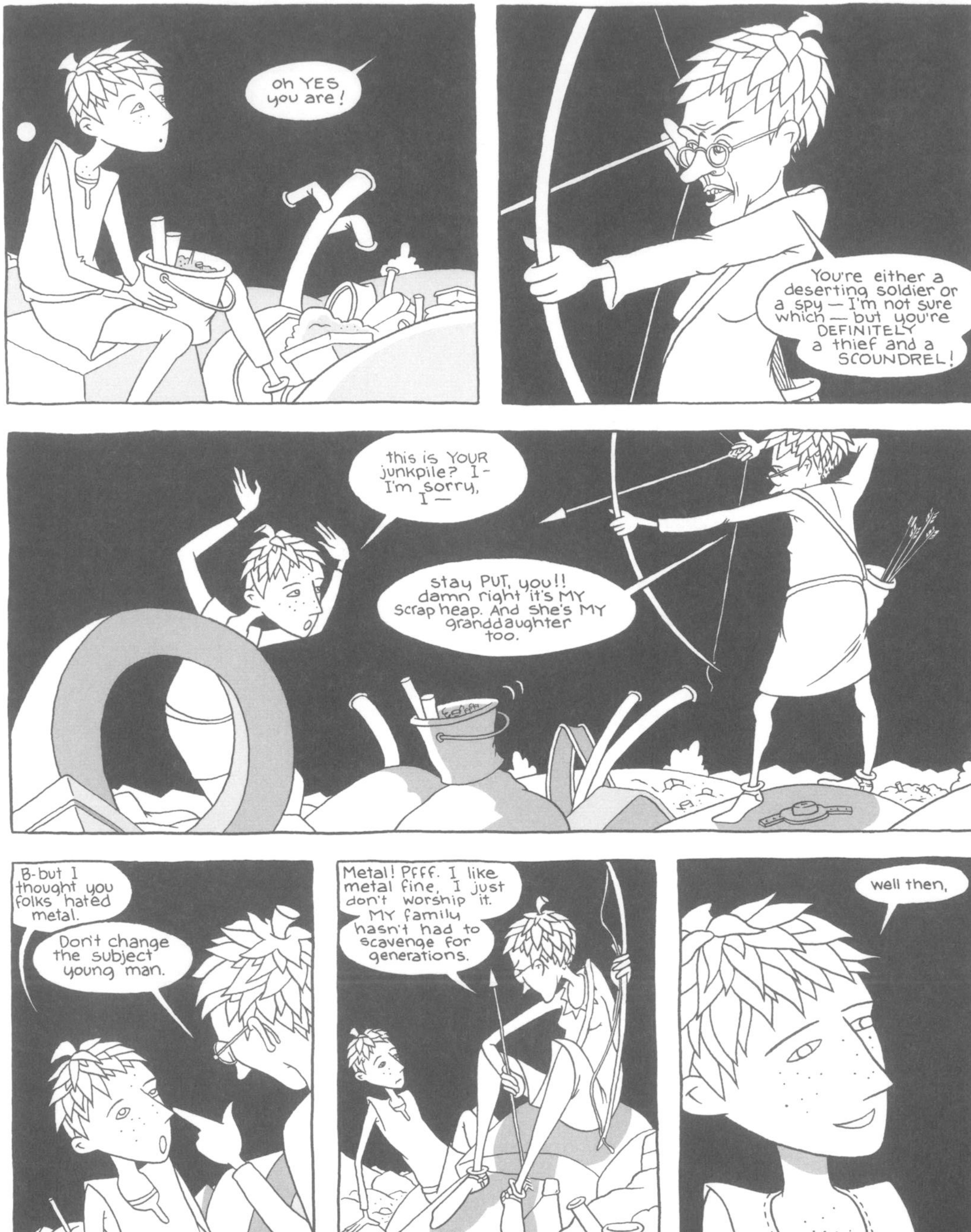
oh YES you are!
You're either a deserting soldier or a spy — I'm not sure which — but you're DEFINITELY a thief and a SCOUNDREL!
this is YOUR junkpile? I- I'm sorry, I—
stay PUT, you!! damn right it's MY scrap heap. And she's MY granddaughter too.
B-but I thought you folks hated metal.
Don't change the subject young man.
Metal! Pfff. I like metal fine, I just don't worship it. MY family hasn't had to scavenge for generations.
well then,

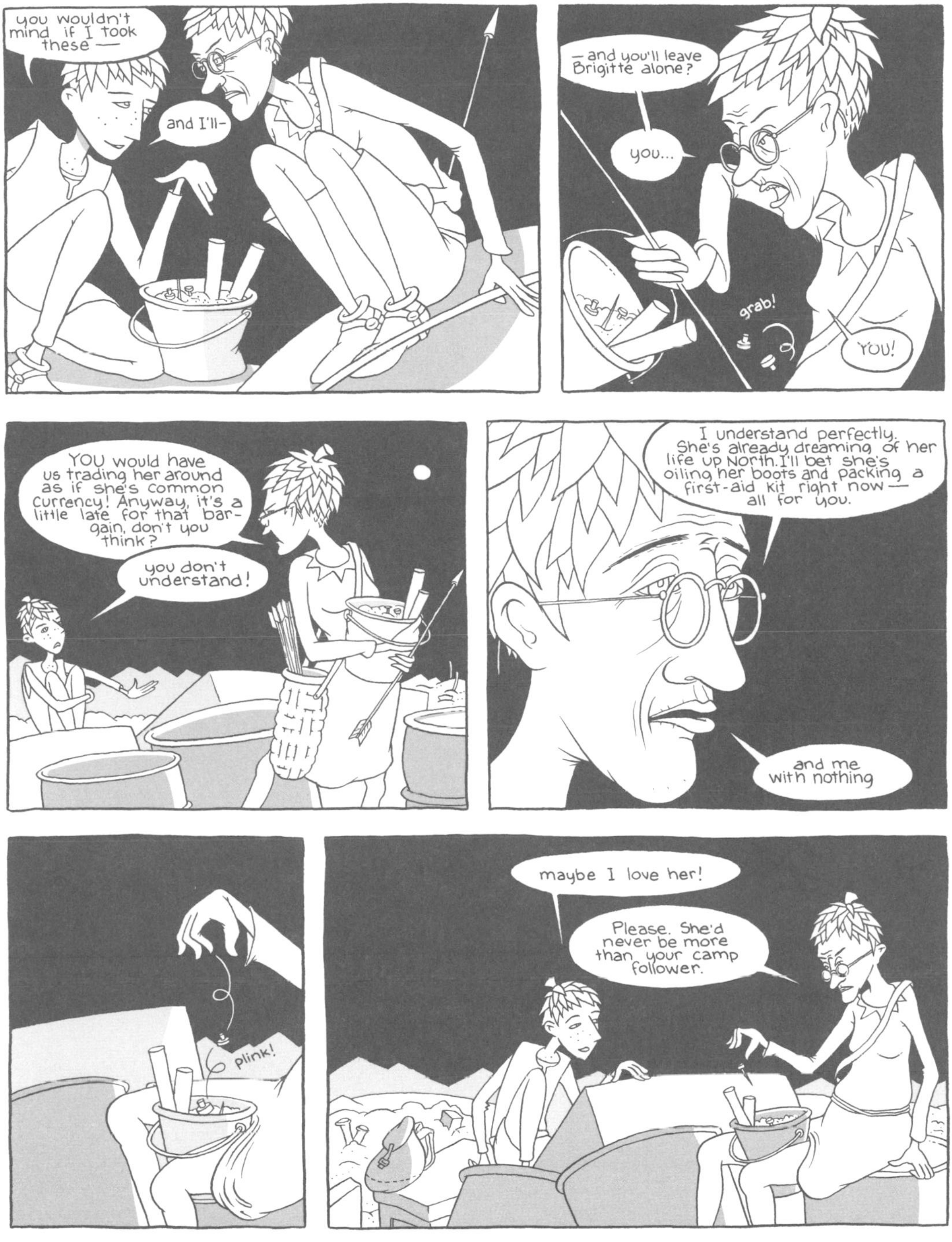
you wouldn't mind if I took these —
and I'll-
— and you'll leave Brigitte alone?
you...
grab!
YOU!
YOU would have us trading her around as if she's common currency! Anyway, it's a little late for that bargain, don't you think?
you don't understand!
I understand perfectly. She's already dreaming of her life up North. I'll bet she's oiling her boots and packing a first-aid kit right now — all for you.
and me with nothing
plink!
maybe I love her!
Please. She'd never be more than your camp follower.

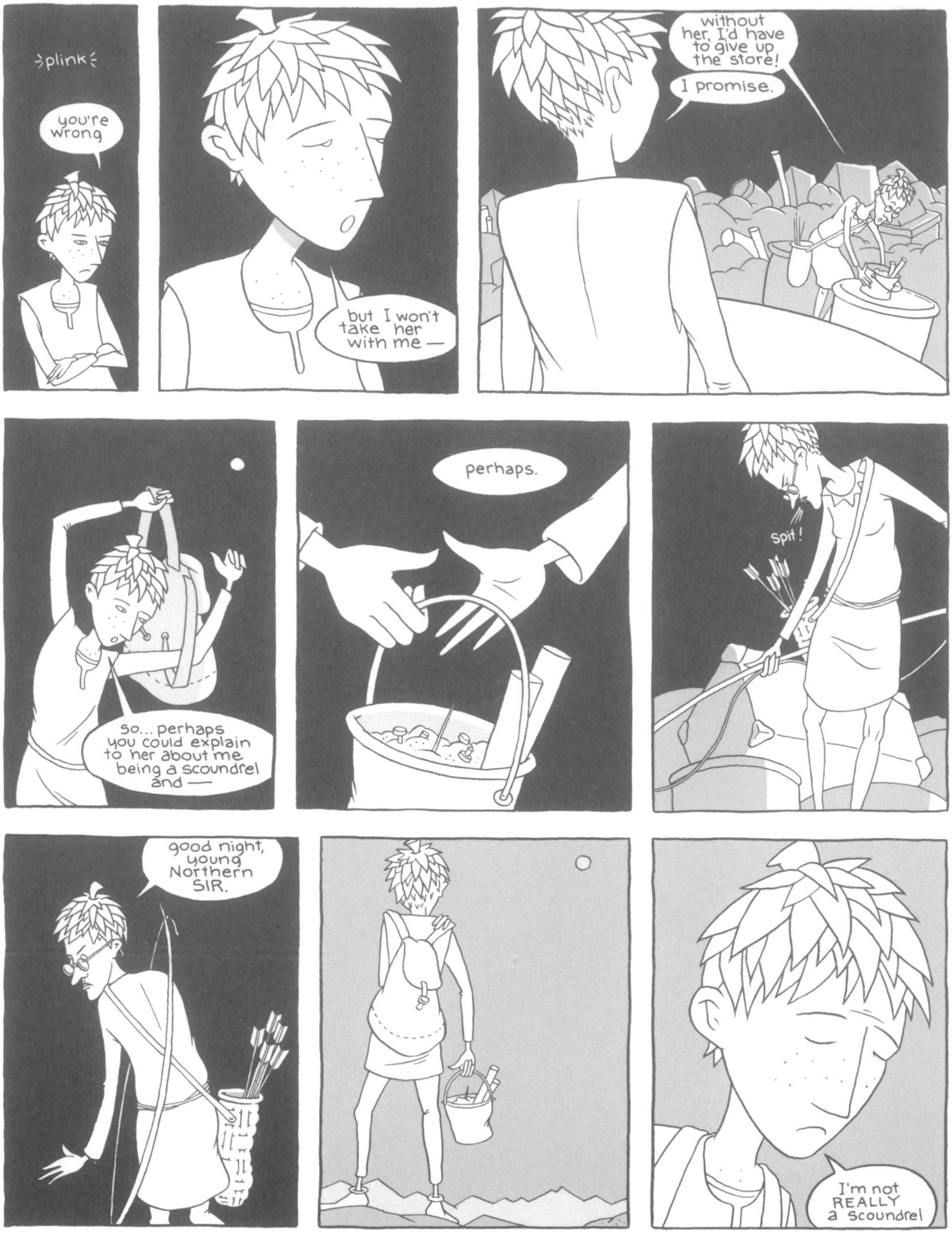
plink
you're wrong
but I won't take her with me —
without her, I'd have to give up the store!
I promise.
so... perhaps you could explain to her about me being a scoundrel and —
perhaps.
Spit!
good night, young Northern SIR.
I'm not REALLY a scoundrel

ow, ow, oww OW!!

surgery day

Dorian, you can't sit on your hindquarters scribbling verse for six months and then walk thirty miles in two days without harming your feet.

ow, OW! So, is it true that Brigitte is consorting with the enemy?

NO.

So it IS true.

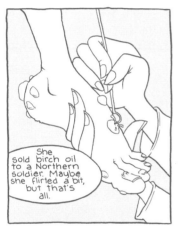

She sold birch oil to a Northern soldier. Maybe she flirted a bit, but that's all.

Charlotte! You shouldn't even do business with those tyrants, let alone expose Brigitte —

mmf-

No nationalist rants, dear boy. Now go get some rest.

Dorian!

Brigitte, could you please pour me a pint of walnut ink? I shall pay with this poem — a Valentine to our threatened land.

Oh, and could you put it in a fallen-pod bottle?

We don't use those anymore.

So I hear you're leaving us — — following the winds of war — so to speak.

don't believe everything you hear, Dorian.

glug! glug!

my advice EXACTLY, dear Brigitte, and don't forget to read it. It's important.

OK, OK!

market day

tink!

tink!

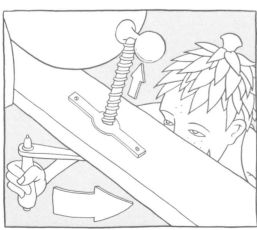

sweet!

30

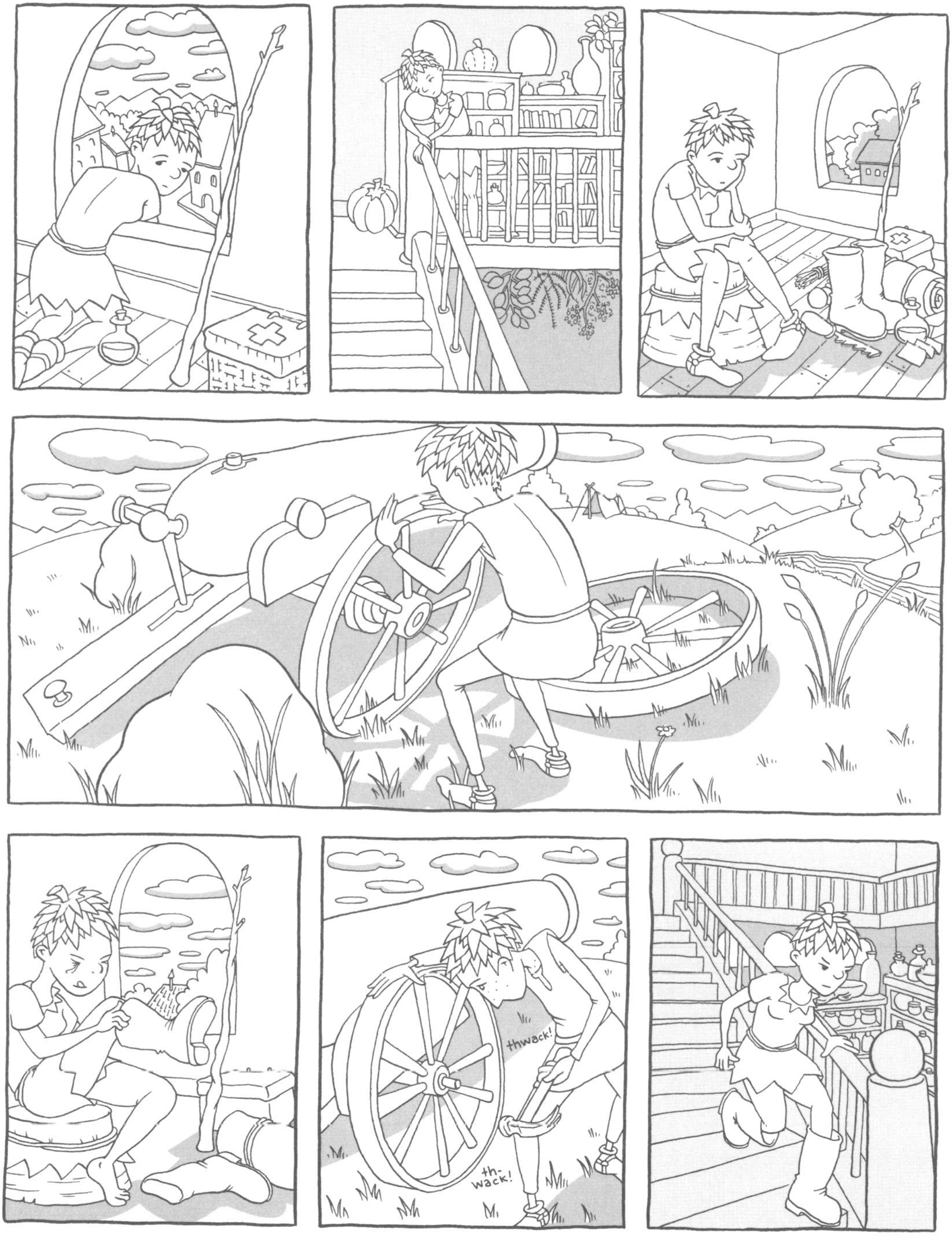
thwack!
th-
wack!

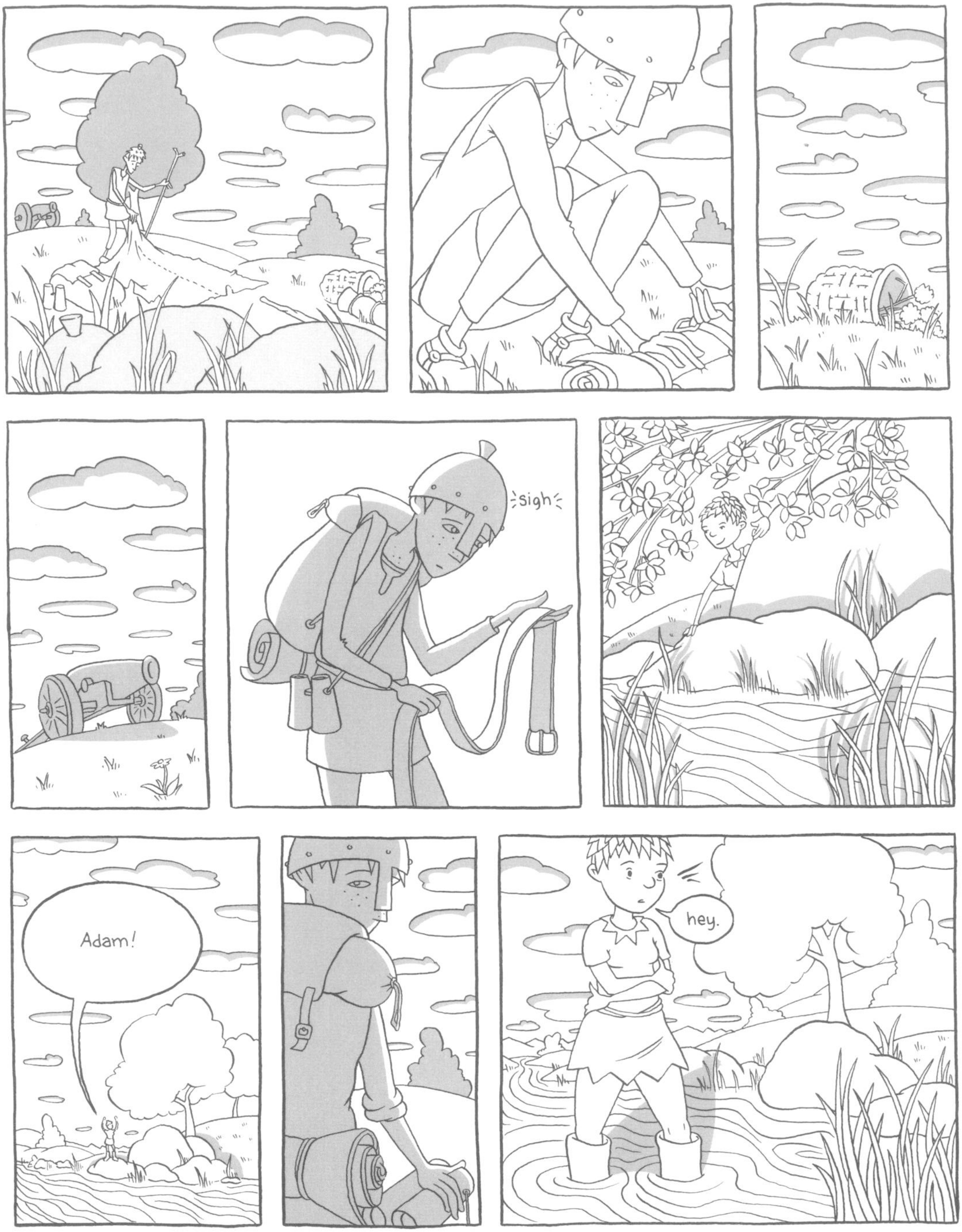
sigh
Adam!
hey.

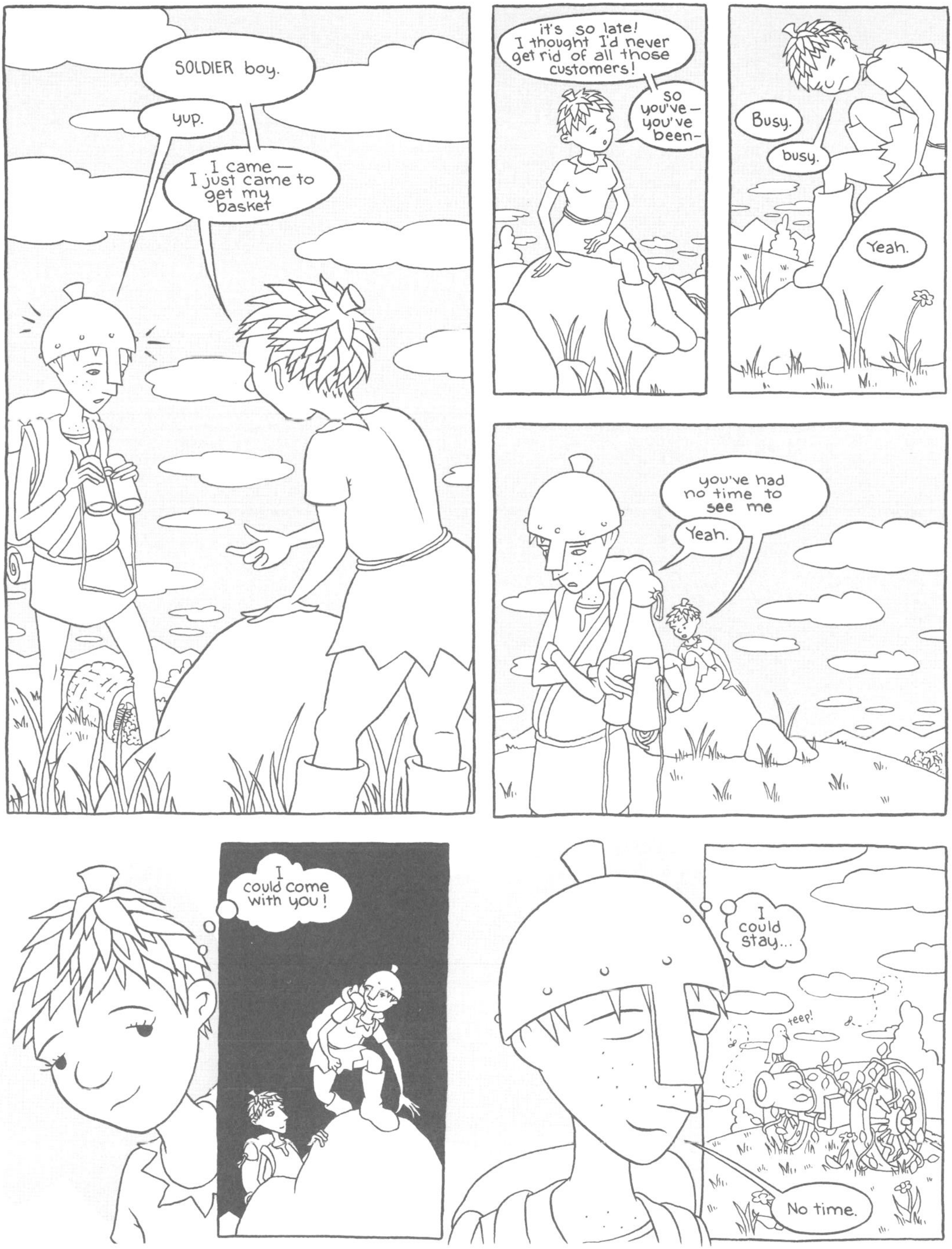
SOLDIER boy.
yup.
I came — I just came to get my basket
it's so late! I thought I'd never get rid of all those customers!
so you've — you've been-
Busy.
busy.
Yeah.
you've had no time to see me
Yeah.
I could come with you!
I could stay...
teep!
No time.

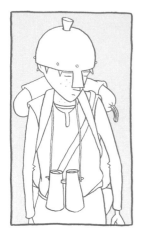

FUCK!

We're on opposite sides, Brigitte, we —

whatever

anyway, I've thought 'n' thought about it. Grandmother needs me here... HERE.

So don't argue with me, Adam!

you're sure.

Nothing you could say will change my mind.

hey,

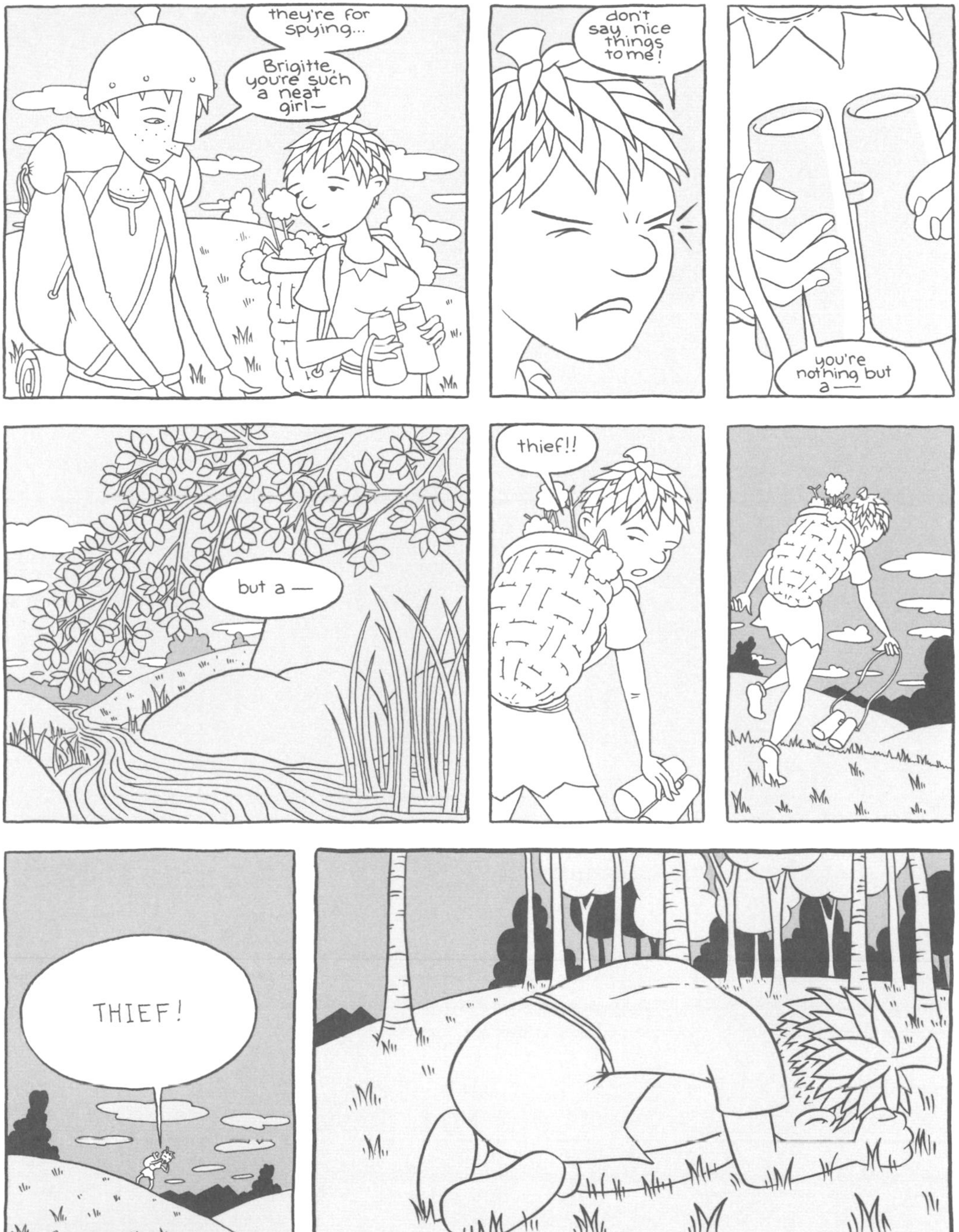
they're for spying...
Brigitte, you're such a neat girl—
don't say nice things to me!
you're nothing but a—
but a—
thief!!
THIEF!

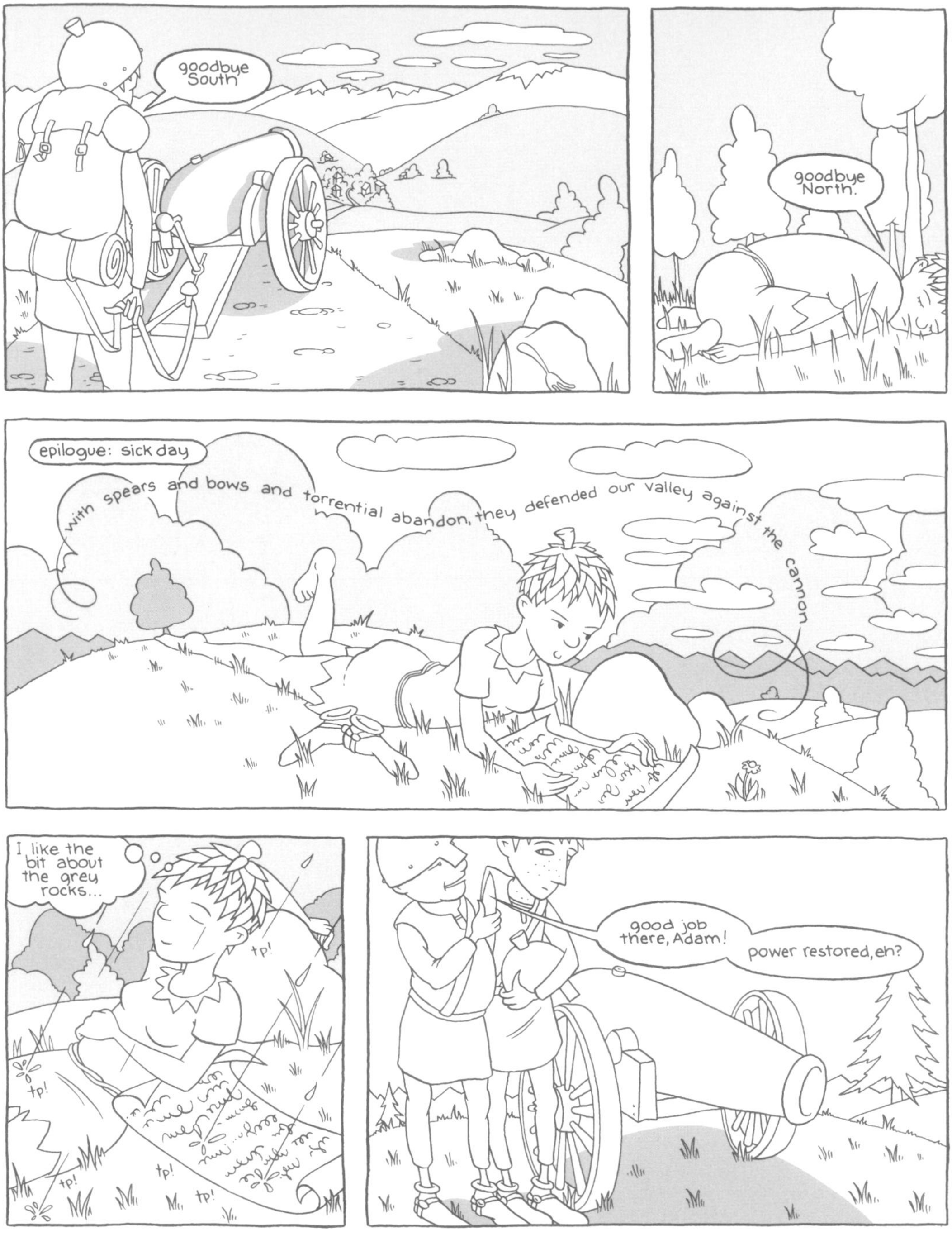
goodbye South
goodbye North.
epilogue: sick day
with spears and bows and torrential abandon, they defended our valley against the cannon
I like the bit about the grey rocks...
tp!
tp!
tp!
tp!
tp!
good job there, Adam!
power restored, eh?

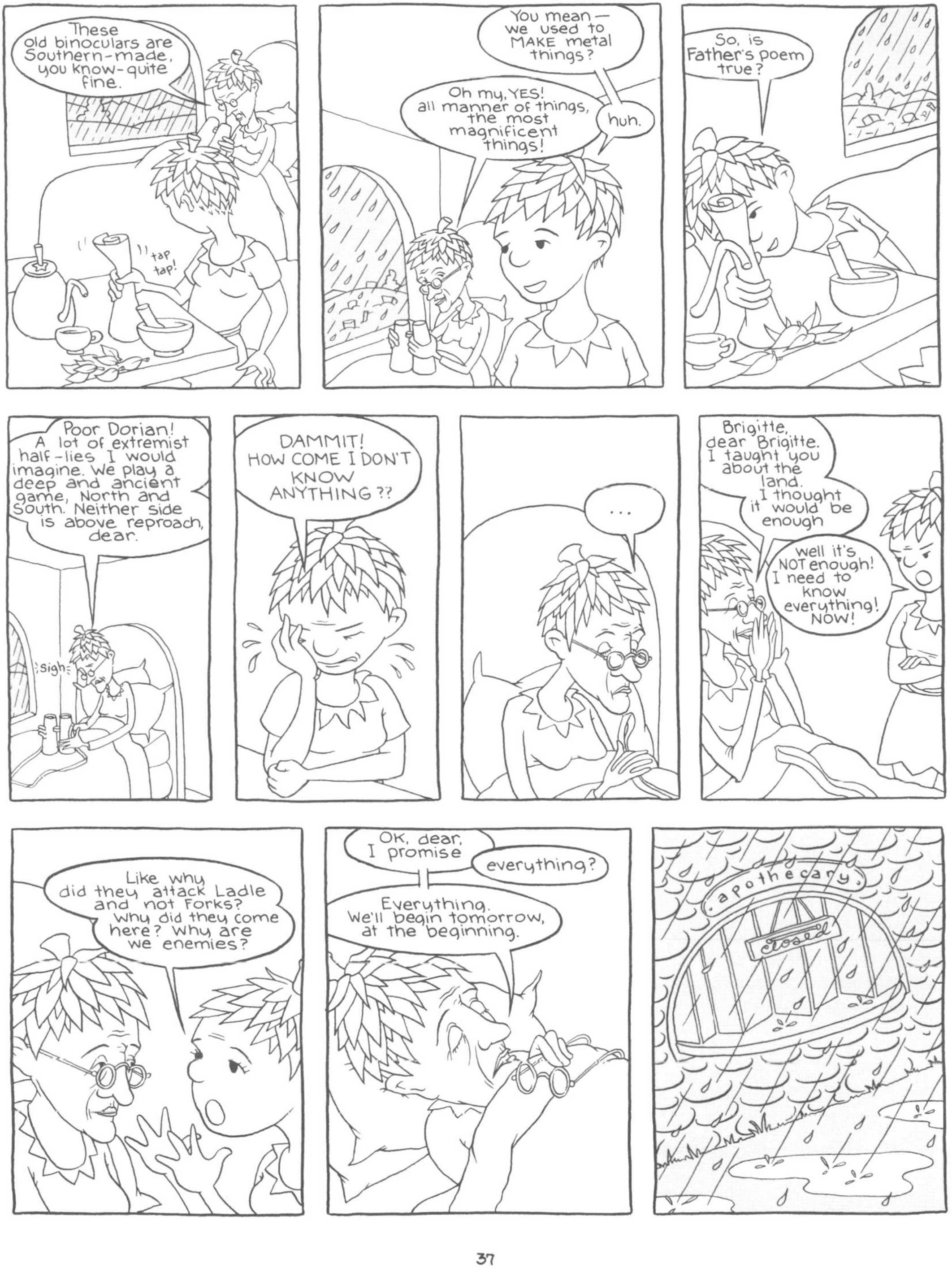
These old binoculars are Southern-made, you know- quite fine.
tap tap!
You mean — we used to MAKE metal things?
Oh my, YES! all manner of things, the most magnificent things!
huh.
So, is Father's poem true?
Poor Dorian! A lot of extremist half-lies I would imagine. We play a deep and ancient game, North and South. Neither side is above reproach, dear.
sigh
DAMMIT! HOW COME I DON'T KNOW ANYTHING??
...
Brigitte, dear Brigitte. I taught you about the land. I thought it would be enough
Well it's NOT enough! I need to know everything! NOW!
Like why did they attack Ladle and not Forks? Why did they come here? Why are we enemies?
OK, dear, I promise
everything?
Everything. We'll begin tomorrow, at the beginning.
apothecary
closed

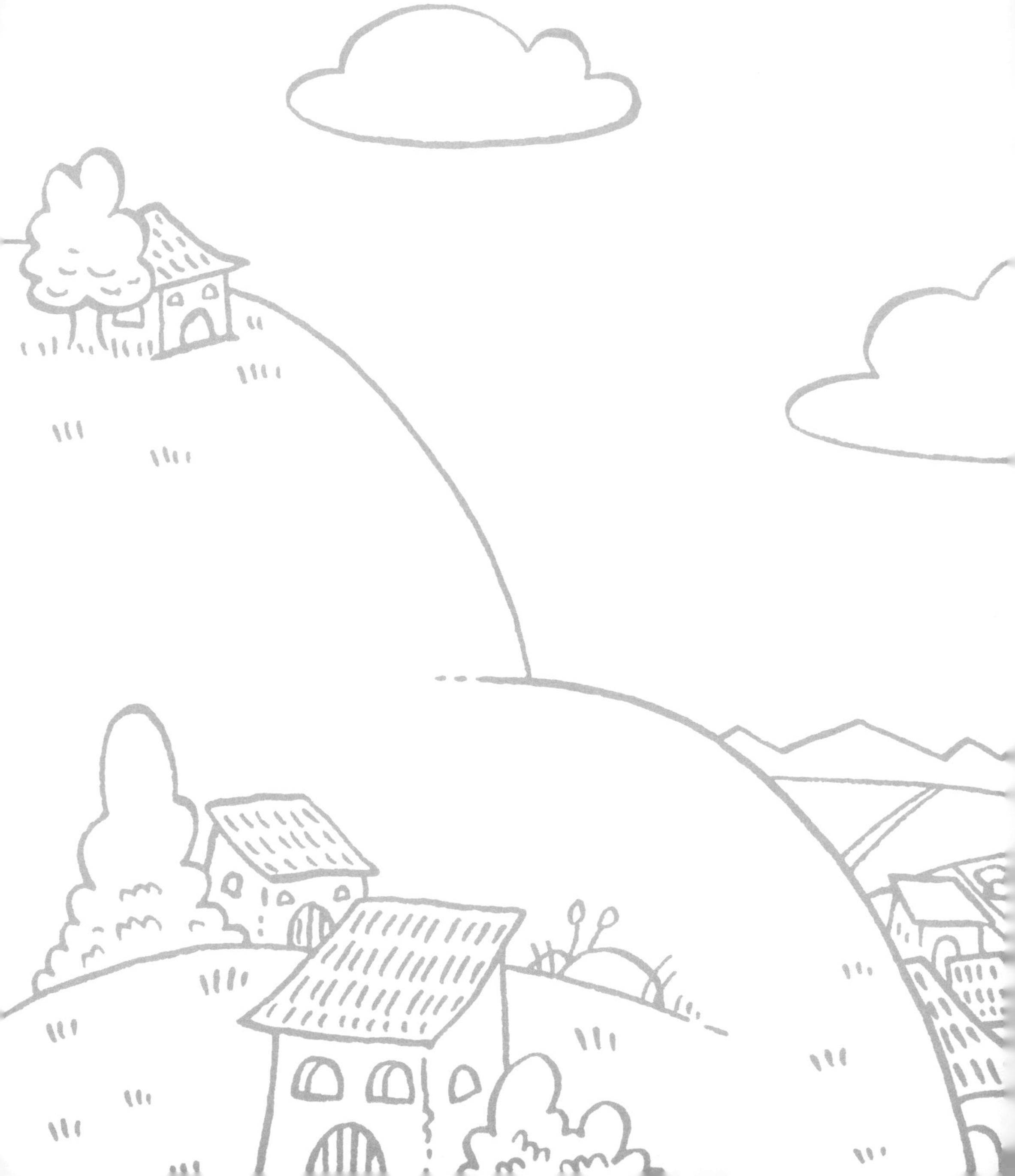

Chapter 2
WARRIOR QUEEN

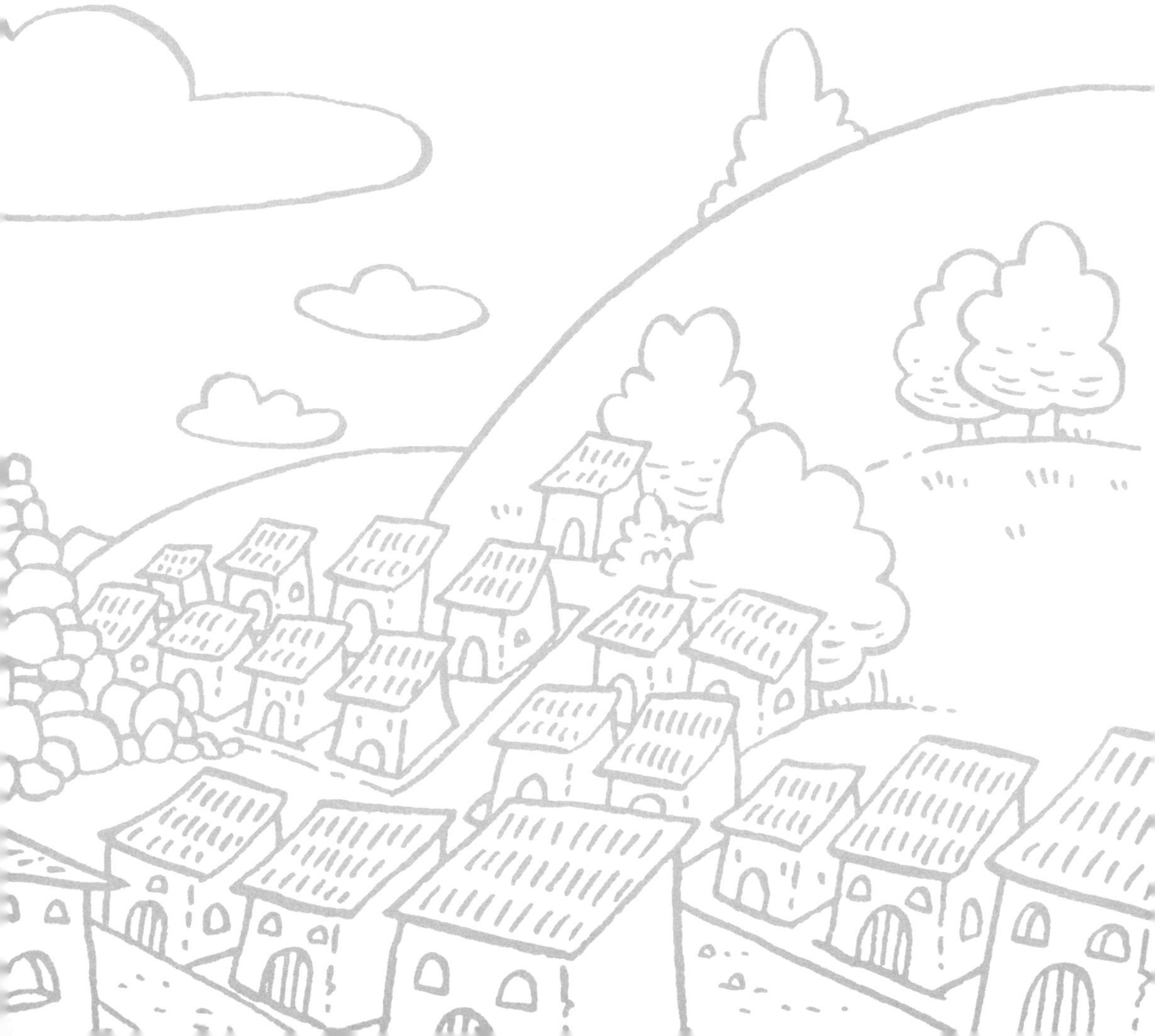

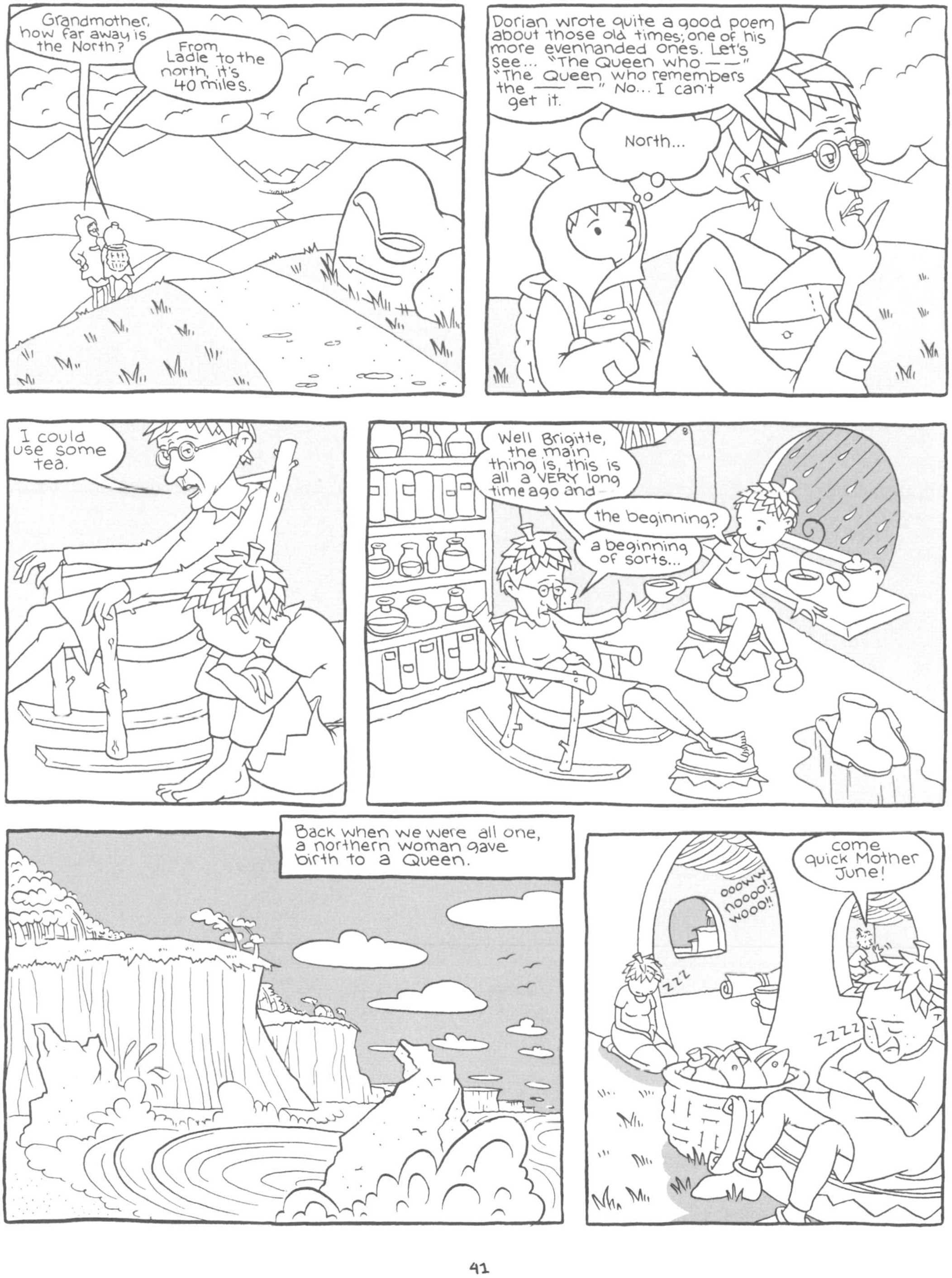
Grandmother, how far away is the North?
From Ladle to the north, it's 40 miles.
Dorian wrote quite a good poem about those old times; one of his more evenhanded ones. Let's see... "The Queen who ——" "The Queen who remembers the —— —" No... I can't get it.
North...
I could use some tea.
Well Brigitte, the main thing is, this is all a VERY long time ago and—
the beginning?
a beginning of sorts...
Back when we were all one, a northern woman gave birth to a Queen.
OOOWW!! NOOOO!! WOOO!!
come quick Mother June!
ZZZ
ZZZZ

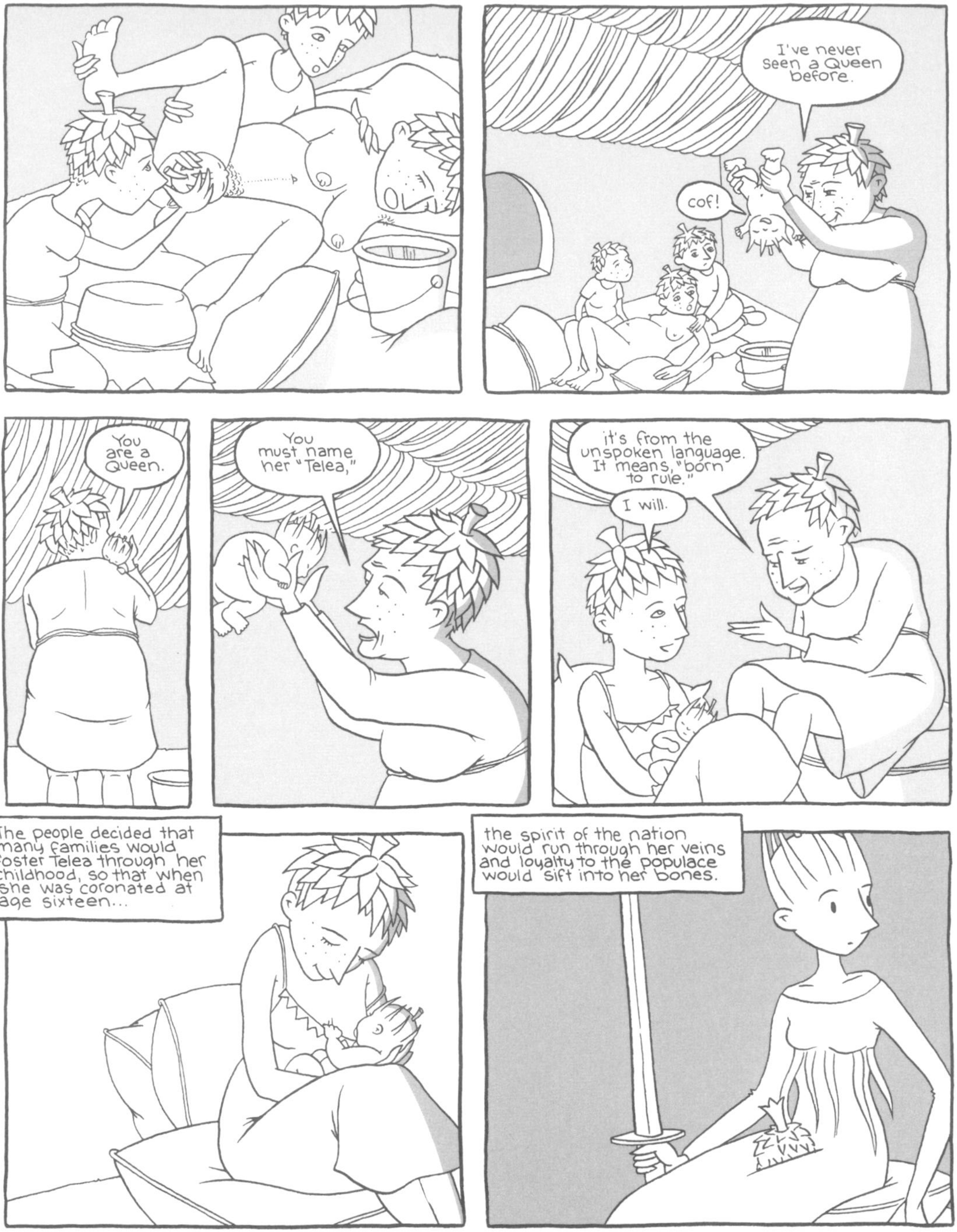
I've never seen a Queen before.
cof!
You are a Queen.
You must name her "Telea,"
it's from the unspoken language. It means, "born to rule."
I will.
The people decided that many families would foster Telea through her childhood, so that when she was coronated at age sixteen...
the spirit of the nation would run through her veins and loyalty to the populace would sift into her bones.

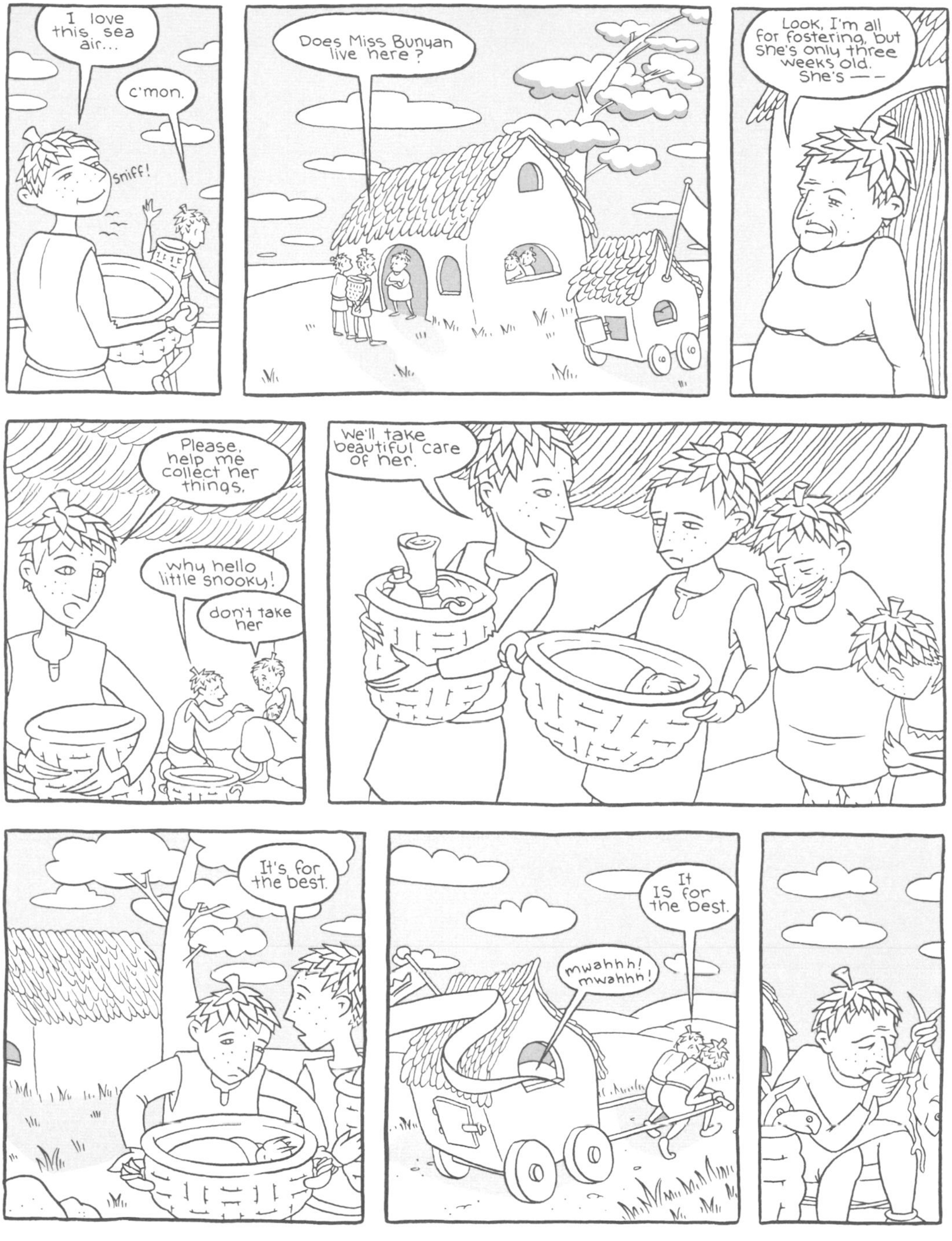
I love this sea air...
c'mon.
Sniff!
Does Miss Bunyan live here ?
Look, I'm all for fostering, but she's only three weeks old. She's ——
Please, help me collect her things.
why hello little snooky!
don't take her
We'll take beautiful care of her.
It's for the best.
It IS for the best.
mwahhh! mwahhh!

Immediately following her coronation at age sixteen, Queen Telea toured the country for a year, collecting keys to the city from every village council in the land.

Telea! Welcome home!

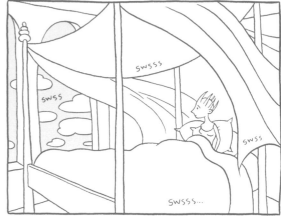

swsss

swss

swss

swsss...

tomorrow.

Telea, you've skipped three Judgement Days already—you can't sit here, for-ever, cloudgazing and empty headed—

tomorrow, please?

OK, but no more procrastination

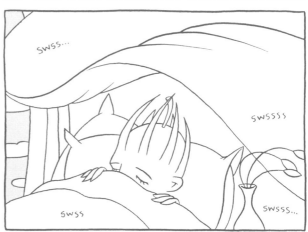

swss...

swssss

swss

swsss...

Rise 'n' shine Telea, it's Judgement Day!

mrrr...

It's so early...and they pinch!

it's eleven, dear.

OK, here I go.

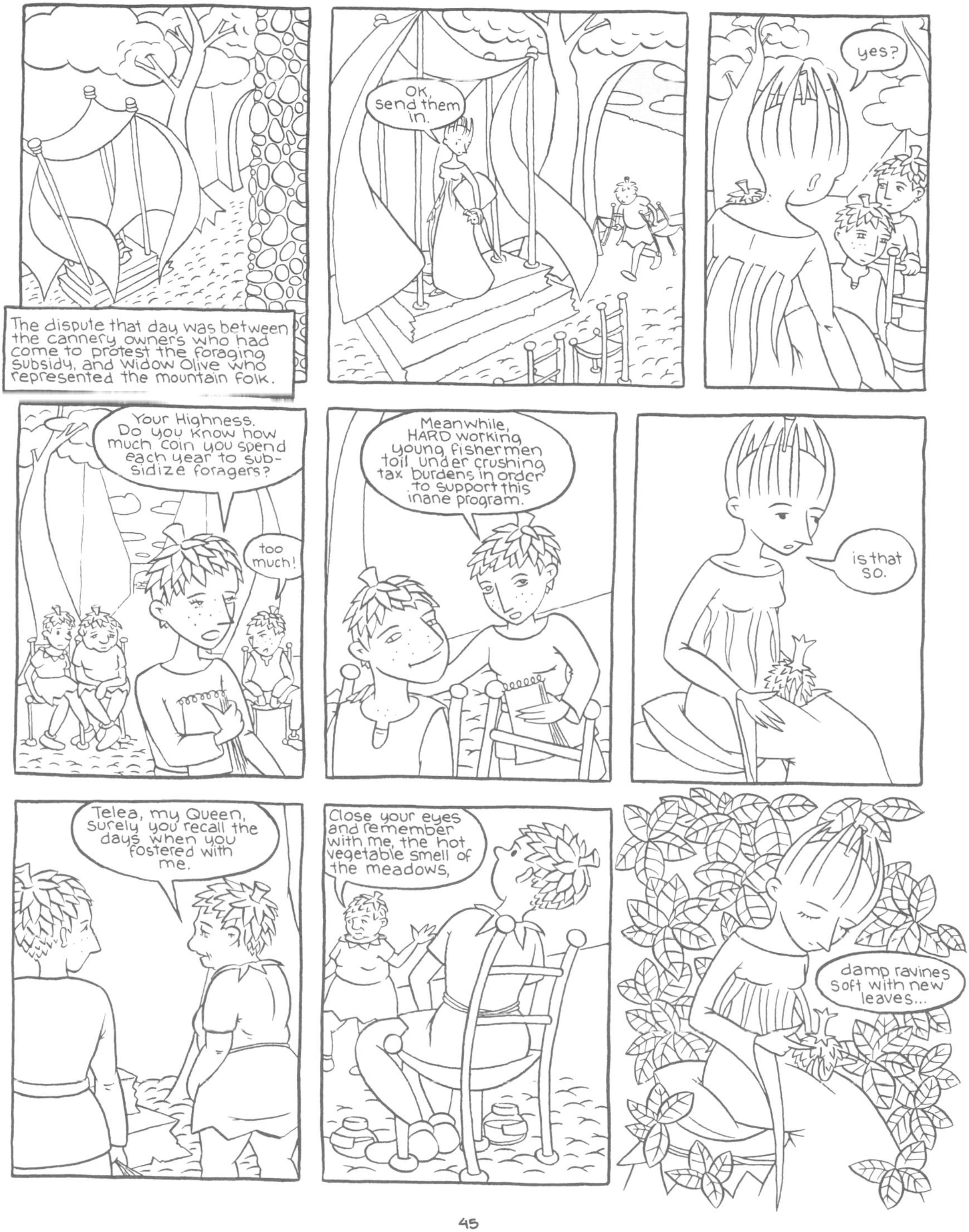
The dispute that day was between the cannery owners who had come to protest the foraging subsidy, and Widow Olive who represented the mountain folk.
Ok, send them in.
yes?
Your Highness. Do you know how much coin you spend each year to subsidize foragers?
too much!
Meanwhile, HARD working young fishermen toil under crushing tax burdens in order to support this inane program.
is that so.
Telea, my Queen, surely you recall the days when you fostered with me.
Close your eyes and remember with me, the hot vegetable smell of the meadows,
damp ravines soft with new leaves...

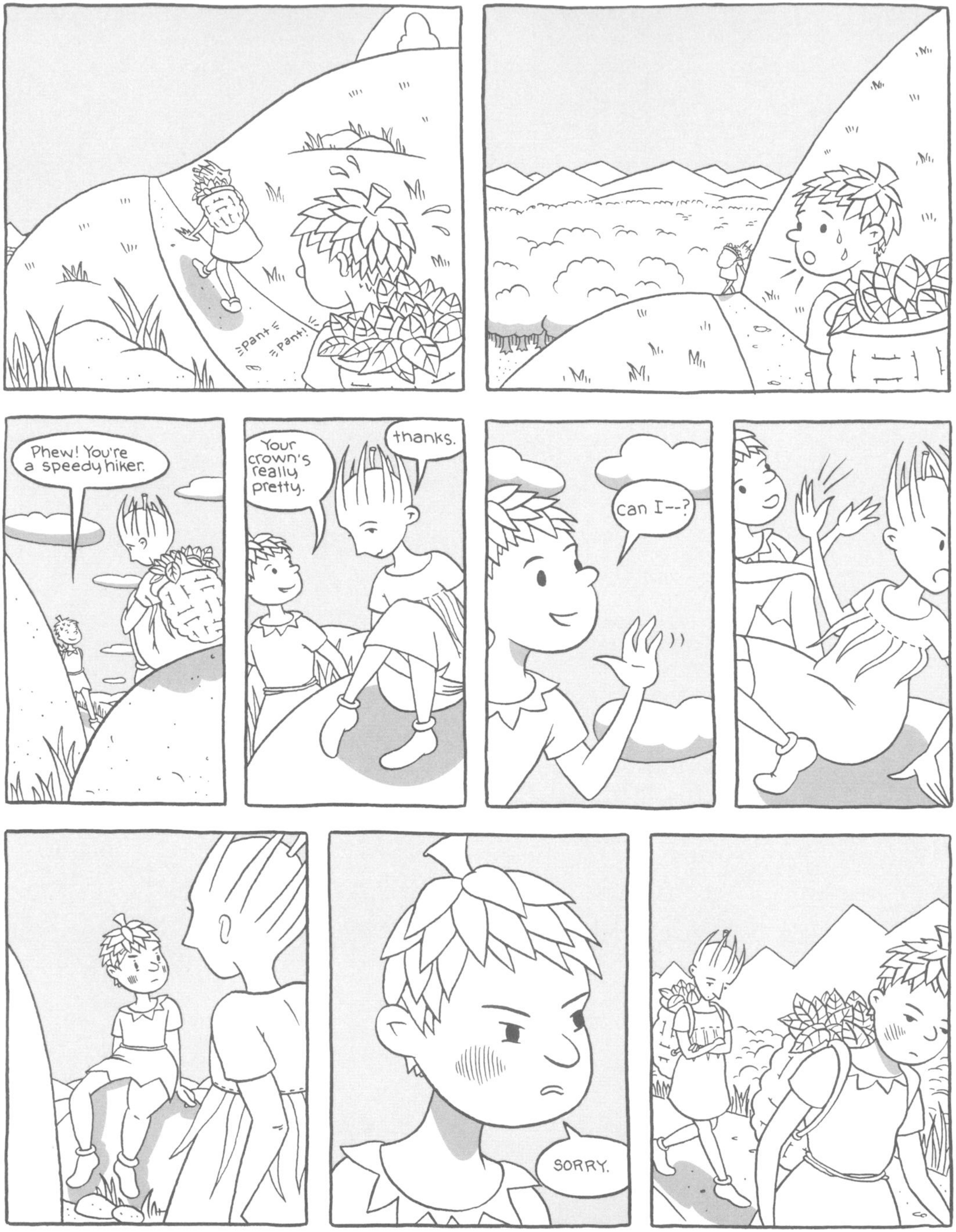
pant
pant!
Phew! You're a speedy hiker.
Your crown's really pretty.
thanks.
can I--?
SORRY.

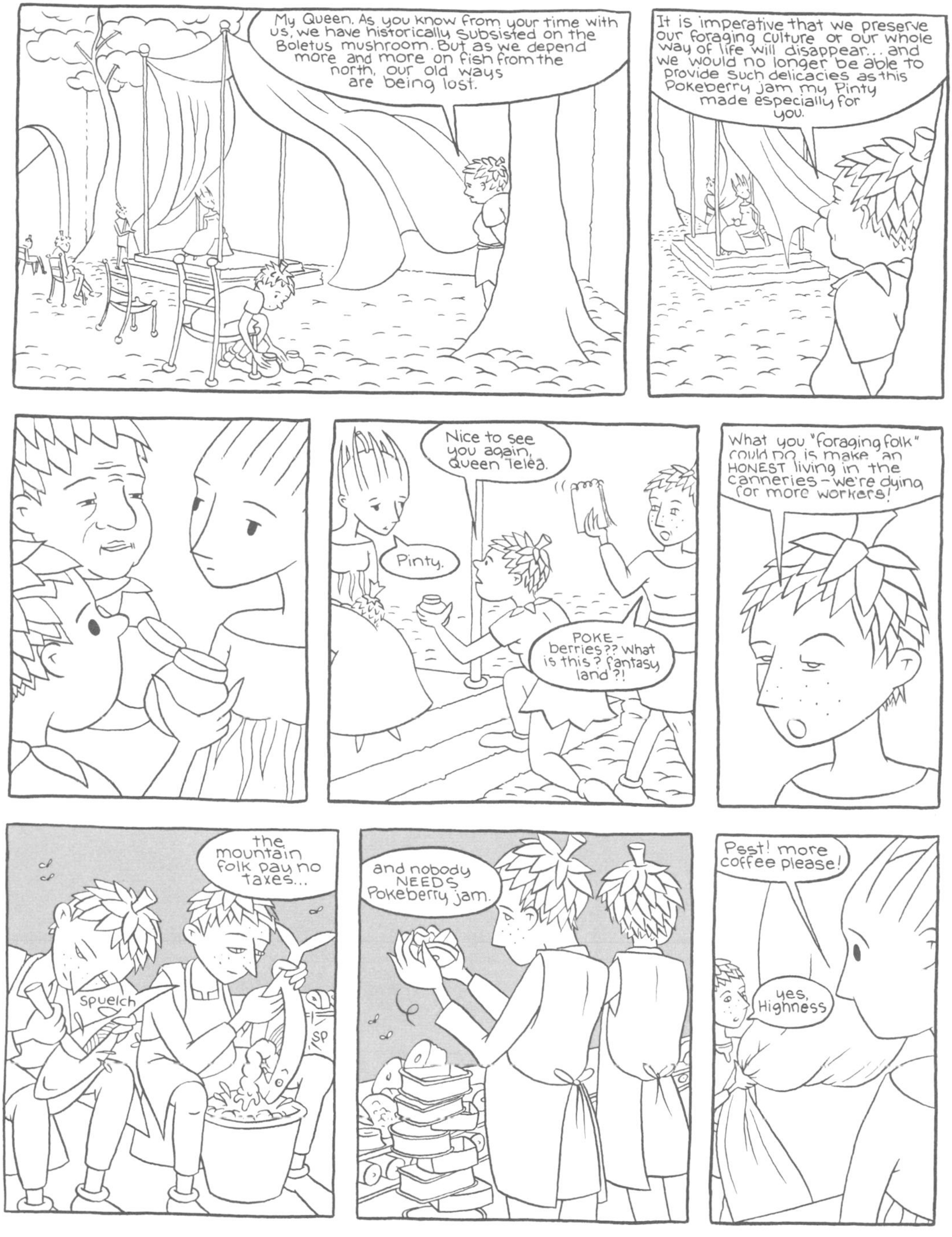
My Queen. As you know from your time with us, we have historically subsisted on the Boletus mushroom. But as we depend more and more on fish from the north, our old ways are being lost.
It is imperative that we preserve our foraging culture or our whole way of life will disappear... and we would no longer be able to provide such delicacies as this Pokeberry jam my Pinty made especially for you.
Nice to see you again, Queen Telea.
Pinty.
POKE-berries?? what is this? fantasy land?!
What you "foraging folk" could do is make an HONEST living in the canneries - we're dying for more workers!
the mountain folk pay no taxes...
spuelch
sp
and nobody NEEDS Pokeberry jam.
Psst! more coffee please!
yes, Highness

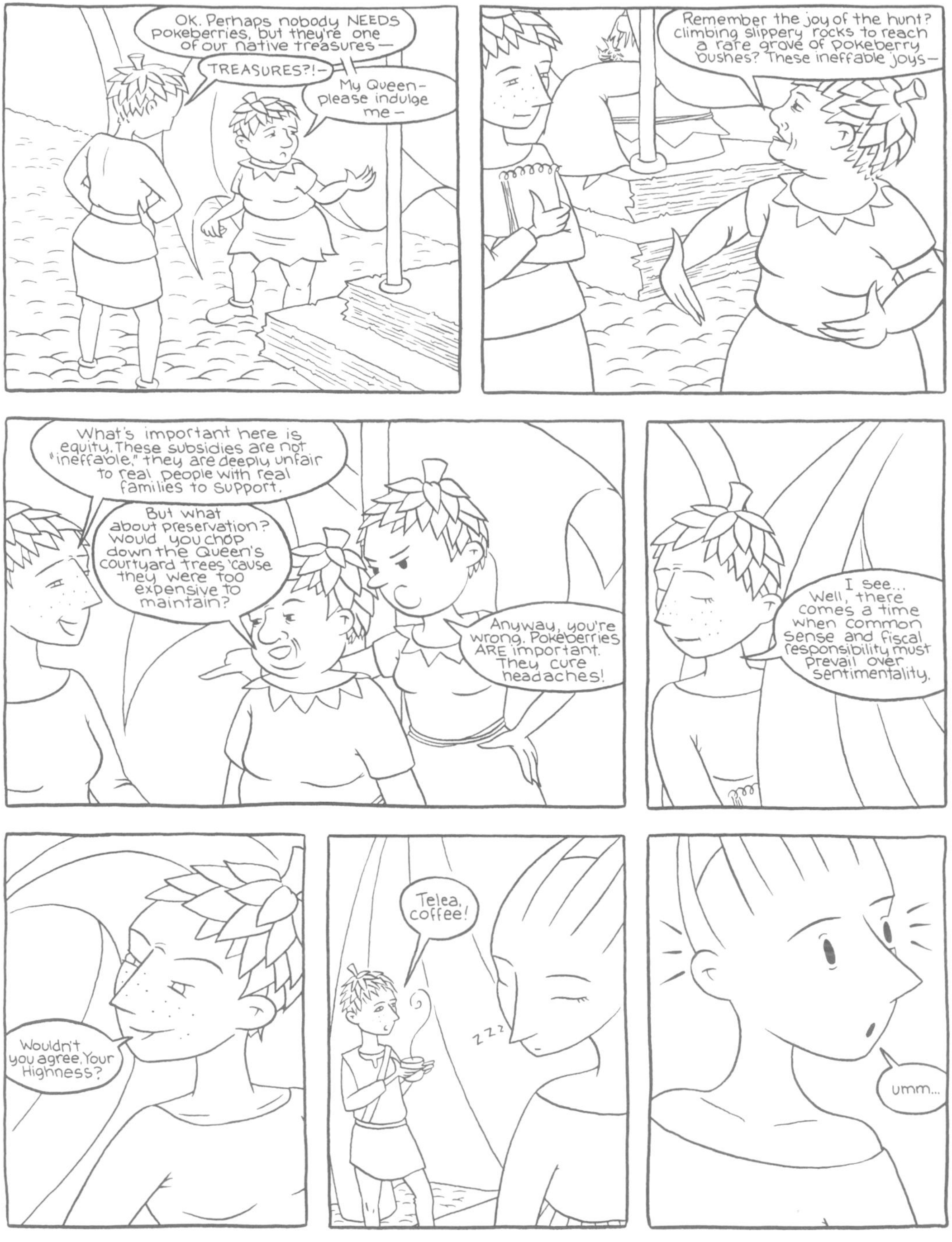
OK. Perhaps nobody NEEDS pokeberries, but they're one of our native treasures—
TREASURES?!—
My Queen—please indulge me—
Remember the joy of the hunt? climbing slippery rocks to reach a rare grove of pokeberry bushes? These ineffable joys—
What's important here is equity. These subsidies are not "ineffable," they are deeply unfair to real people with real families to support.
But what about preservation? Would you chop down the Queen's courtyard trees 'cause they were too expensive to maintain?
Anyway, you're wrong. Pokeberries ARE important. They cure headaches!
I see... Well, there comes a time when common sense and fiscal responsibility must prevail over sentimentality.
Wouldn't you agree, Your Highness?
Telea, coffee!
Z Z Z
umm...

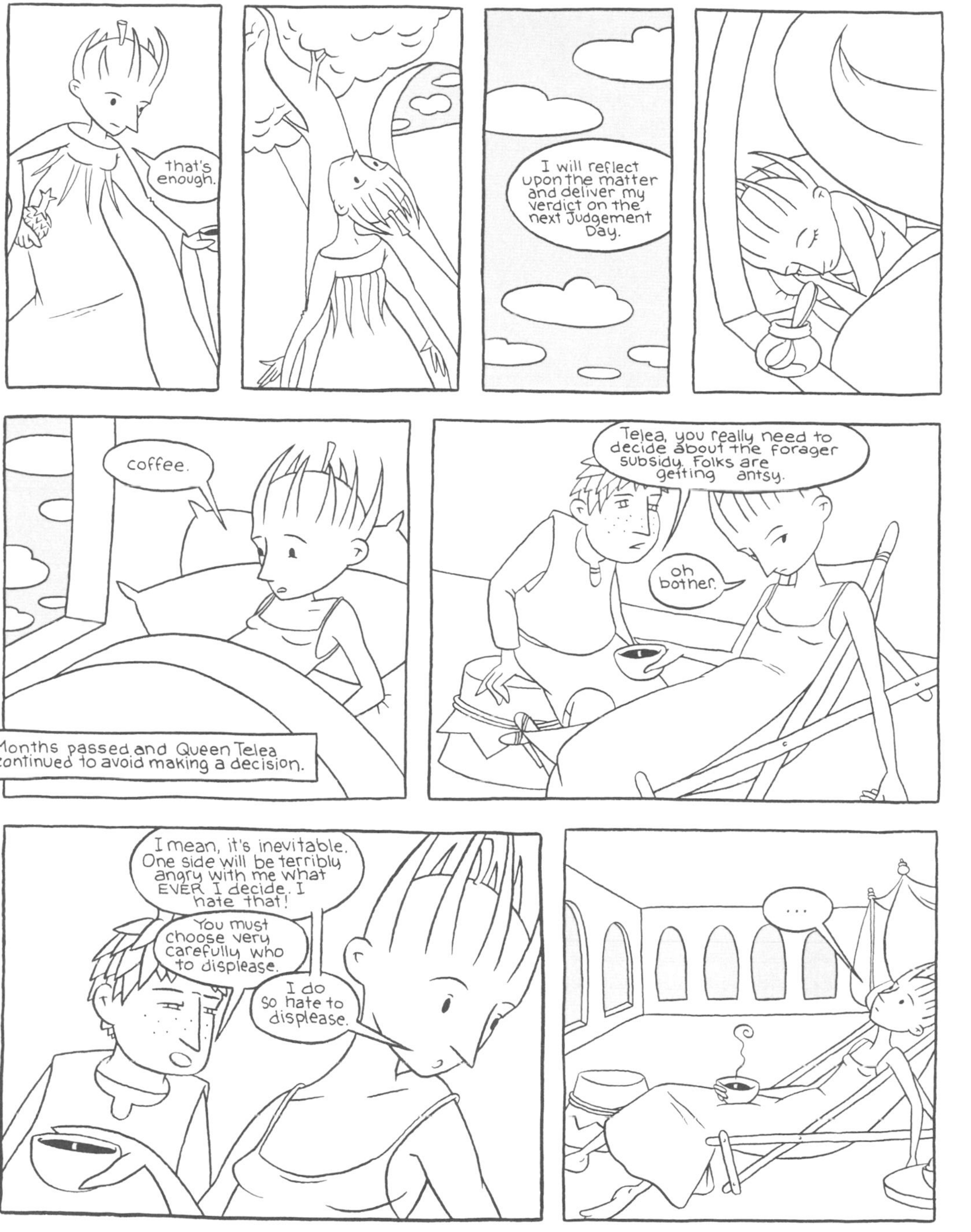

that's enough.
I will reflect upon the matter and deliver my verdict on the next Judgement Day.
coffee.
Months passed and Queen Telea continued to avoid making a decision.
Telea, you really need to decide about the forager subsidy. Folks are getting antsy.
oh bother.
I mean, it's inevitable. One side will be terribly angry with me what EVER I decide. I hate that!
You must choose very carefully who to displease.
I do so hate to displease.
...

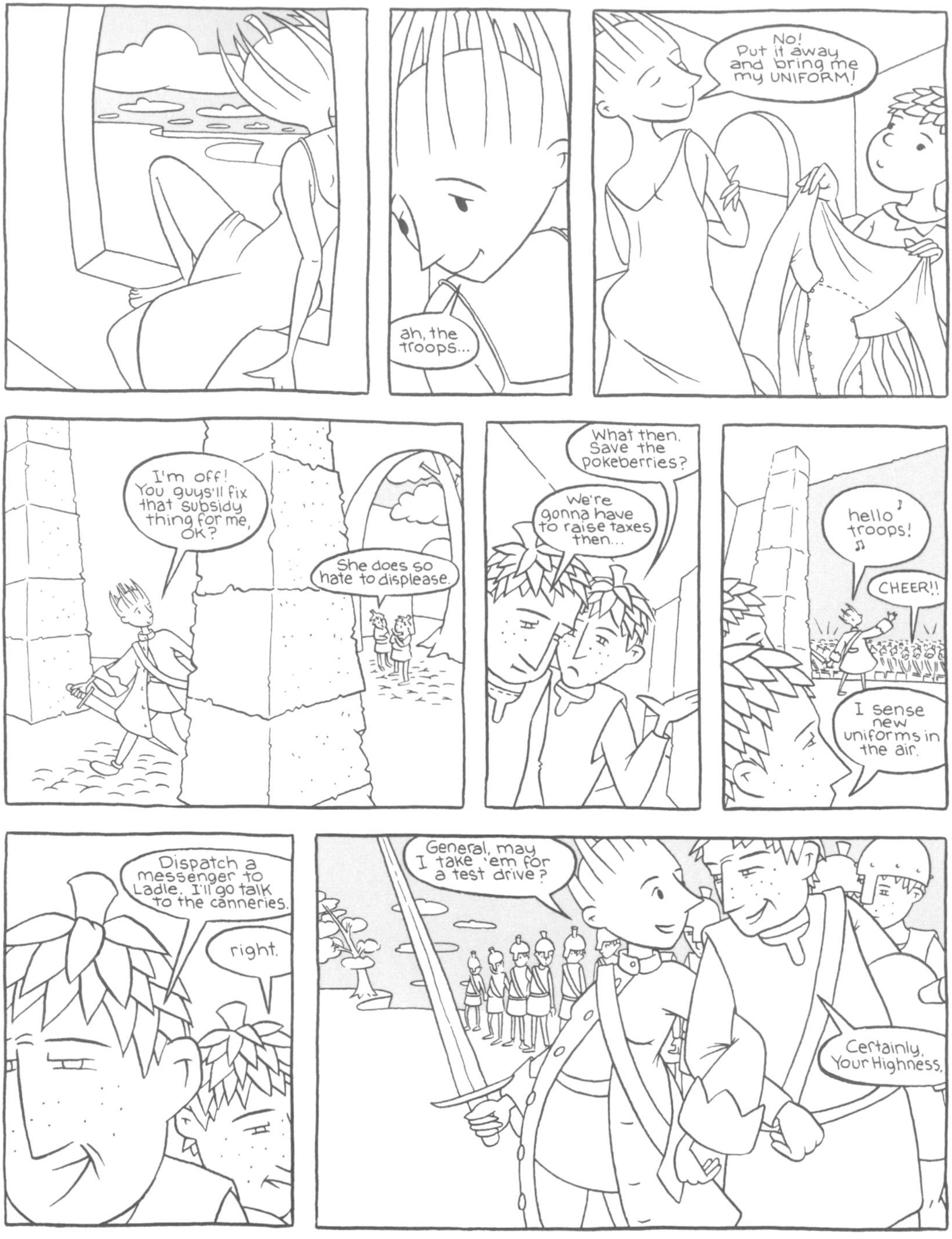
ah, the troops...
No! Put it away and bring me my UNIFORM!
I'm off! You guys'll fix that subsidy thing for me, OK?
She does so hate to displease.
What then. Save the pokeberries?
We're gonna have to raise taxes then...
hello troops!
CHEER!!
I sense new uniforms in the air.
Dispatch a messenger to Ladle. I'll go talk to the canneries.
right.
General, may I take 'em for a test drive?
Certainly, Your Highness.

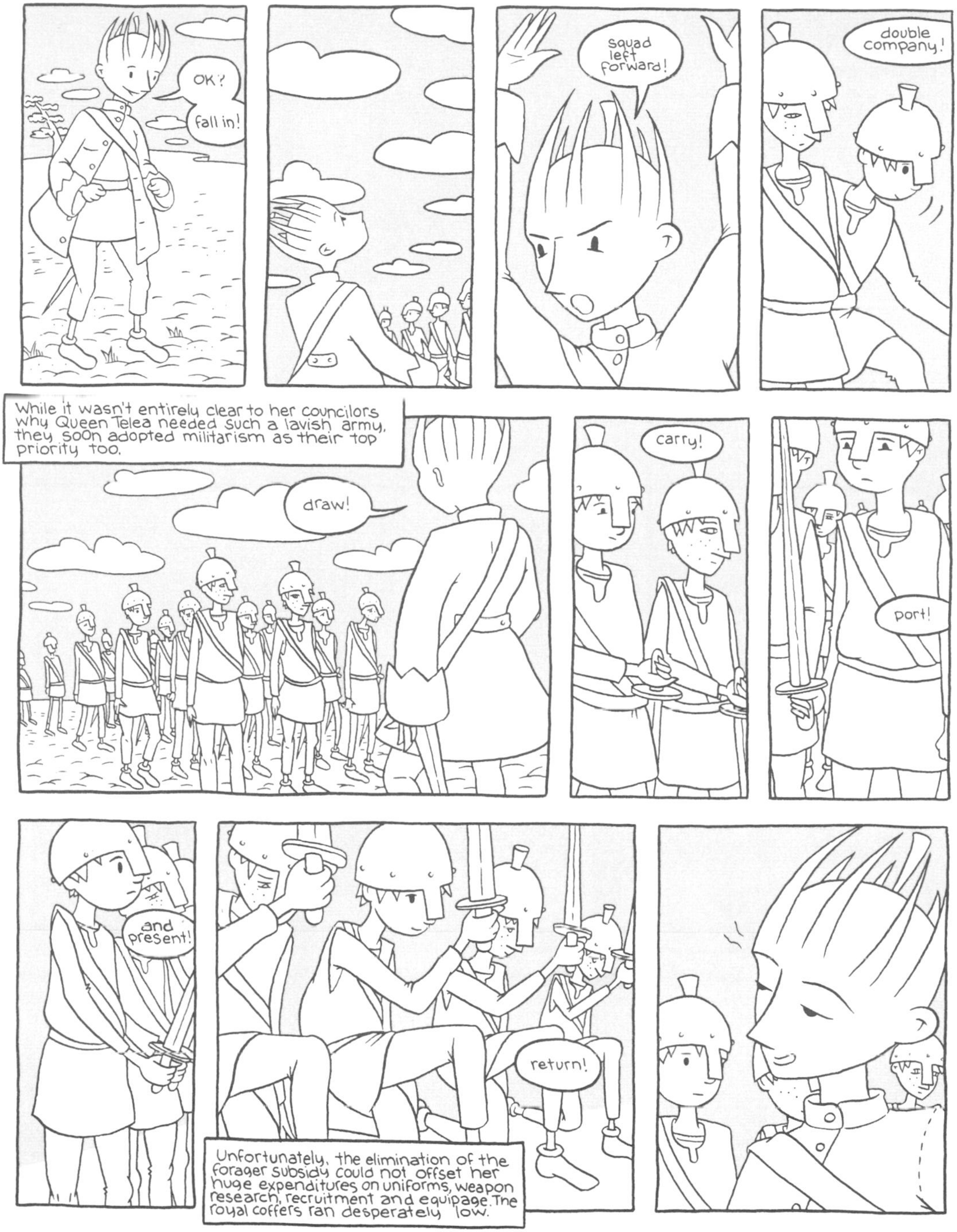
OK?
fall in!
squad left forward!
double company!
While it wasn't entirely clear to her councilors why Queen Telea needed such a lavish army, they soon adopted militarism as their top priority too.
draw!
carry!
port!
and present!
return!
Unfortunately, the elimination of the forager subsidy could not offset her huge expenditures on uniforms, weapon research, recruitment and equipage. The royal coffers ran desperately low.

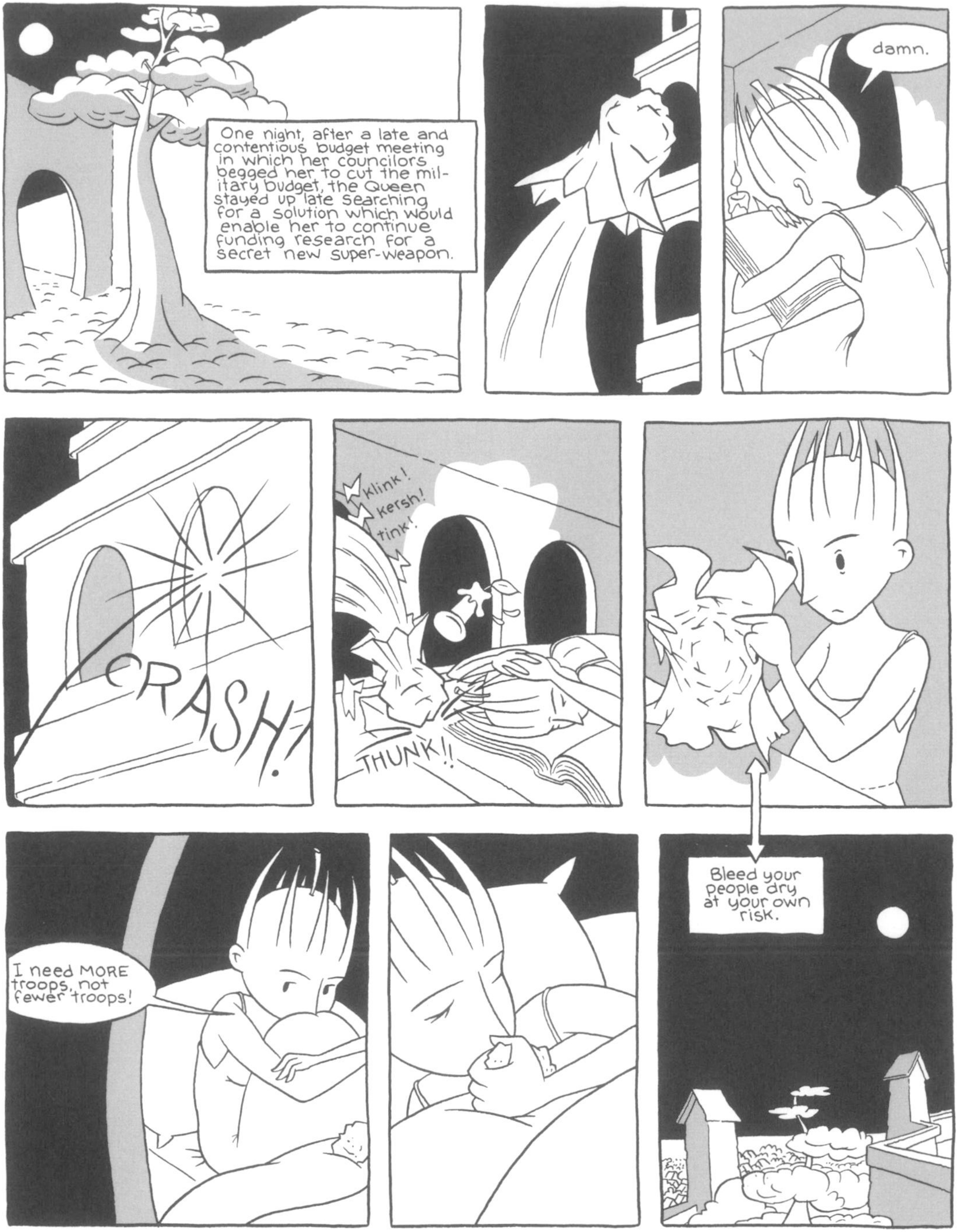
One night, after a late and contentious budget meeting in which her councilors begged her to cut the military budget, the Queen stayed up late searching for a solution which would enable her to continue funding research for a secret new super-weapon.
damn.
CRASH!!
klink!
kersh!
tink!
THUNK!!
Bleed your people dry at your own risk.
I need MORE troops, not fewer troops!

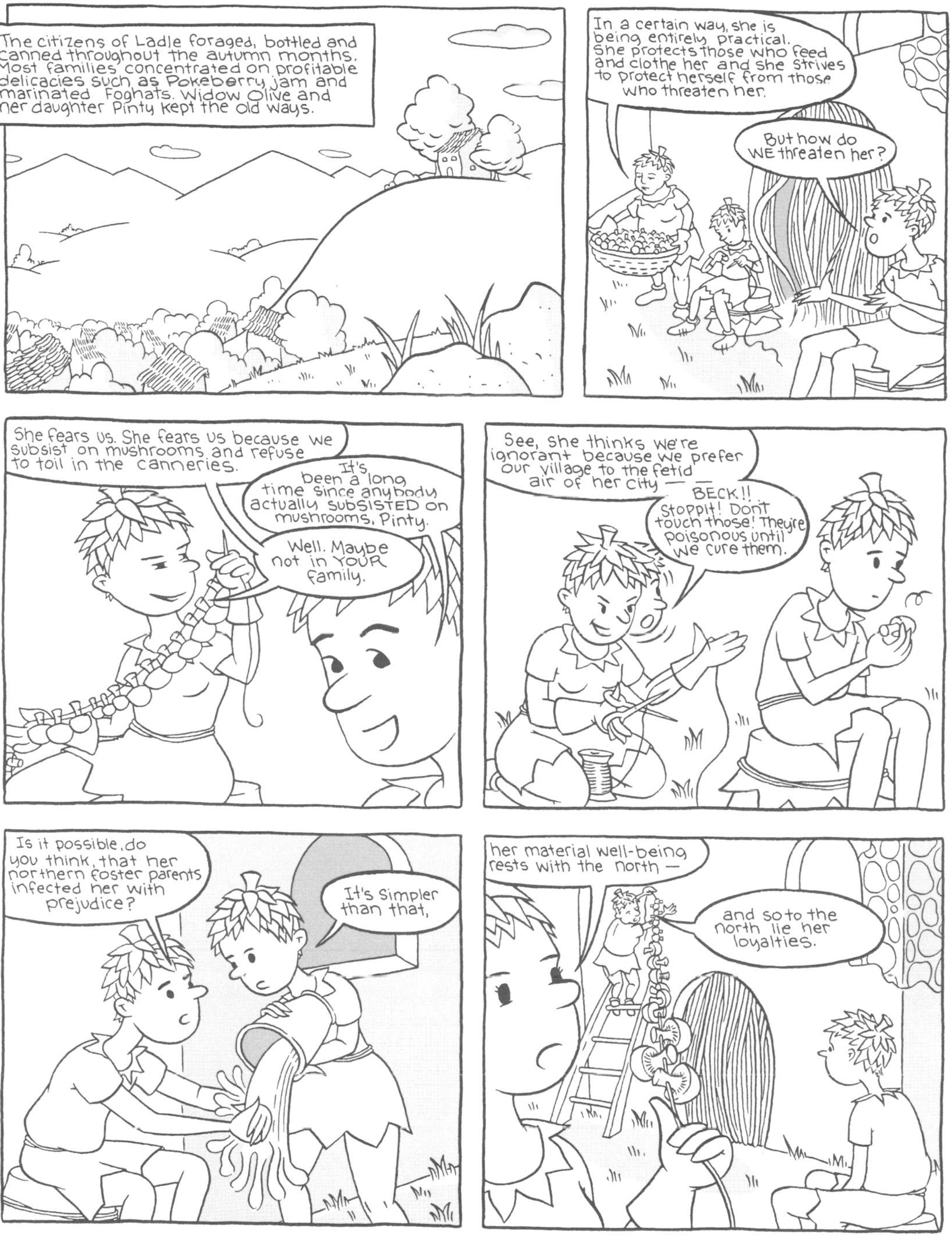
The citizens of Ladle foraged, bottled and canned throughout the autumn months. Most families concentrated on profitable delicacies such as Pokeberry jam and marinated Foghats. Widow Olive and her daughter Pinty kept the old ways.
In a certain way, she is being entirely practical. She protects those who feed and clothe her and she strives to protect herself from those who threaten her.
But how do WE threaten her?
She fears us. She fears us because we subsist on mushrooms and refuse to toil in the canneries.
It's been a long time since anybody actually SUBSISTED on mushrooms, Pinty.
Well. Maybe not in YOUR family.
See, she thinks we're ignorant because we prefer our village to the fetid air of her city — —
BECK!! Stoppit! Don't touch those! They're poisonous until we cure them.
Is it possible, do you think, that her northern foster parents infected her with prejudice?
It's simpler than that,
her material well-being rests with the north —
and so to the north lie her loyalties.

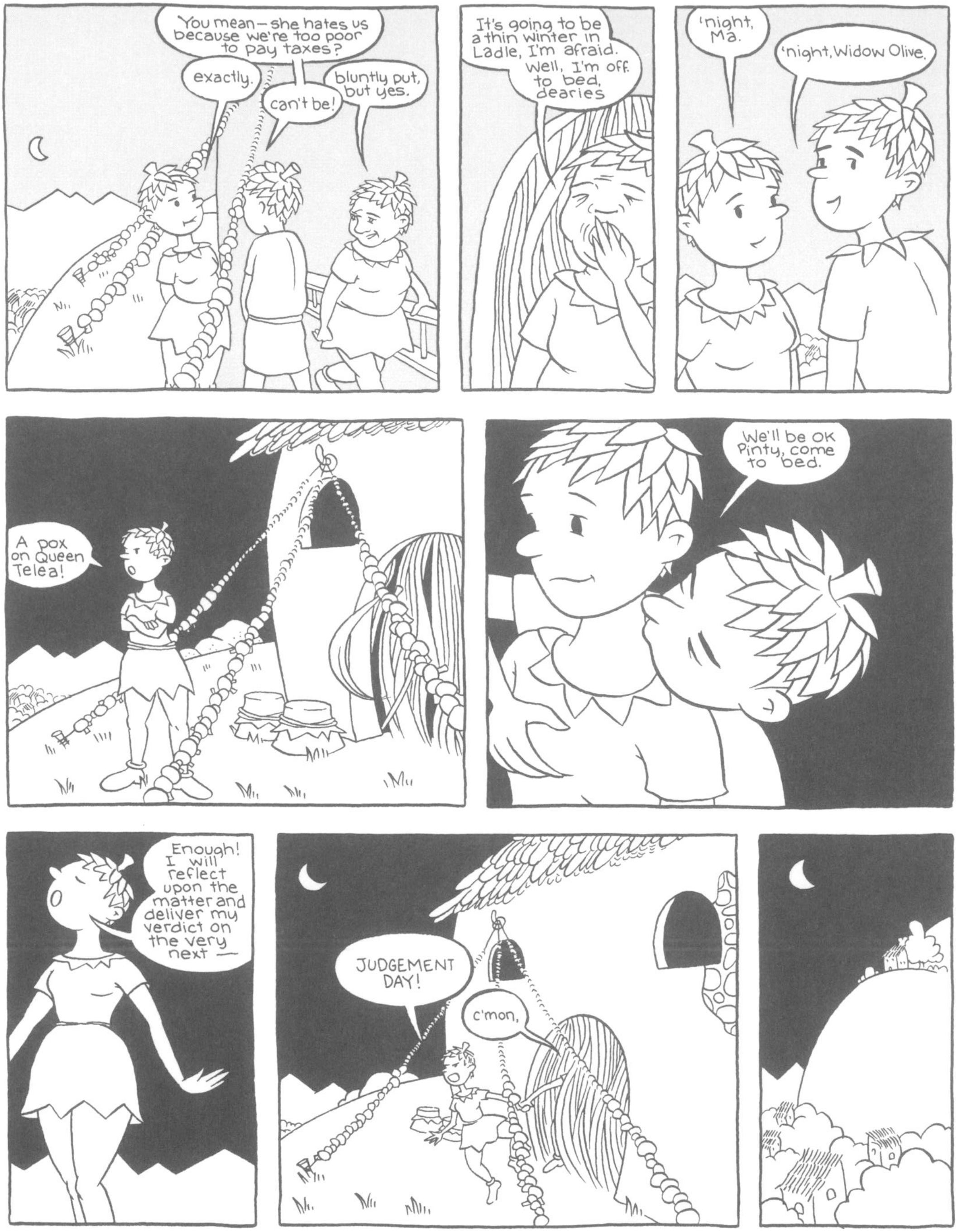
You mean—she hates us because we're too poor to pay taxes?
exactly.
can't be!
bluntly put, but yes.
It's going to be a thin winter in Ladle, I'm afraid.
Well, I'm off to bed, dearies
'night, Ma.
'night, Widow Olive.
A pox on Queen Telea!
We'll be OK Pinty, come to bed.
Enough! I will reflect upon the matter and deliver my verdict on the very next —
JUDGEMENT DAY!
c'mon,

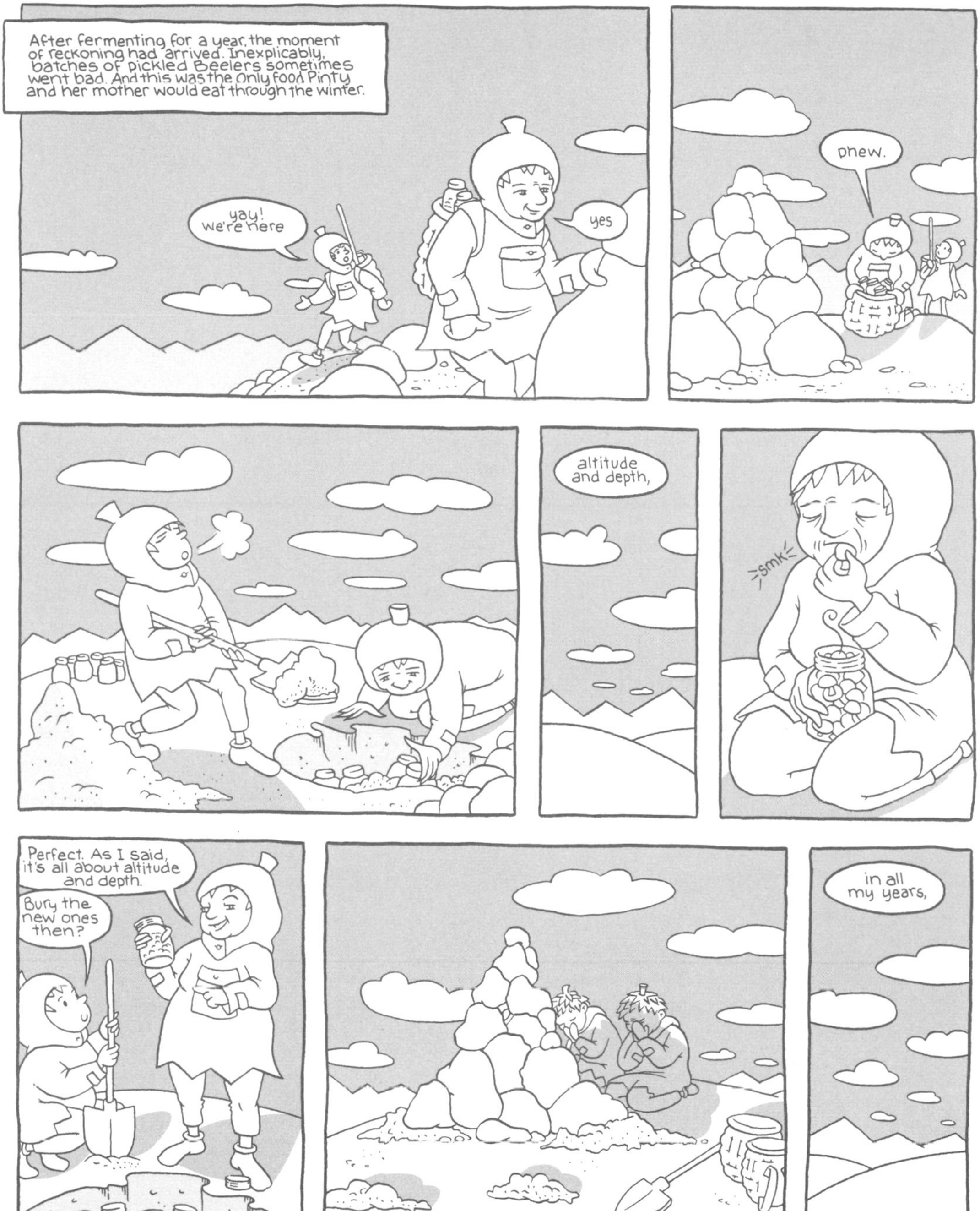
After fermenting for a year, the moment of reckoning had arrived. Inexplicably, batches of pickled Beelers sometimes went bad. And this was the only food Pinty and her mother would eat through the winter.
yay! we're here
yes
phew.
altitude and depth,
SMK
Perfect. As I said, it's all about altitude and depth.
Bury the new ones then?
in all my years,

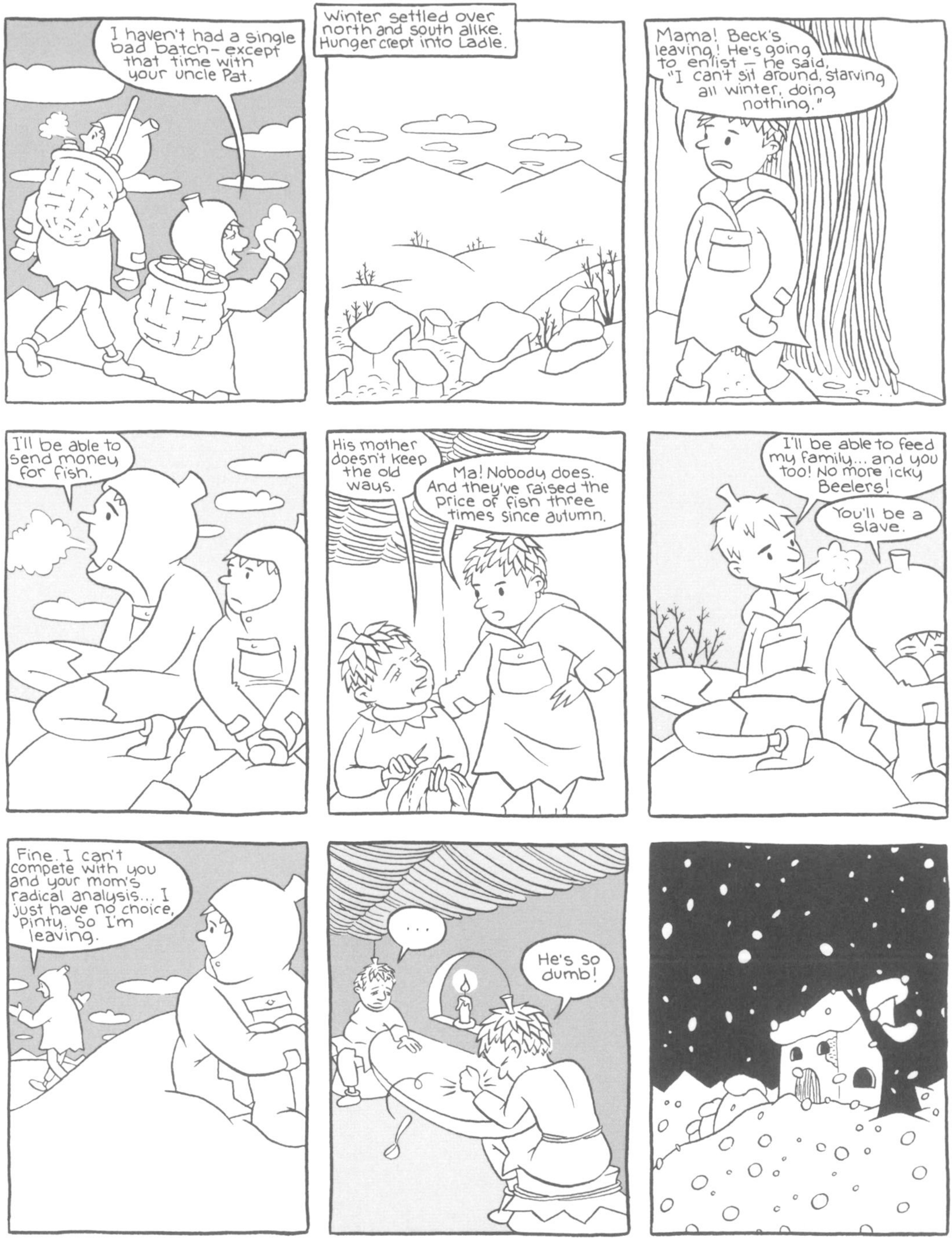
I haven't had a single bad batch- except that time with your uncle Pat.
Winter settled over north and south alike. Hunger crept into Ladle.
Mama! Beck's leaving! He's going to enlist — he said, "I can't sit around, starving all winter, doing nothing."
I'll be able to send money for fish.
His mother doesn't keep the old ways.
Ma! Nobody does. And they've raised the price of fish three times since autumn.
I'll be able to feed my family... and you too! No more icky Beelers!
You'll be a slave.
Fine. I can't compete with you and your mom's radical analysis... I just have no choice, Pinty. So I'm leaving.
...
He's so dumb!

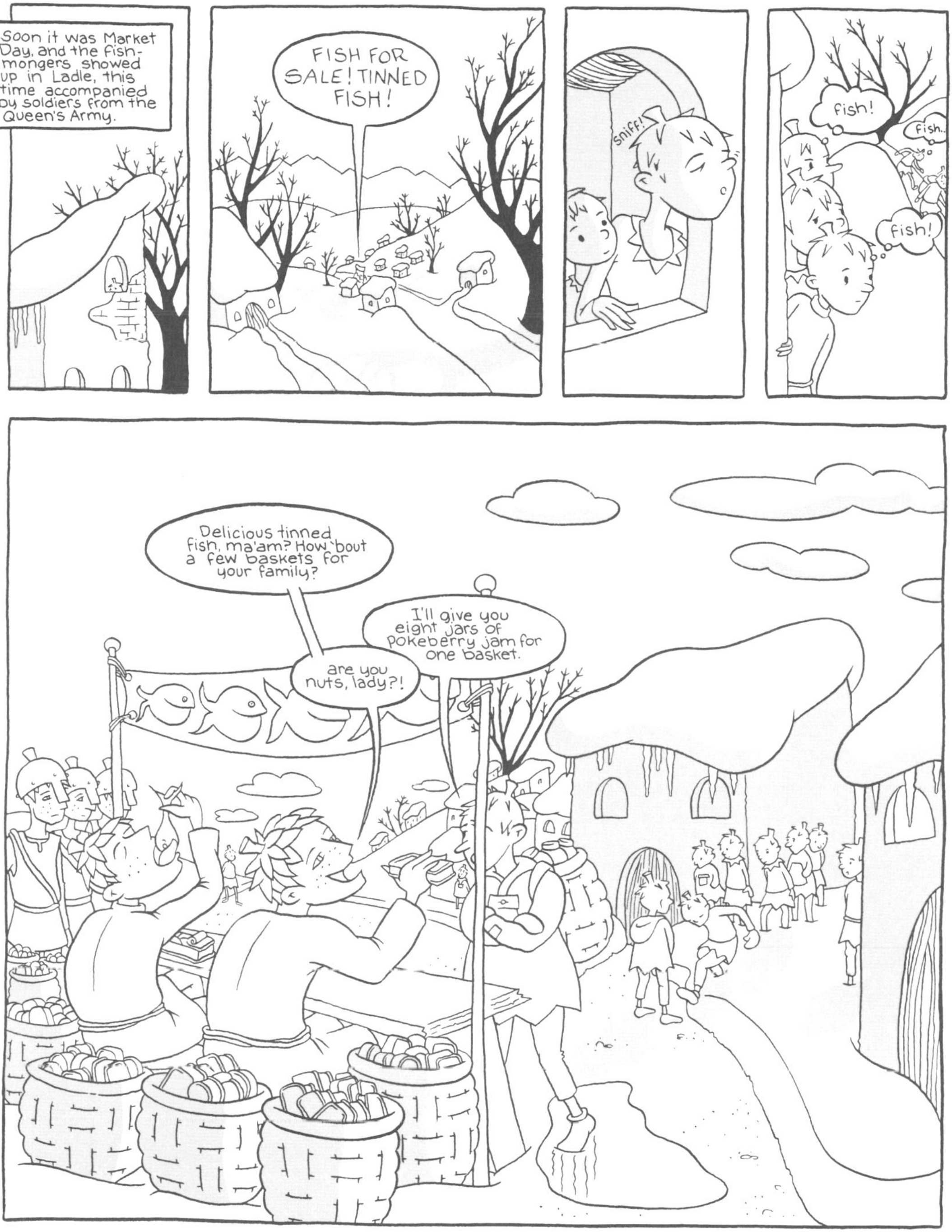

Soon it was Market Day, and the fishmongers showed up in Ladle, this time accompanied by soldiers from the Queen's Army.
FISH FOR SALE! TINNED FISH!
Sniff!
fish!
Fish..
fish!
Delicious tinned fish, ma'am? How 'bout a few baskets for your family?
I'll give you eight jars of pokeberry jam for one basket.
are you nuts, lady?!

ATTENSHUN!

OK then, 8 for ½ a case.

Don't waste my time —

Who wants to serve with honor in the Queen's uniform? Who wants a belly full of fish?

Please sir, it's — it's all I have

sorry, patchy.

C'mon over, boys!

Hey, relax, fellas

They're pretty spindly...

um,

Uh, sir? My name is Beck and—

What IS IT?!

I mean— I'll sign the contract— I WANT to sign, but if I could take fish to my family first—?

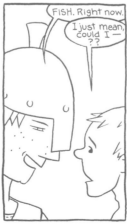

FISH. Right now.

I just mean, could I — ??

oh Beck!
oof!
Pinty? Calm.
you FUCKERS! you — —
BONK!!
mmpff!
Now listen here, young lady,

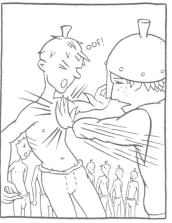

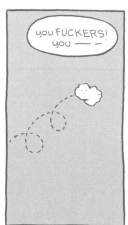

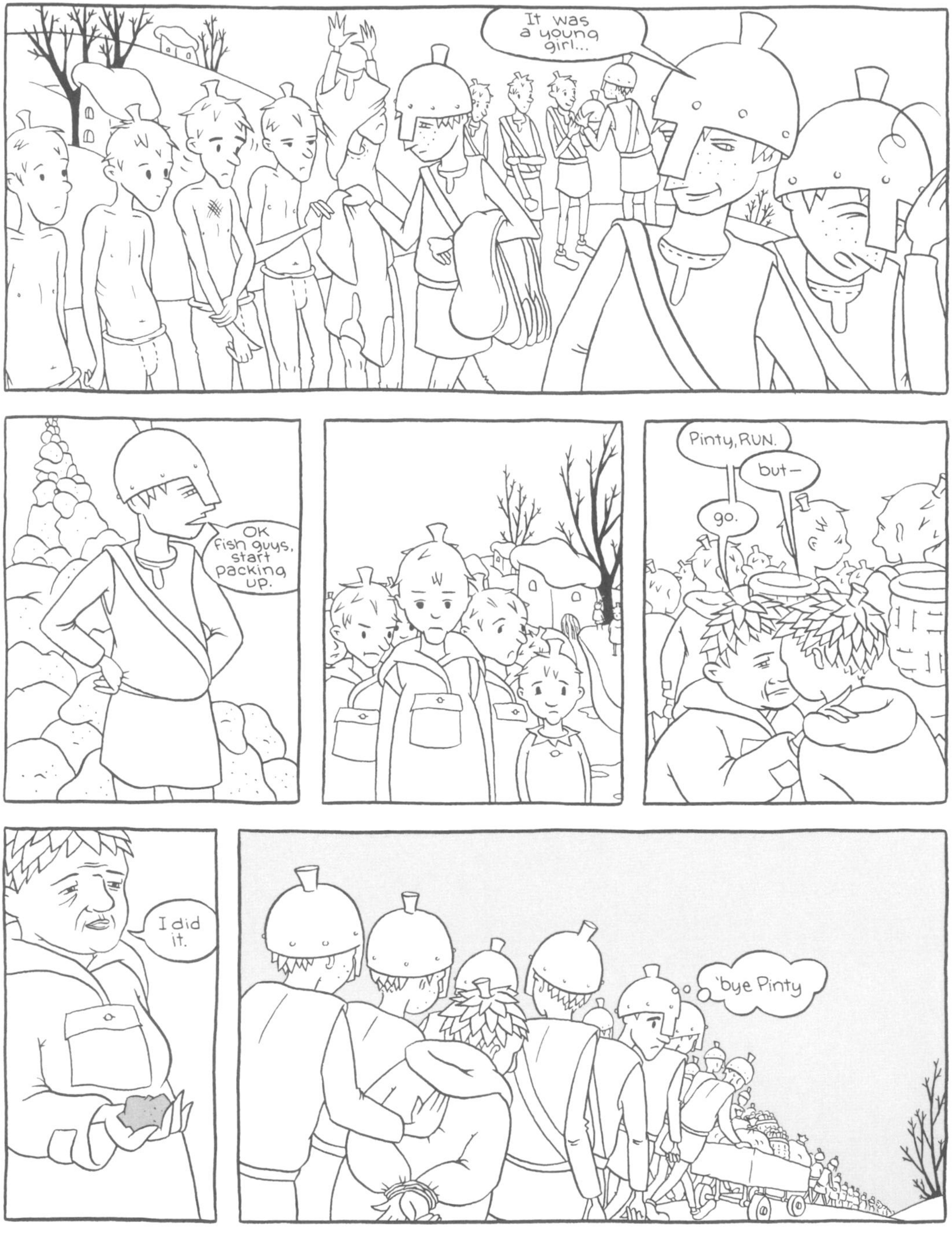
It was a young girl...
OK fish guys, start packing up.
Pinty, RUN.
but—
go.
I did it.
'bye Pinty

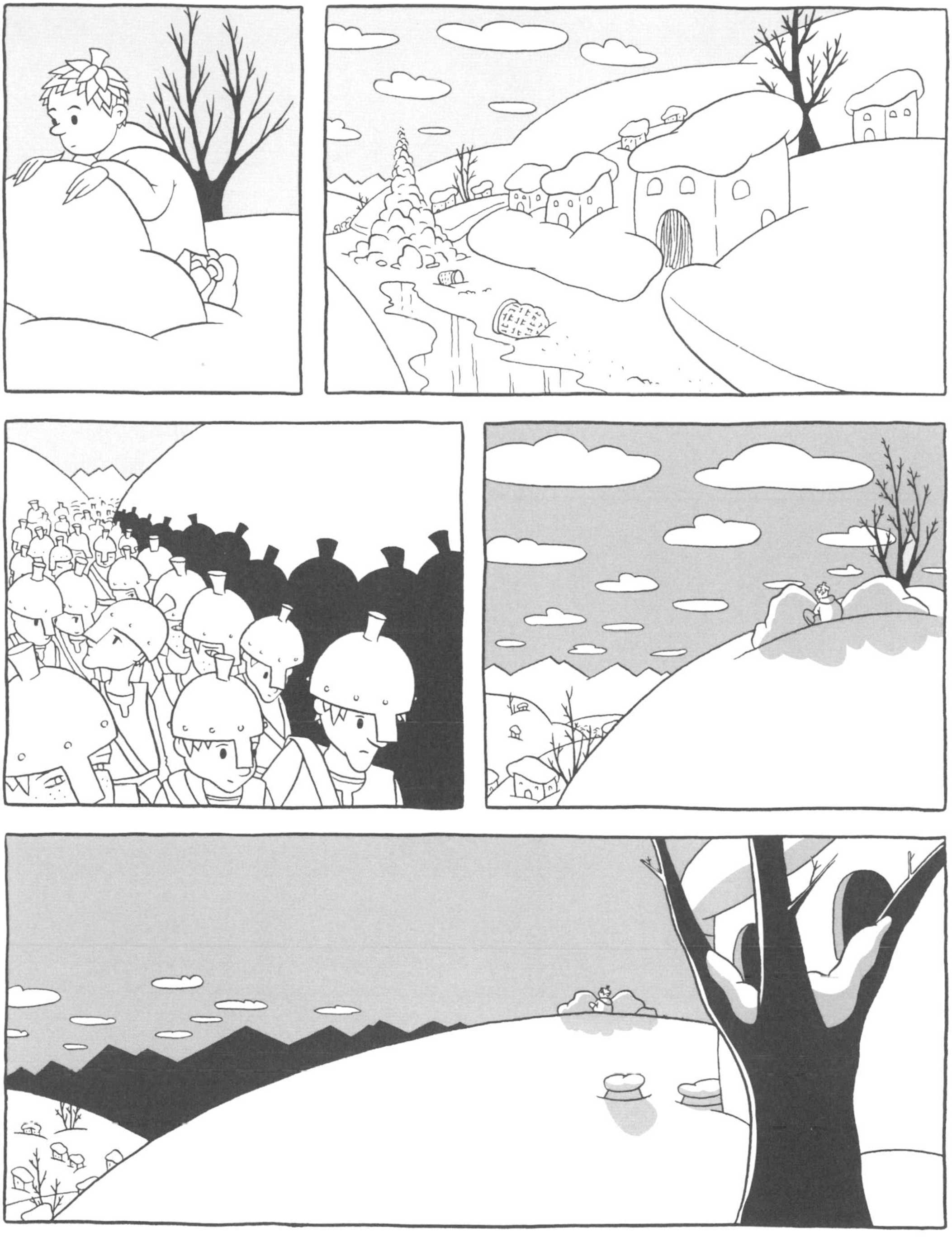

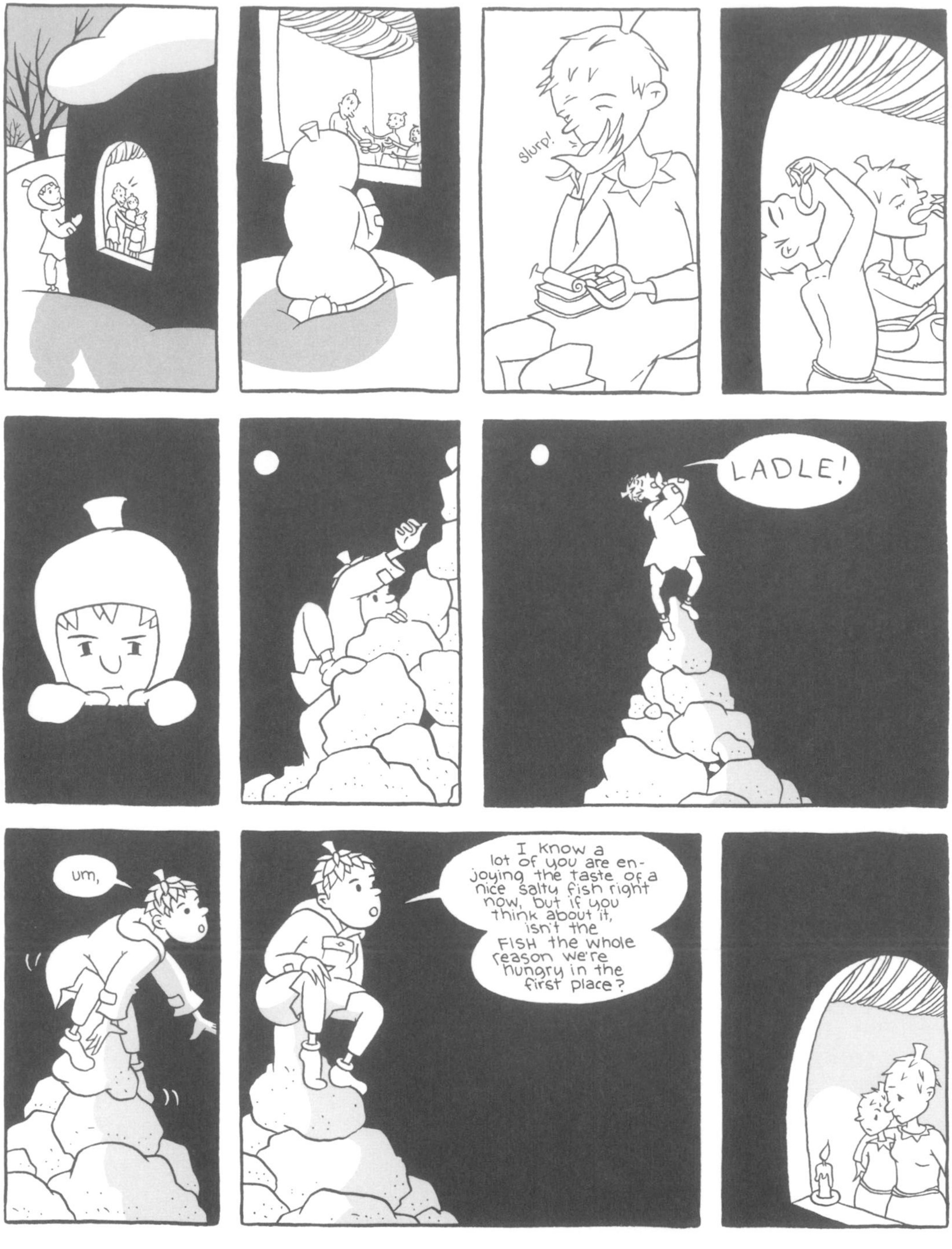
slurp!
LADLE!
um,
I know a lot of you are enjoying the taste of a nice salty fish right now, but if you think about it, isn't the FISH the whole reason we're hungry in the first place?

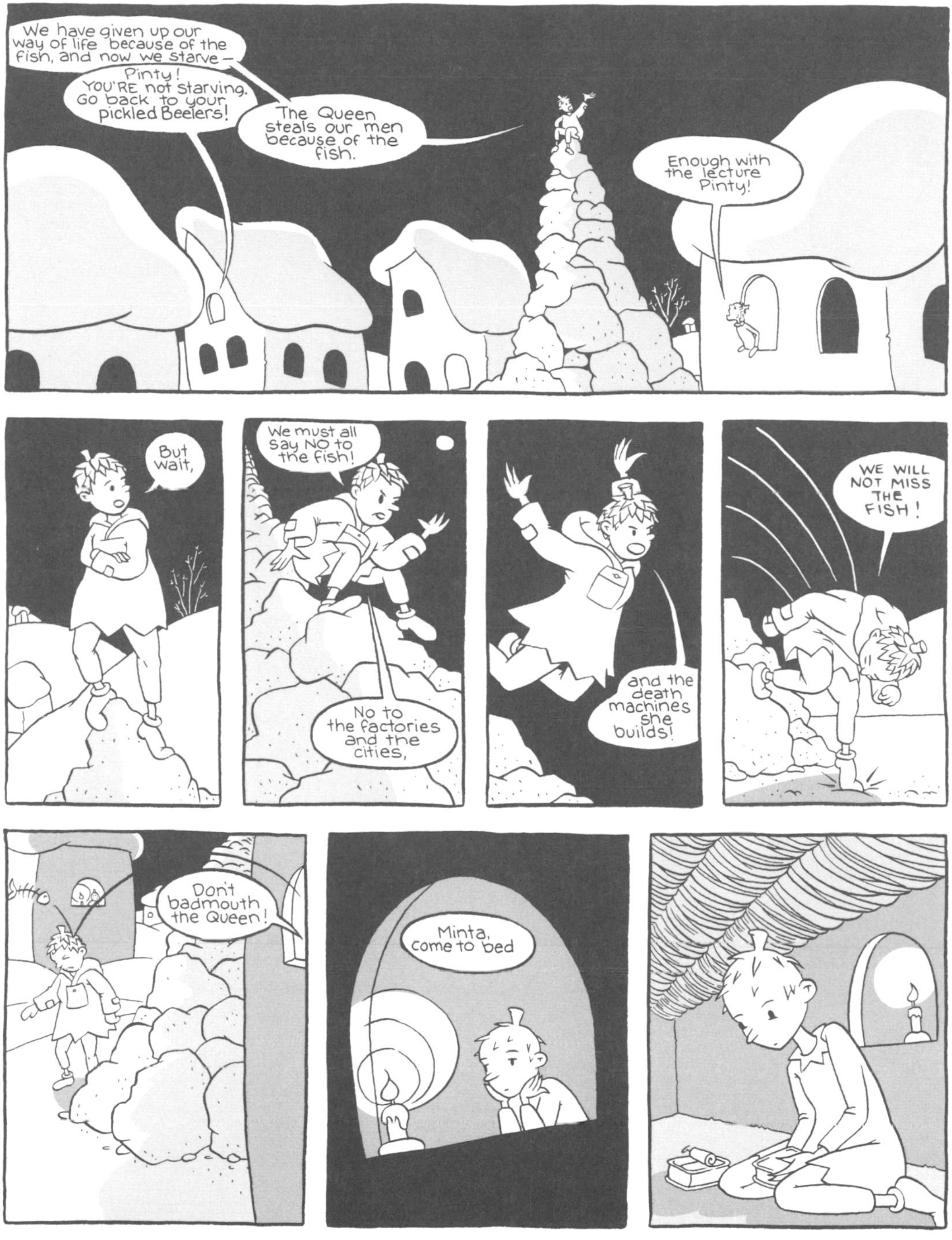
We have given up our way of life because of the fish, and now we starve—
Pinty! YOU'RE not starving. Go back to your pickled Beelers!
The Queen steals our men because of the fish.
Enough with the lecture Pinty!
But wait,
We must all say NO to the fish!
No to the factories and the cities,
and the death machines she builds!
WE WILL NOT MISS THE FISH!
Don't badmouth the Queen!
Minta, come to bed

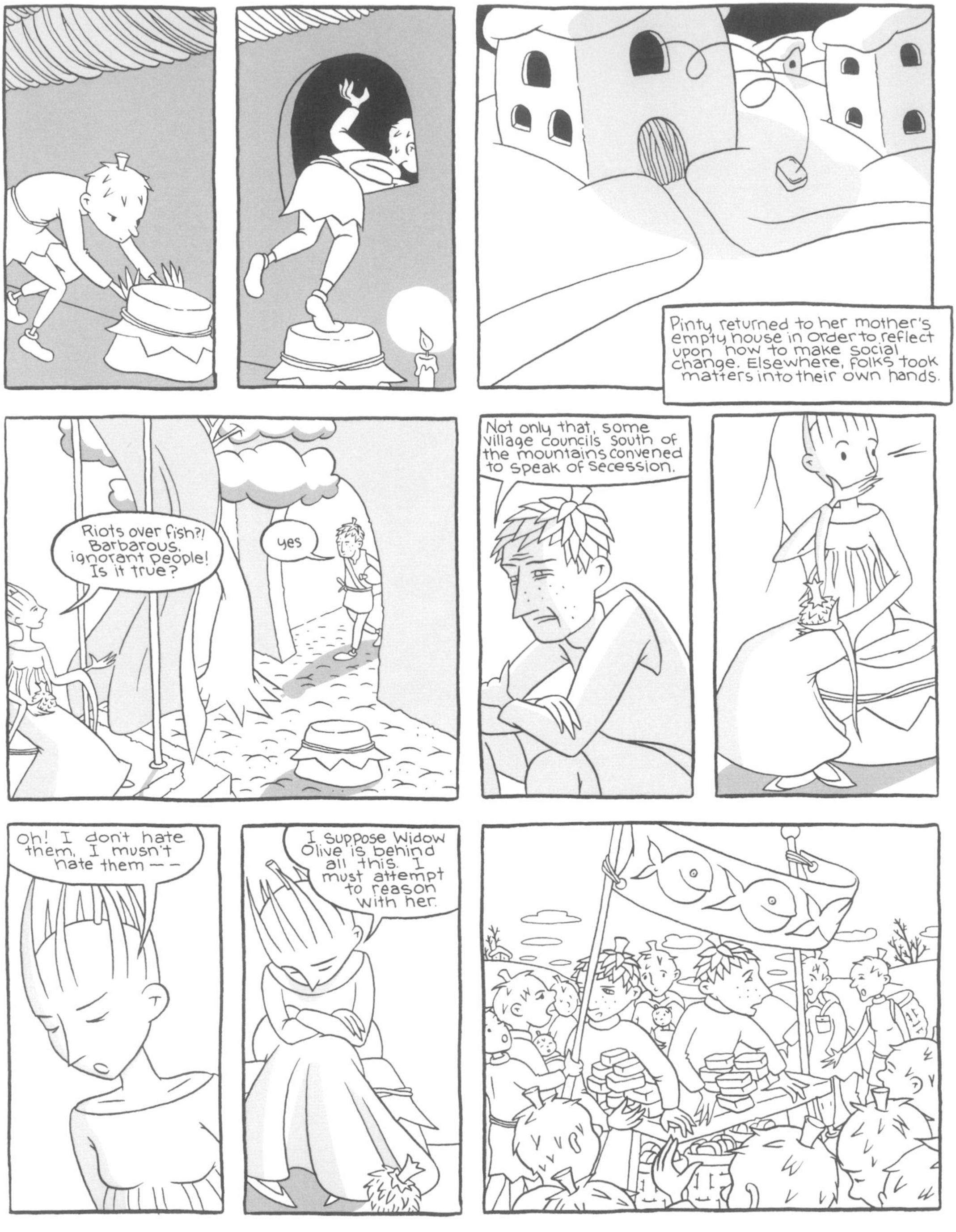
Pinty returned to her mother's empty house in order to reflect upon how to make social change. Elsewhere, folks took matters into their own hands.
Riots over fish?! Barbarous, ignorant people! Is it true?
yes
Not only that, some village councils south of the mountains convened to speak of secession.
Oh! I don't hate them, I musn't hate them --
I suppose Widow Olive is behind all this. I must attempt to reason with her.

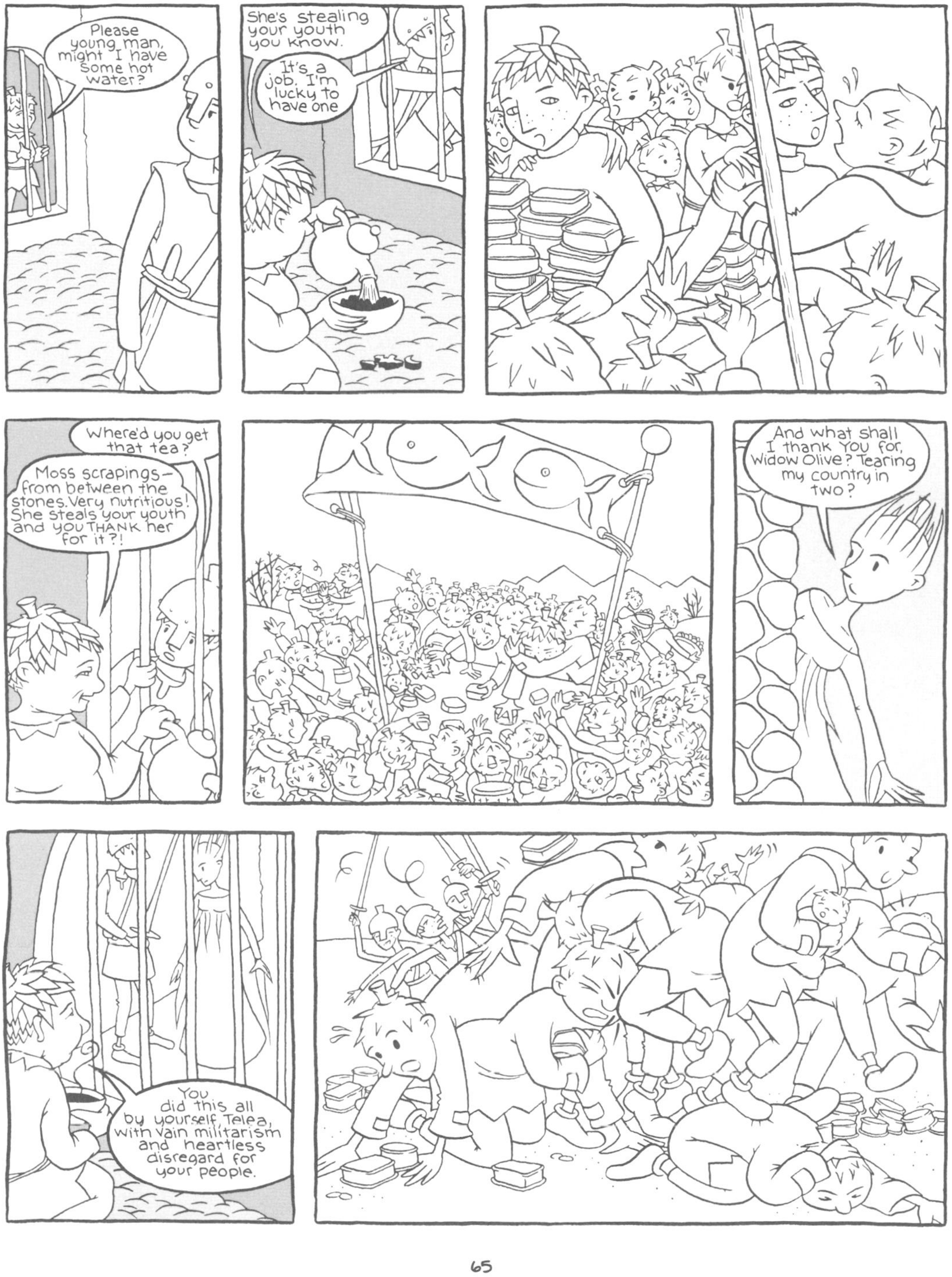
Please young man, might I have some hot water?
She's stealing your youth you know.
It's a job. I'm lucky to have one
Where'd you get that tea?
Moss scrapings– from between the stones. Very nutritious! She steals your youth and you THANK her for it?!
And what shall I thank You for, Widow Olive? Tearing my country in two?
You did this all by yourself, Telea, with vain militarism and heartless disregard for your people.

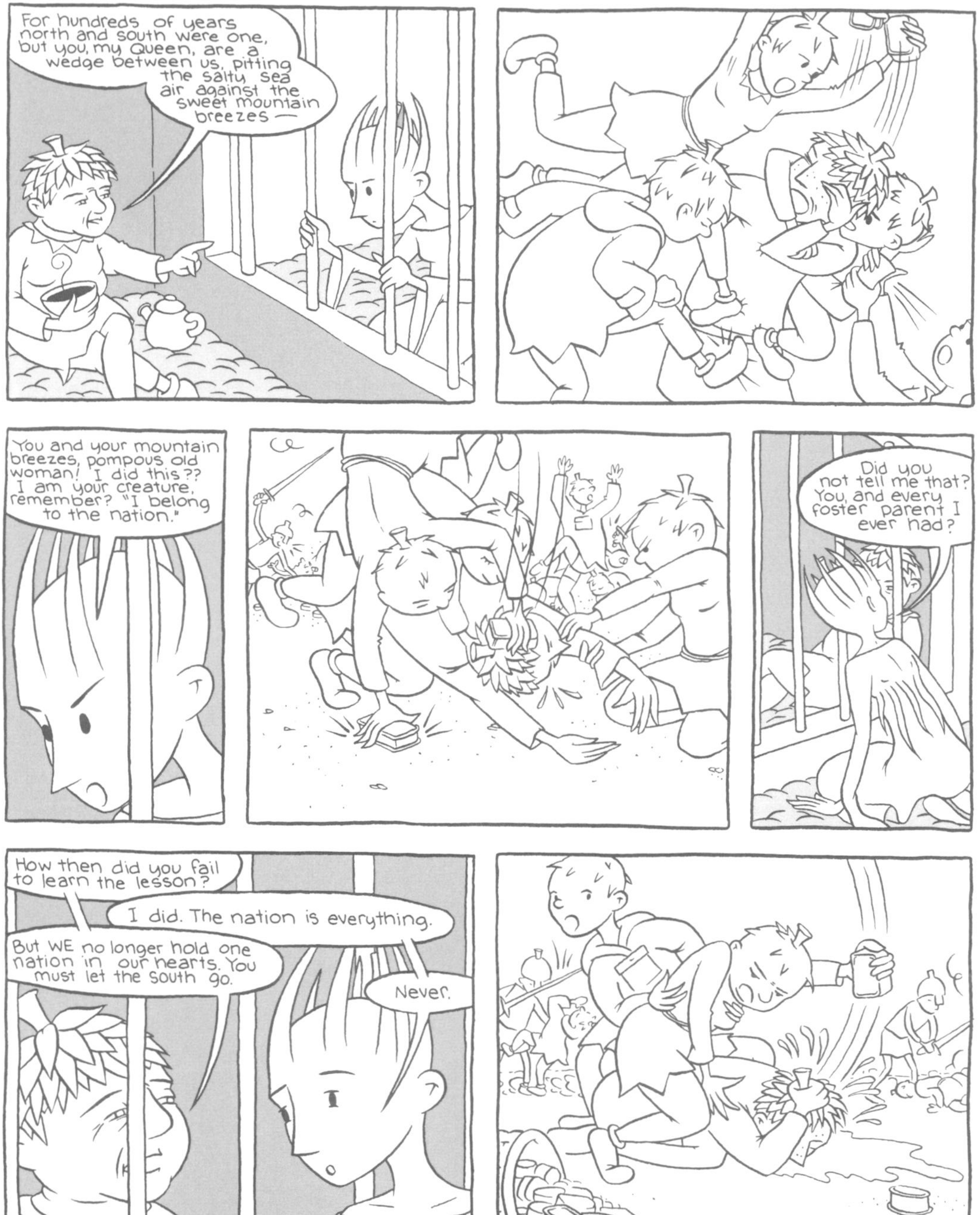
For hundreds of years north and south were one, but you, my Queen, are a wedge between us, pitting the salty sea air against the sweet mountain breezes —
You and your mountain breezes, pompous old woman! I did this?? I am your creature, remember? "I belong to the nation."
Did you not tell me that? You, and every foster parent I ever had?
How then did you fail to learn the lesson?
I did. The nation is everything.
But WE no longer hold one nation in our hearts. You must let the south go.
Never.

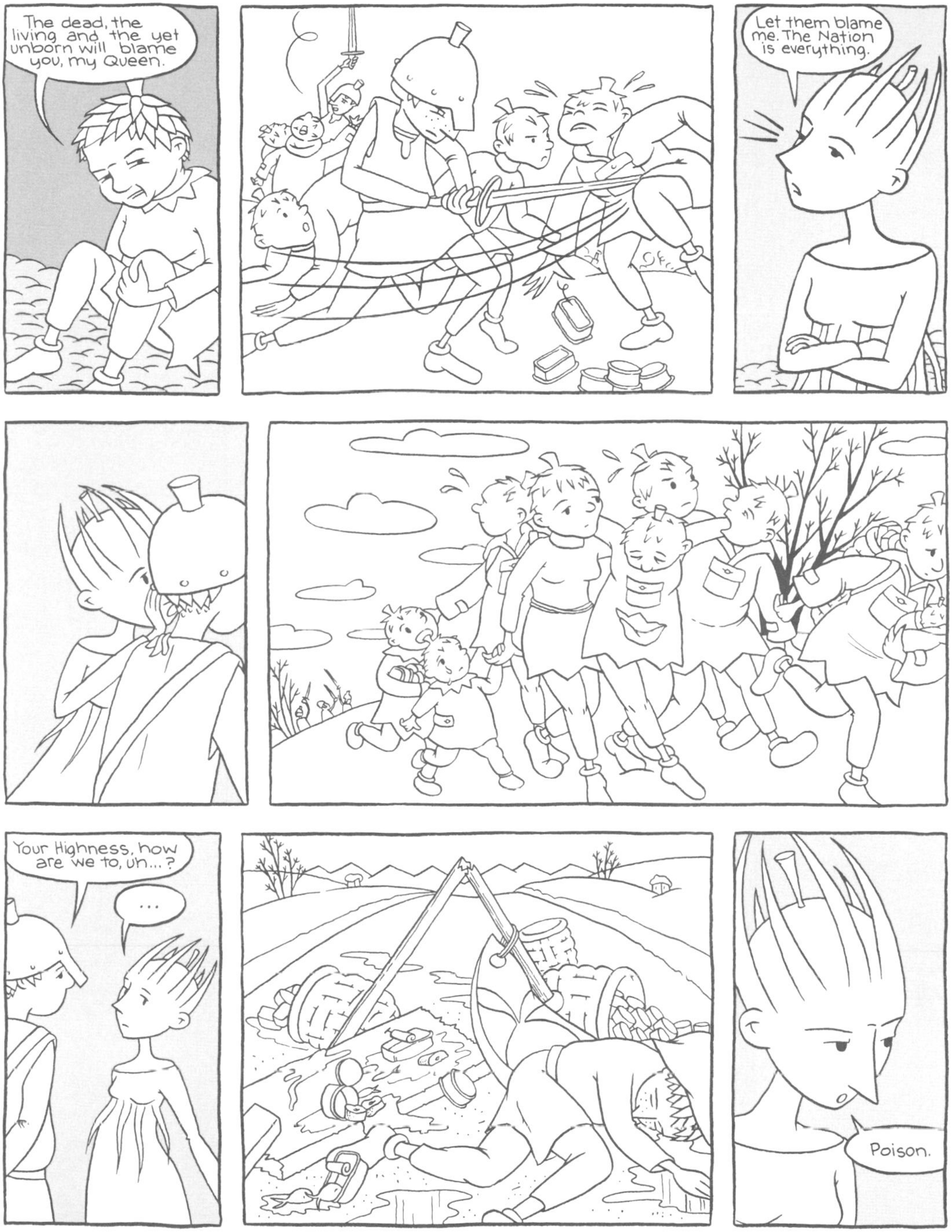
The dead, the living and the yet unborn will blame you, my Queen.
Let them blame me. The Nation is everything.
Your Highness, how are we to, uh...?
...
Poison.

When does a riot turn into a war? Perhaps it is when the rioters figure out who the true enemy is.

Minta! I'm glad you're here!

Y'know, part of me is glad to hear about the fish riots — but a non-violent boycott will be so much more effective. It will show the north our value as a market—

It'll give us bargaining power and moral authority.

sniff

The Queen killed your mama.

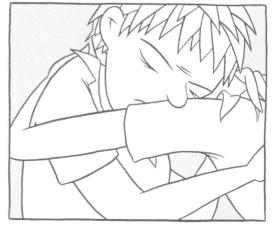

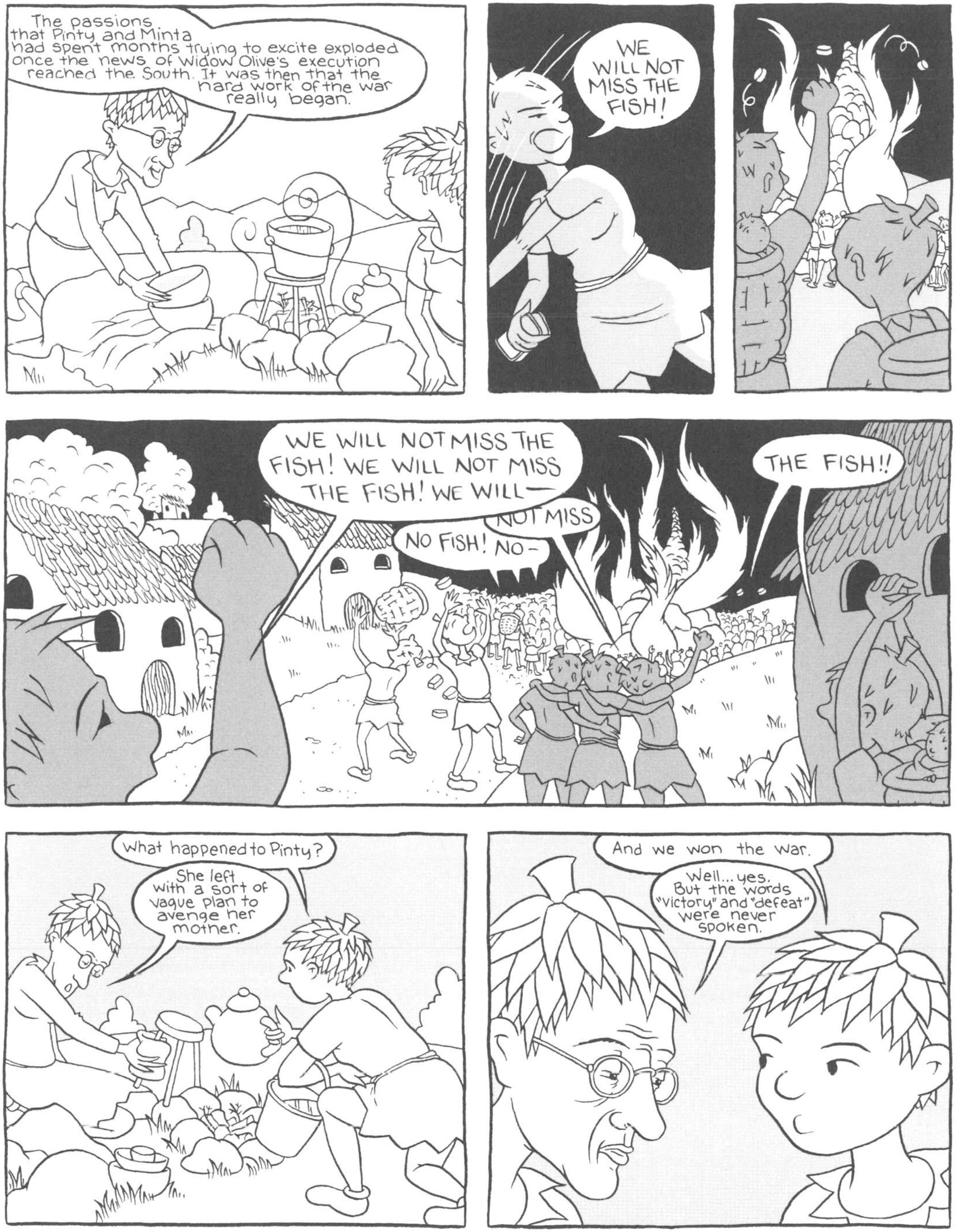
The passions that Pinty and Minta had spent months trying to excite exploded once the news of Widow Olive's execution reached the South. It was then that the hard work of the war really began.
WE WILL NOT MISS THE FISH!
WE WILL NOT MISS THE FISH! WE WILL NOT MISS THE FISH! WE WILL—
NOT MISS
NO FISH! NO-
THE FISH!!
What happened to Pinty?
She left with a sort of vague plan to avenge her mother.
And we won the war.
Well... yes. But the words "victory" and "defeat" were never spoken.

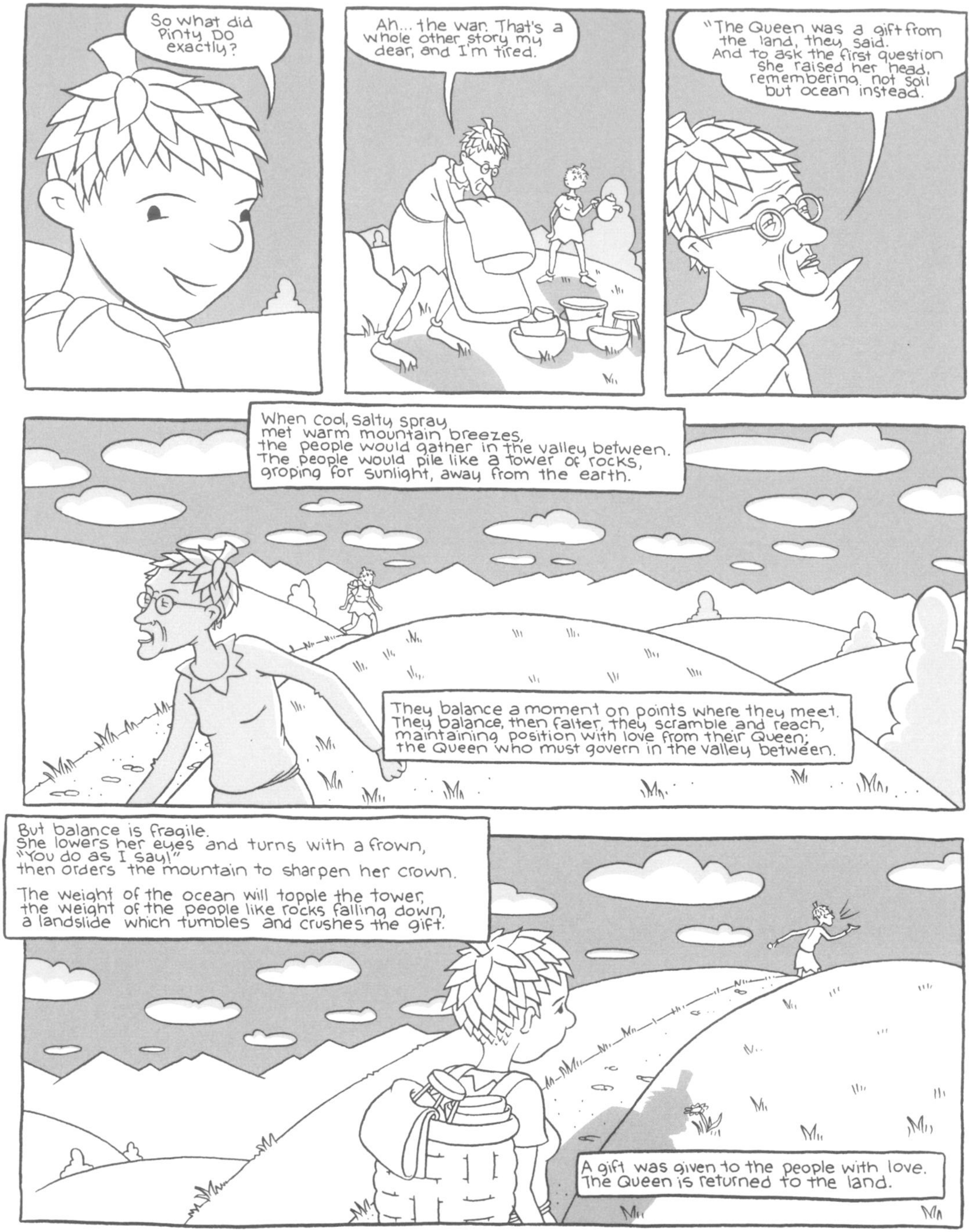
So what did Pinty Do exactly?
Ah... the war. That's a whole other story my dear, and I'm tired.
"The Queen was a gift from the land, they said. And to ask the first question she raised her head, remembering, not soil but ocean instead.
When cool, salty spray met warm mountain breezes, the people would gather in the valley between. The people would pile like a tower of rocks, groping for sunlight, away from the earth.
They balance a moment on points where they meet. They balance, then falter, they scramble and reach, maintaining position with love from their Queen; the Queen who must govern in the valley between.
But balance is fragile. She lowers her eyes and turns with a frown, "You do as I say!" then orders the mountain to sharpen her crown.
The weight of the ocean will topple the tower, the weight of the people like rocks falling down, a landslide which tumbles and crushes the gift.
A gift was given to the people with love. The Queen is returned to the land.

ground floor
shop/livingroom

second floor
work room

Chapter 3
JIMMY & CHARLOTTE

Charlotte &
Jimmy's room

Ramona's
room

third floor
bedrooms

attic
storage

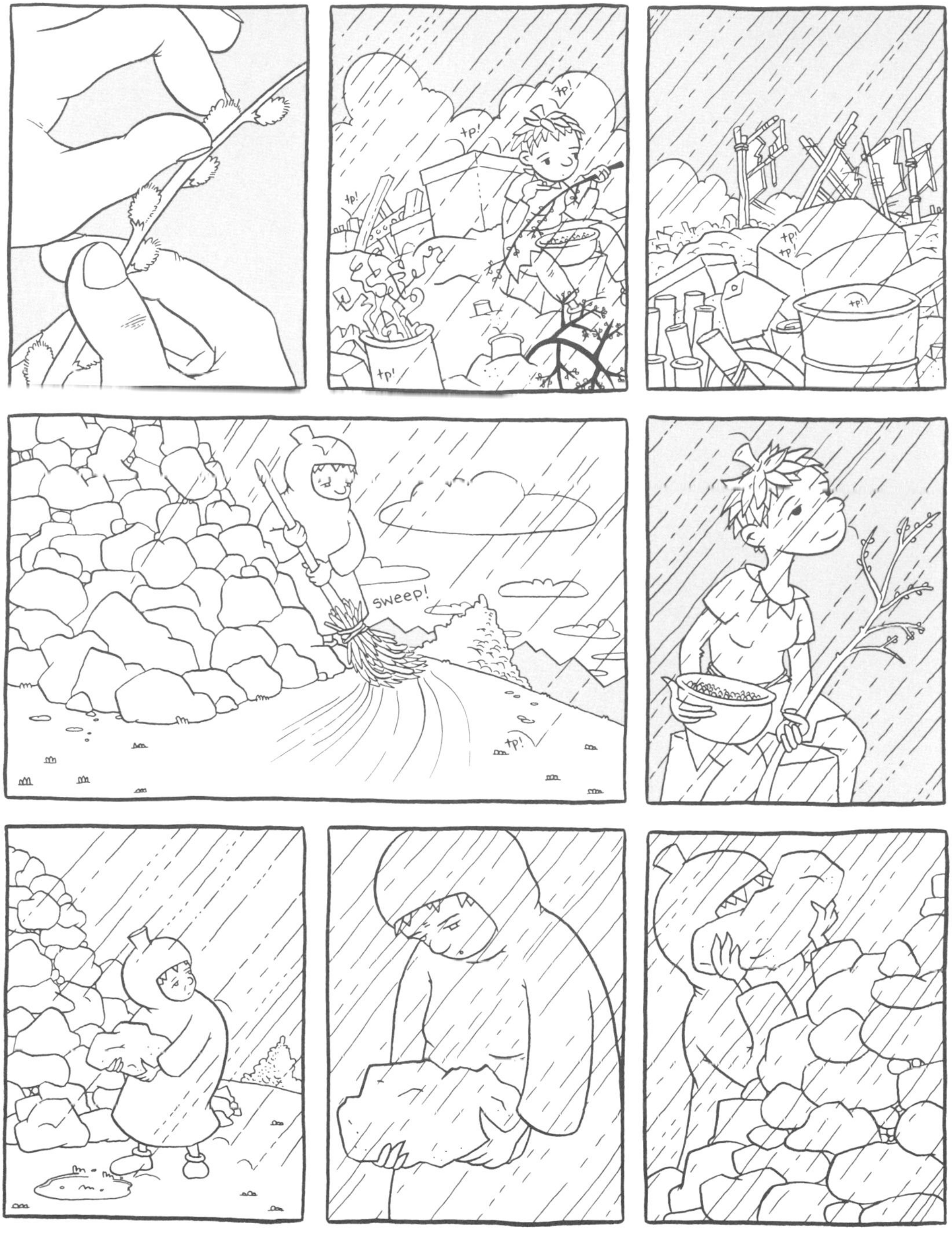
tp!
tp!
tp!
tp!
tp!
tp!
tp!
tp!
SWEEP!
tp!

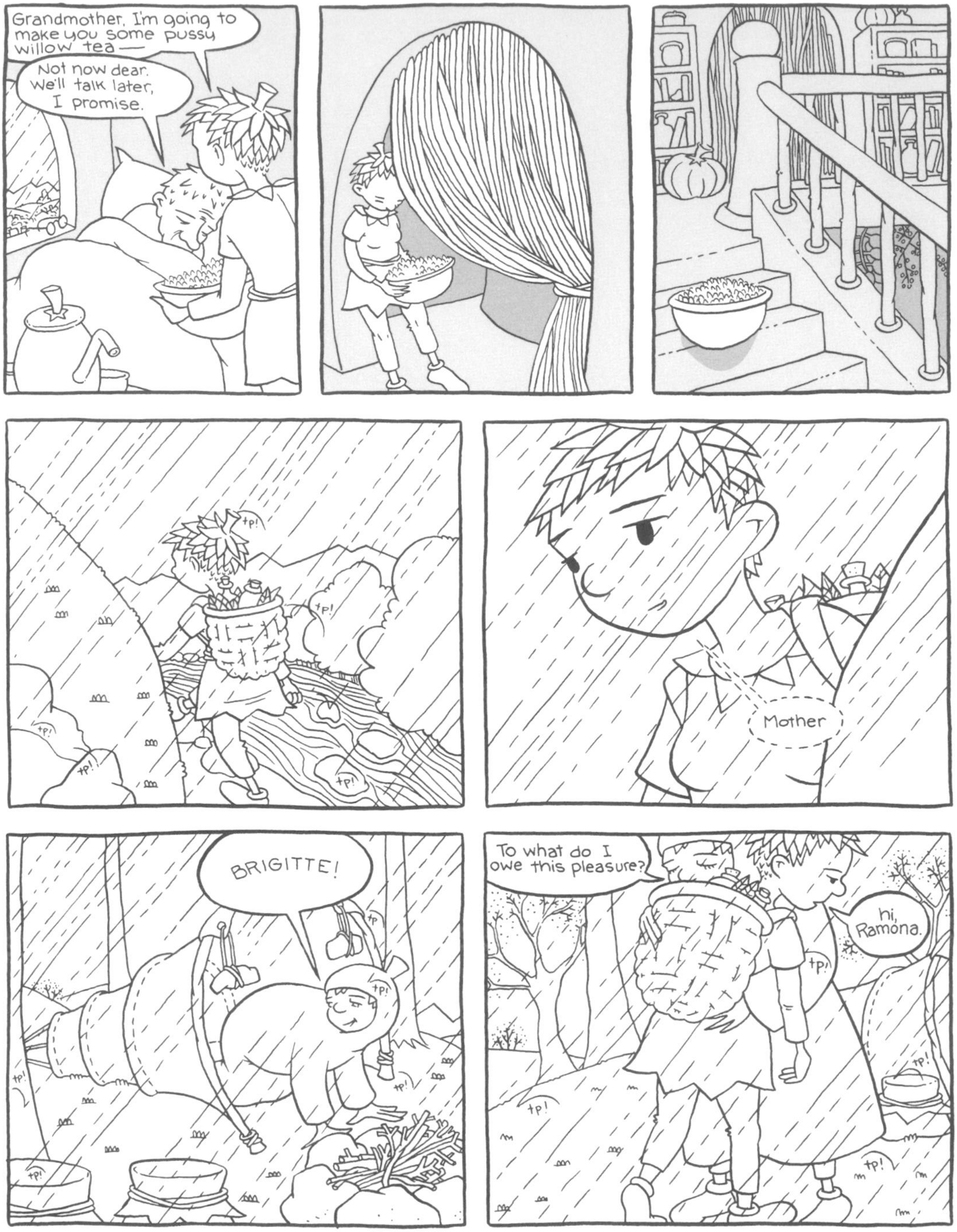
Grandmother, I'm going to make you some pussy willow tea —
Not now dear. We'll talk later, I promise.
tp!
tp!
tp!
tp!
tp!
Mother
BRIGITTE!
tp
tp!
tp!
tp!
tp!
To what do I owe this pleasure?
hi, Ramona.
tp!
tp!
tp!
tp!

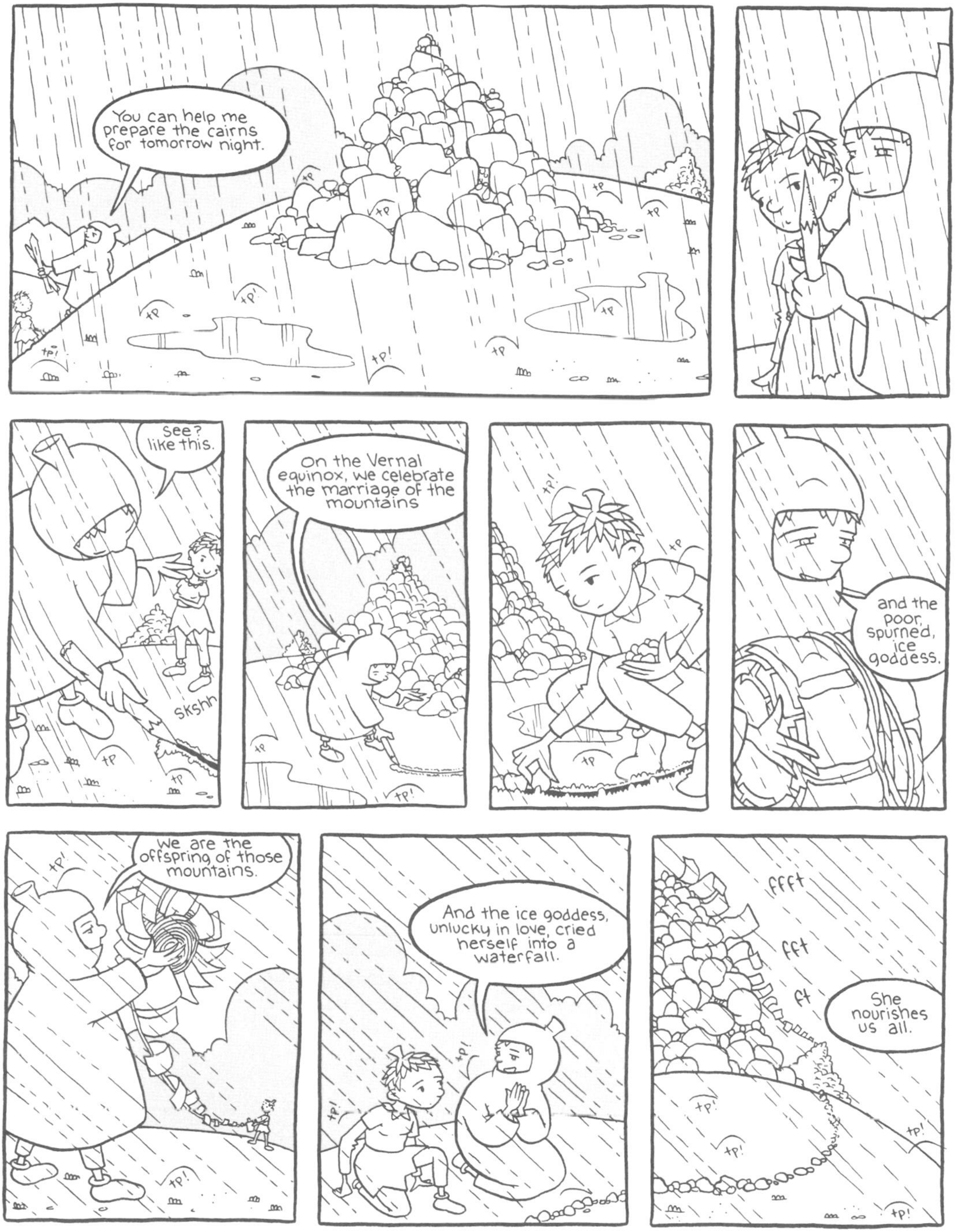
You can help me prepare the cairns for tomorrow night.
tp!
see? like this.
SKshh
On the Vernal equinox, we celebrate the marriage of the mountains
and the poor, spurned, ice goddess.
We are the offspring of those mountains.
And the ice goddess, unlucky in love, cried herself into a waterfall.
ffft
fft
ft
She nourishes us all.

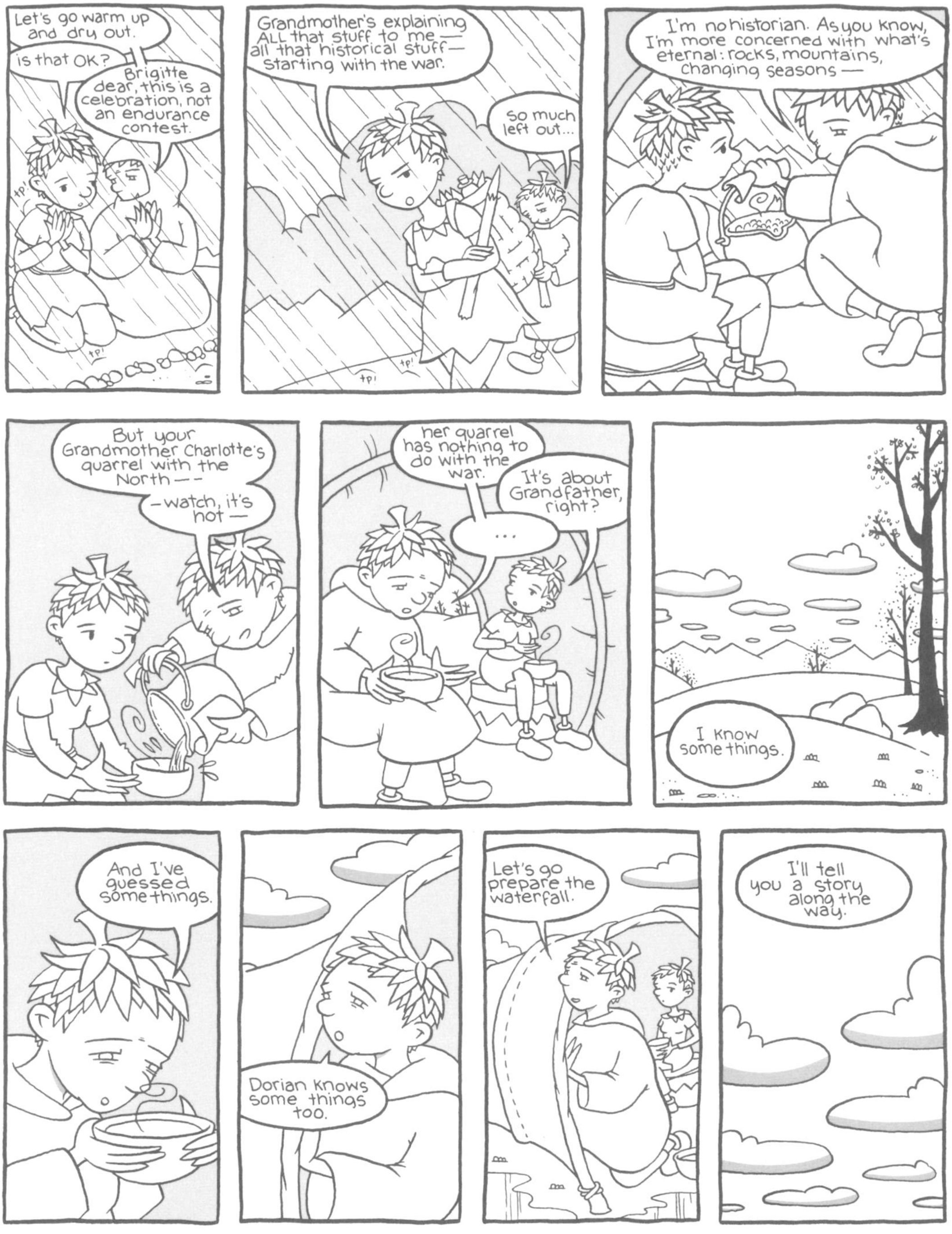
Let's go warm up and dry out.
is that OK?
Brigitte dear, this is a celebration, not an endurance contest.
tp!
Grandmother's explaining ALL that stuff to me— all that historical stuff— starting with the war.
So much left out...
I'm no historian. As you know, I'm more concerned with what's eternal: rocks, mountains, changing seasons—
But your Grandmother Charlotte's quarrel with the North--
—watch, it's hot—
her quarrel has nothing to do with the war.
It's about Grandfather, right?
...
I know some things.
And I've guessed some things.
Dorian knows some things too.
Let's go prepare the waterfall.
I'll tell you a story along the way.

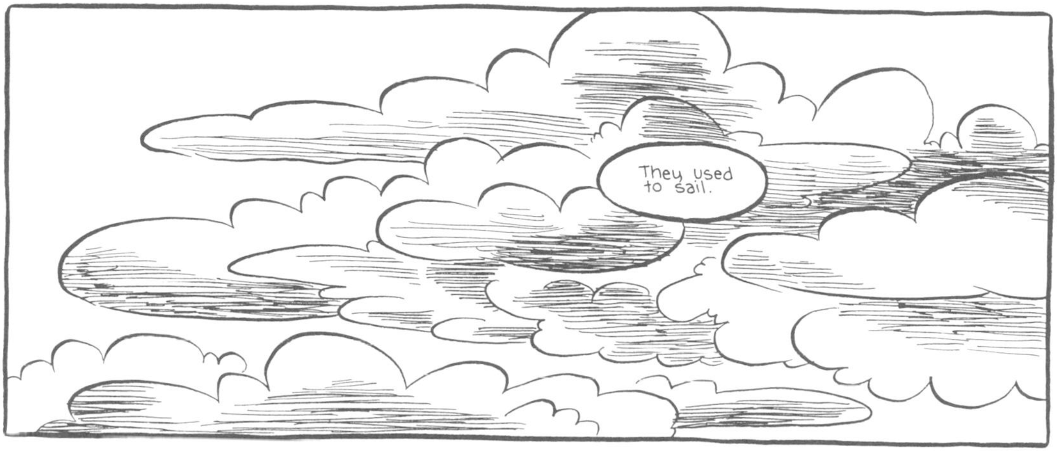
They used to sail.

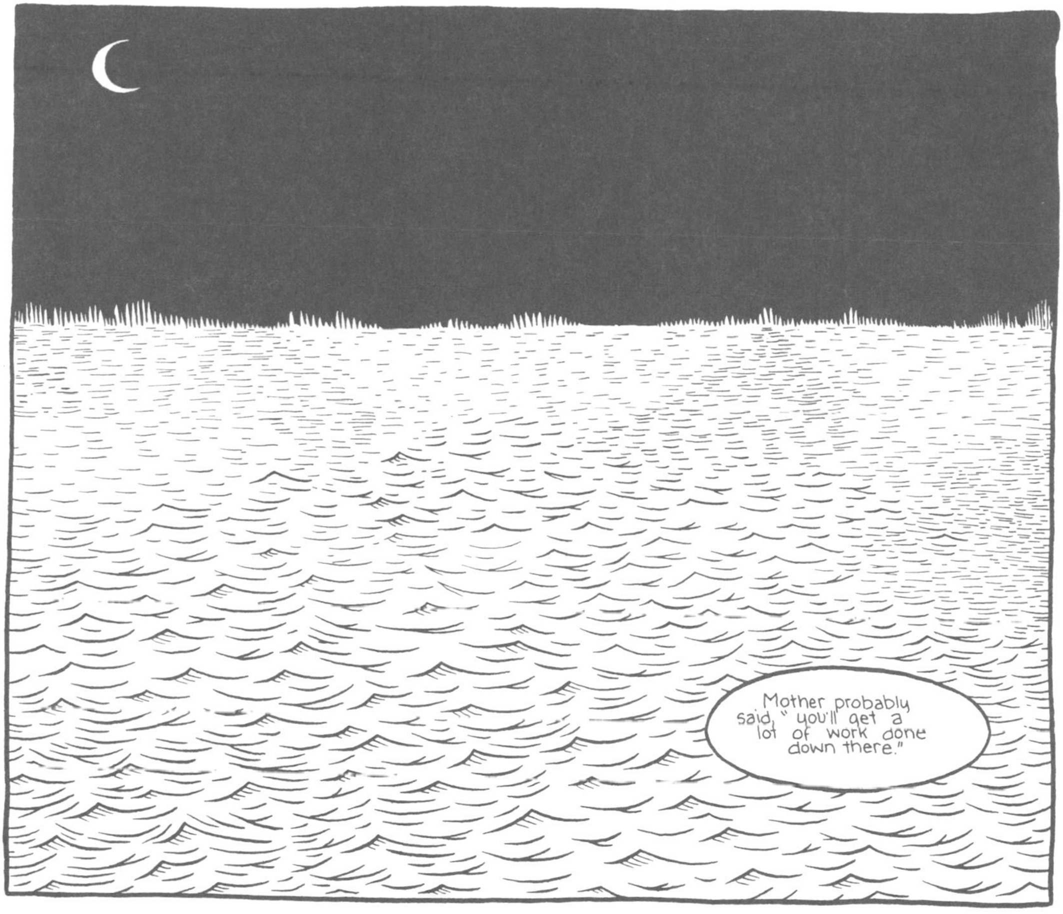
Mother probably said, "you'll get a lot of work done down there."

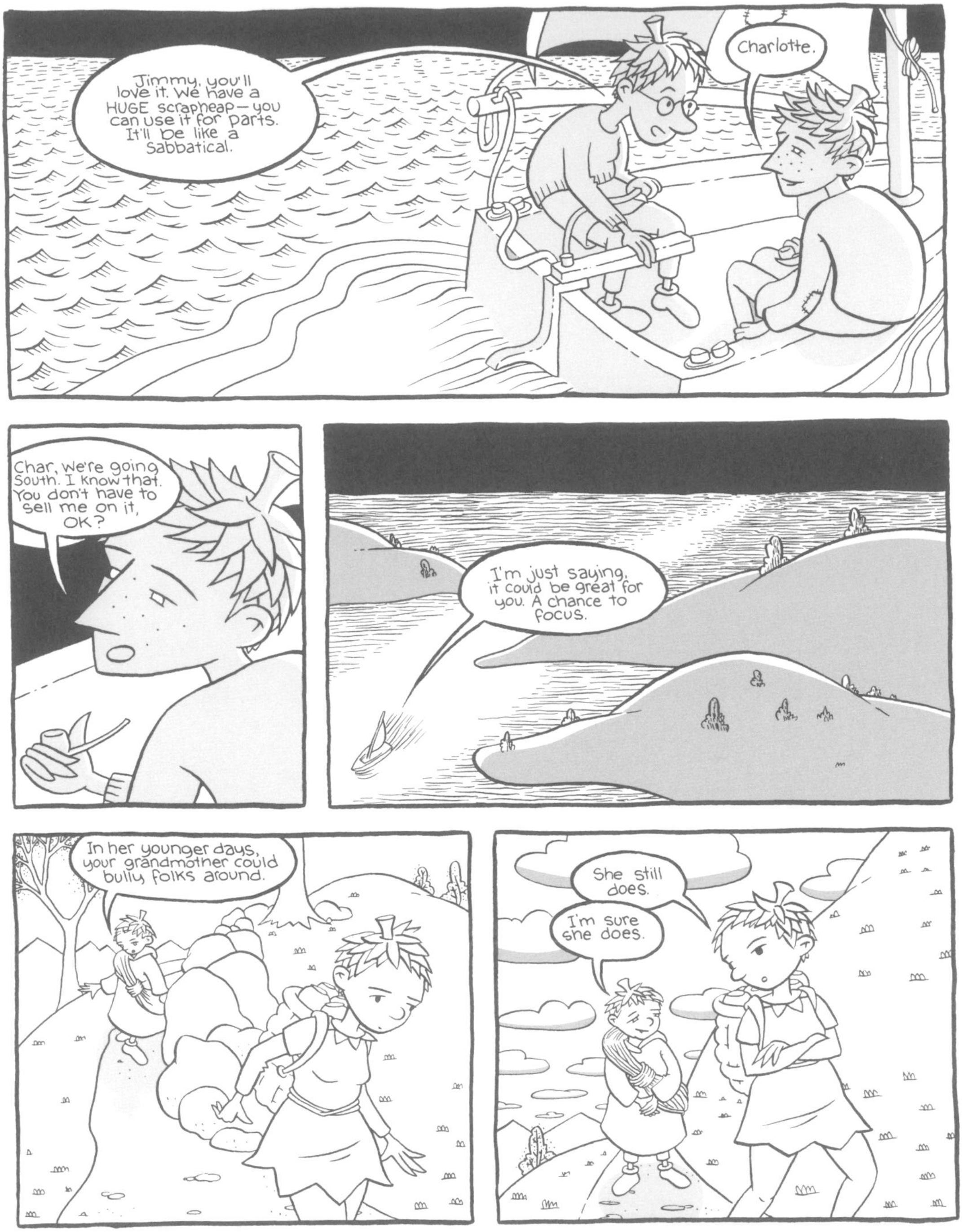
Jimmy, you'll love it. We have a HUGE scrapheap—you can use it for parts. It'll be like a sabbatical.
Charlotte.
Char, we're going South. I know that. You don't have to sell me on it, OK?
I'm just saying, it could be great for you. A chance to focus.
In her younger days, your grandmother could bully folks around.
She still does.
I'm sure she does.

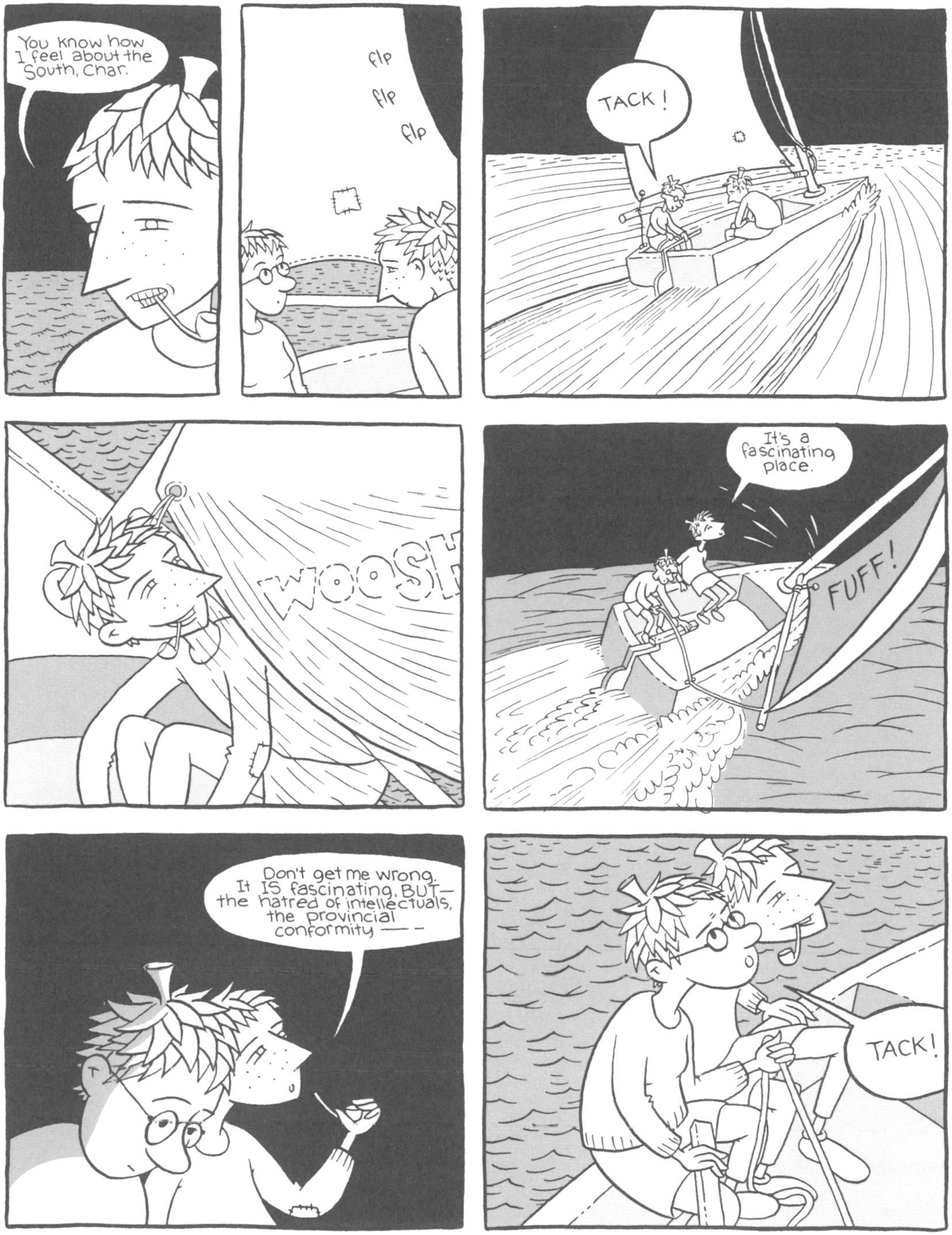
You know how I feel about the South, Char.
flp
flp
flp
TACK!
WOOSH
It's a fascinating place.
FUFF!
Don't get me wrong. It IS fascinating, BUT— the hatred of intellectuals, the provincial conformity ———
TACK!

WOOSH!

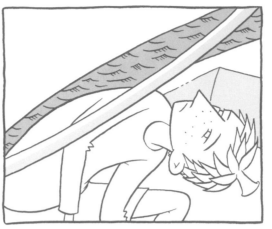

KUNCH!!

Hey! Take it easy, sailor girl!

I'll be a pariah there.

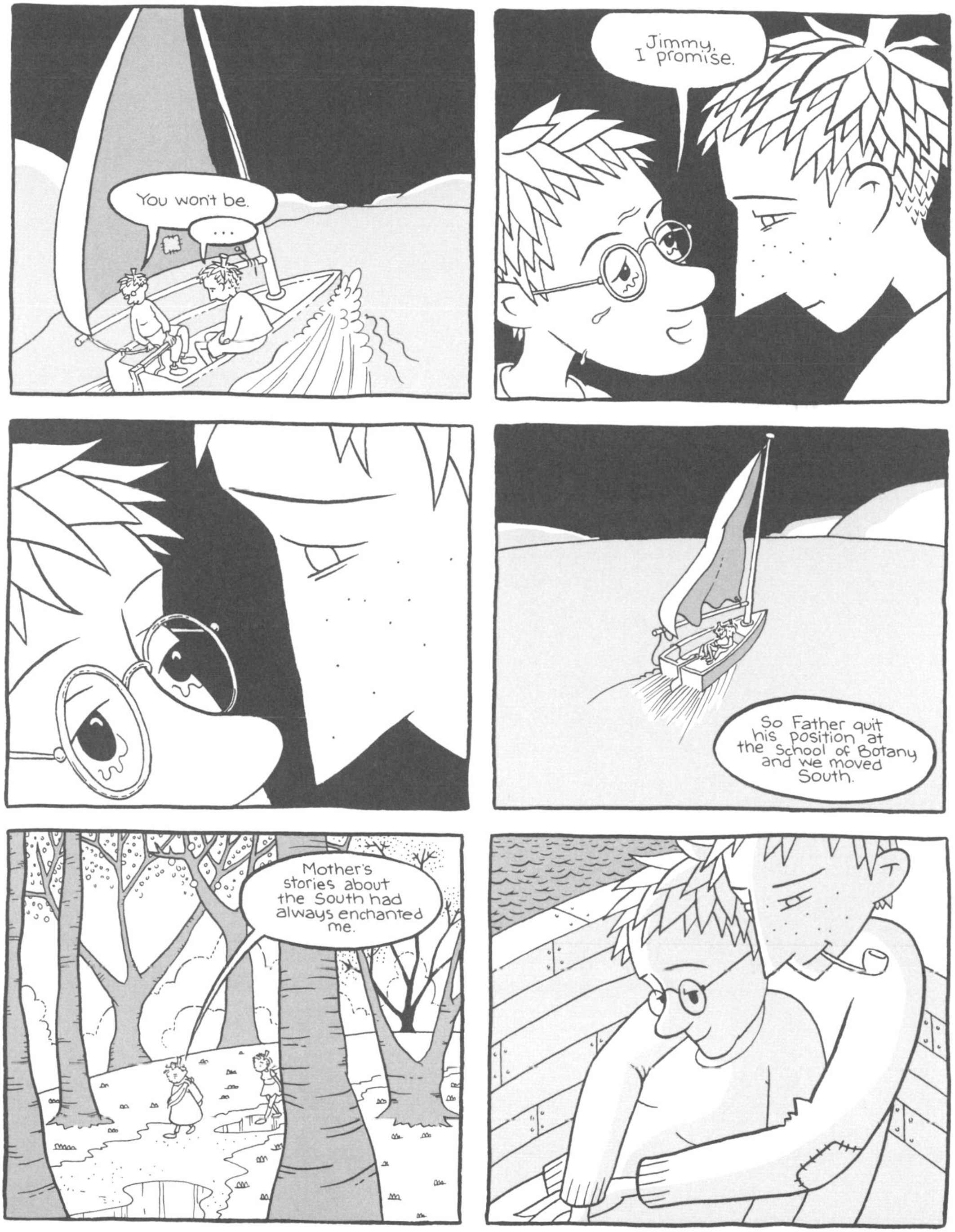
You won't be.
. . .
Jimmy, I promise.
So Father quit his position at the School of Botany and we moved South.
Mother's stories about the South had always enchanted me.

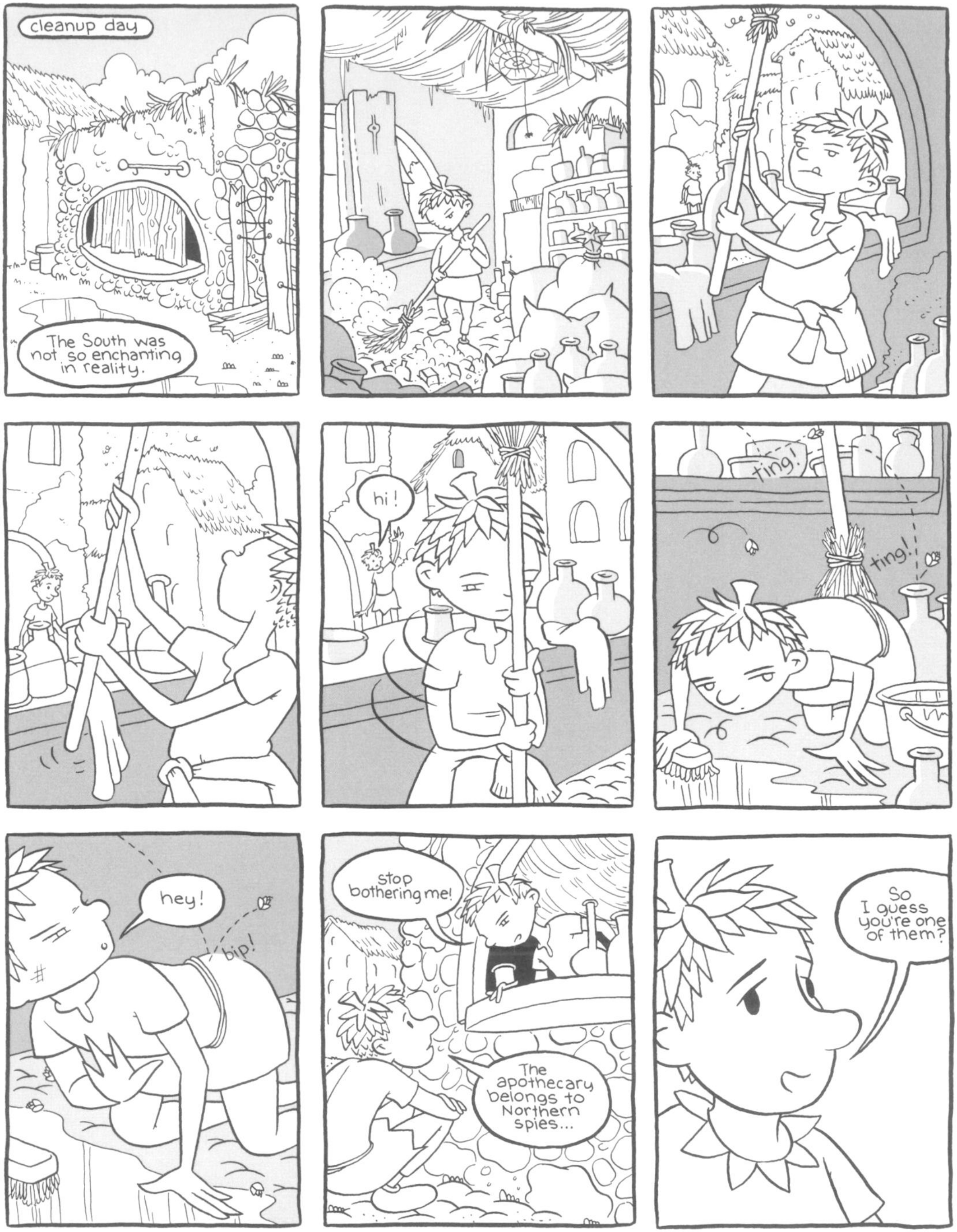
cleanup day
The South was not so enchanting in reality.
hi!
ting!
ting!
hey!
bip!
stop bothering me!
The apothecary belongs to Northern spies...
So I guess you're one of them?

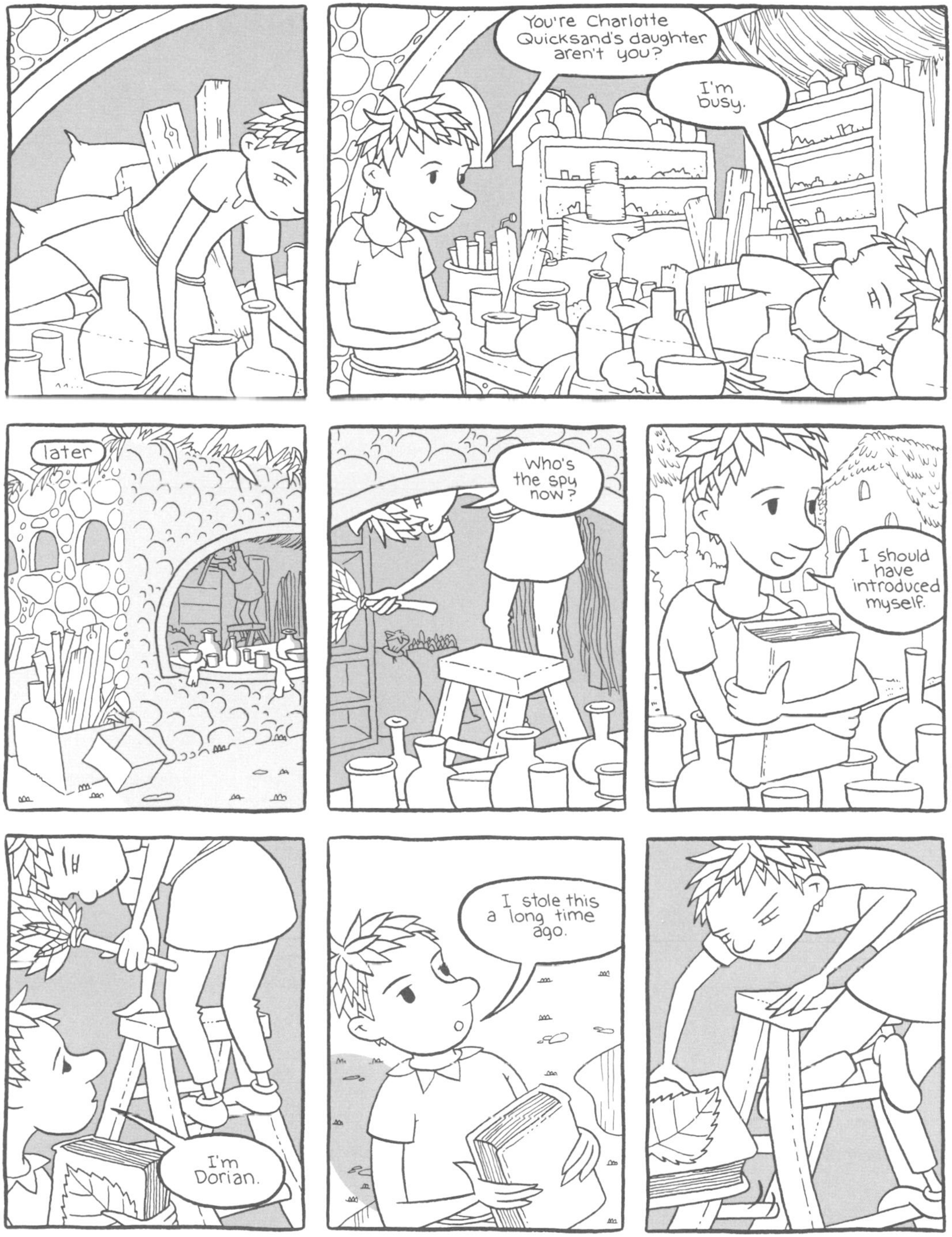
You're Charlotte Quicksand's daughter aren't you?
I'm busy.
later
Who's the spy now?
I should have introduced myself.
I'm Dorian.
I stole this a long time ago.

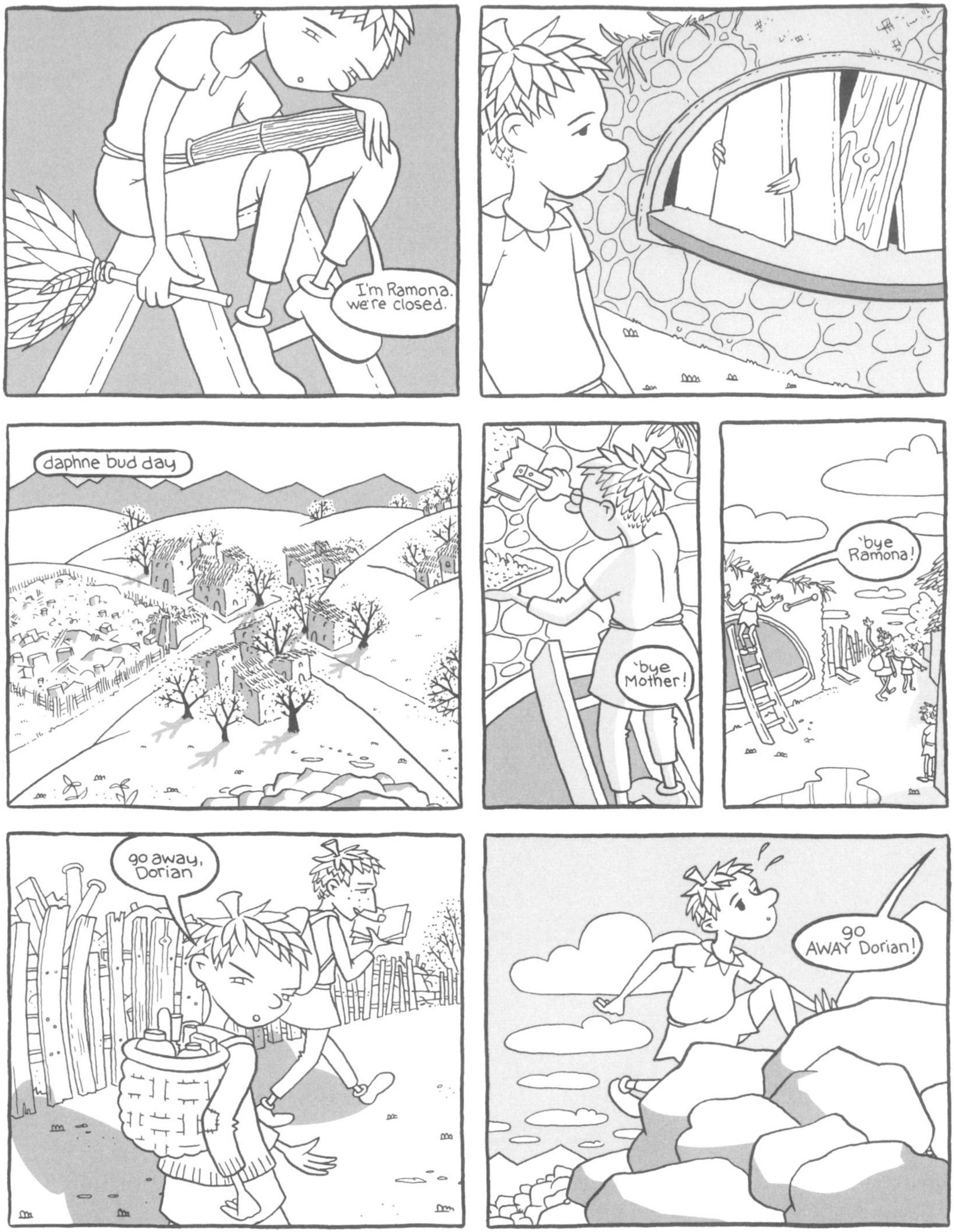
I'm Ramona.
we're closed.
daphne bud day
`bye Mother!
`bye Ramona!
go away, Dorian
go AWAY Dorian!

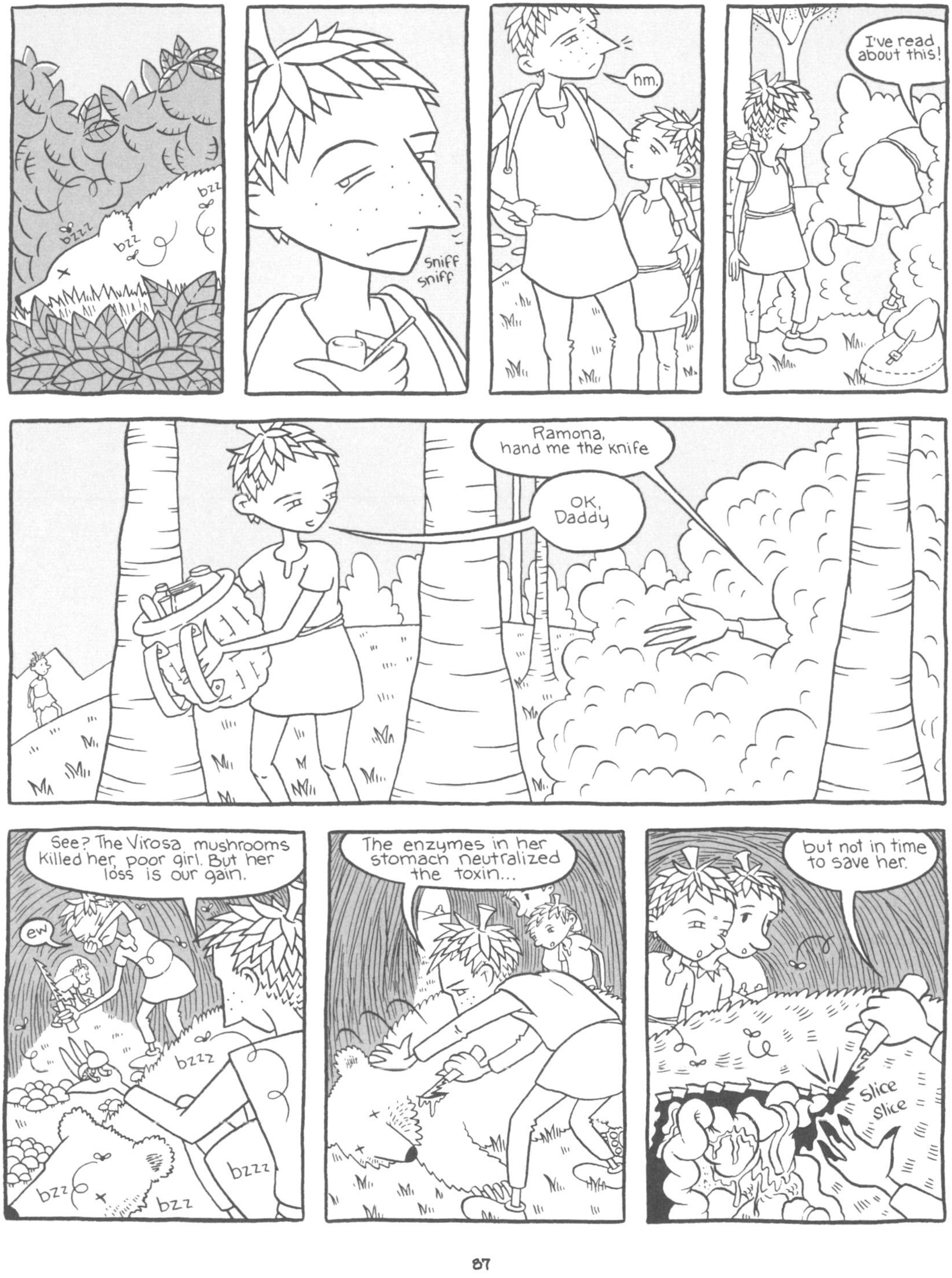
bzz
bzzz
bzz
bzzz
sniff
sniff
hm.
I've read about this!
Ramona, hand me the knife
OK, Daddy
See? The Virosa mushrooms killed her, poor girl. But her loss is our gain.
ew
bzzz
bzz
bzz
bzzz
The enzymes in her stomach neutralized the toxin...
but not in time to save her.
Slice
Slice

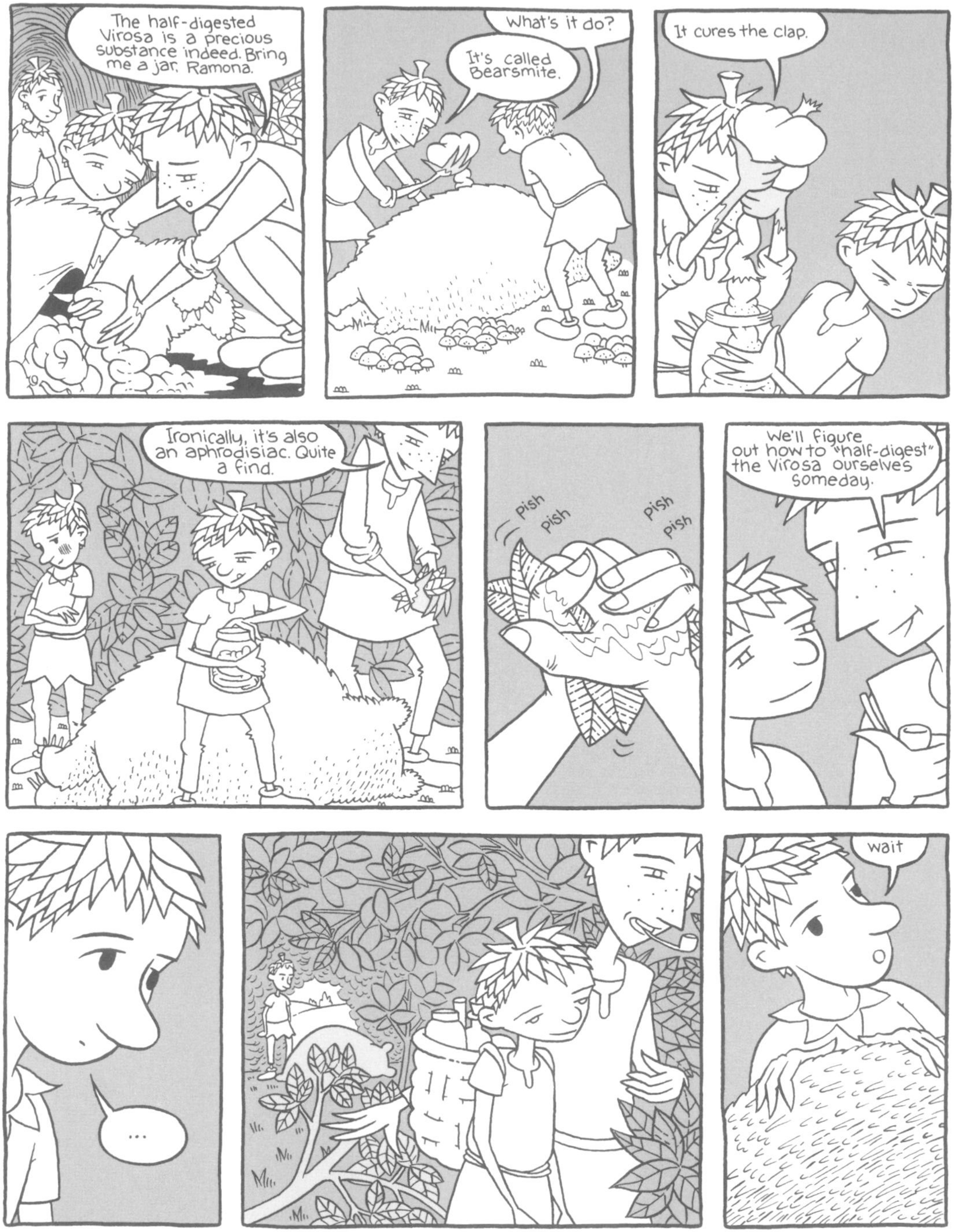
The half-digested Virosa is a precious substance indeed. Bring me a jar, Ramona.
What's it do?
It's called Bearsmite.
It cures the clap.
Ironically, it's also an aphrodisiac. Quite a find.
pish
pish
pish
pish
We'll figure out how to "half-digest" the Virosa ourselves someday.
...
wait

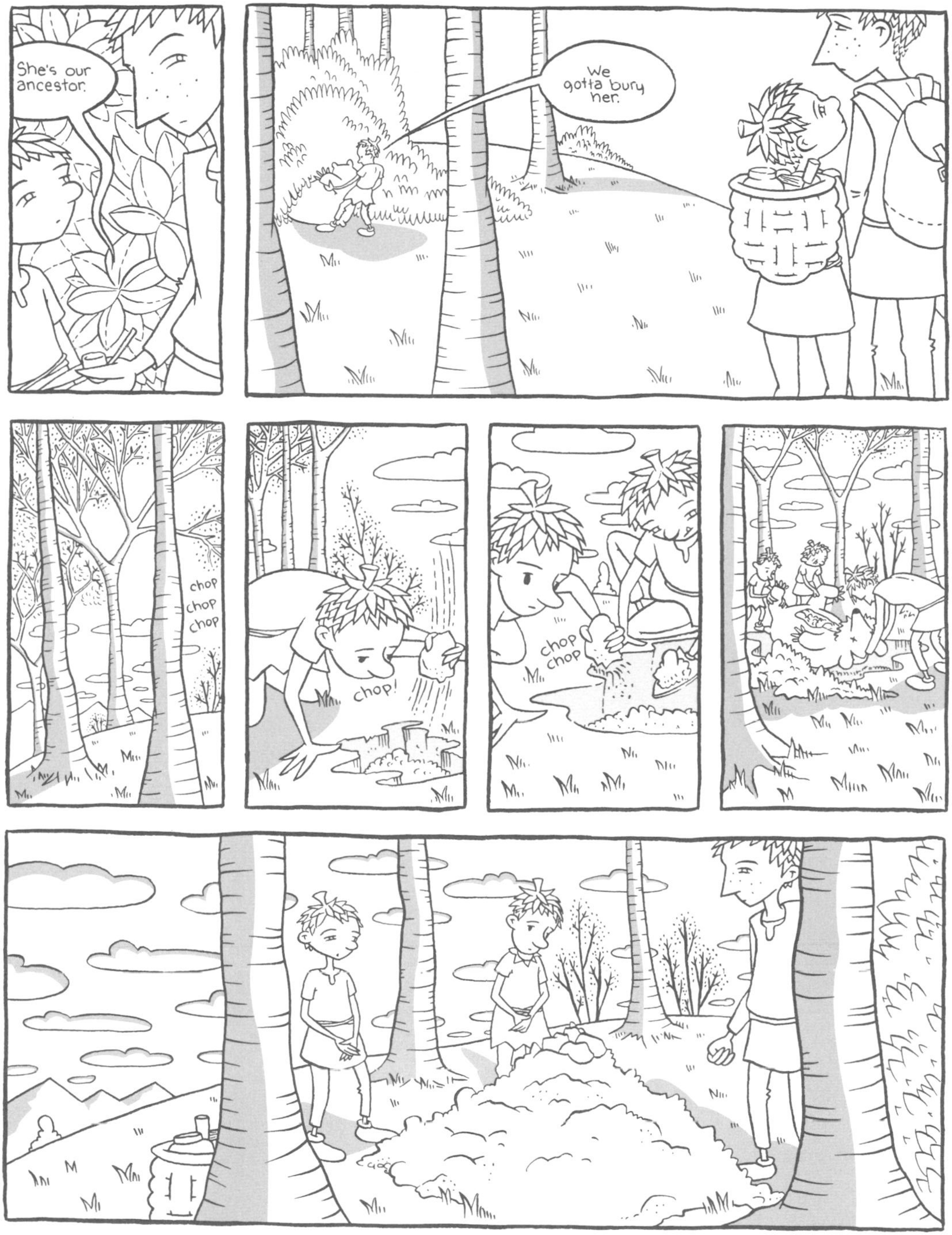

She's our ancestor.
We gotta bury her.
chop
chop
chop
chop!
chop
chop

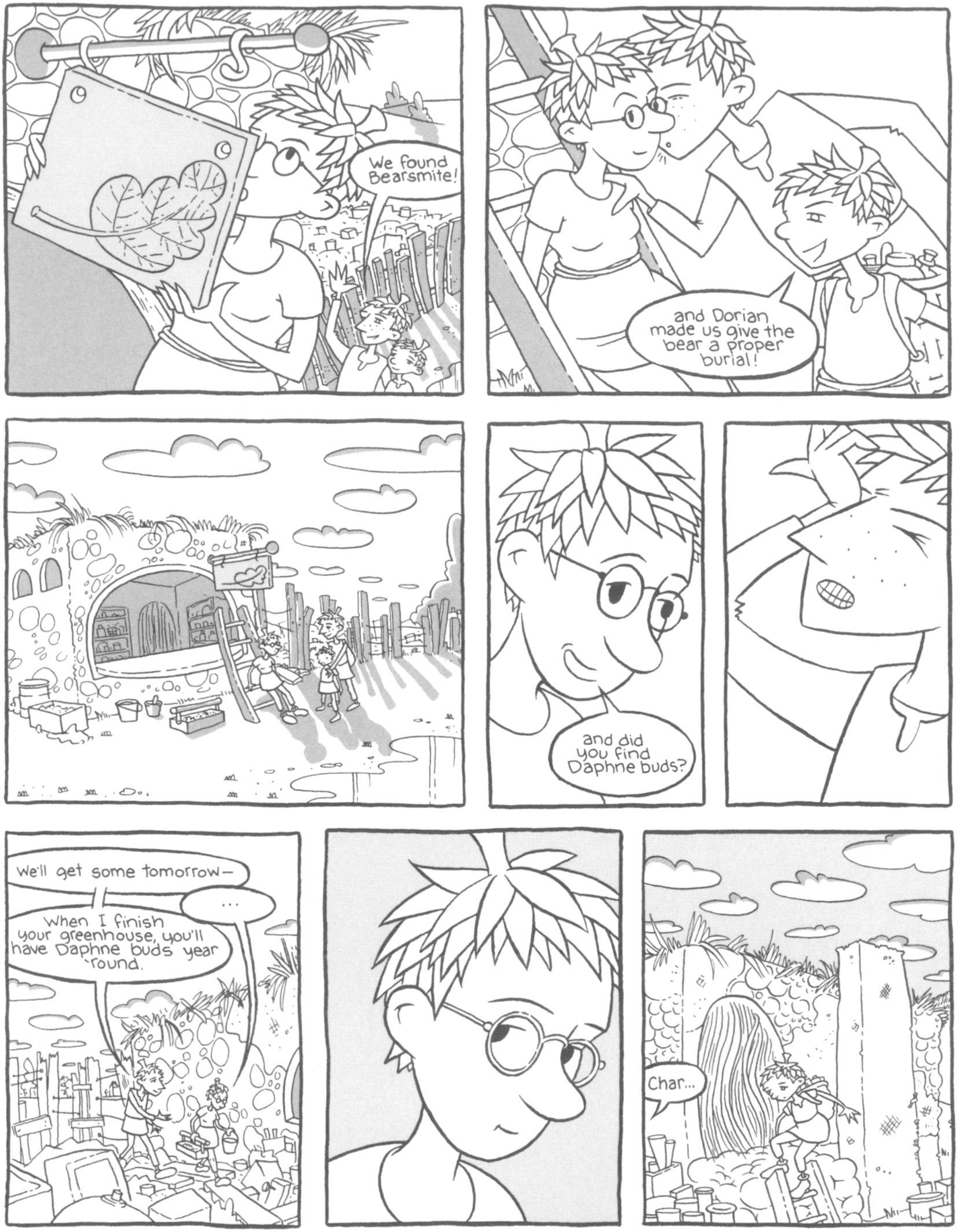
We found Bearsmite!
and Dorian made us give the bear a proper burial!
and did you find Daphne buds?
We'll get some tomorrow—
When I finish your greenhouse, you'll have Daphne buds year 'round.
...
Char...

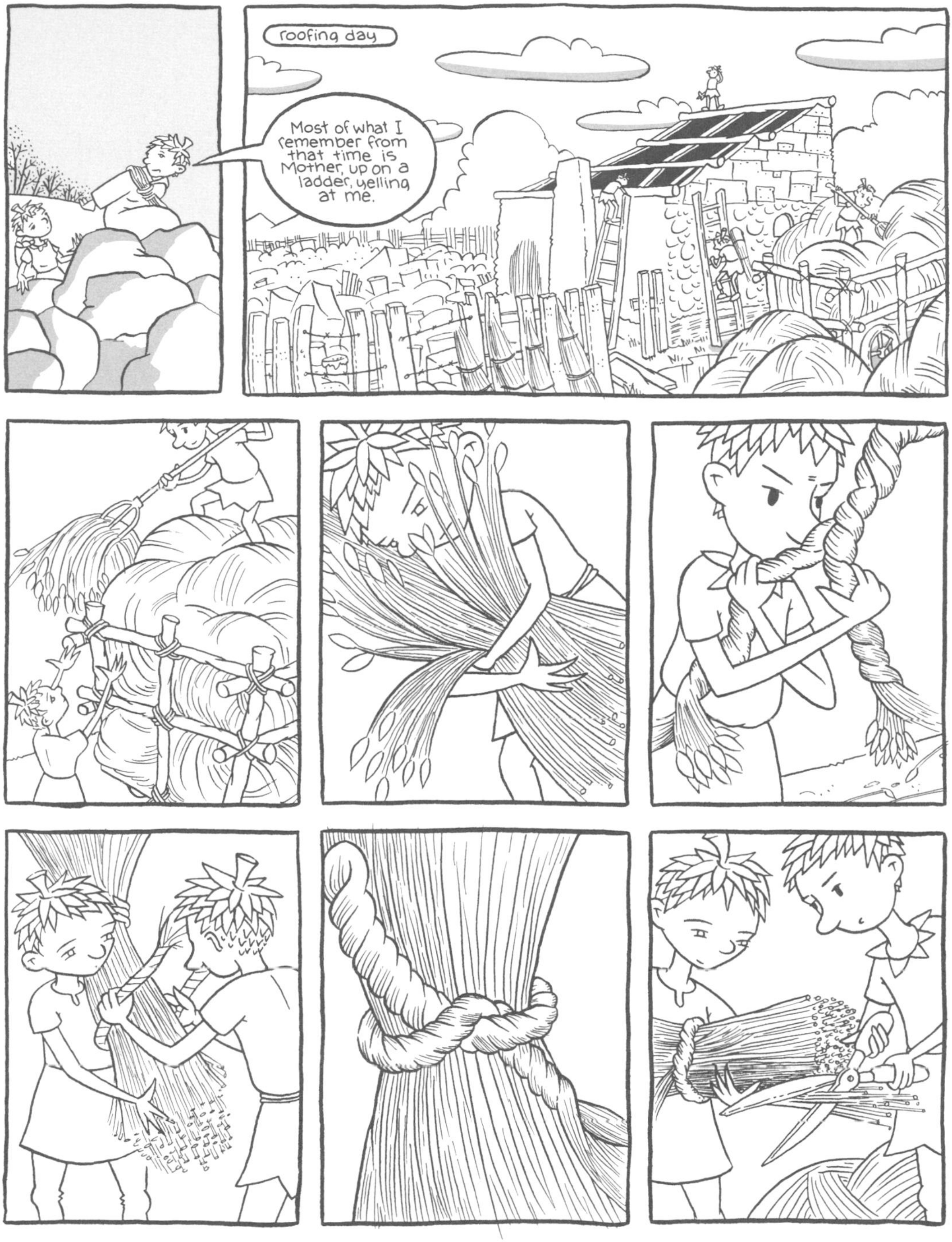
roofing day
Most of what I remember from that time is Mother, up on a ladder, yelling at me.

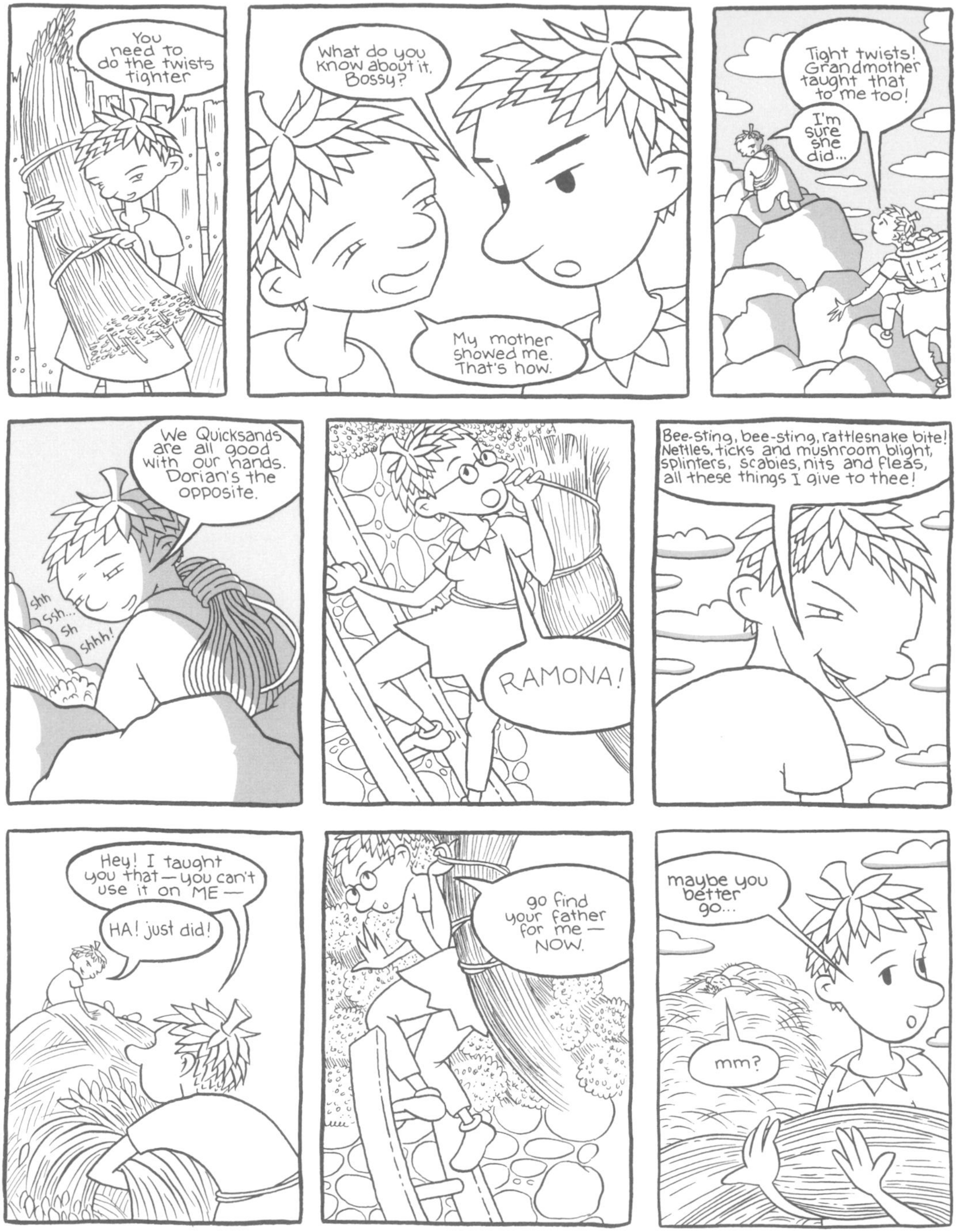

You need to do the twists tighter
What do you know about it, Bossy?
My mother showed me. That's how.
Tight twists! Grandmother taught that to me too!
I'm sure she did...
We Quicksands are all good with our hands. Dorian's the opposite.
shh
ssh...
sh
shhh!
RAMONA!
Bee-sting, bee-sting, rattlesnake bite! Nettles, ticks and mushroom blight, splinters, scabies, nits and fleas, all these things I give to thee!
Hey! I taught you that—you can't use it on ME—
HA! just did!
go find your father for me—NOW.
maybe you better go...
mm?

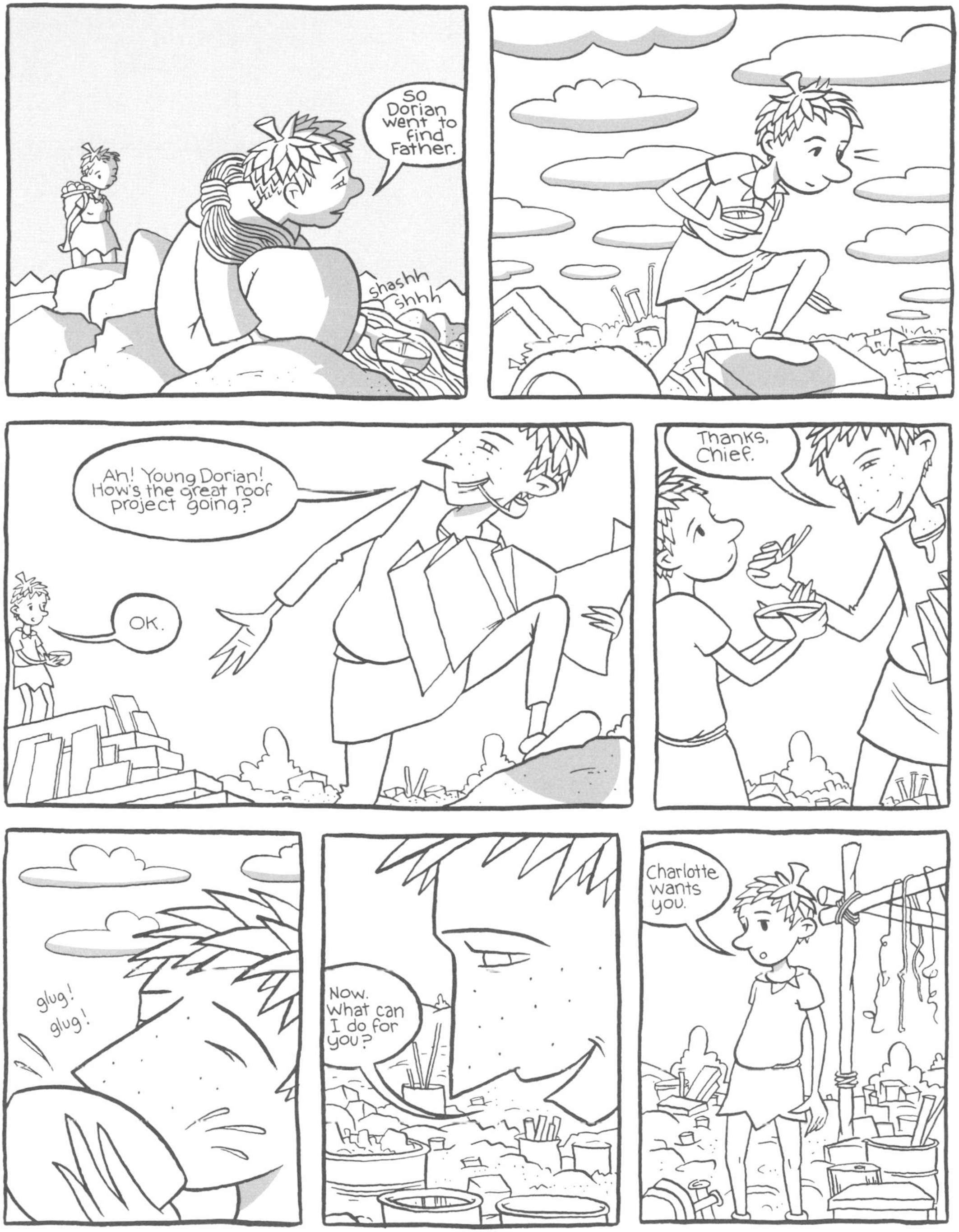
So Dorian went to find Father.
shashh
shhh
Ah! Young Dorian! How's the great roof project going?
OK.
Thanks, Chief.
glug!
glug!
Now. What can I do for you?
Charlotte wants you.

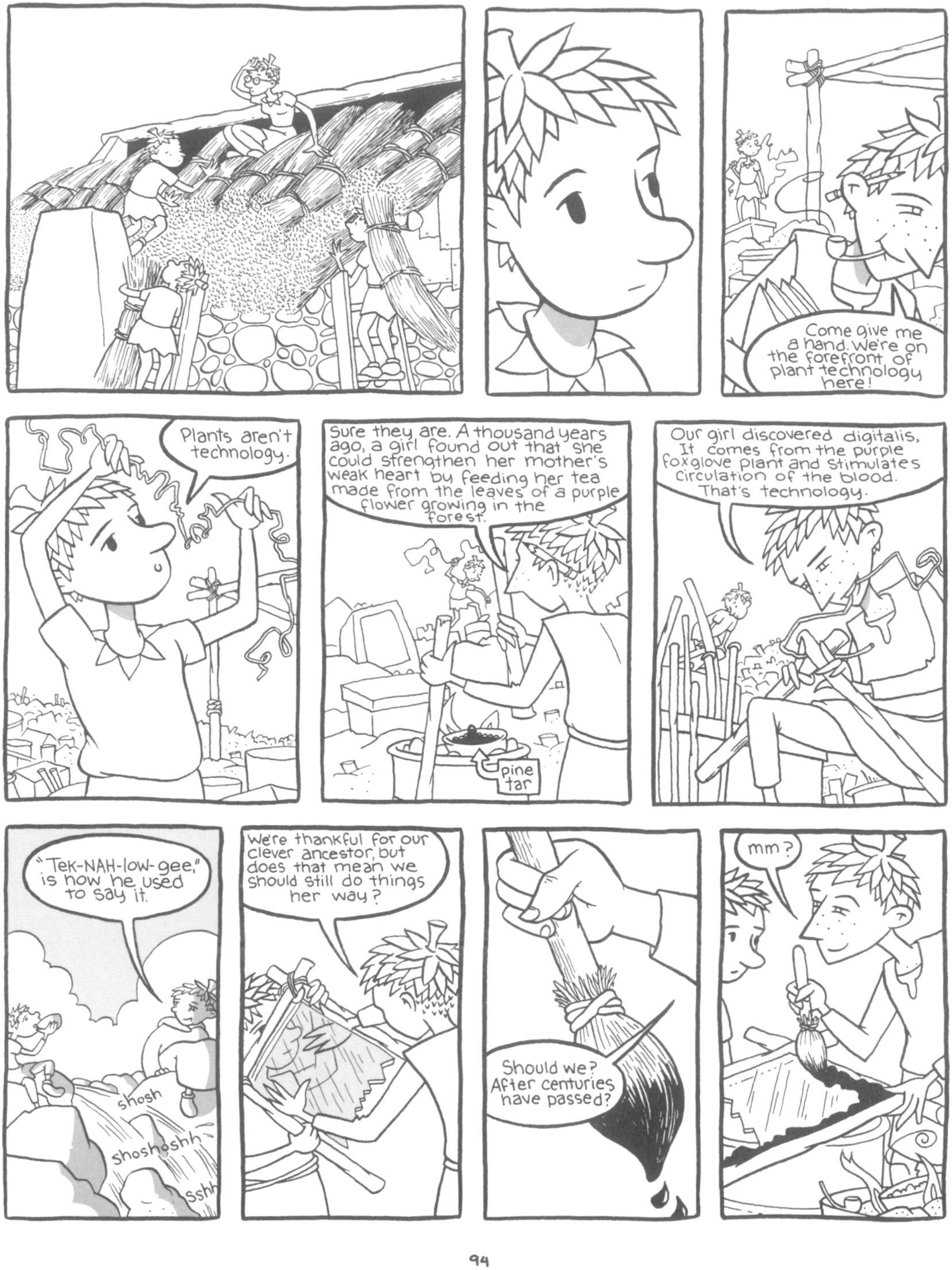
Come give me a hand. We're on the forefront of plant technology here!
Plants aren't technology.
Sure they are. A thousand years ago, a girl found out that she could strengthen her mother's weak heart by feeding her tea made from the leaves of a purple flower growing in the forest.
pine tar
Our girl discovered digitalis, It comes from the purple foxglove plant and stimulates circulation of the blood. That's technology.
"Tek-NAH-low-gee," is how he used to say it.
shosh
shoshoshh
sshh
We're thankful for our clever ancestor, but does that mean we should still do things her way?
Should we? After centuries have passed?
mm?

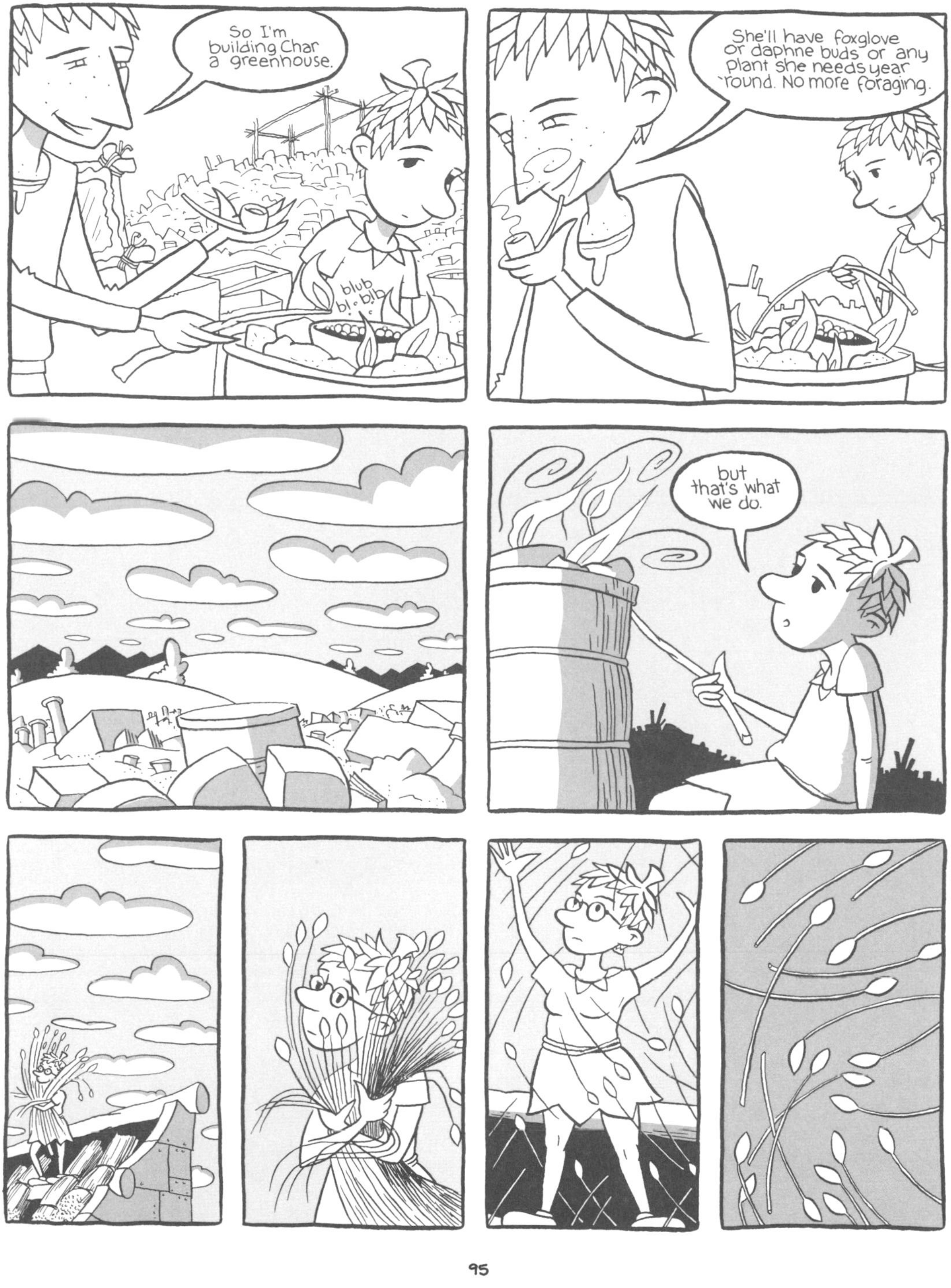
So I'm building Char a greenhouse.
blub bl blb
She'll have foxglove or daphne buds or any plant she needs year 'round. No more foraging.
but that's what we do.

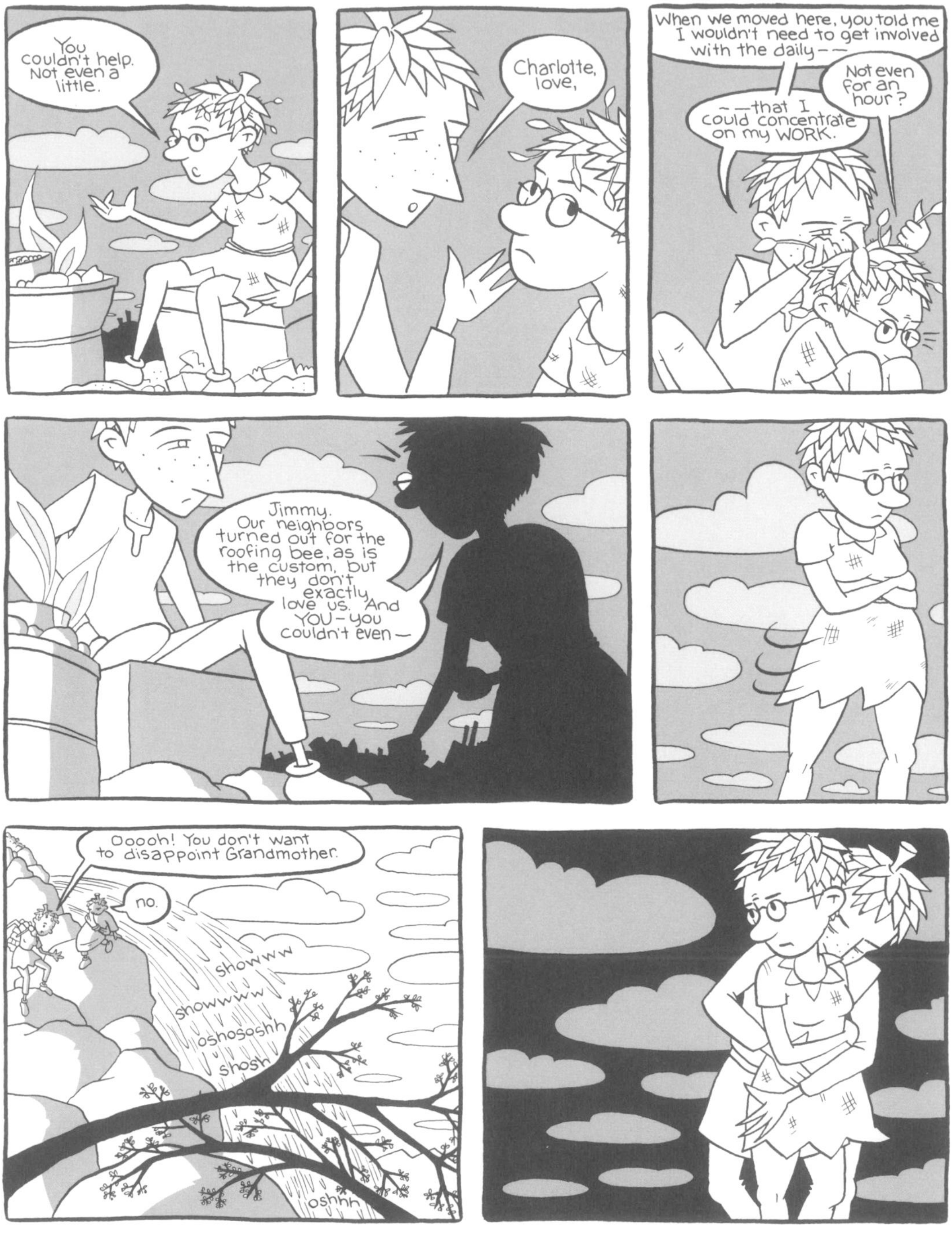
You couldn't help. Not even a little.
Charlotte, love,
When we moved here, you told me I wouldn't need to get involved with the daily--
--that I could concentrate on my WORK.
Not even for an hour?
Jimmy. Our neighbors turned out for the roofing bee, as is the custom, but they don't exactly love us. And YOU-you couldn't even-
Ooooh! You don't want to disappoint Grandmother.
no.
showww
showwww
oshososhh
shosh
oshhh

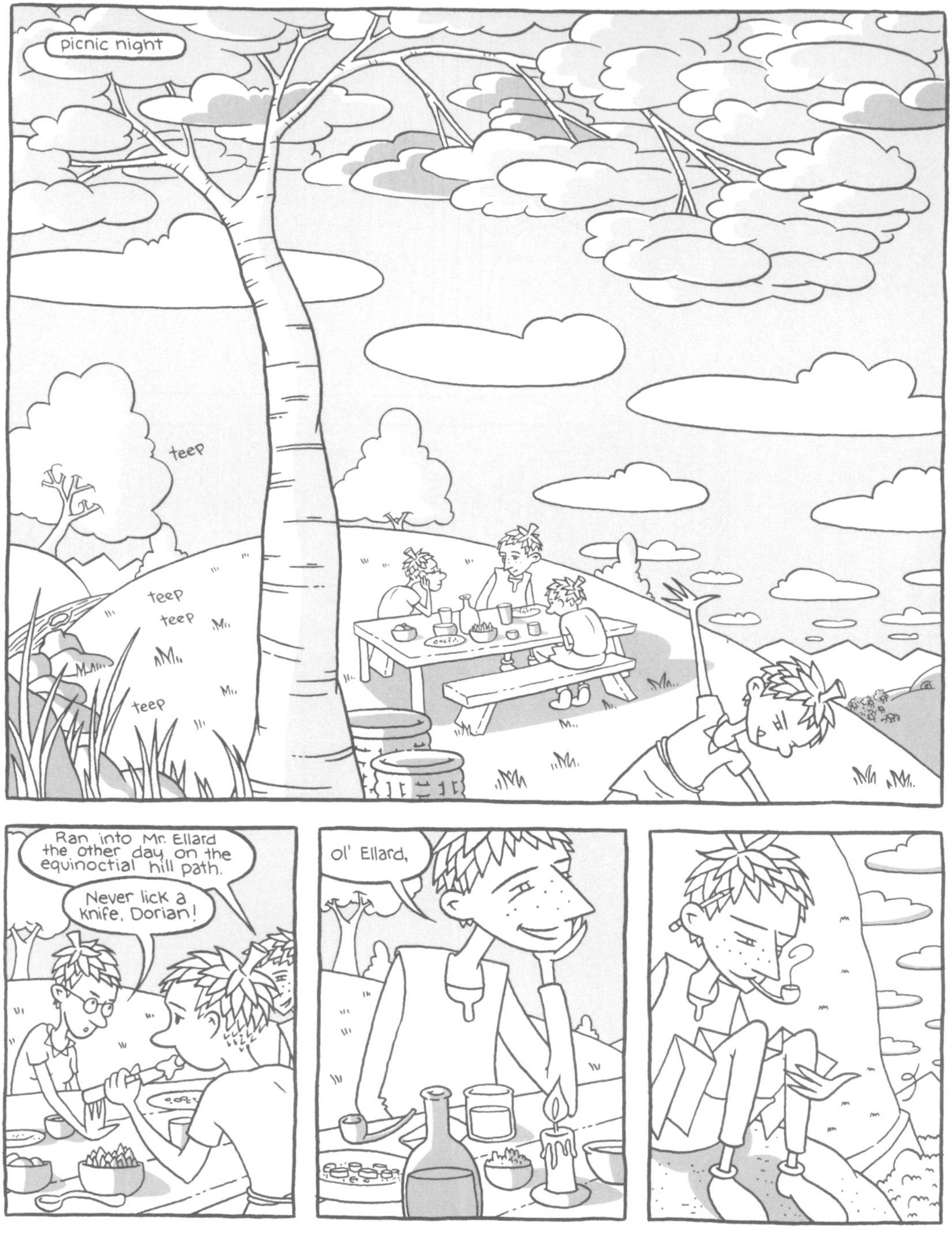
picnic night
teep
teep
teep
teep
Ran into Mr. Ellard the other day on the equinoctial hill path.
Never lick a knife, Dorian!
Ol' Ellard,

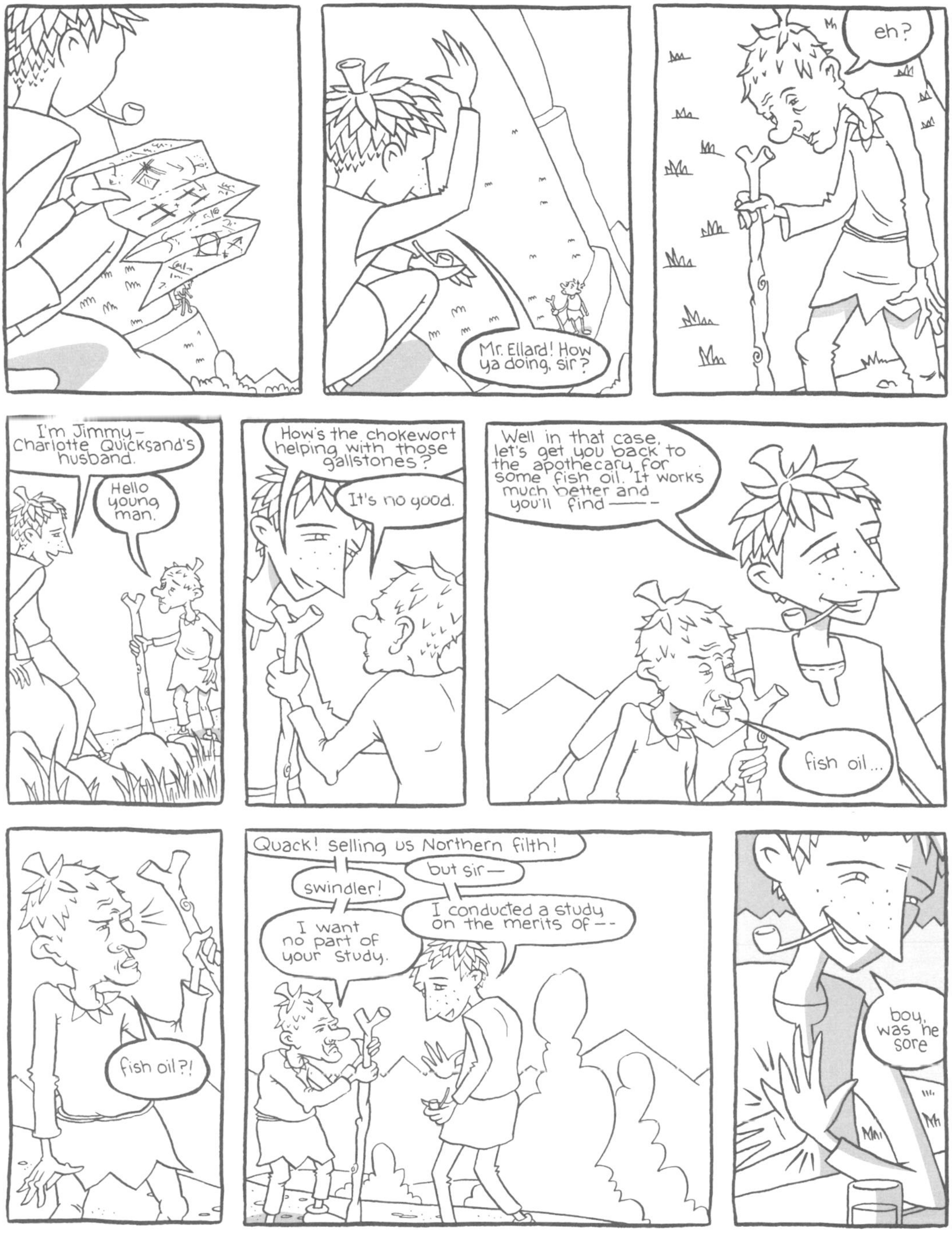
Mr. Ellard! How ya doing, sir?
eh?
I'm Jimmy– Charlotte Quicksand's husband.
Hello young man.
How's the chokewort helping with those gallstones?
It's no good.
Well in that case, let's get you back to the apothecary for some fish oil. It works much better and you'll find ——
fish oil...
fish oil?!
Quack! selling us Northern filth!
but sir—
swindler!
I conducted a study on the merits of --
I want no part of your study.
boy, was he sore

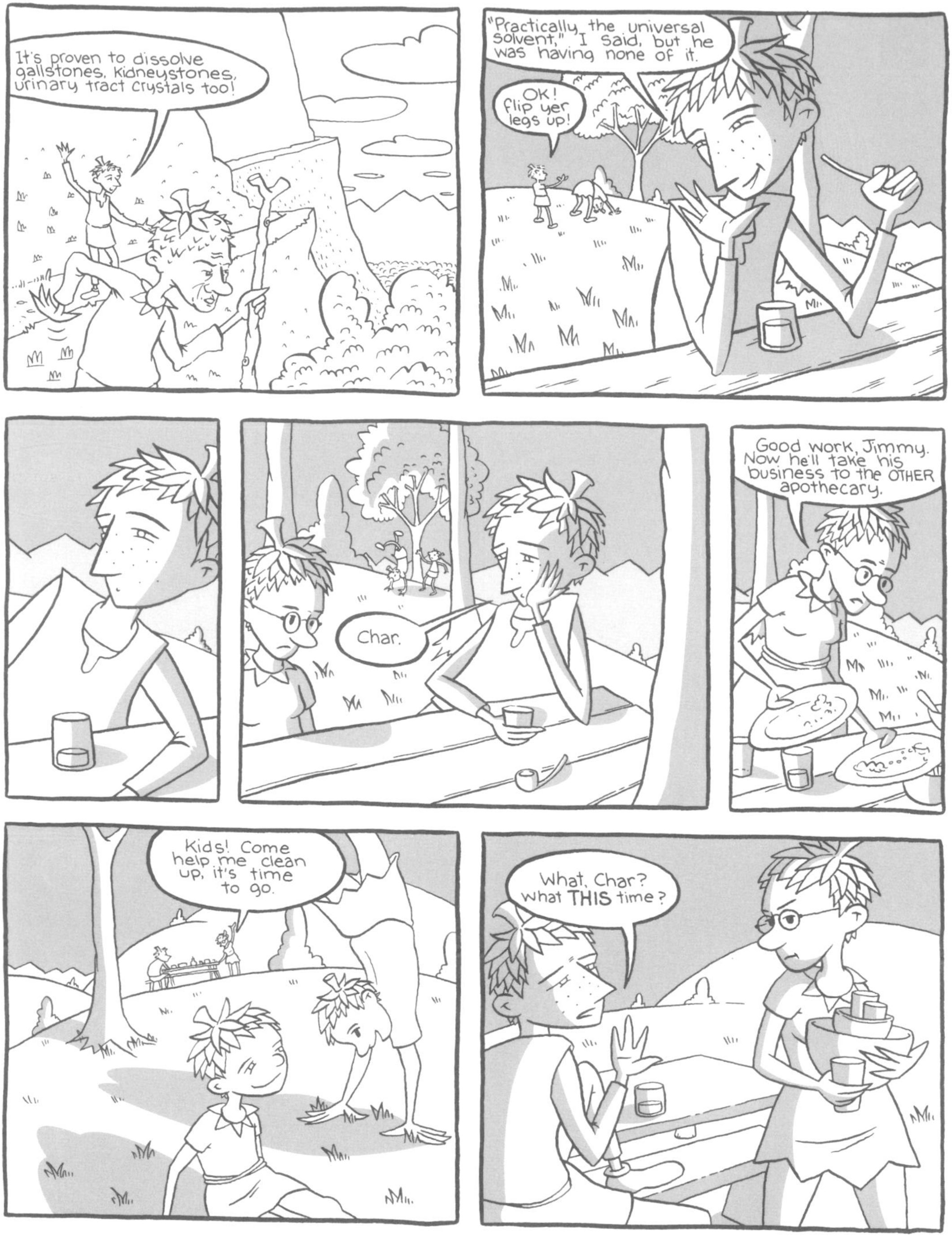
It's proven to dissolve gallstones, kidneystones, urinary tract crystals too!
"Practically the universal solvent," I said, but he was having none of it.
OK! flip yer legs up!
Char.
Good work, Jimmy. Now he'll take his business to the OTHER apothecary.
Kids! Come help me clean up, it's time to go.
What, Char? what THIS time?

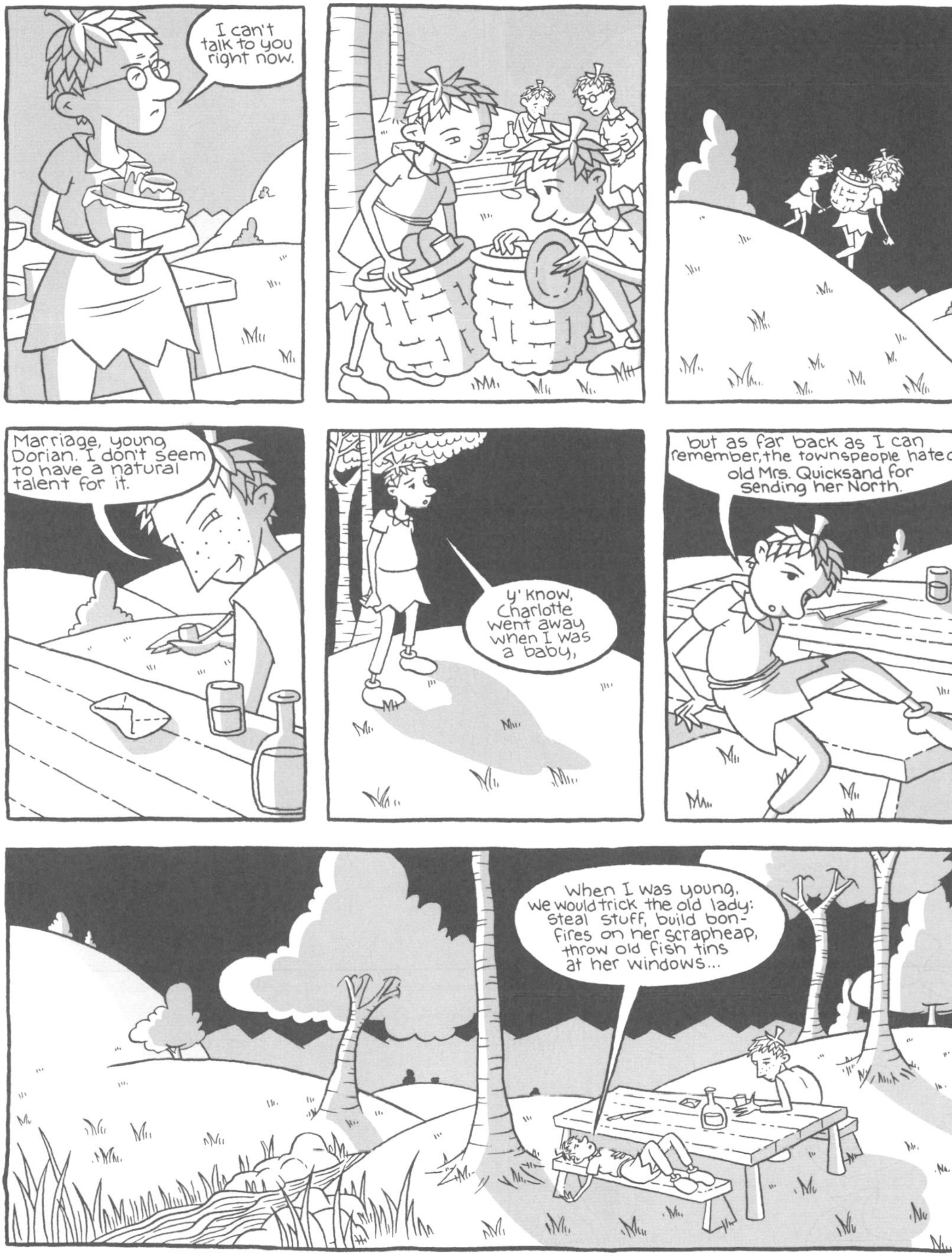
I can't talk to you right now.
Marriage, young Dorian. I don't seem to have a natural talent for it.
y' know, Charlotte went away when I was a baby,
but as far back as I can remember, the townspeople hated old Mrs. Quicksand for sending her North.
When I was young, we would trick the old lady: Steal stuff, build bon-fires on her scrapheap, throw old fish tins at her windows...

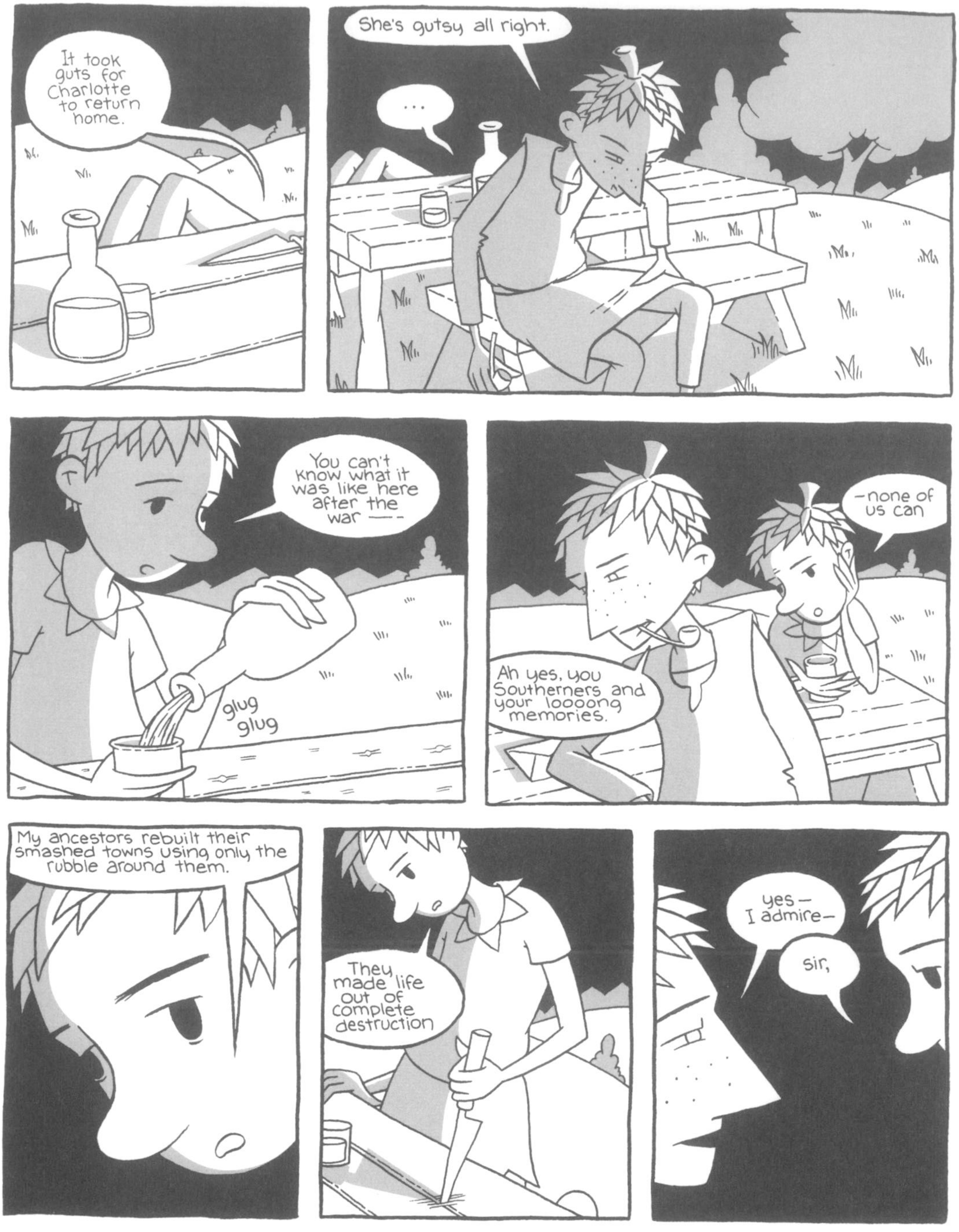
It took guts for Charlotte to return home.
She's gutsy all right.
...
You can't know what it was like here after the war —-
glug glug
-none of us can
Ah yes, you Southerners and your loooong memories.
My ancestors rebuilt their smashed towns using only the rubble around them.
They made life out of complete destruction
yes — I admire—
sir,

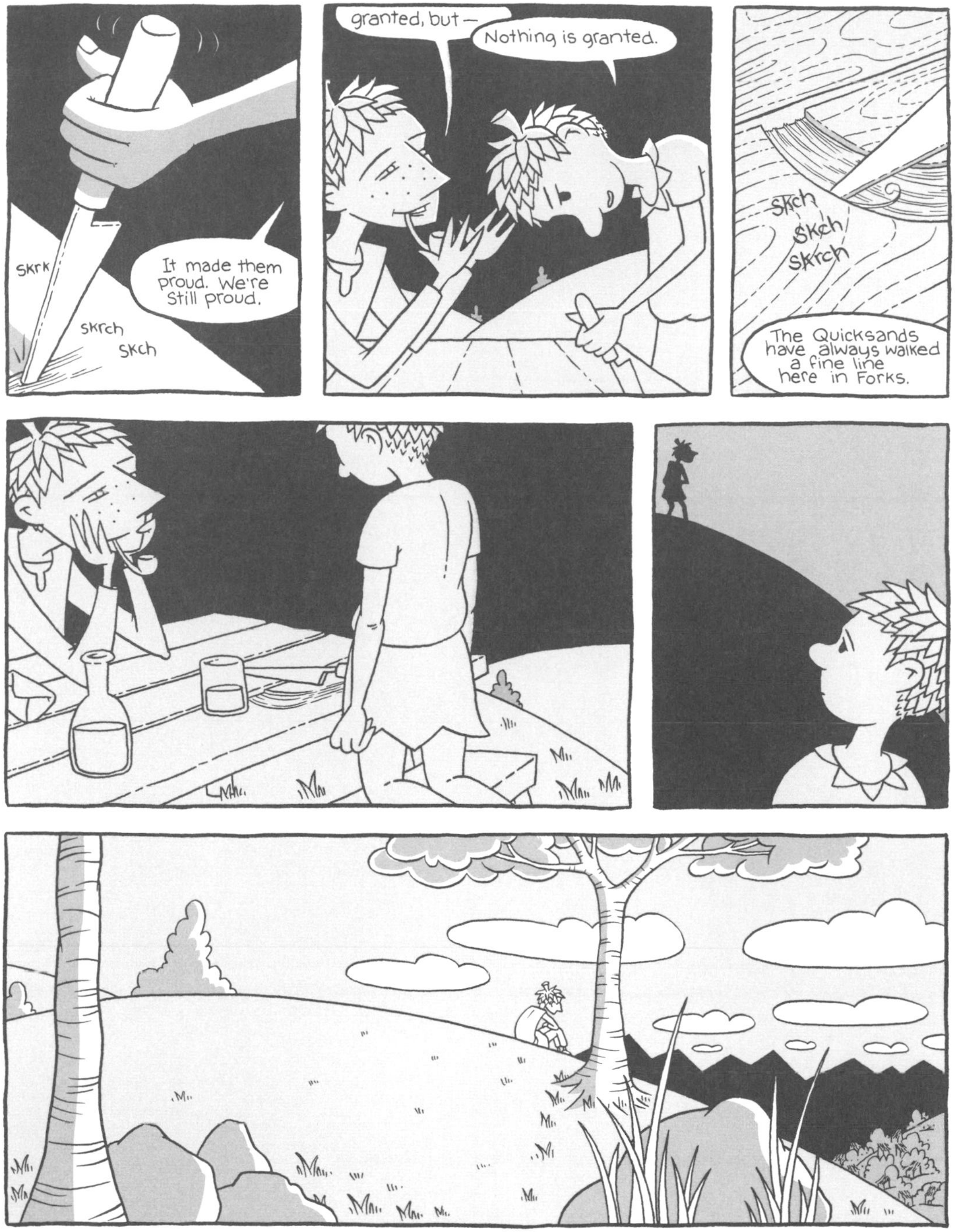
SKRK
SKRCH
SKCH
It made them proud. We're still proud.
granted, but—
Nothing is granted.
SKCH
SKCH
SKRCH
The Quicksands have always walked a fine line here in Forks.

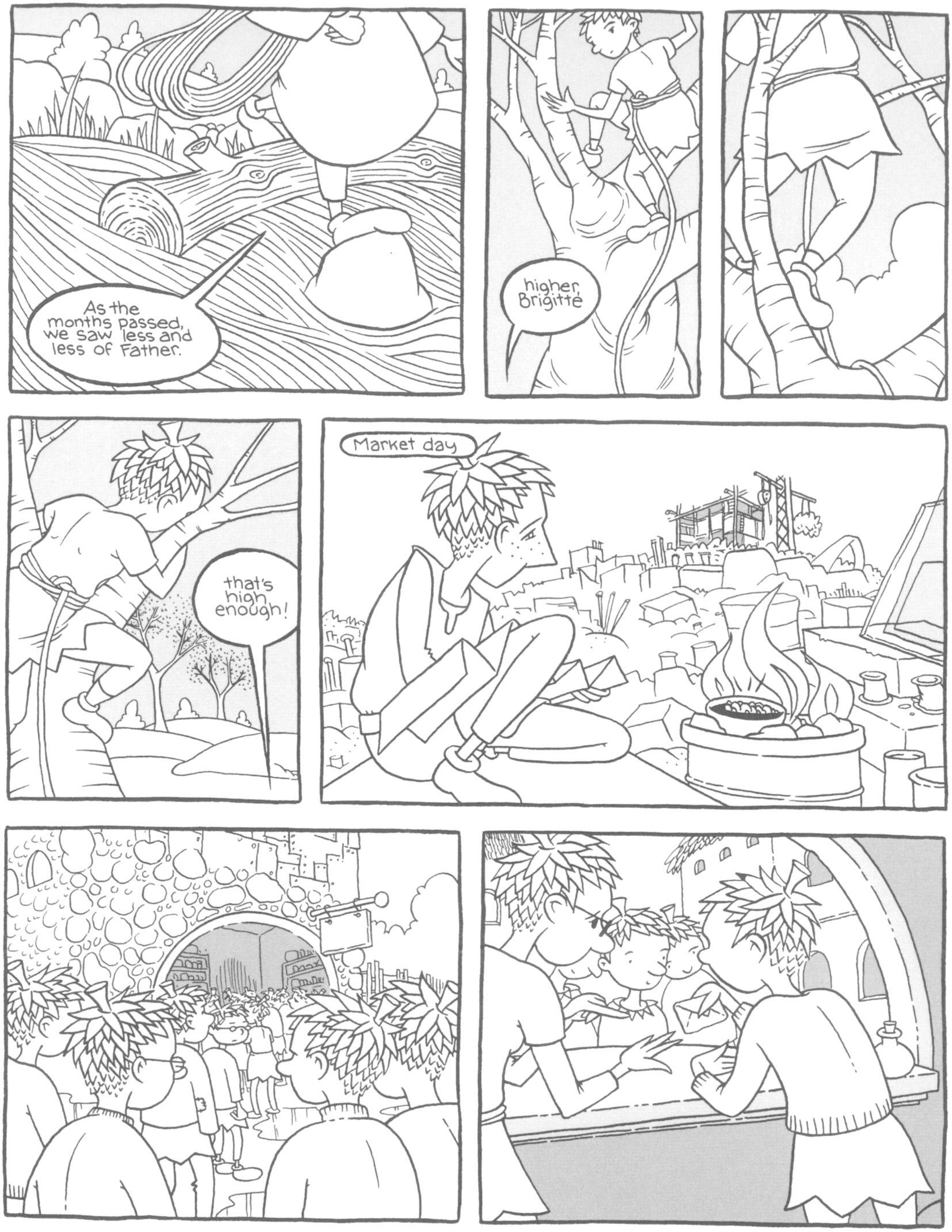
As the months passed, we saw less and less of Father.
higher, Brigitte
that's high enough!
Market day

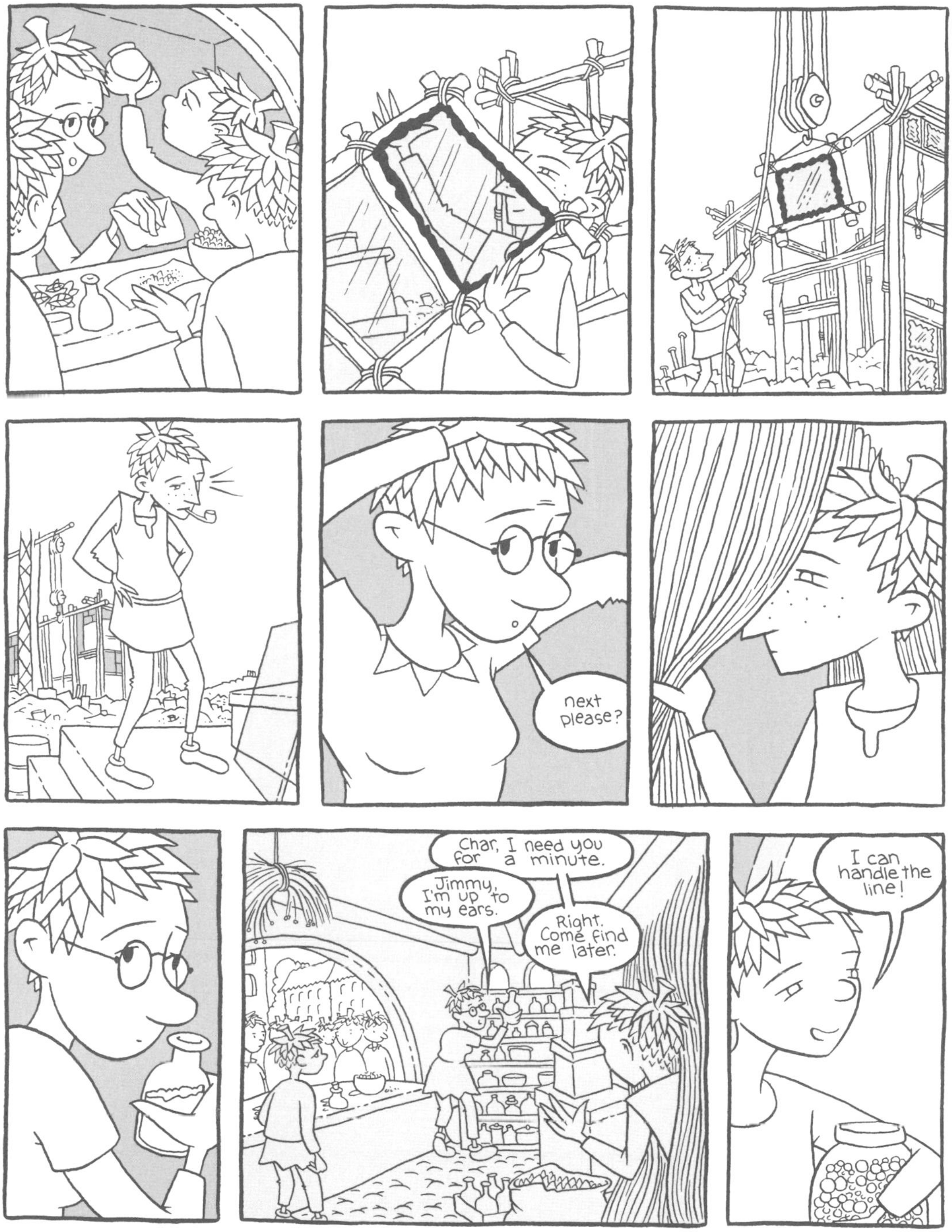

next please?
Char, I need you for a minute.
Jimmy, I'm up to my ears.
Right. Come find me later.
I can handle the line!

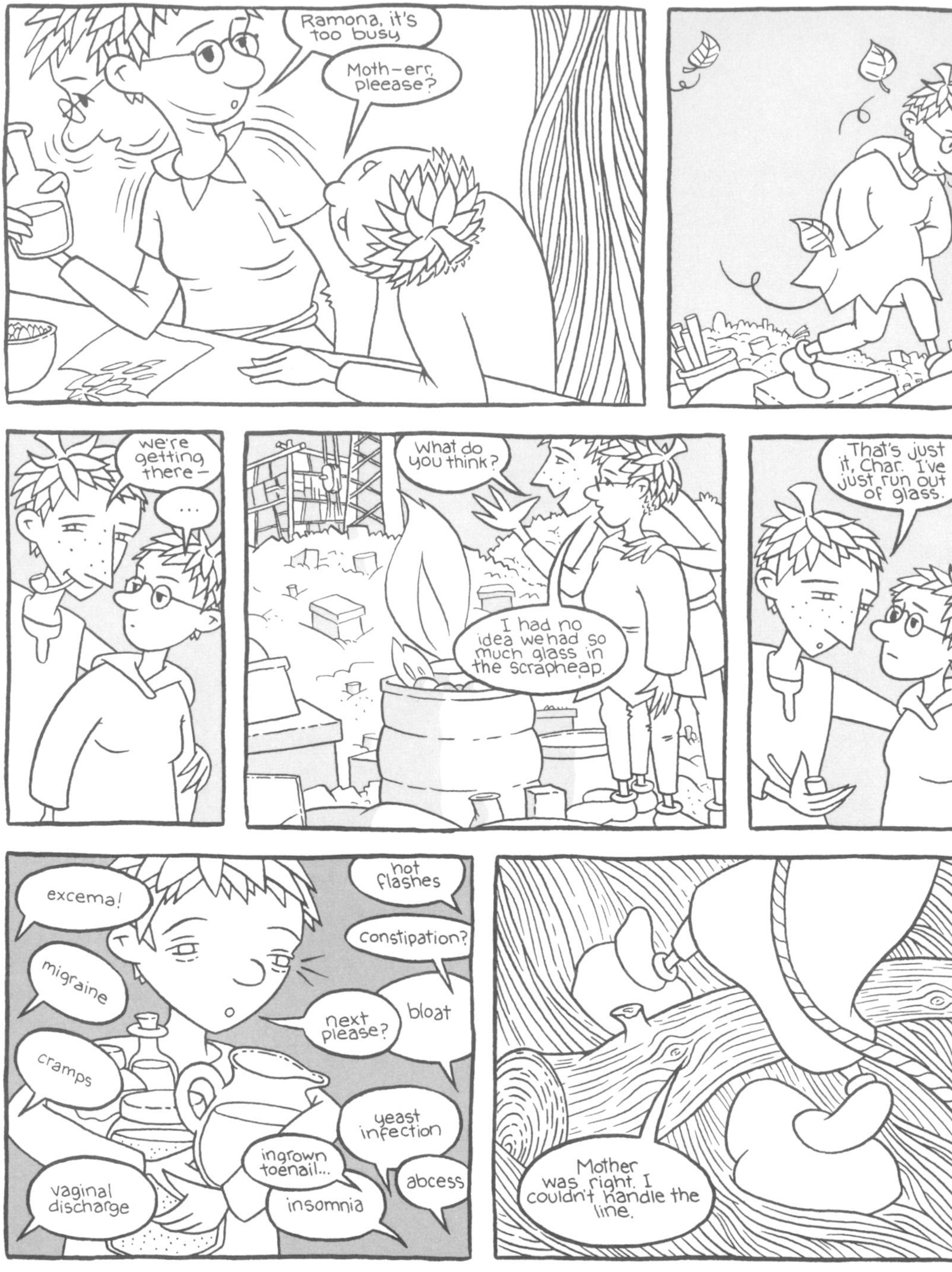
Ramona, it's too busy
Moth-err, pleease?
we're getting there-
...
What do you think?
I had no idea we had so much glass in the scrapheap.
That's just it, Char. I've just run out of glass.
excema!
hot flashes
constipation?
migraine
next please?
bloat
cramps
yeast infection
ingrown toenail...
abcess
vaginal discharge
insomnia
Mother was right. I couldn't handle the line.

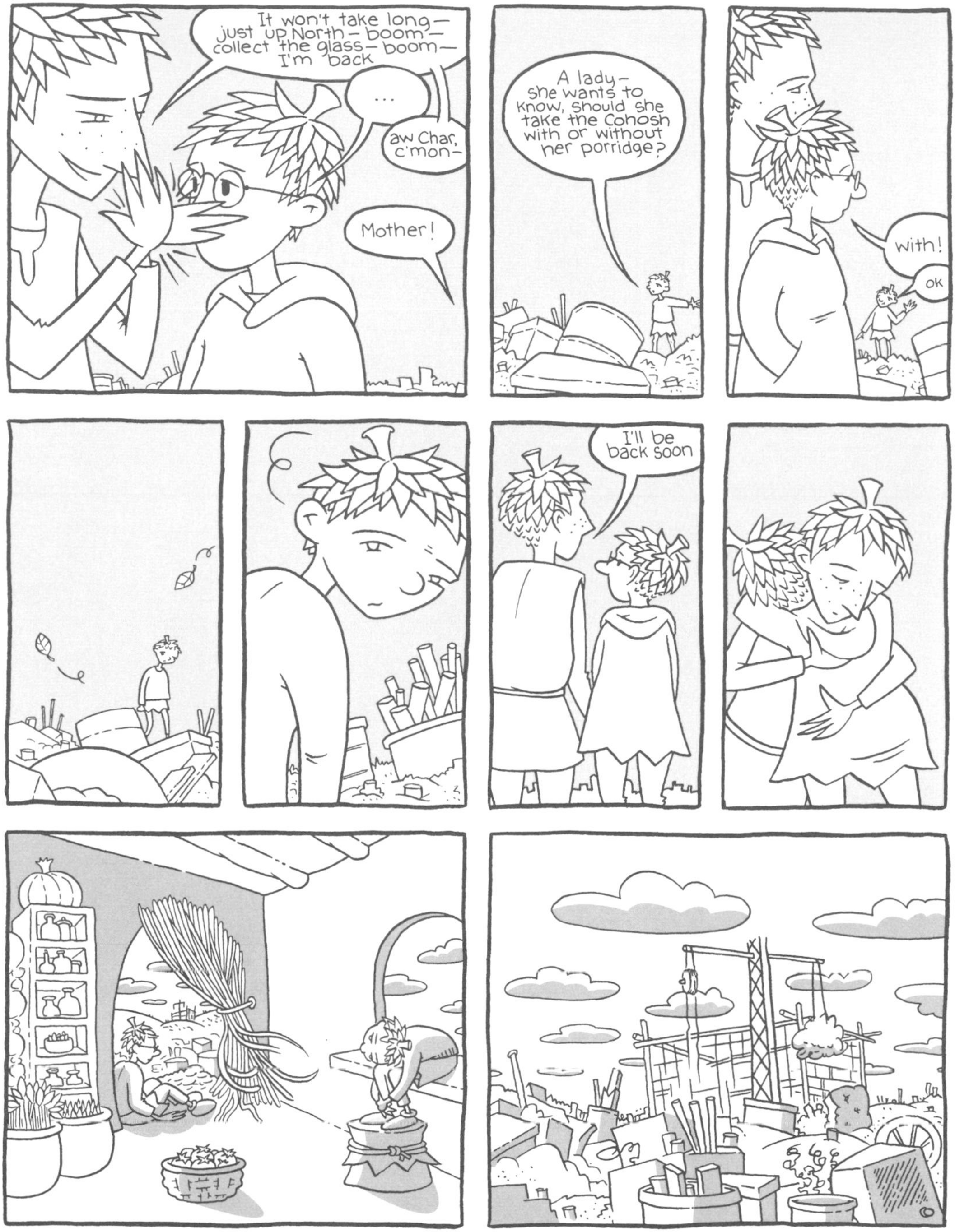
It won't take long— just up North—boom— collect the glass—boom— I'm back
...
aw Char, c'mon—
Mother!
A lady— she wants to know, should she take the Cohosh with or without her porridge?
With!
ok
I'll be back soon

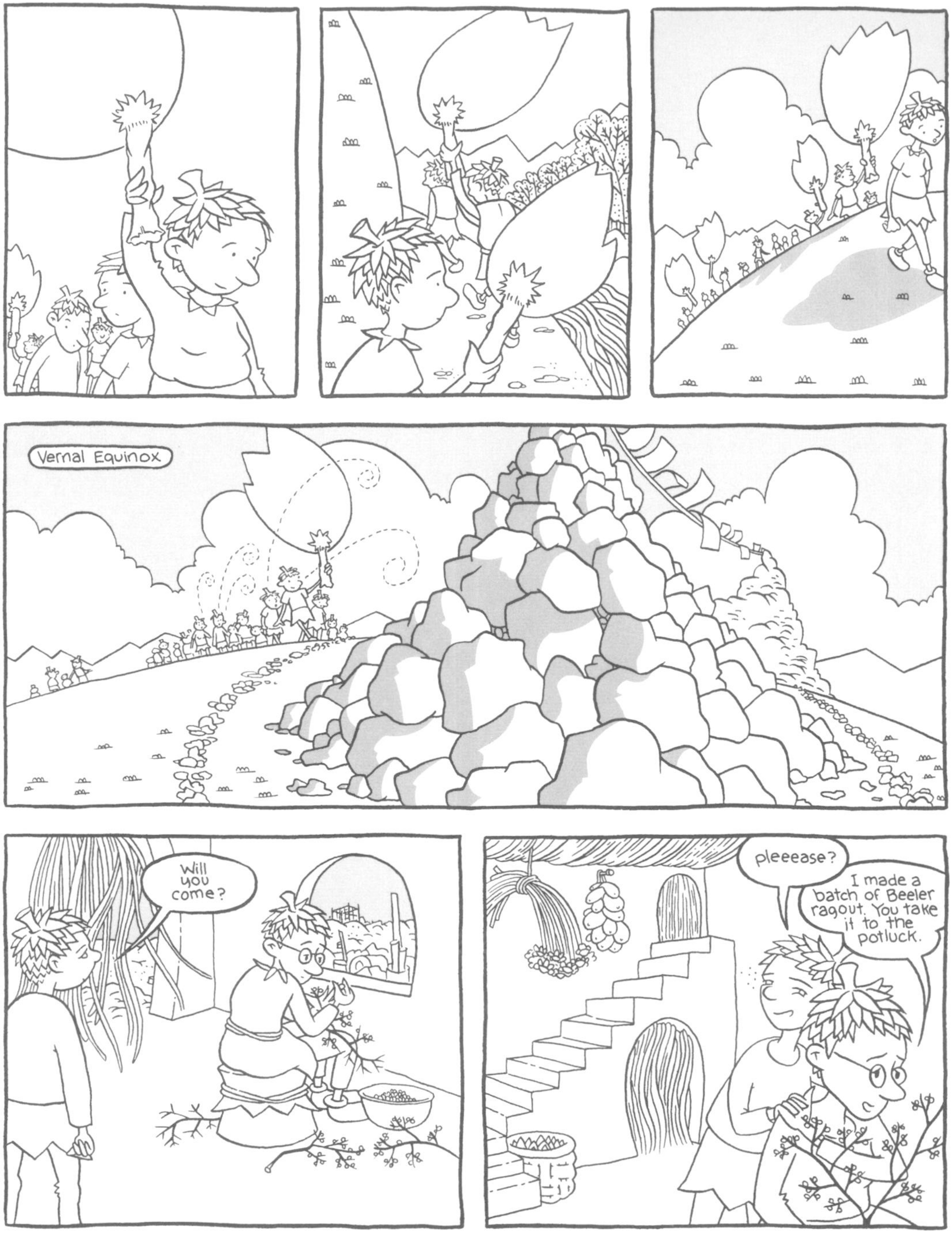
Vernal Equinox
Will you come?
pleeease?
I made a batch of Beeler ragout. You take it to the potluck.

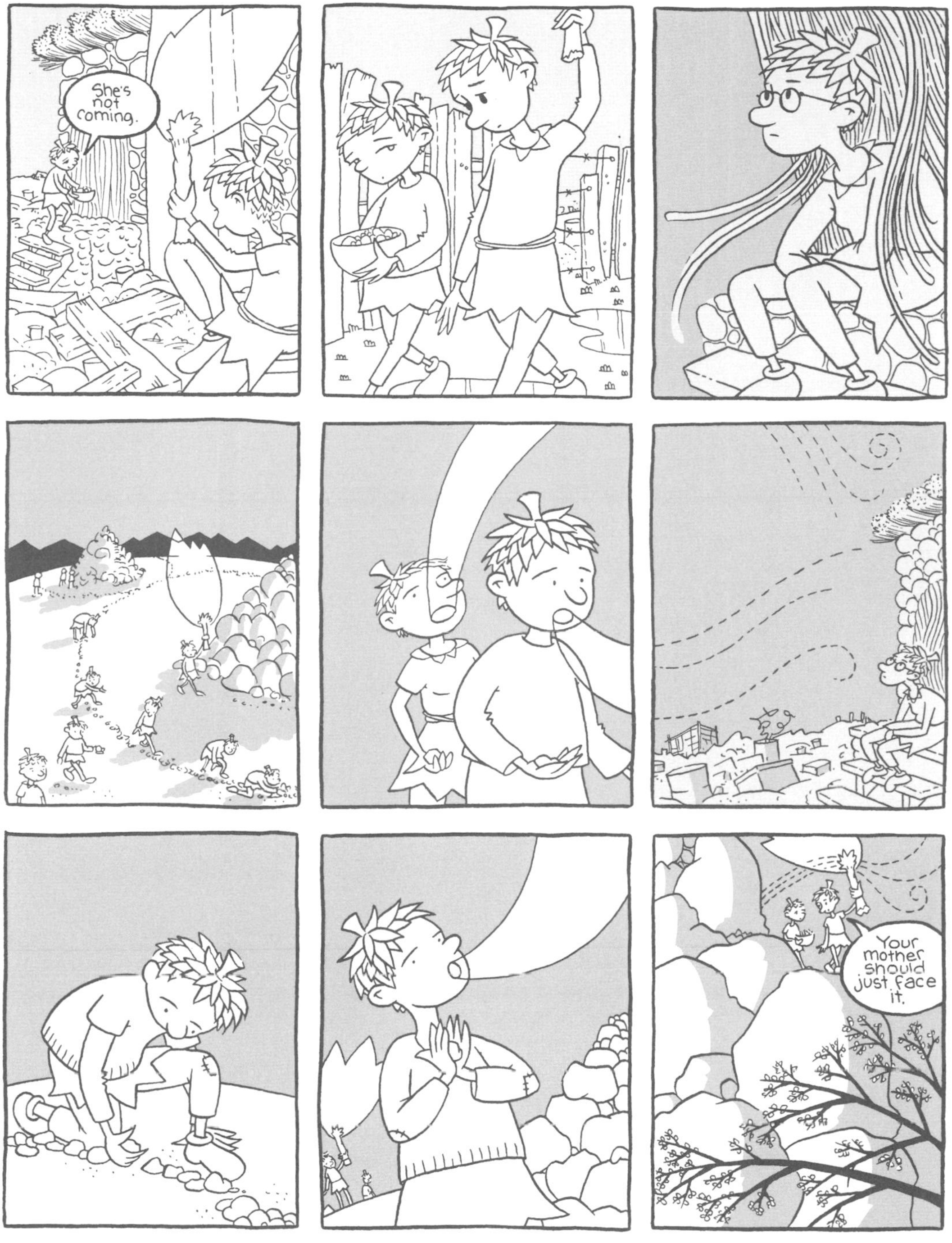
She's not coming.
Your mother should just face it.

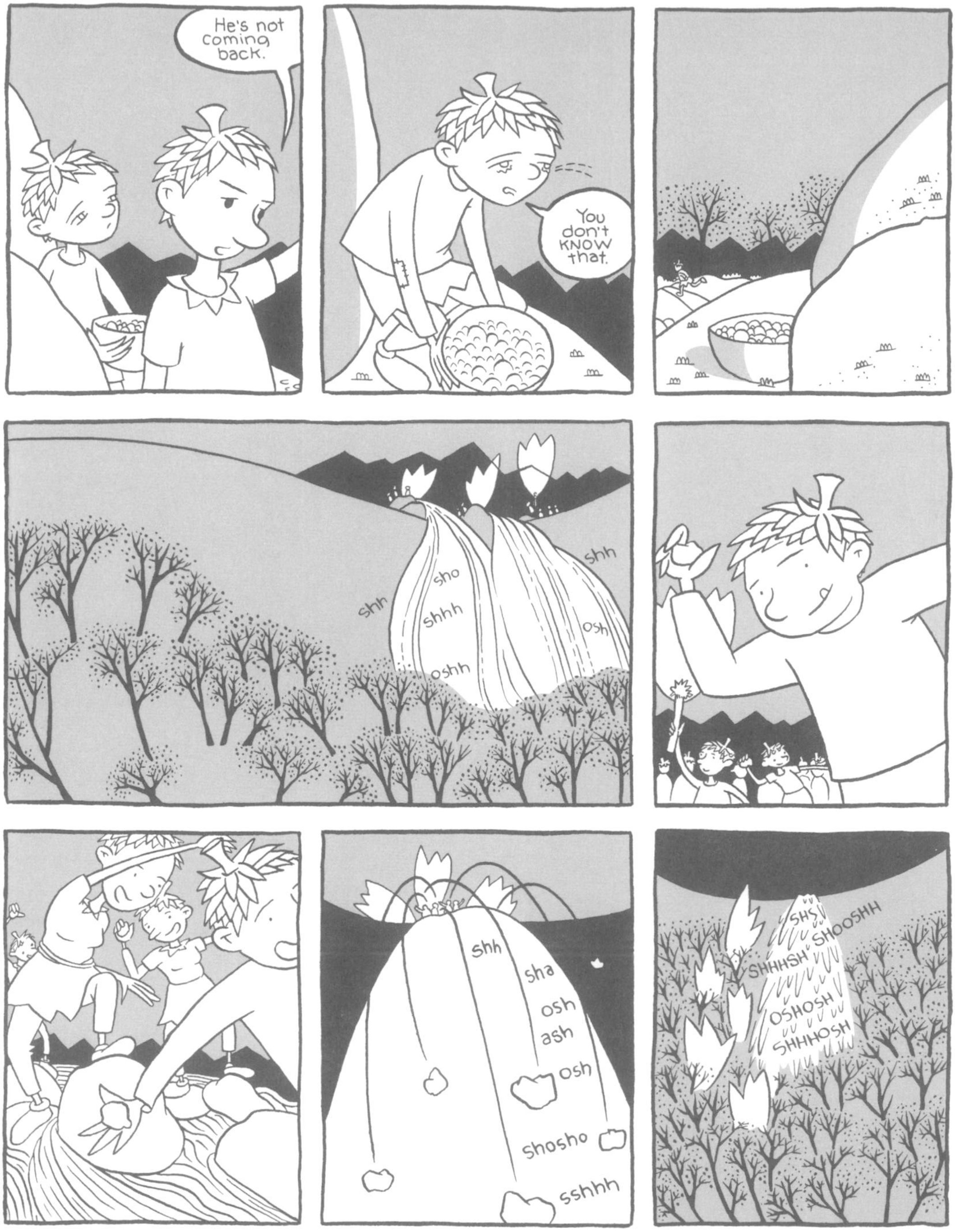
He's not coming back.
You don't KNOW that.
shh
sho
shhh
oshh
shh
osh
shh
sha
osh
ash
osh
shosho
sshhh
SHS
SHOOSHH
SHHHSH
OSHOSH
SHHHOSH

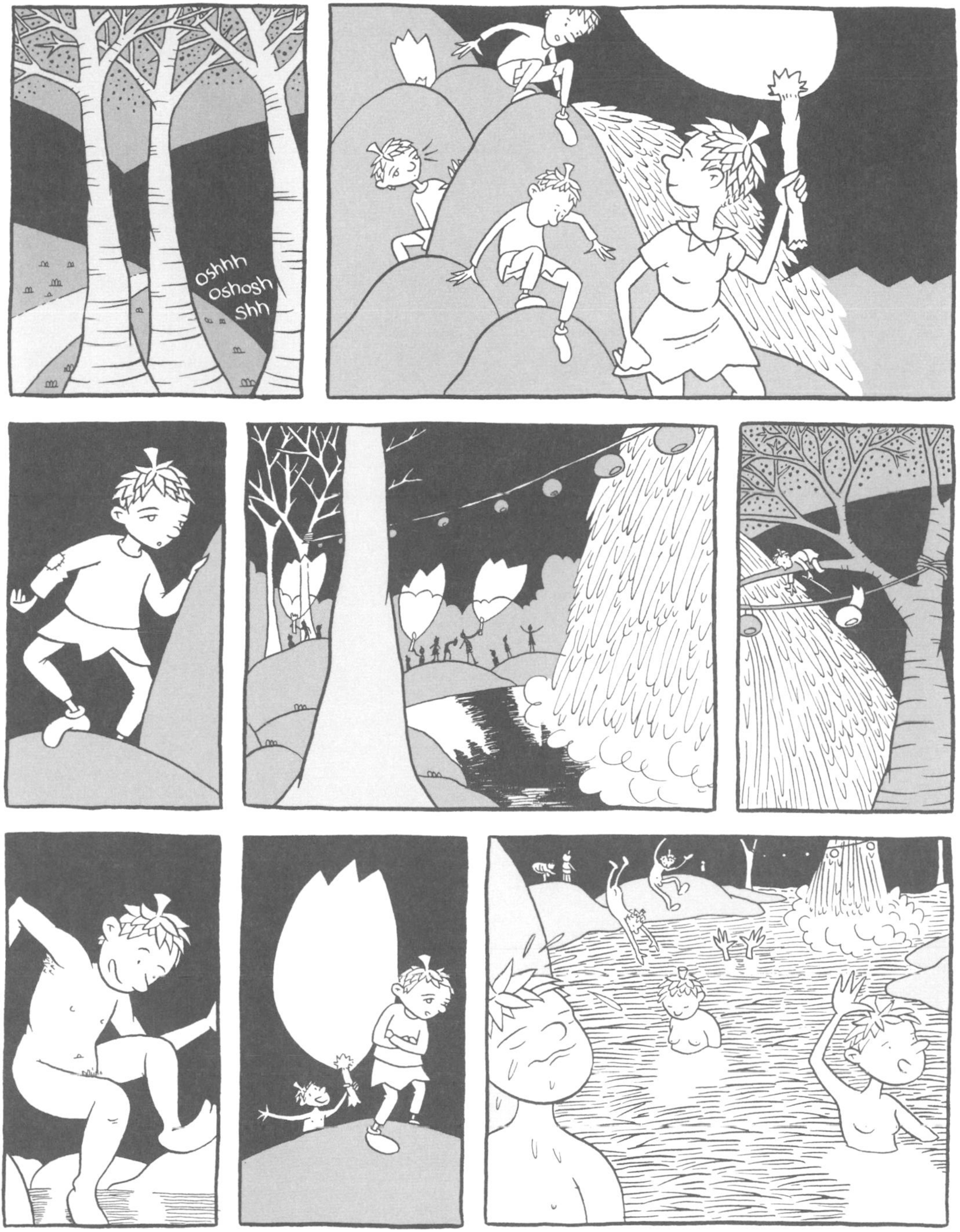
oshhh
oshosh
shh

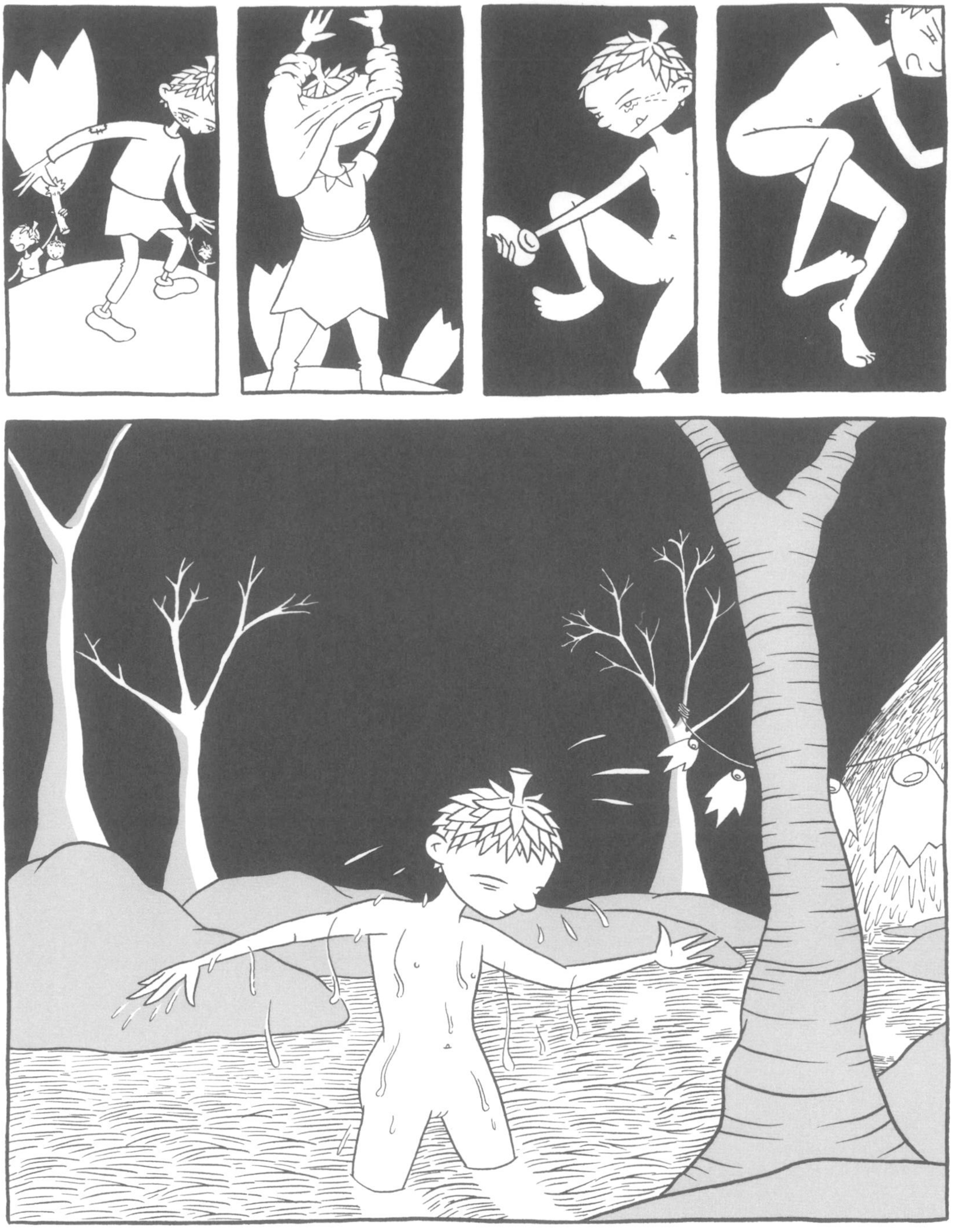

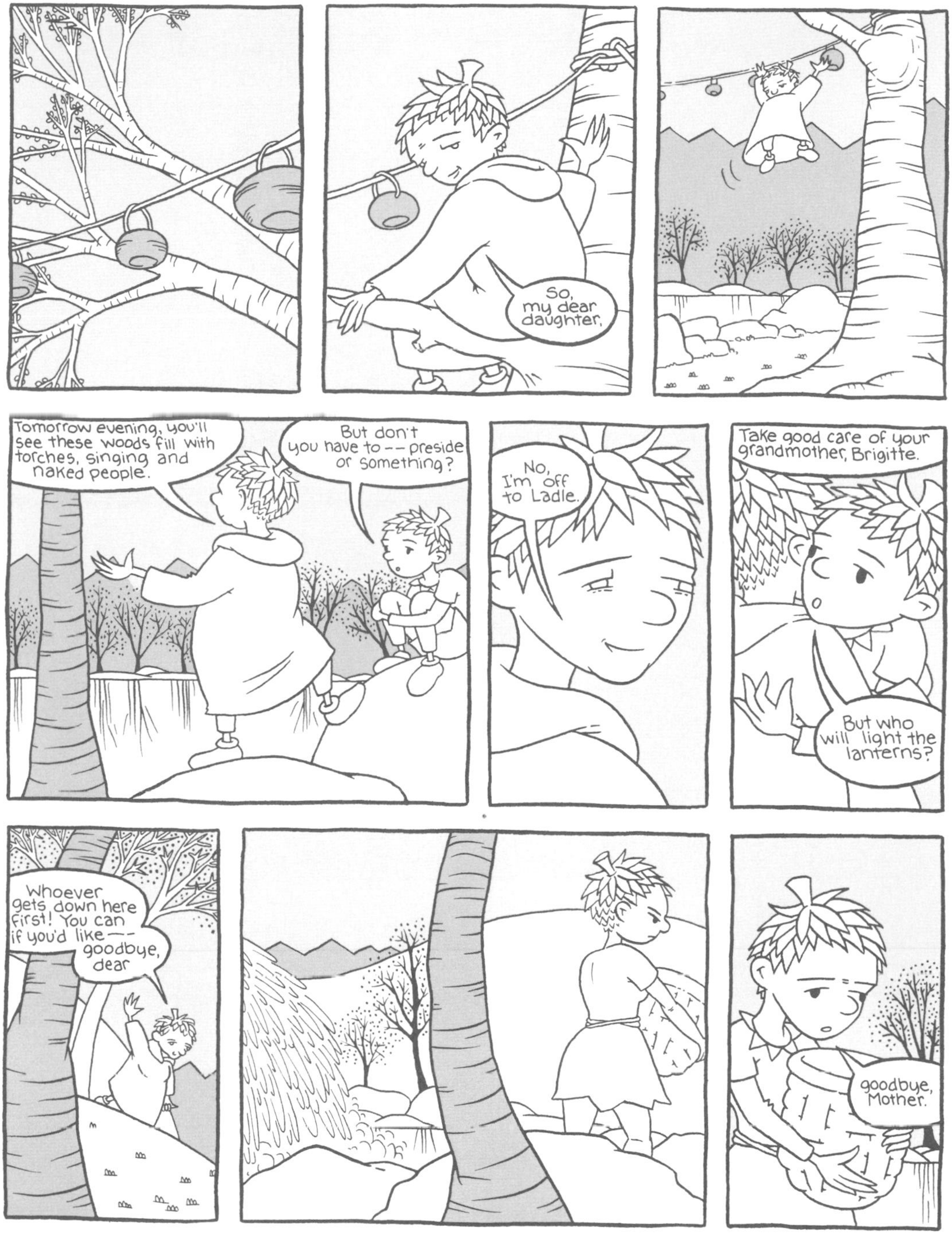
So, my dear daughter,
Tomorrow evening, you'll see these woods fill with torches, singing and naked people.
But don't you have to -- preside or something?
No, I'm off to Ladle.
Take good care of your grandmother, Brigitte.
But who will light the lanterns?
Whoever gets down here first! You can if you'd like --
goodbye, dear
goodbye, Mother.

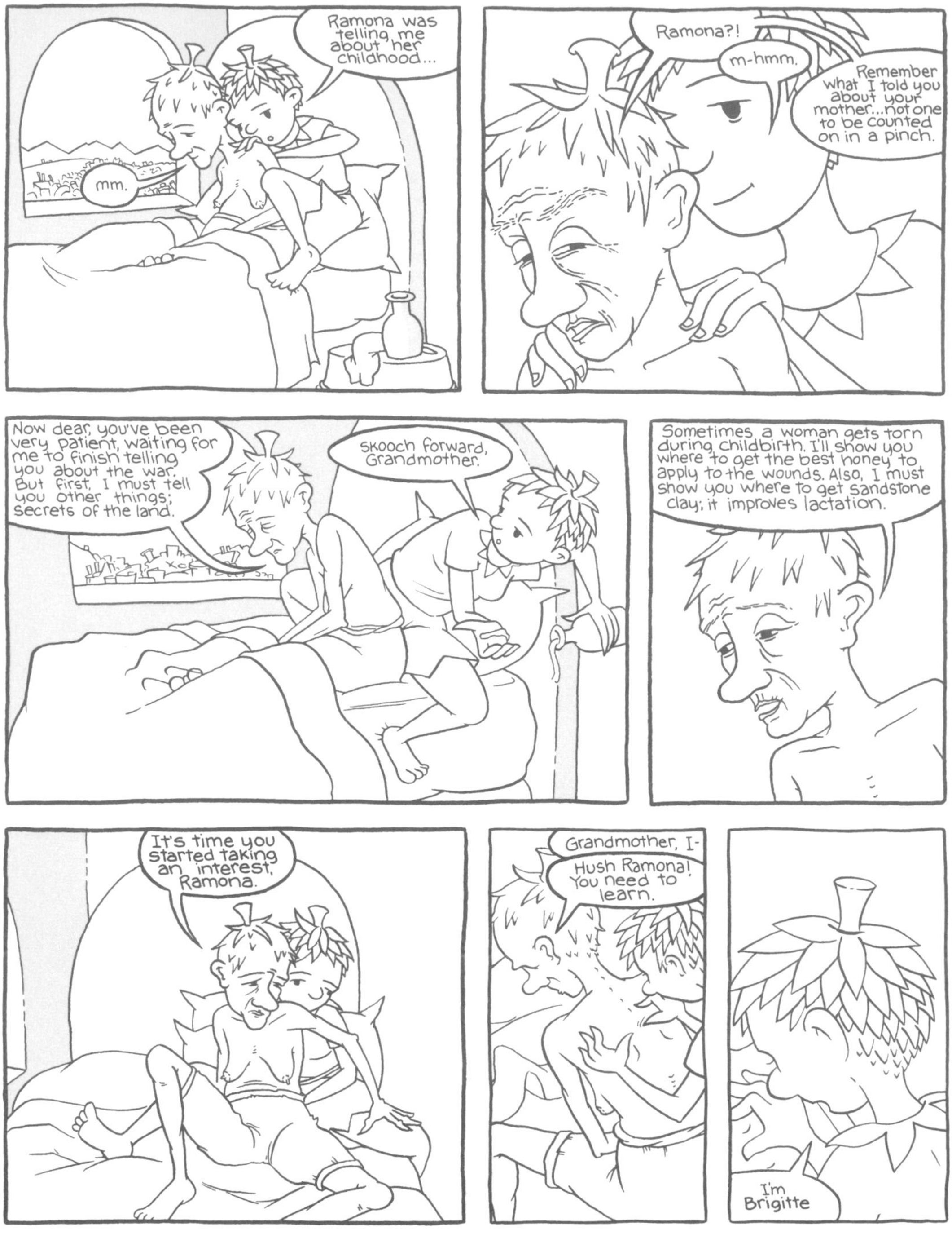
Ramona was telling me about her childhood...
mm.
Ramona?!
m-hmm.
Remember what I told you about your mother...not one to be counted on in a pinch.
Now dear, you've been very patient, waiting for me to finish telling you about the war. But first, I must tell you other things; secrets of the land.
Skooch forward, Grandmother.
Sometimes a woman gets torn during childbirth. I'll show you where to get the best honey to apply to the wounds. Also, I must show you where to get sandstone clay; it improves lactation.
It's time you started taking an interest, Ramona.
Grandmother, I-
Hush Ramona! You need to learn.
I'm Brigitte

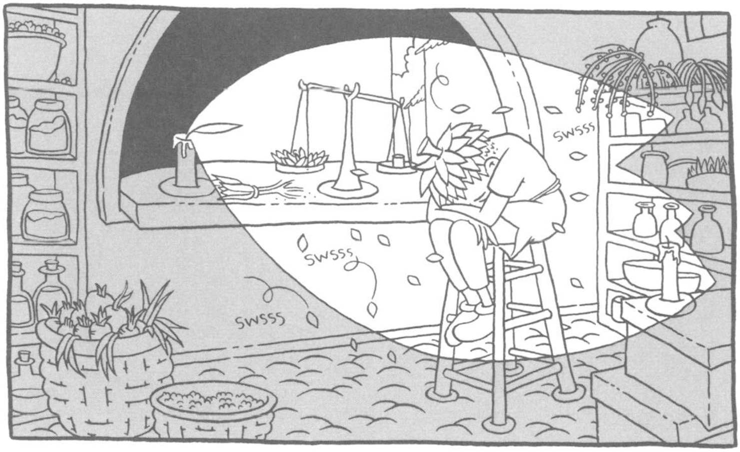
SWSSS
SWSSS
SWSSS

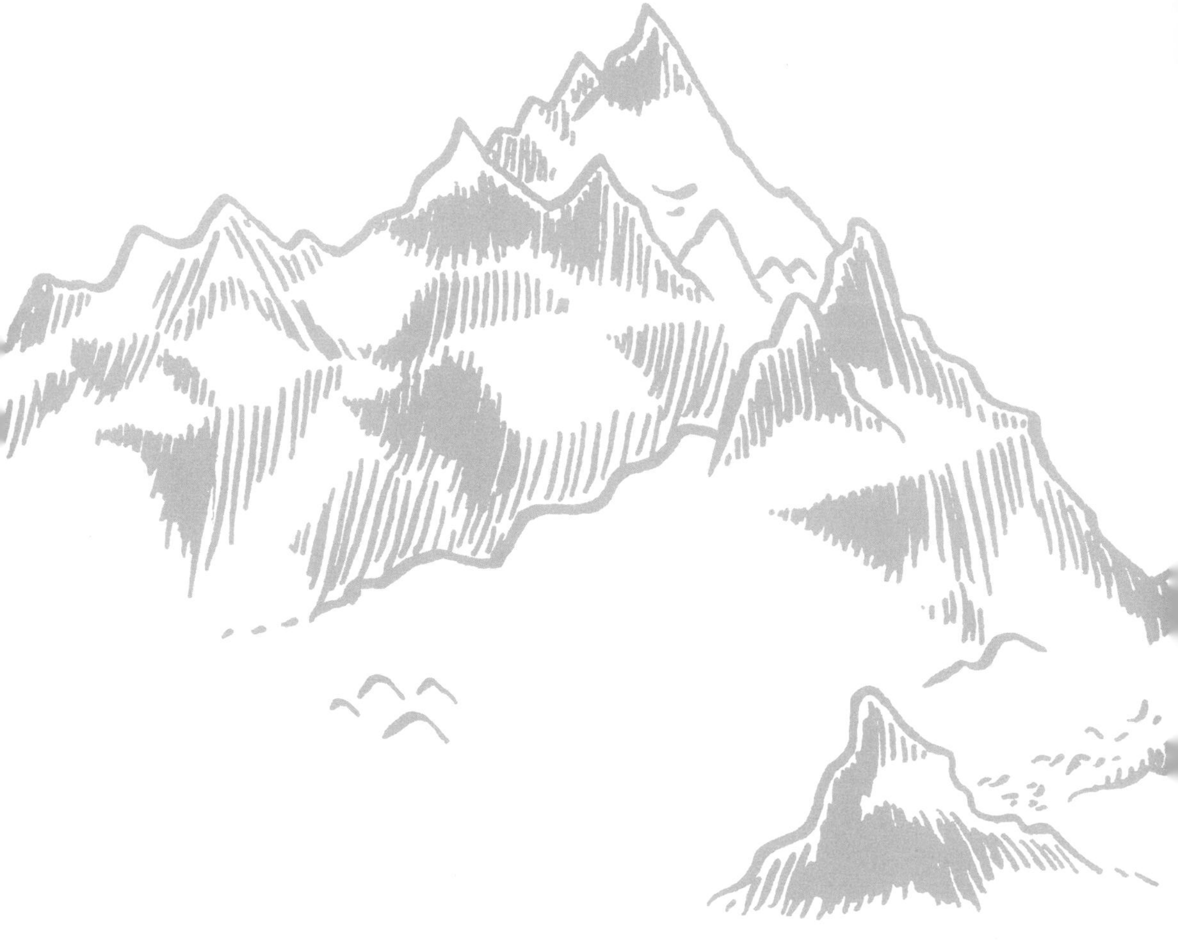

Chapter 4
RAMONA & DORIAN

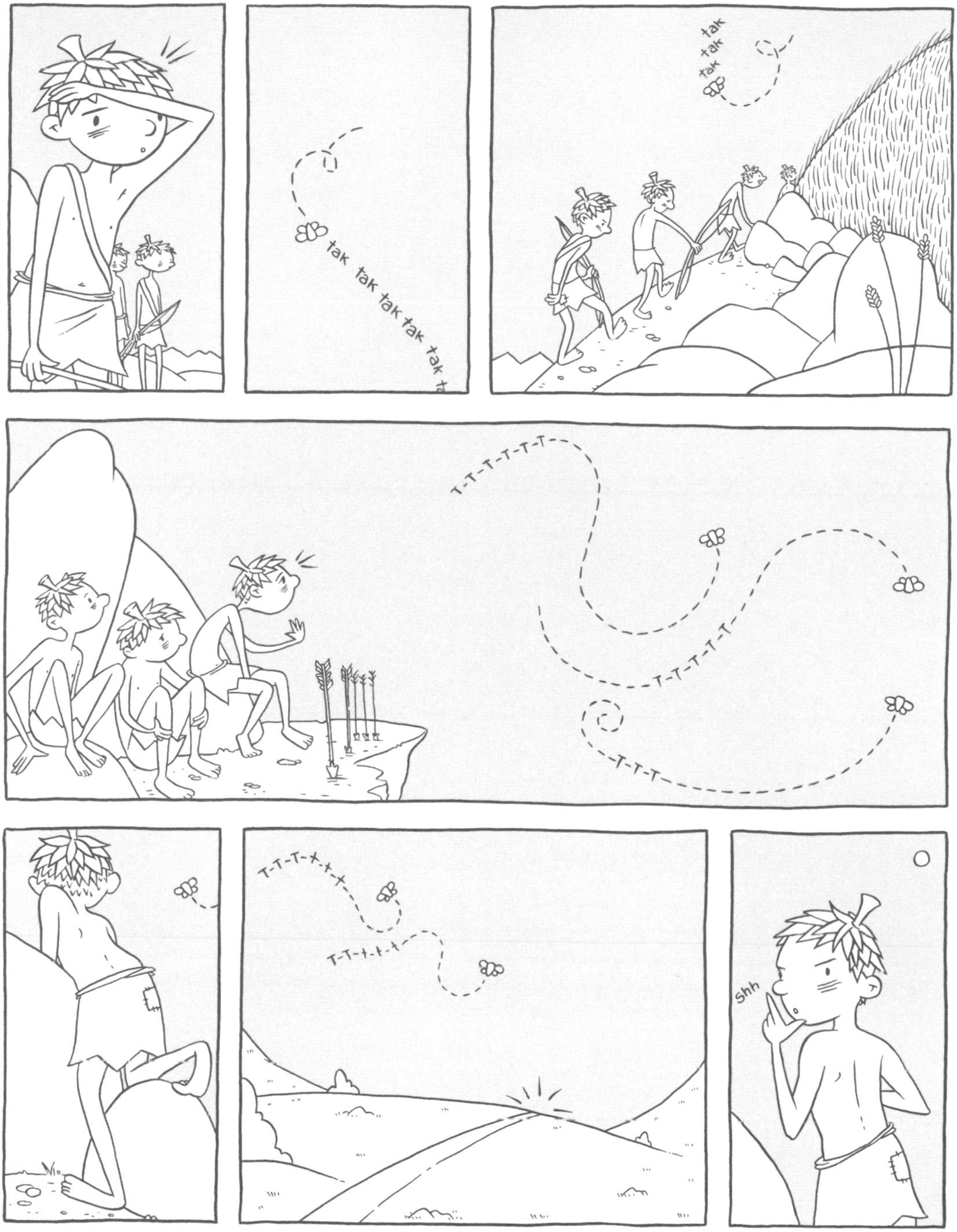
tak tak tak tak tak ta
tak tak tak
T-T-T-T-T-T-T
T-T-T-T-T-T
T-T-T
T-T-T-t-t-t
T-T-t-t-t
Shh

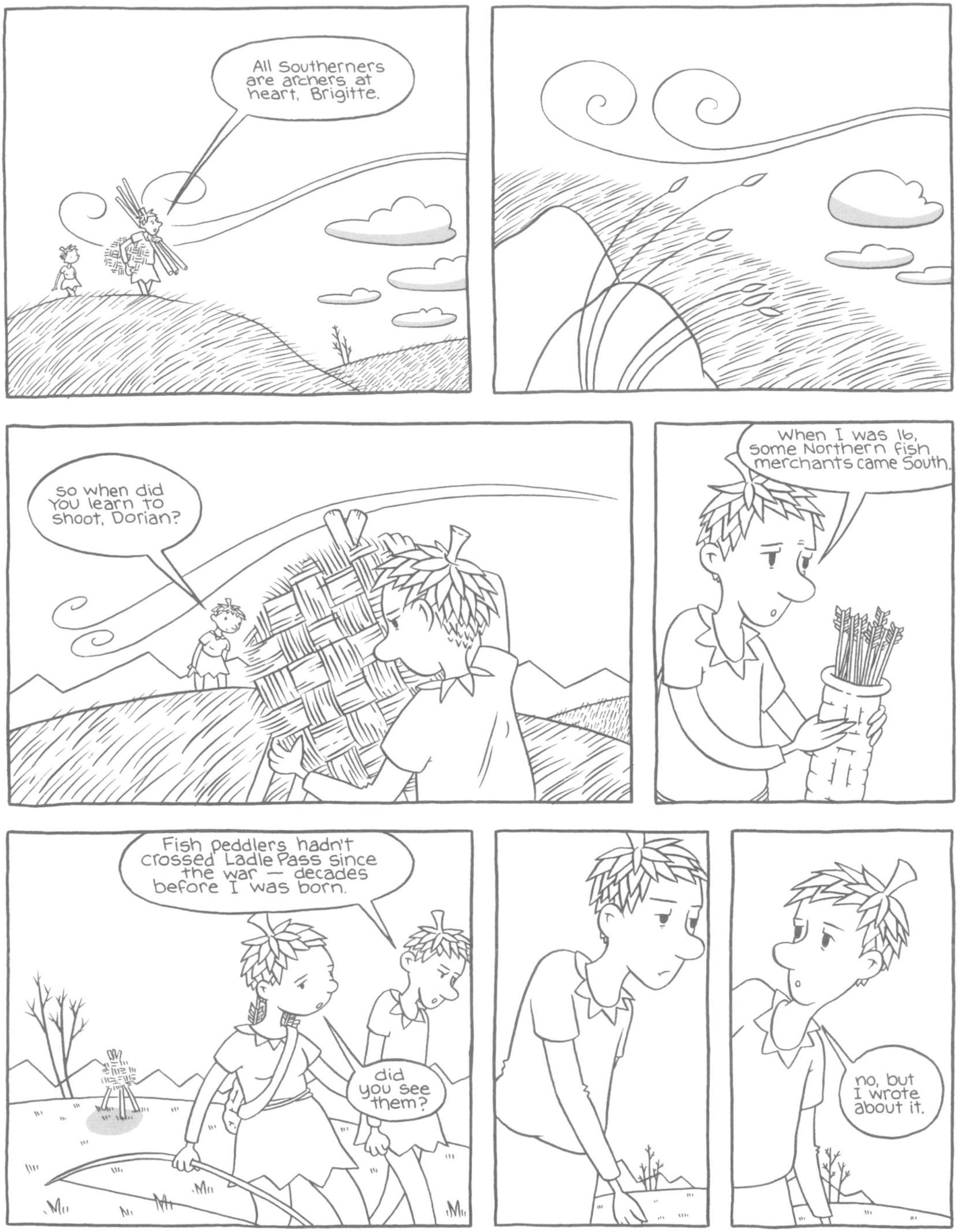
All Southerners are archers at heart, Brigitte.
So when did you learn to shoot, Dorian?
When I was 16, some Northern fish merchants came South.
Fish peddlers hadn't crossed Ladle Pass since the war — decades before I was born.
did you see them?
no, but I wrote about it.

T-T-T-T
tak-tak-tak-tak
let's break!

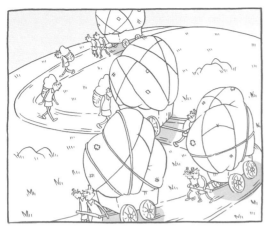

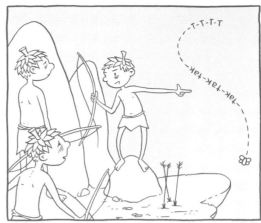

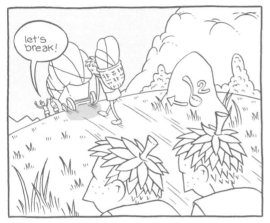

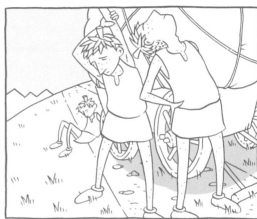

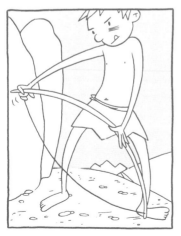

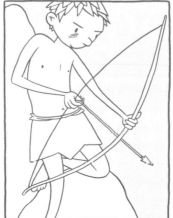

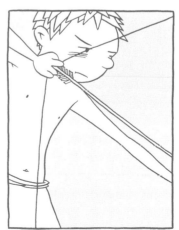

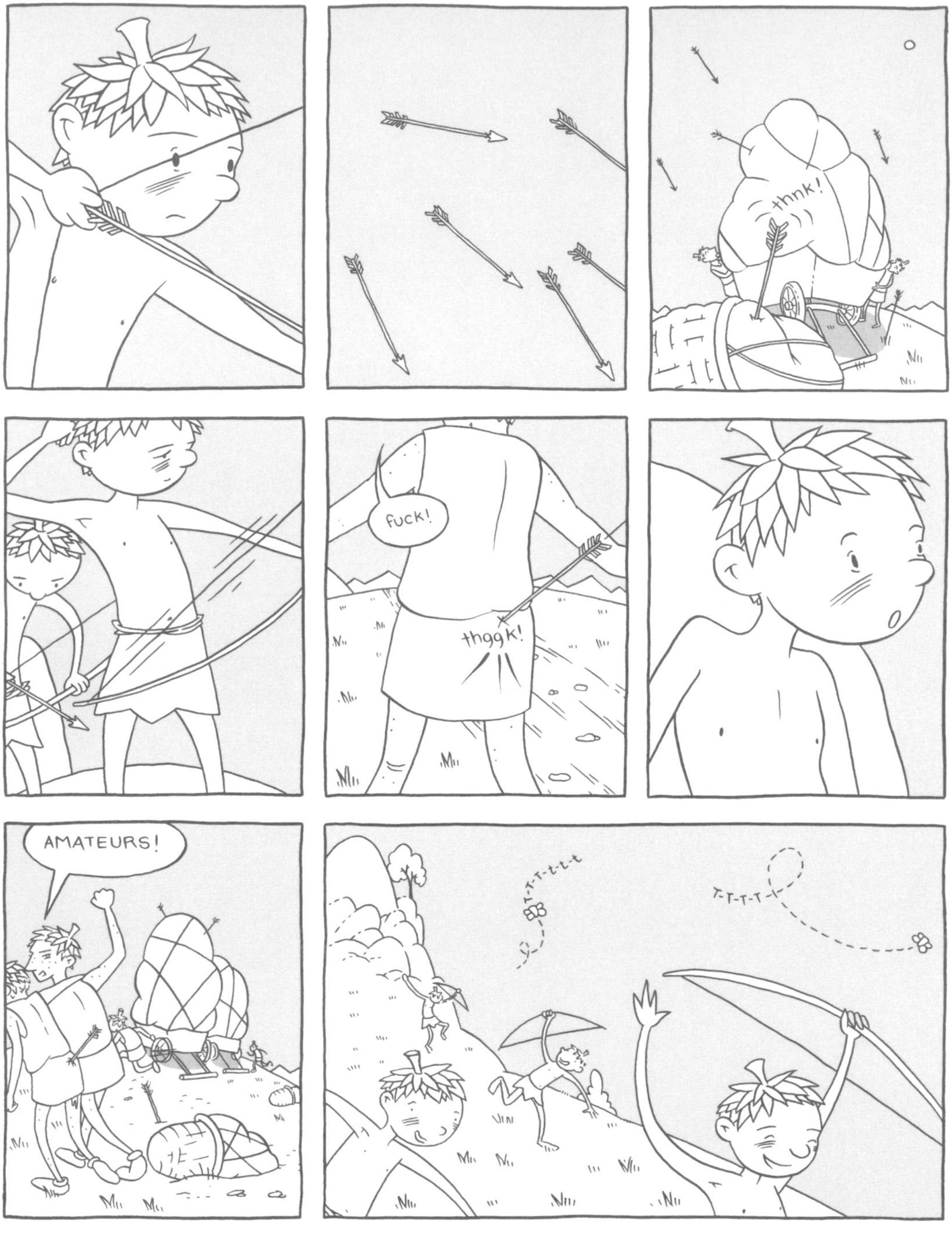
thnk!
fuck!
thggk!
AMATEURS!
T-T-T-t-t-t
T-T-T-T-

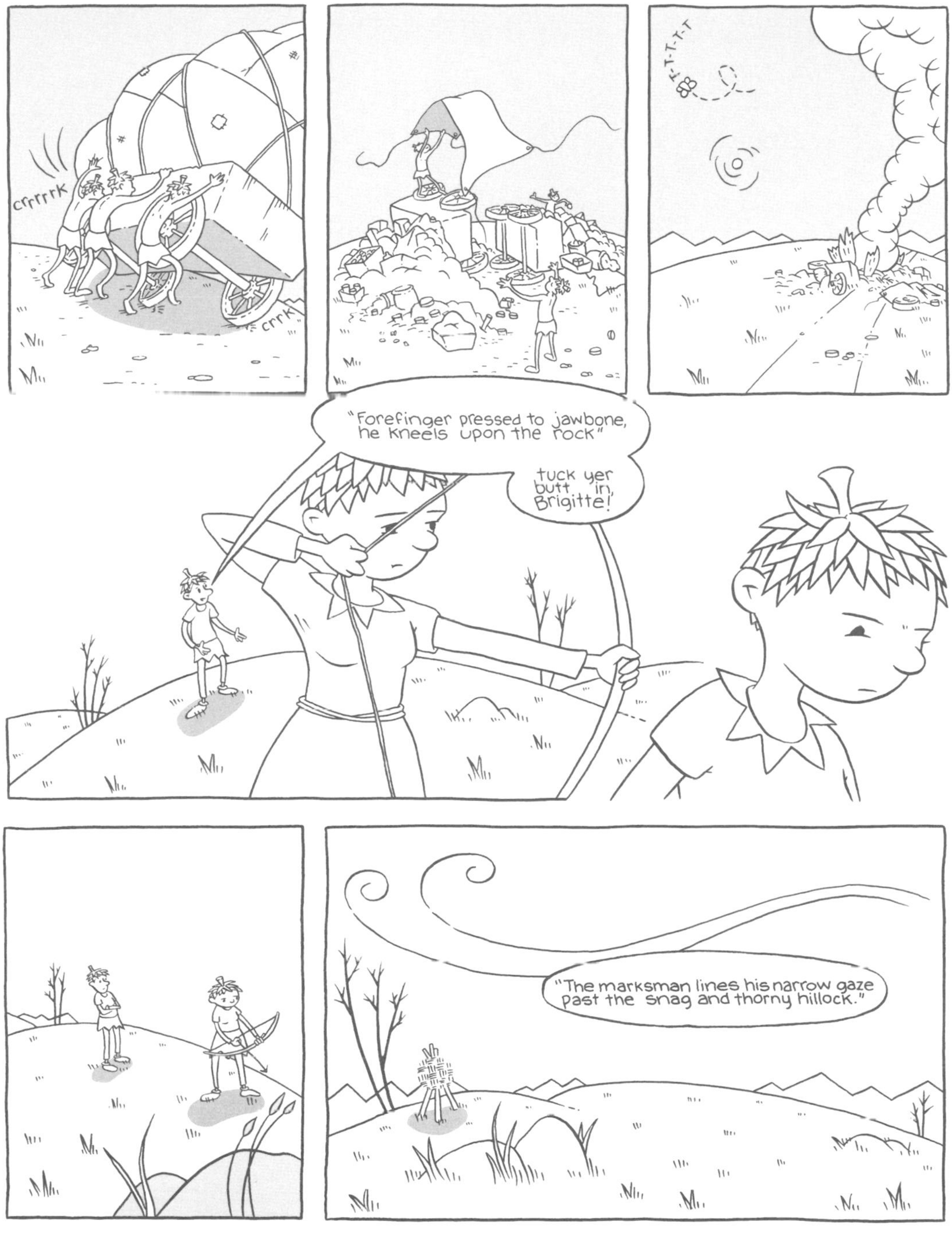
crrrrrk
crrk
T-T-T-T-T
"Forefinger pressed to jawbone, he kneels upon the rock"
tuck yer butt in, Brigitte!
"The marksman lines his narrow gaze past the snag and thorny hillock."

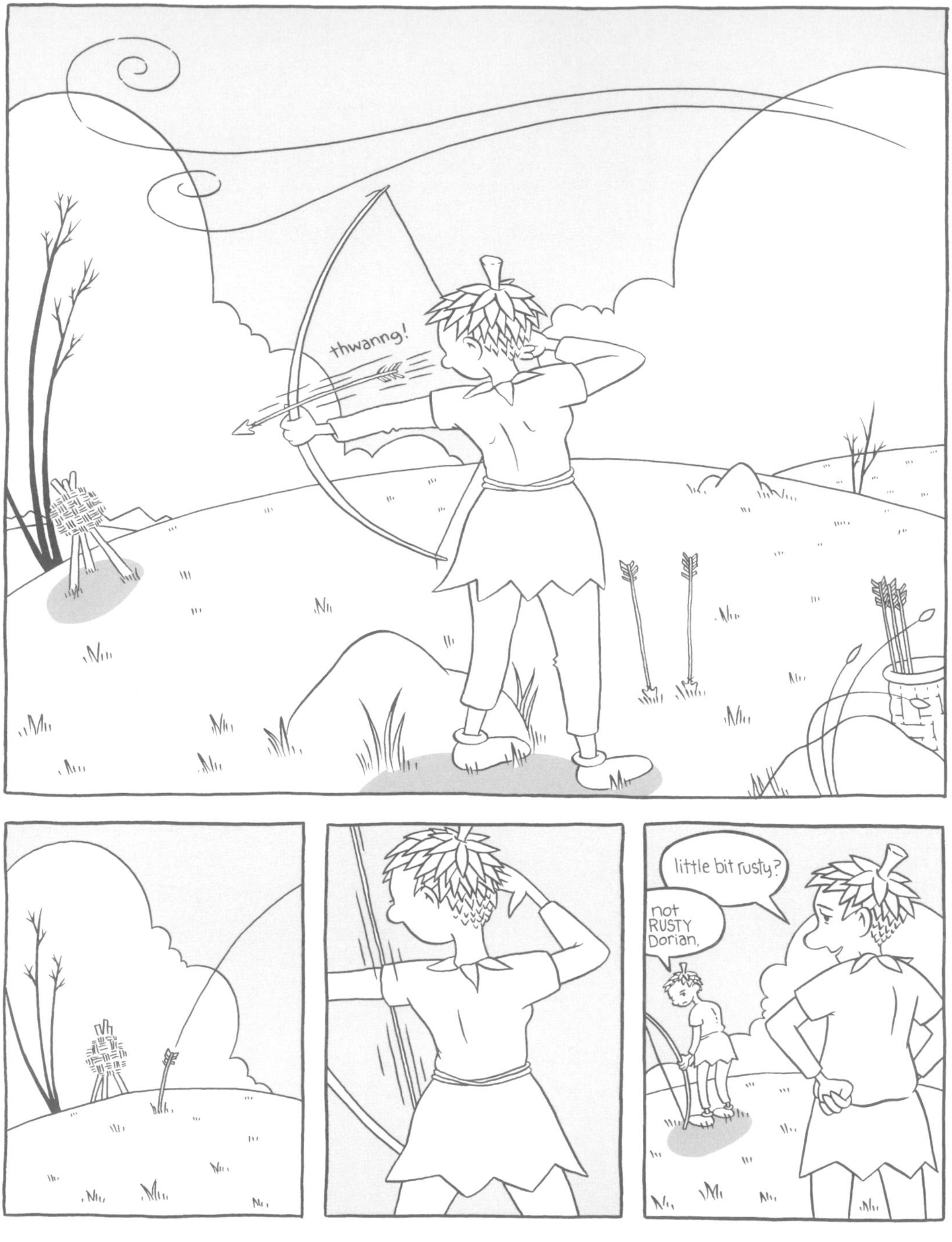
thwanng!
little bit rusty?
not
RUSTY
Dorian,

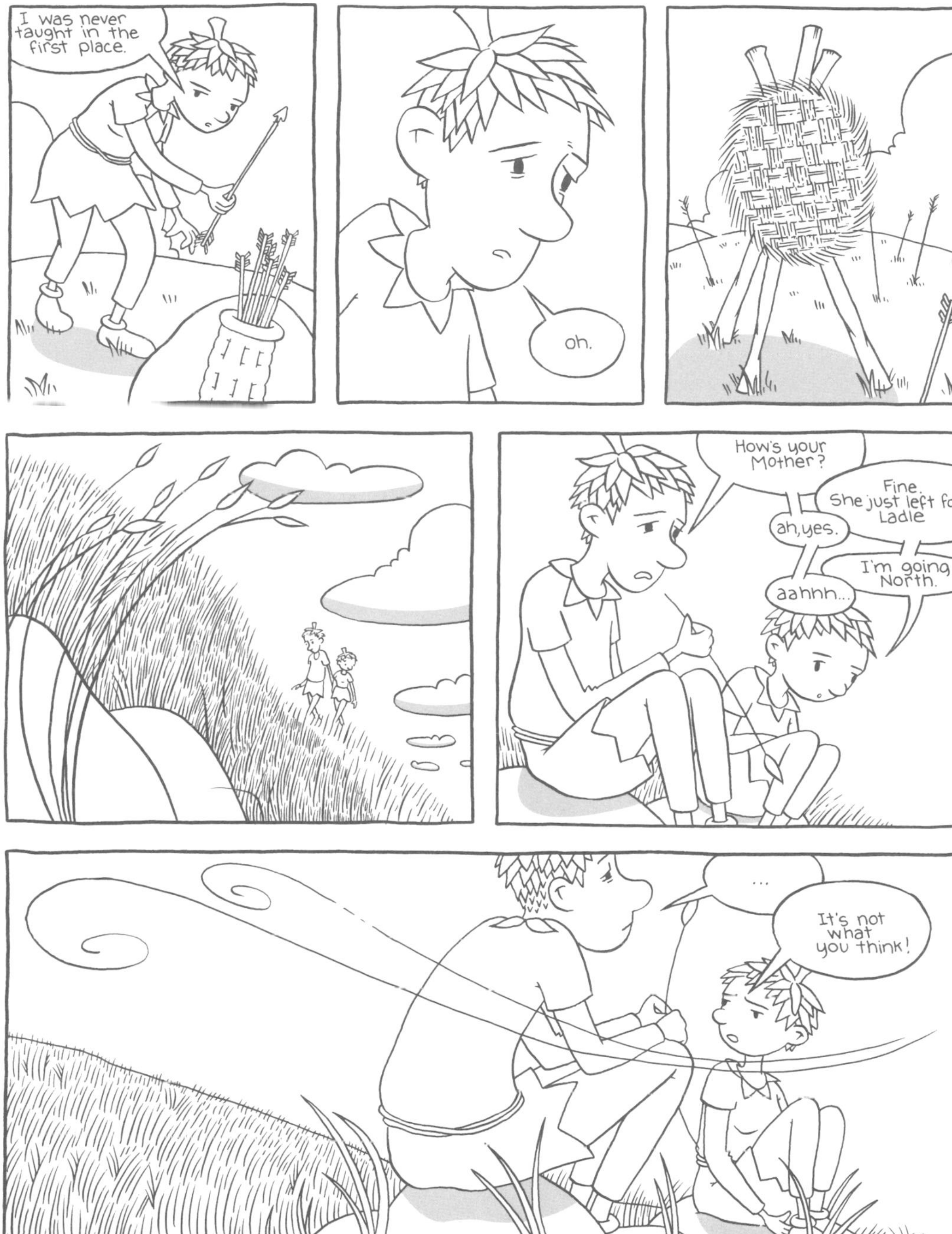
I was never taught in the first place.
oh.
How's your Mother?
Fine. She just left for Ladle
ah, yes.
I'm going North.
aahhh...
...
It's not what you think!

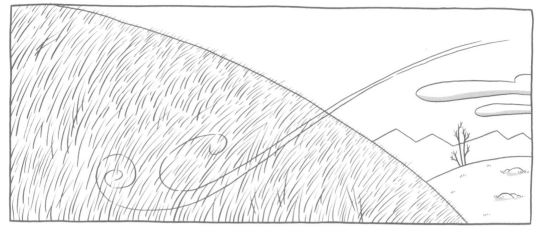

I want to look around up there — find my roots —

roots! the best of YOUR roots are right here. Your Grandmother—

Don't talk to me about Grandmother, she's — she doesn't even know who I am anymore

You want to talk about roots? You were conceived in that cabin up there. Middle of a snowstorm, seventeen years ago.

Yeah, and then Grandmother had to come save me.

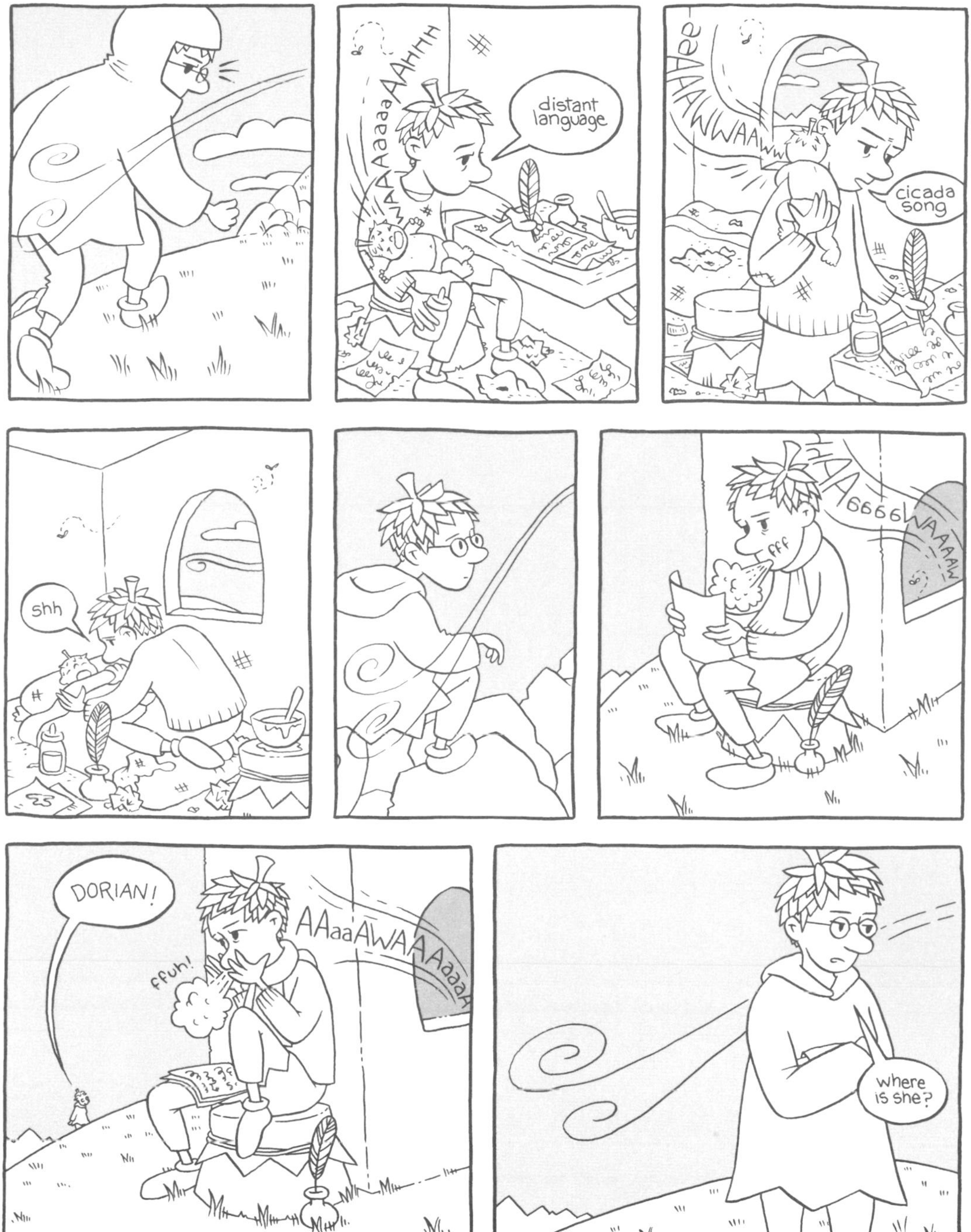
distant language
cicada song
shh
fff
DORIAN!
ffuh!
AAaaAWAAAaaaaA
where is she?

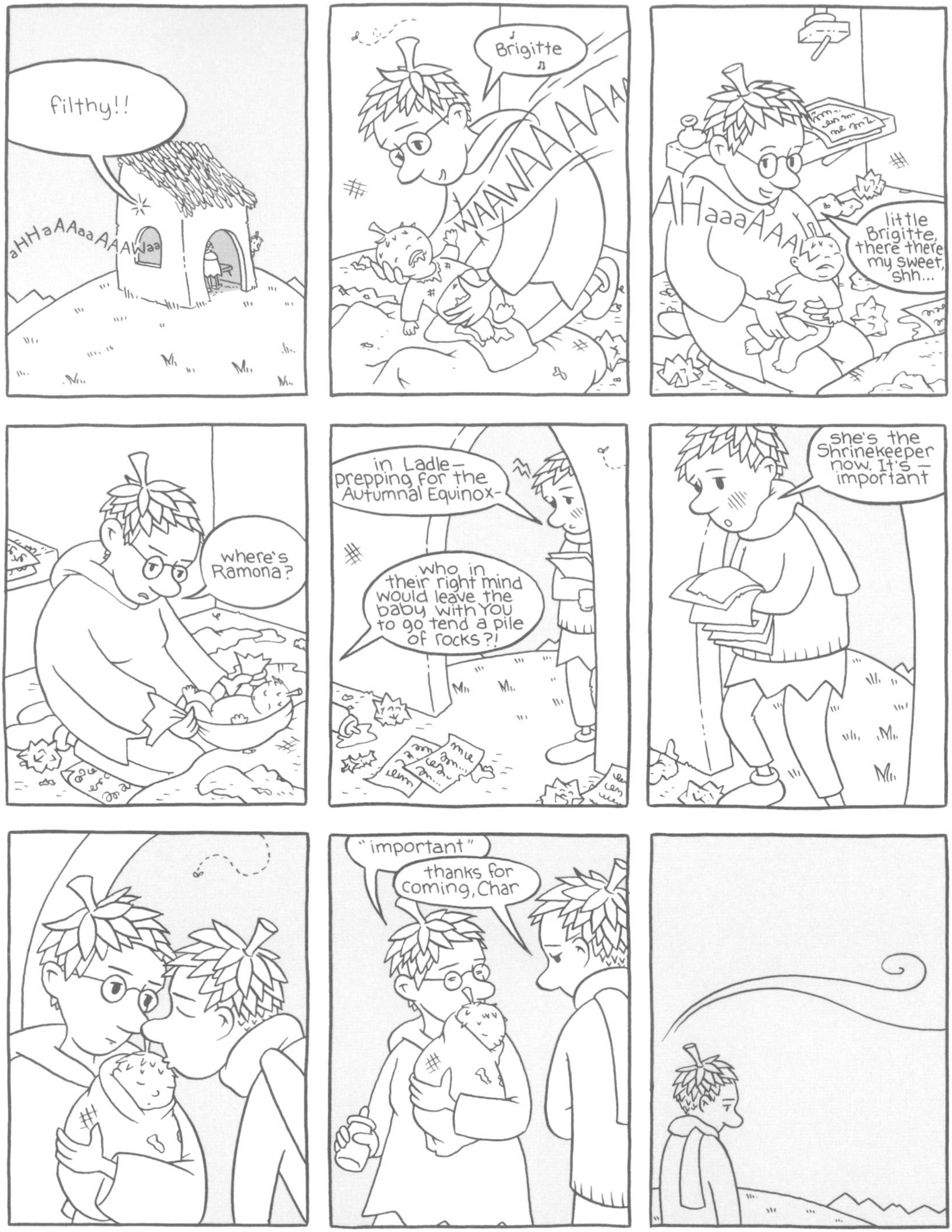
filthy!!
aHHaAAaaAAAWaa
Brigitte
WAAWAAAAAAA
AHaaaAAAW
little Brigitte, there there my sweet, shh...
where's Ramona?
in Ladle—prepping for the Autumnal Equinox—
who in their right mind would leave the baby with YOU to go tend a pile of rocks?!
she's the Shrinekeeper now. It's—important
"important"
thanks for coming, Char

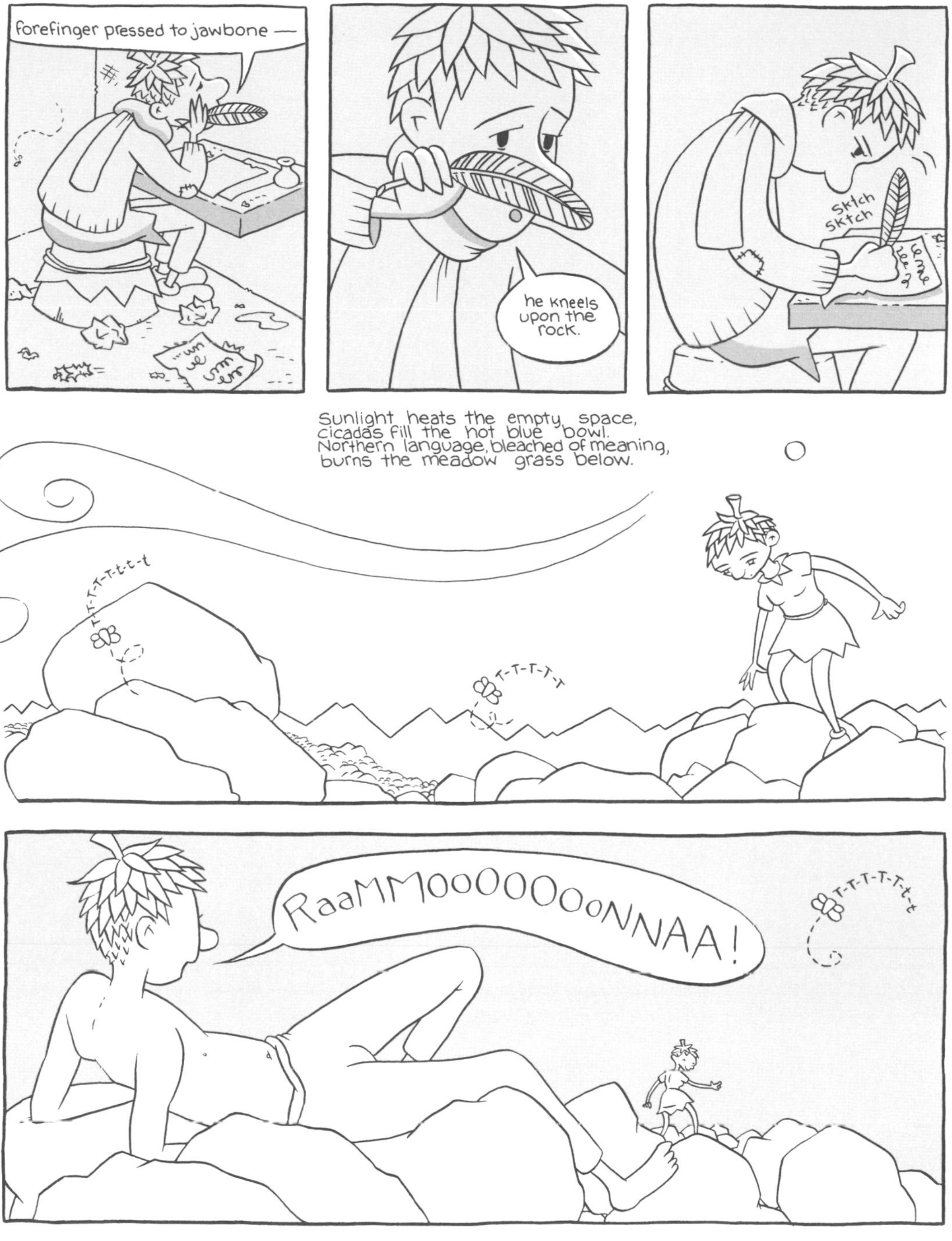
forefinger pressed to jawbone —
he kneels upon the rock.
Sktch Sktch
Sunlight heats the empty space,
cicadas fill the hot blue bowl.
Northern language, bleached of meaning,
burns the meadow grass below.
T-T-T-T-T-t-t-t
T-T-T-T-T
RaaMMOoOOOOOoNNAA!
T-T-T-T-T-t-t

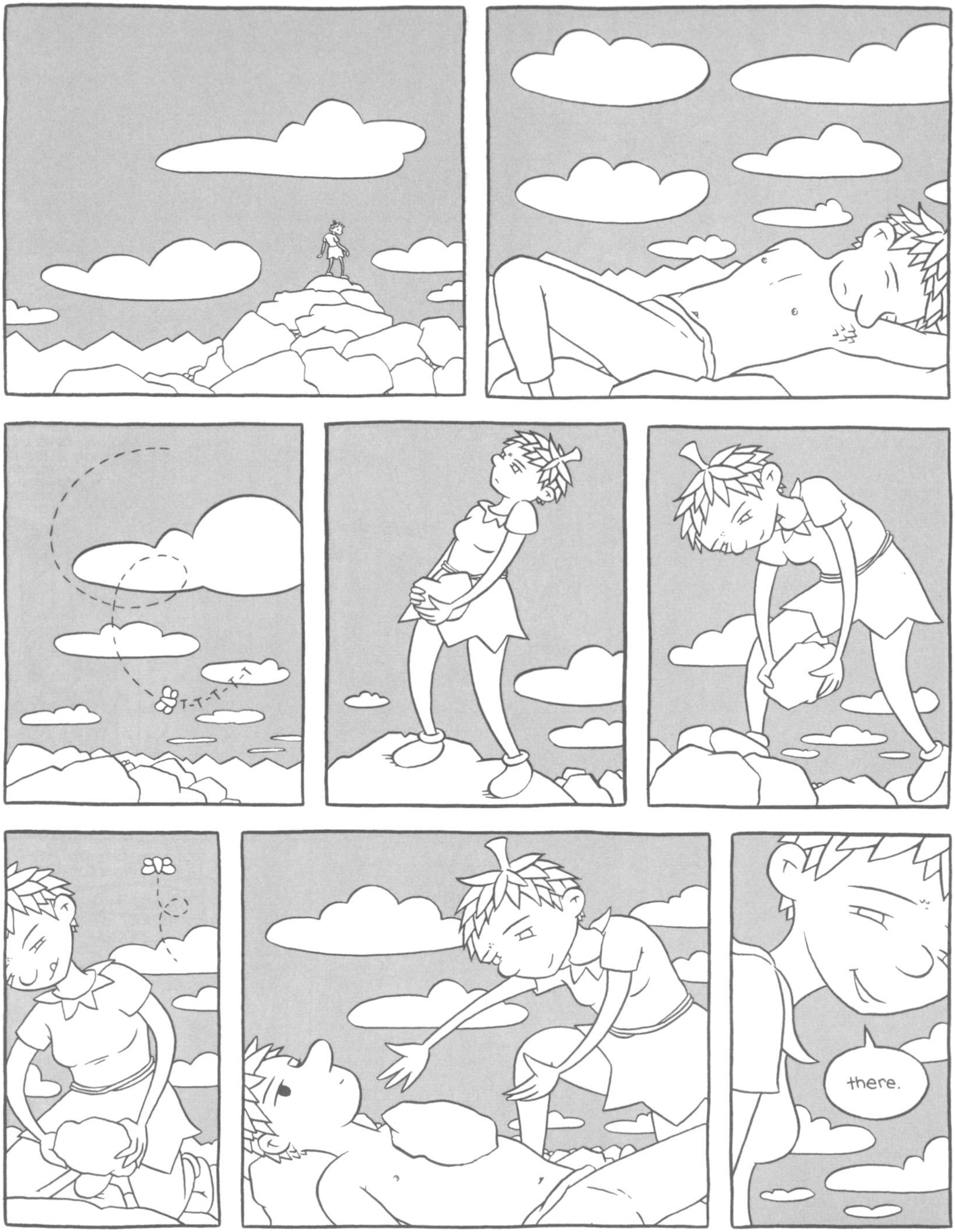
T-T-T-T-T
there.

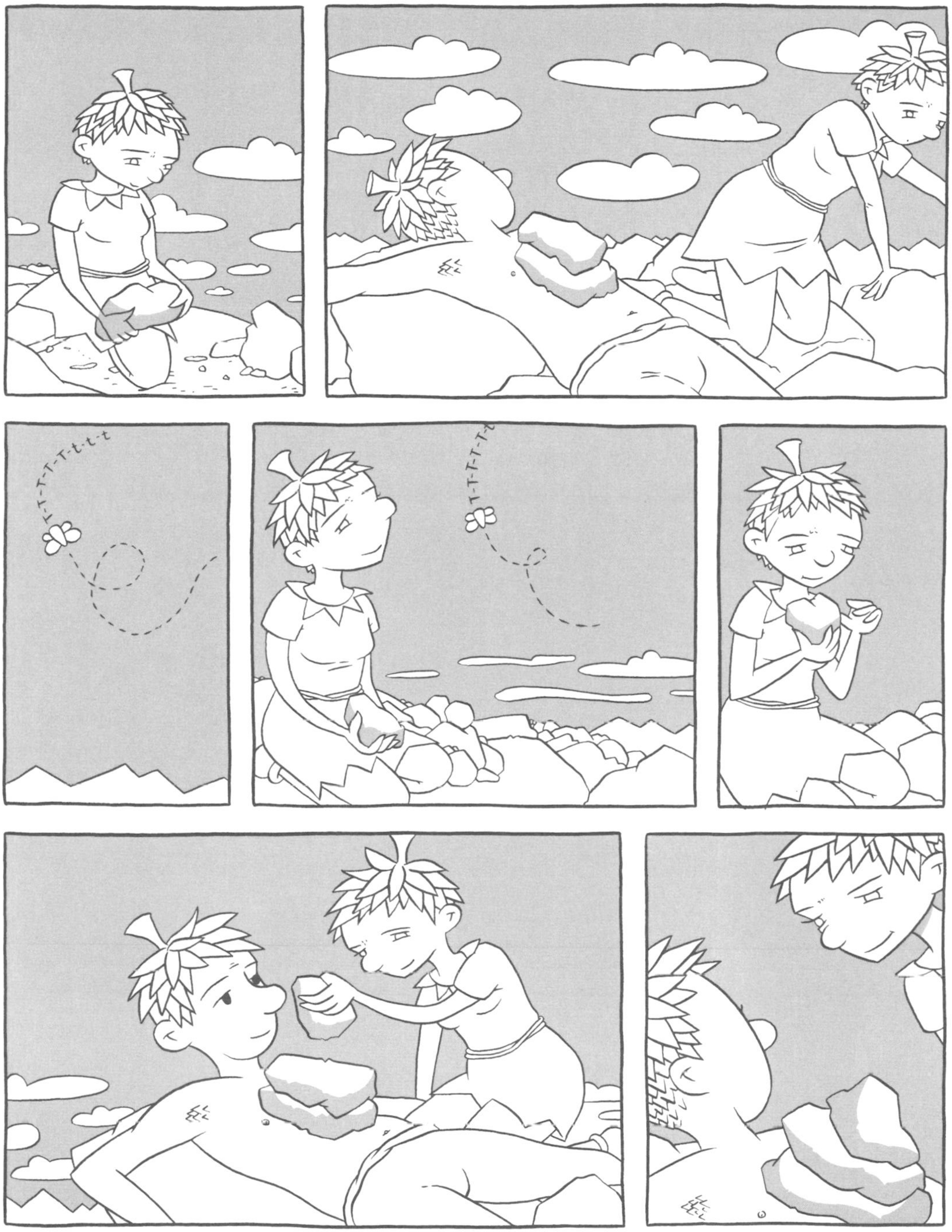

T-T-T-T-T-T-t-t-t
T-T-T-T-T-t

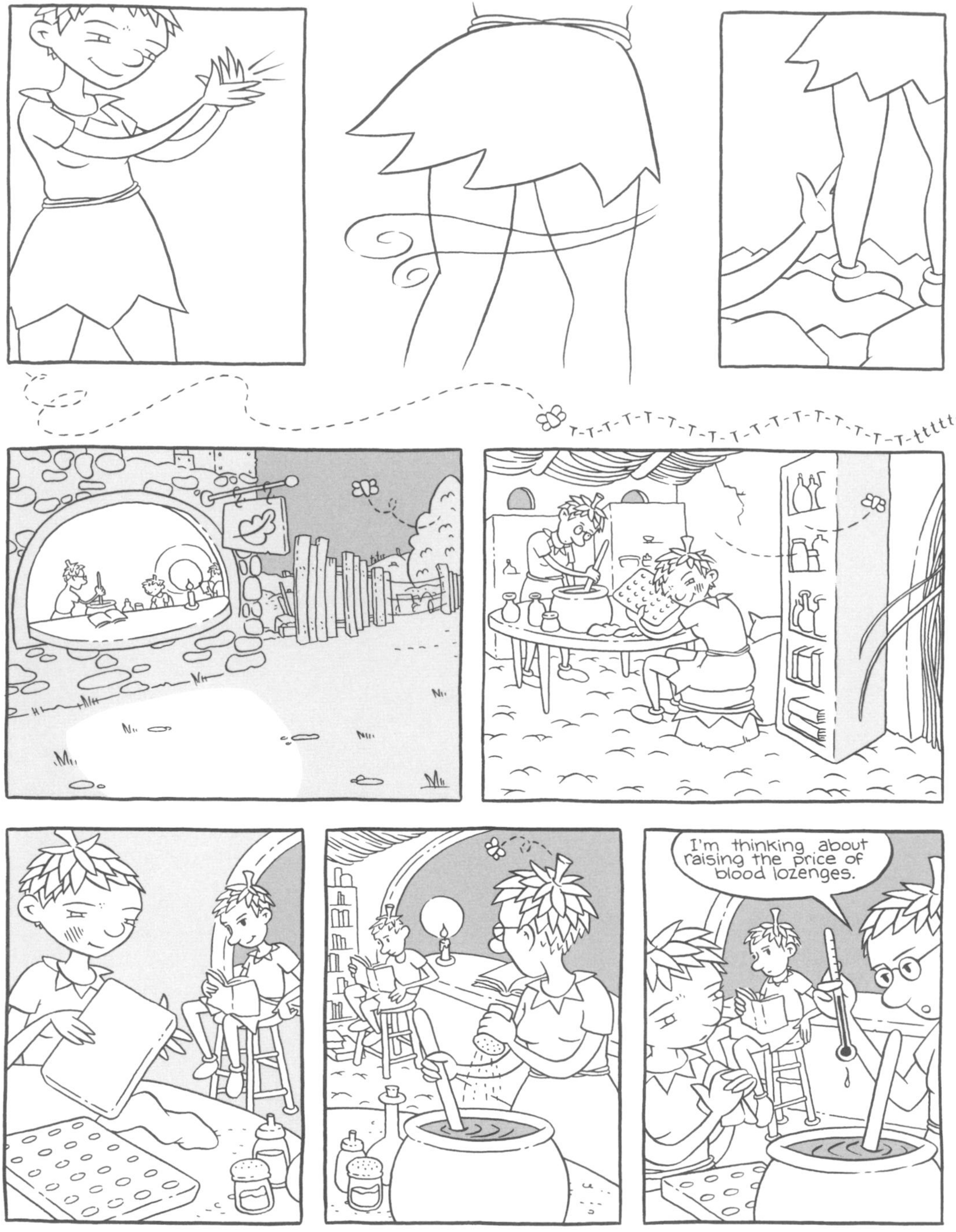
T-T-T-T-T-T-T-T-T-T-T-T-T-T-T-T-T-T-tttttt
I'm thinking about raising the price of blood lozenges.

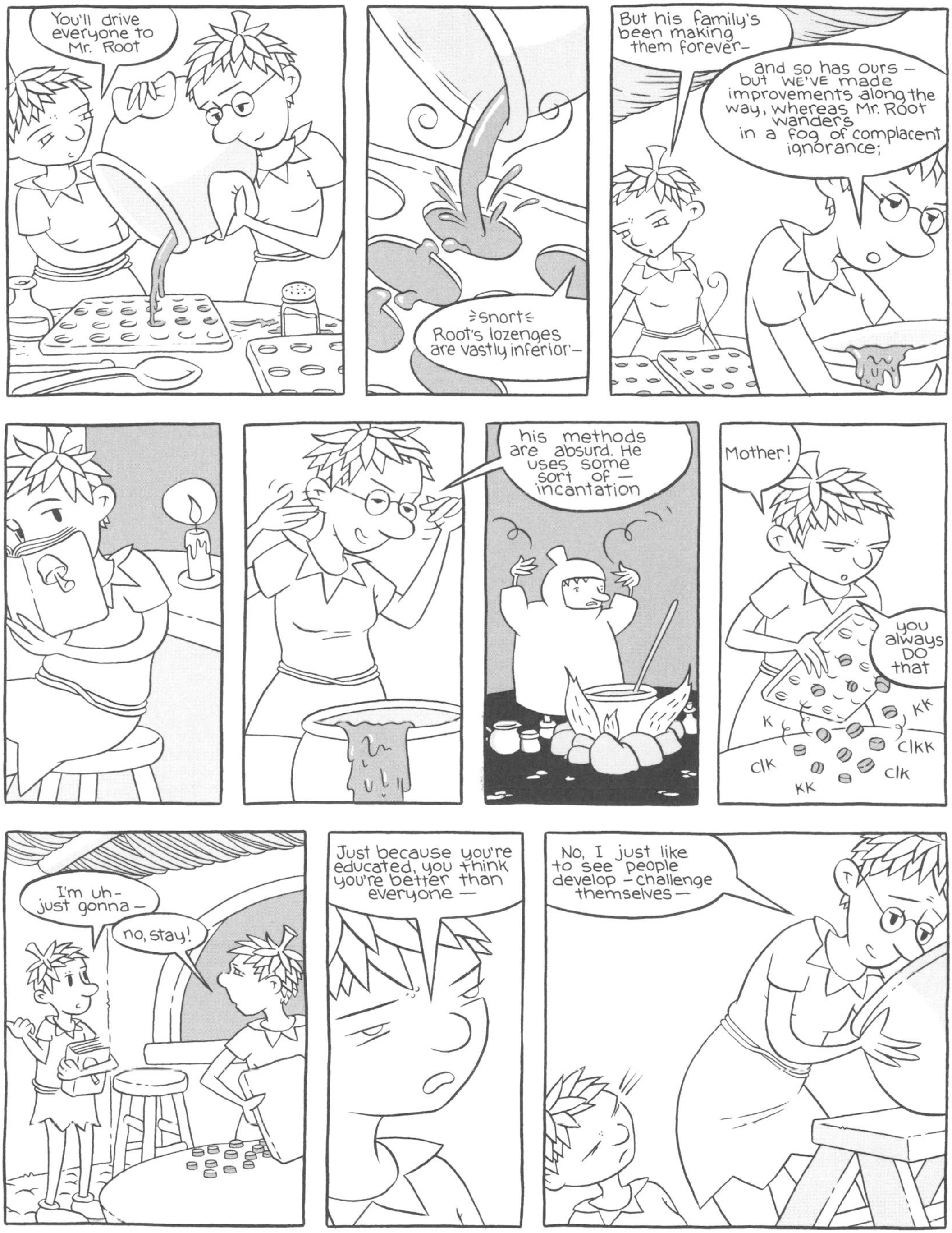
You'll drive everyone to Mr. Root
snort
Root's lozenges are vastly inferior—
But his family's been making them forever—
and so has ours — but WE'VE made improvements along the way, whereas Mr. Root wanders in a fog of complacent ignorance;
his methods are absurd. He uses some sort of — incantation
Mother!
you always DO that
K
KK
ClKK
ClK
KK
ClK
I'm uh- just gonna —
no, stay!
Just because you're educated, you think you're better than everyone —
No, I just like to see people develop — challenge themselves —

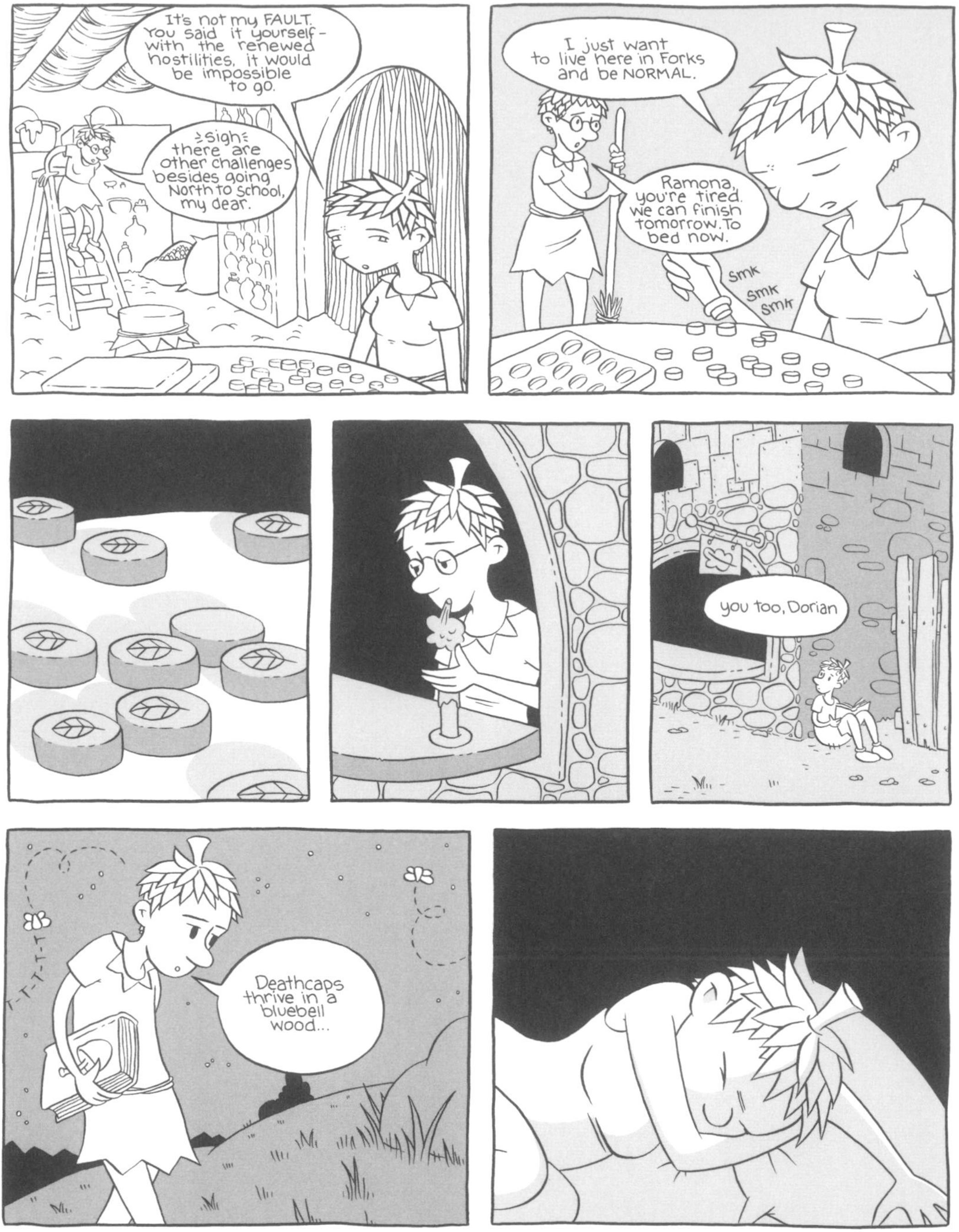
It's not my FAULT. You said it yourself - with the renewed hostilities, it would be impossible to go.
≷sigh≶ there are other challenges besides going North to school, my dear.
I just want to live here in Forks and be NORMAL.
Ramona, you're tired. We can finish tomorrow. To bed now.
smk smk smk
you too, Dorian
Deathcaps thrive in a bluebell wood...

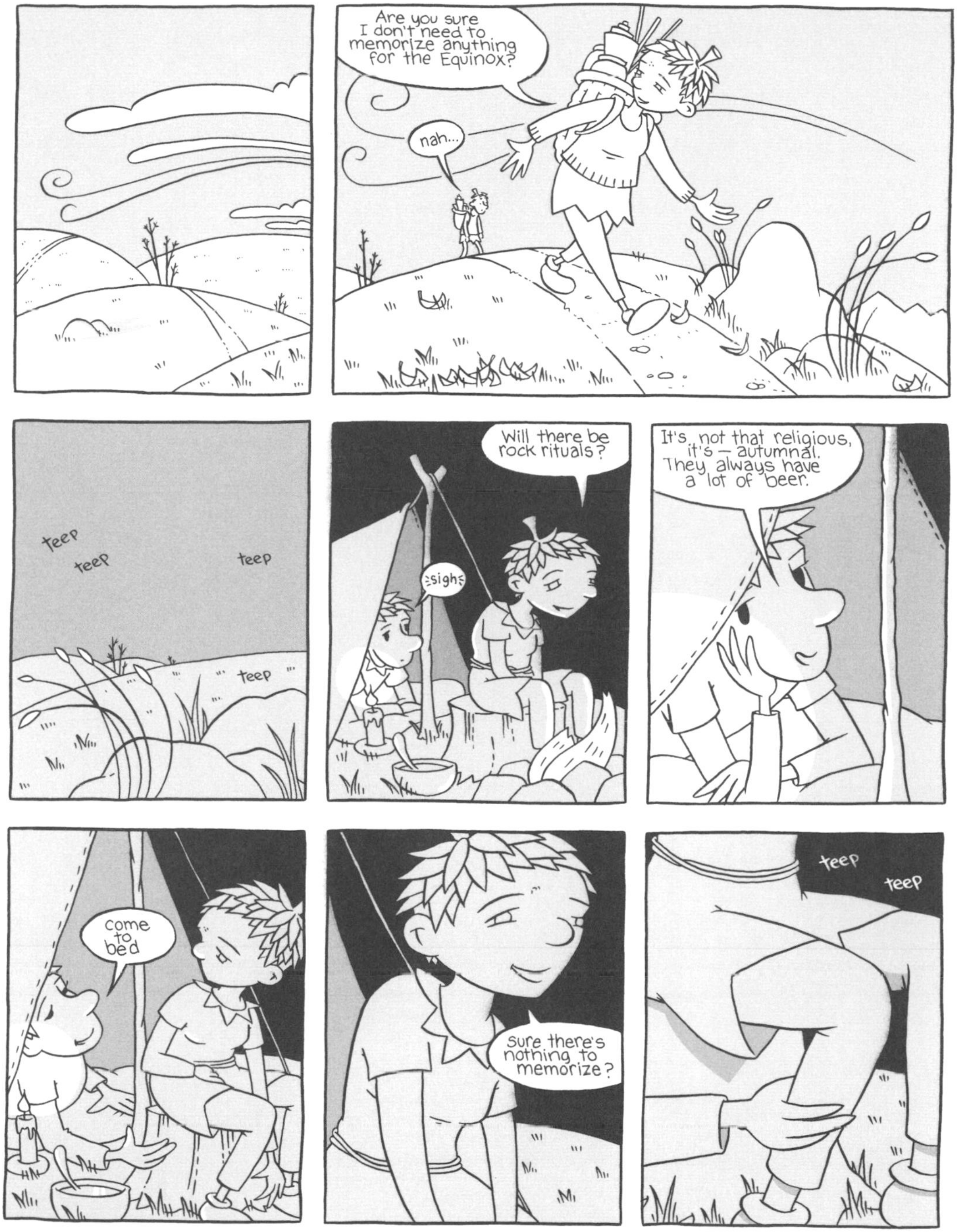
Are you sure I don't need to memorize anything for the Equinox?
nah...
teep
teep
teep
teep
Will there be rock rituals?
sigh
It's not that religious, it's — autumnal. They always have a lot of beer.
come to bed
Sure there's nothing to memorize?
teep
teep

a girl went walking
in a bluebell wood.

picking up deathcaps
wherever she could —

snif

snif
snif

um—

wait
here

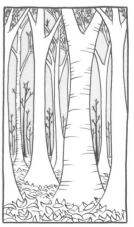

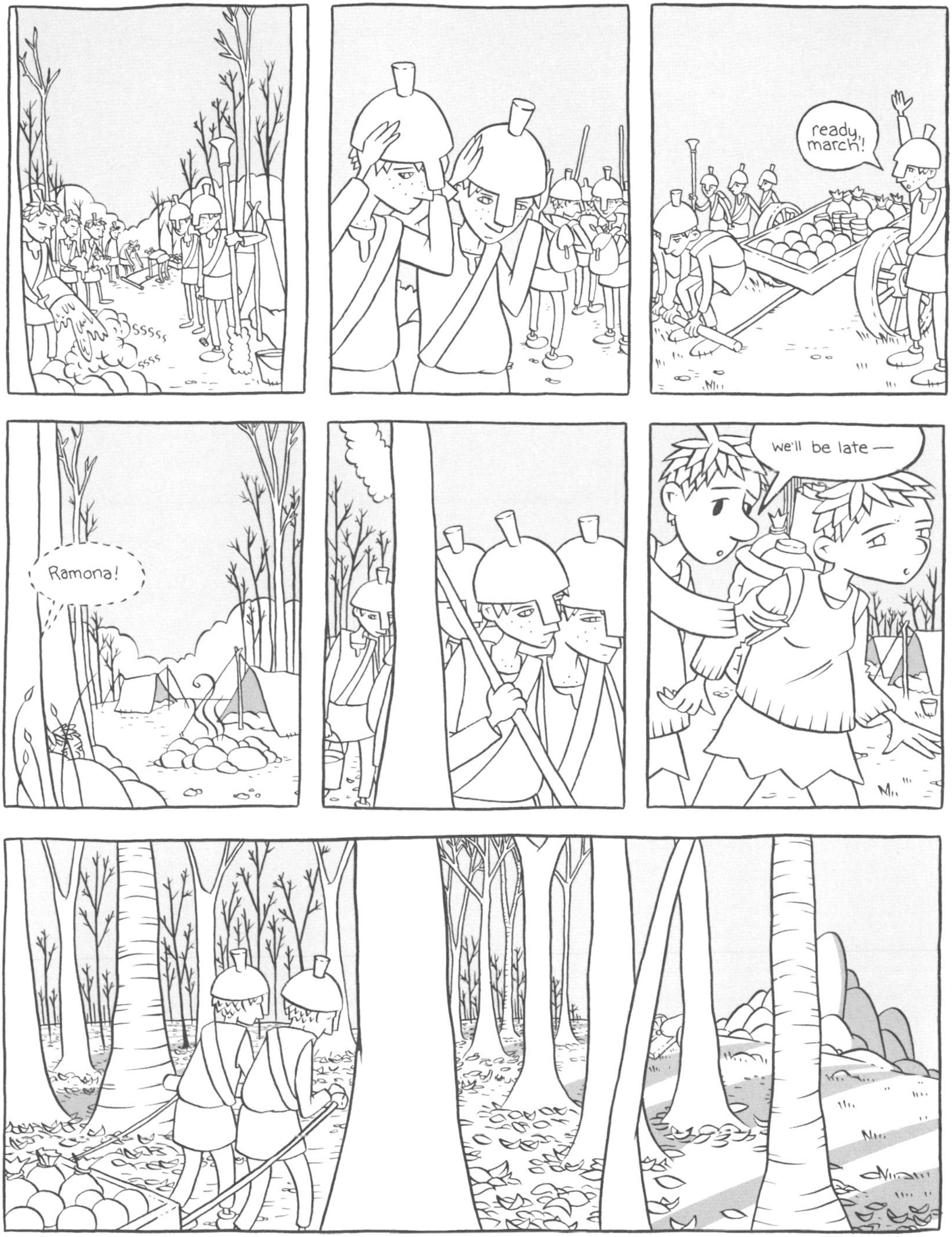
sssss
ssss
ready, march!
Ramona!
we'll be late —

ammunition runner
ventsman
gunner chief
loader 1
loader 2
sponger/rammer
1.
salt peter
2.
elm
3.
iron
4.
sponge
rammer
now Spongeman!
now load!

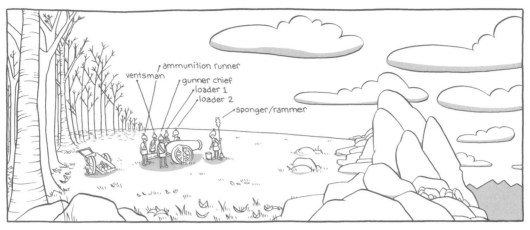

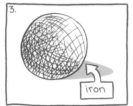

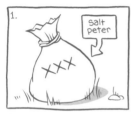

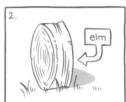

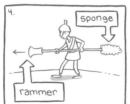

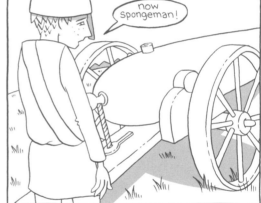

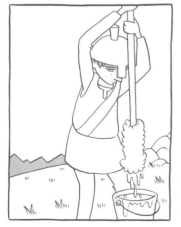

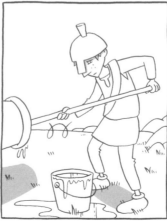

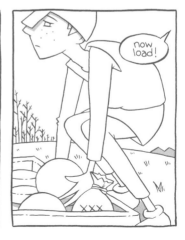

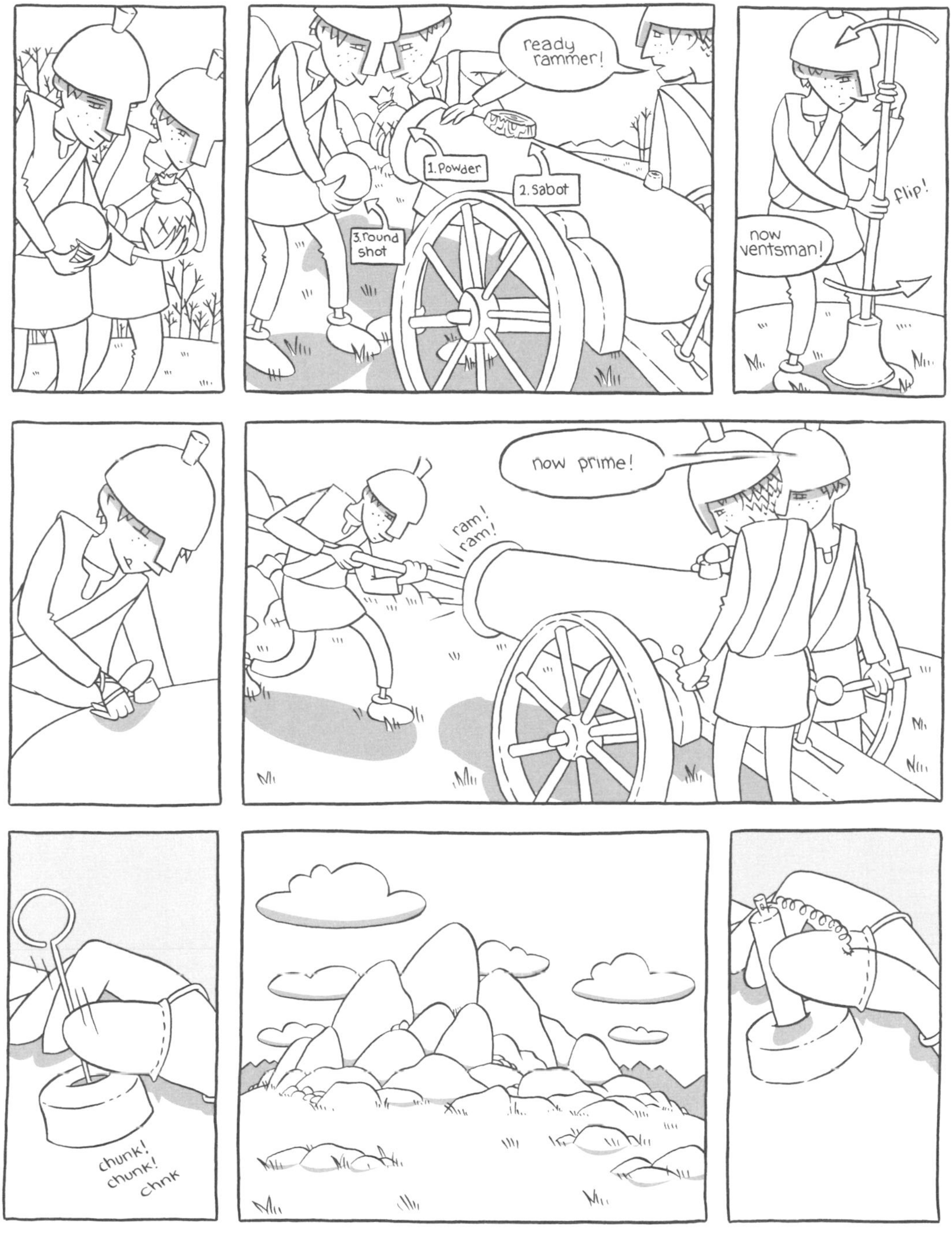
ready rammer!
1. Powder
2. Sabot
3. round shot
now ventsman!
flip!
now prime!
ram! ram!
chunk! chunk! chnk

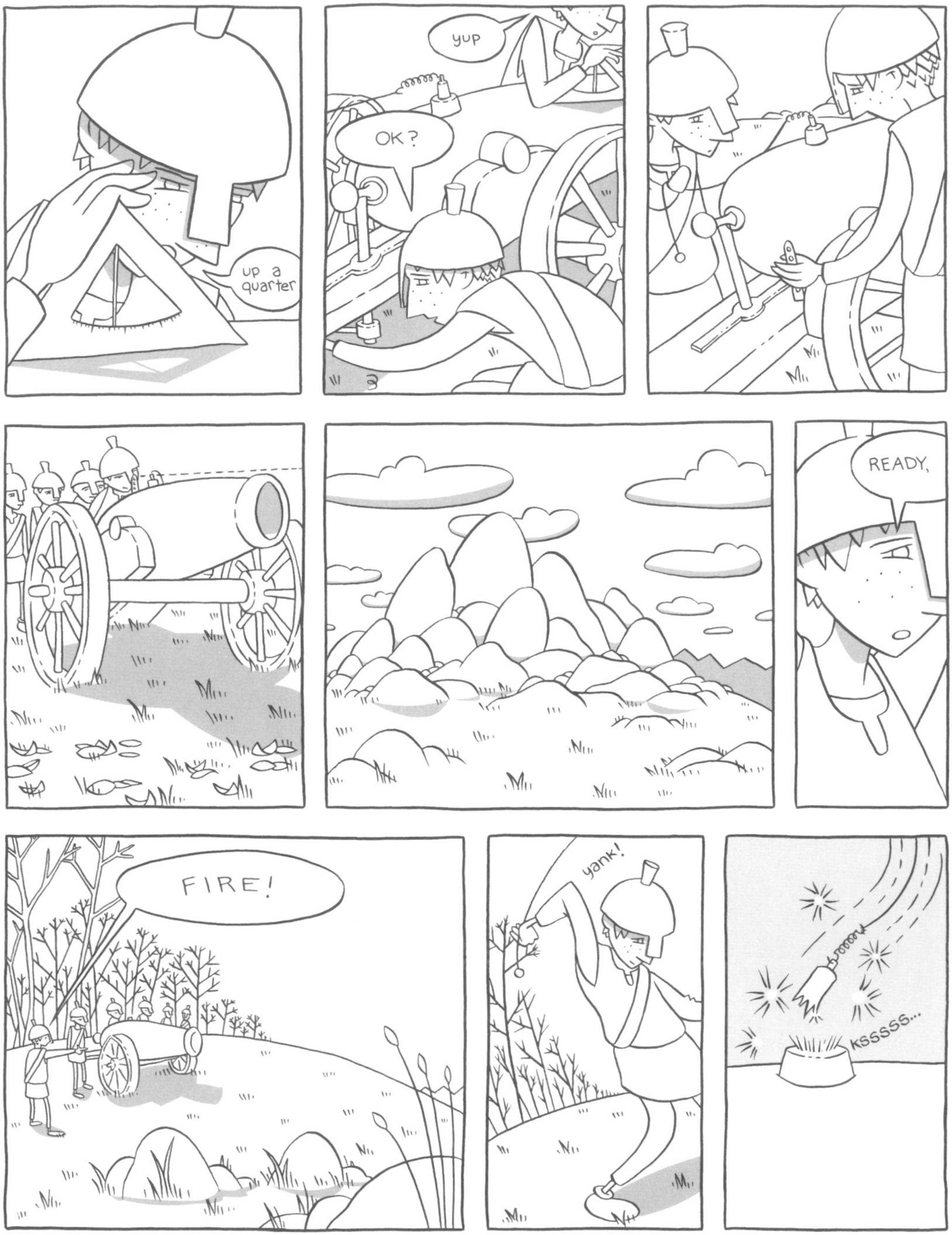
up a quarter
yup
OK?
READY,
FIRE!
yank!
KSSSSS...

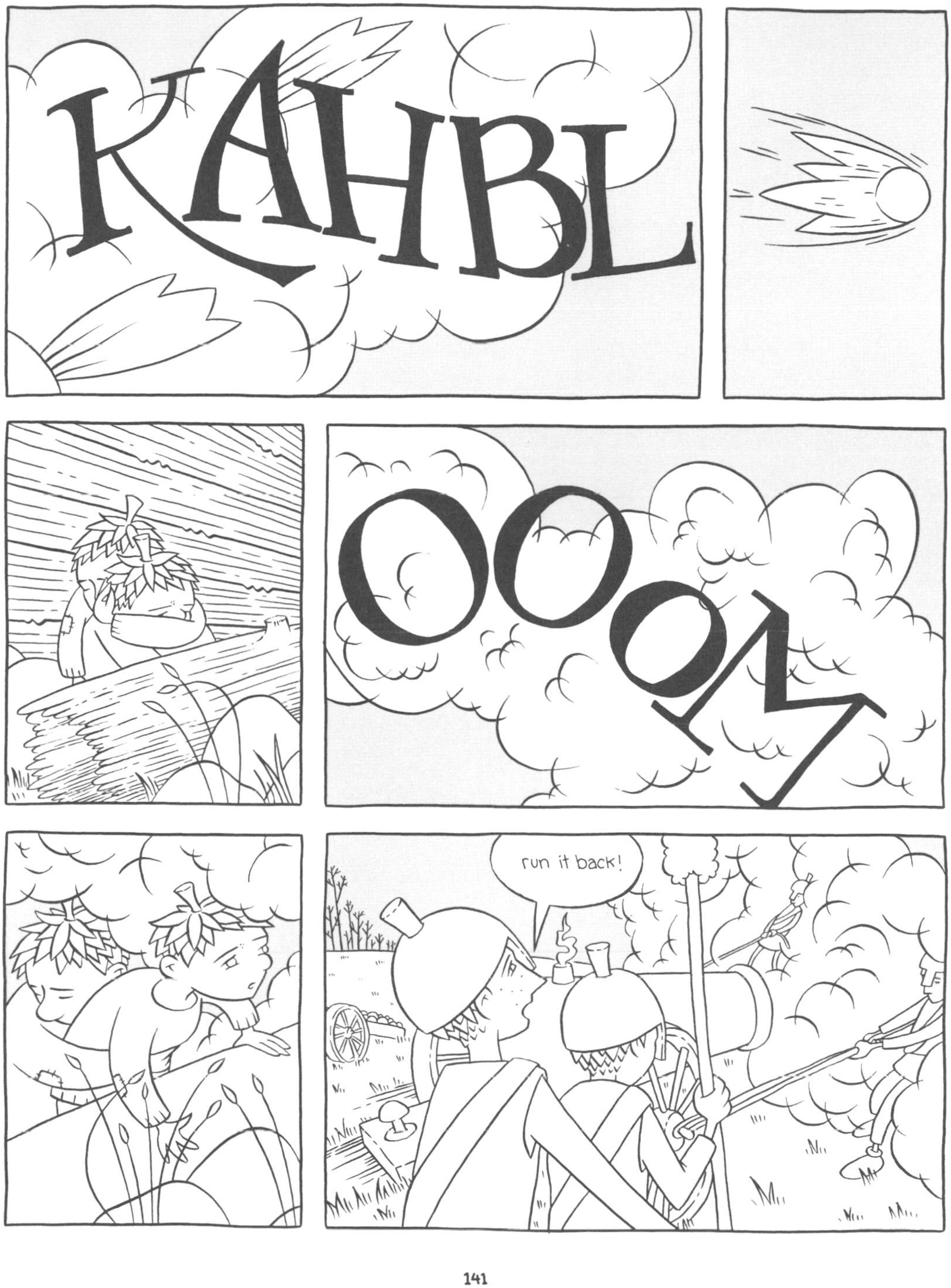
KAHBL
OOOOM
run it back!

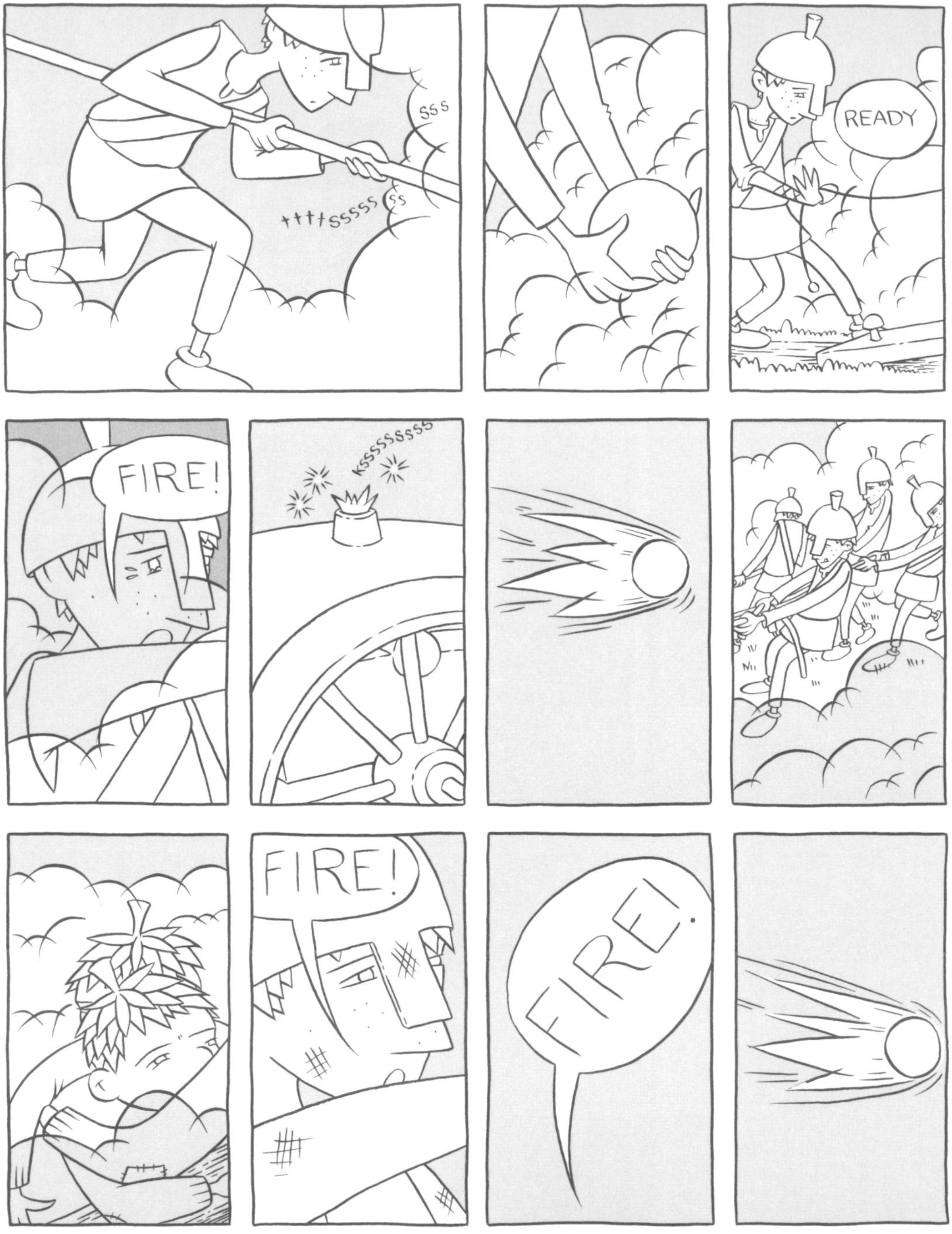
SSS
ttttSSSSS SS
READY
FIRE!
KSSSSSSSSS
FIRE!
FIRE!

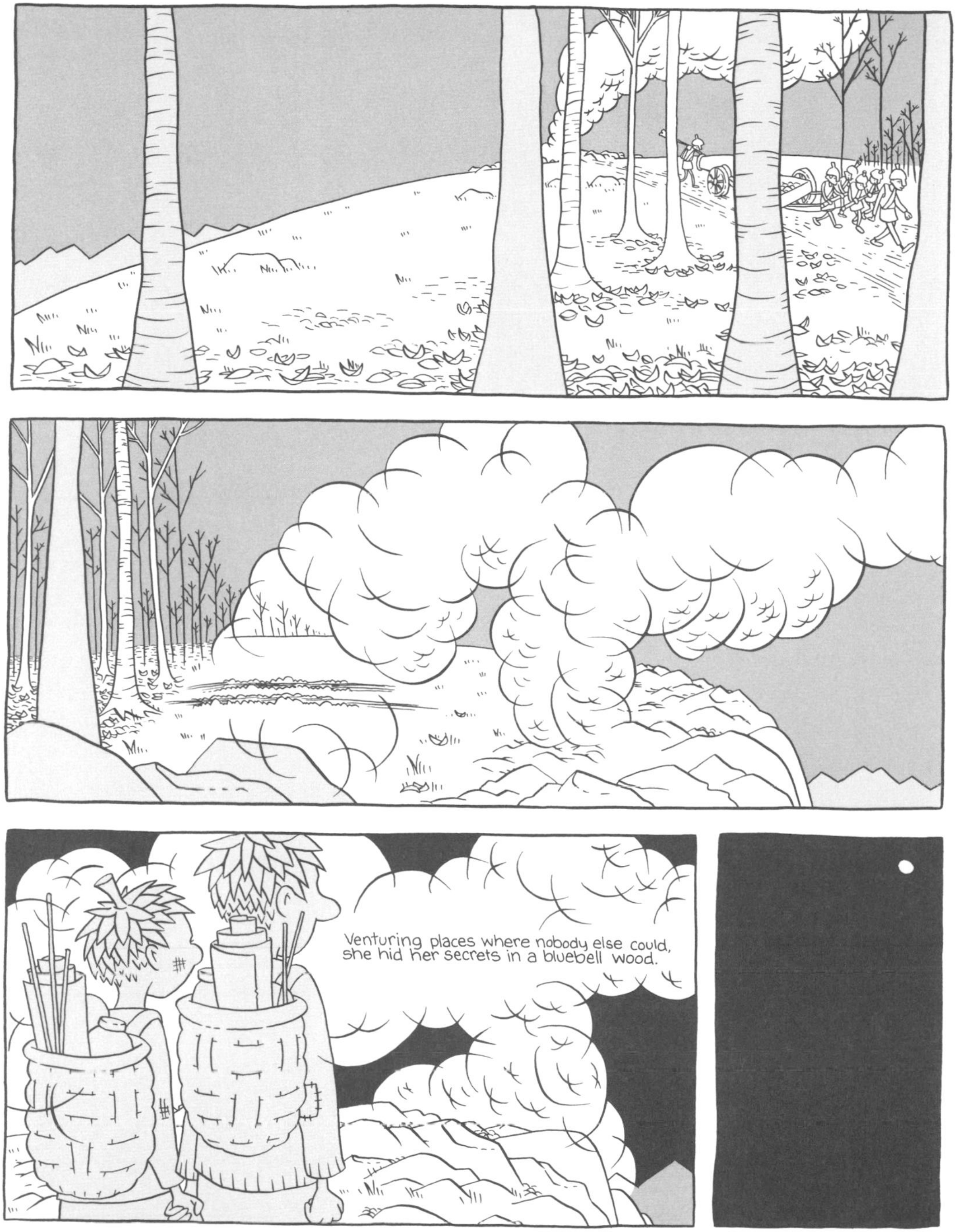
Venturing places where nobody else could, she hid her secrets in a bluebell wood.

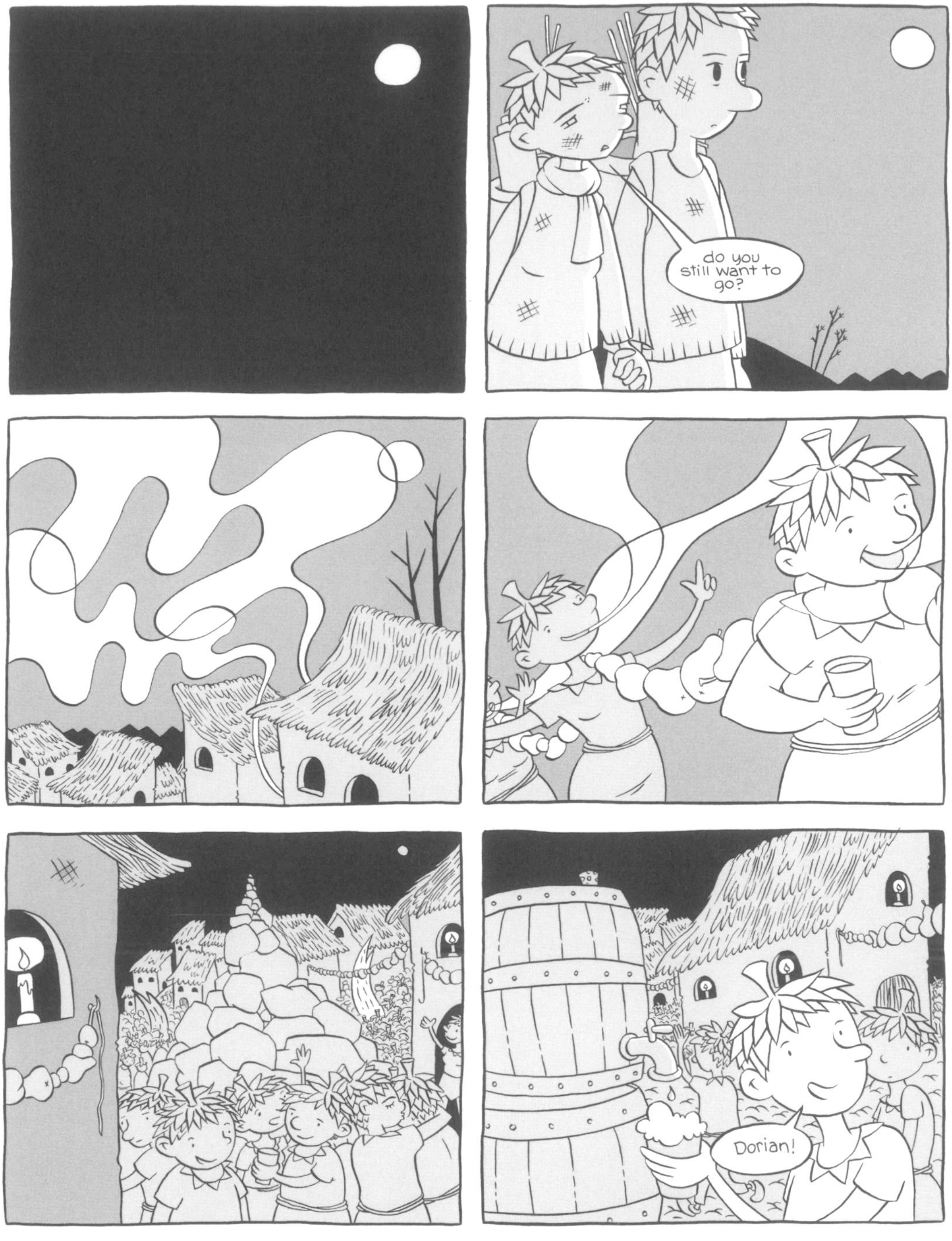
do you still want to go?
Dorian!

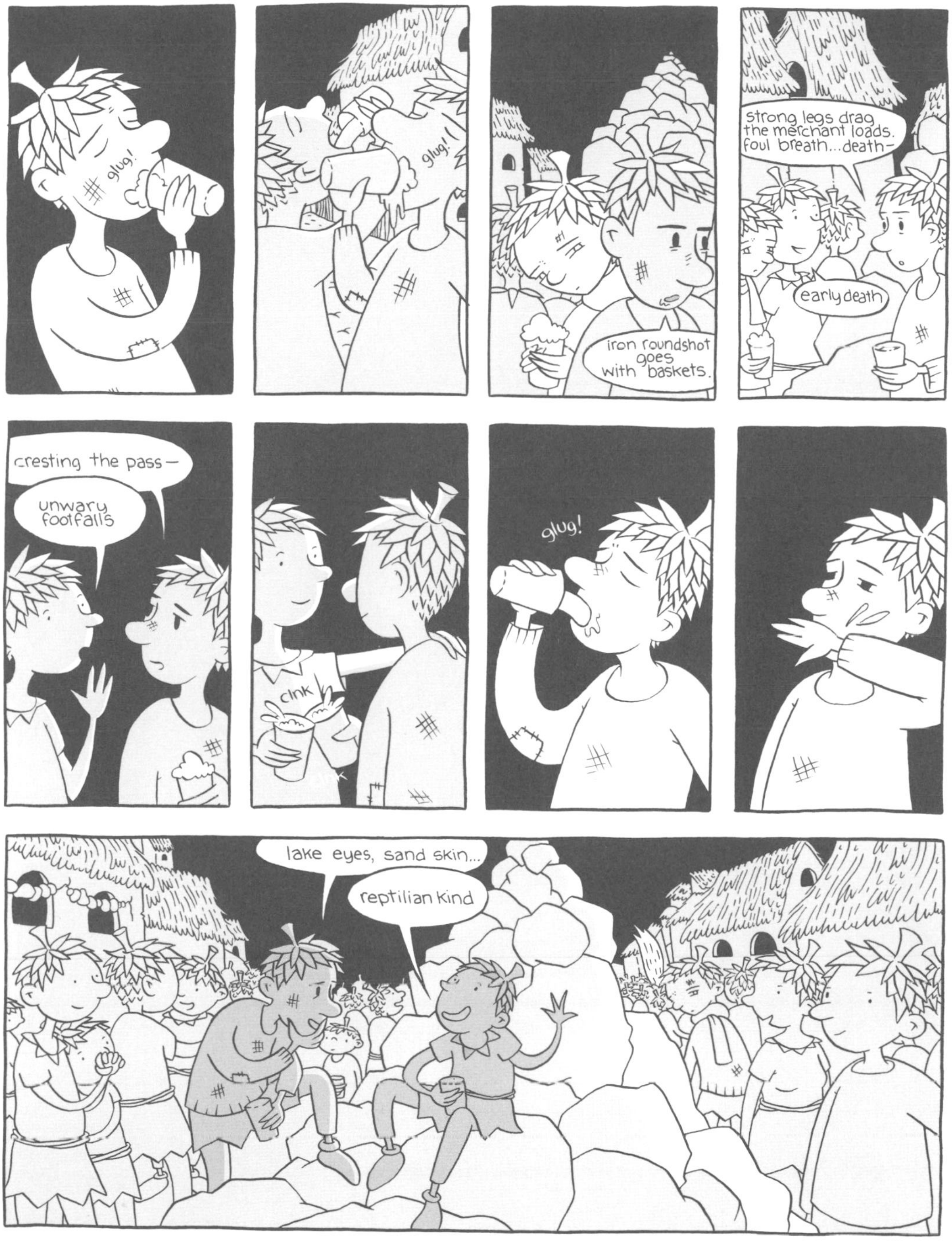
glug!
glug!
iron roundshot goes with baskets.
strong legs drag the merchant loads. foul breath...death-
early death
cresting the pass—
unwary footfalls
clnk
glug!
lake eyes, sand skin...
reptilian kind

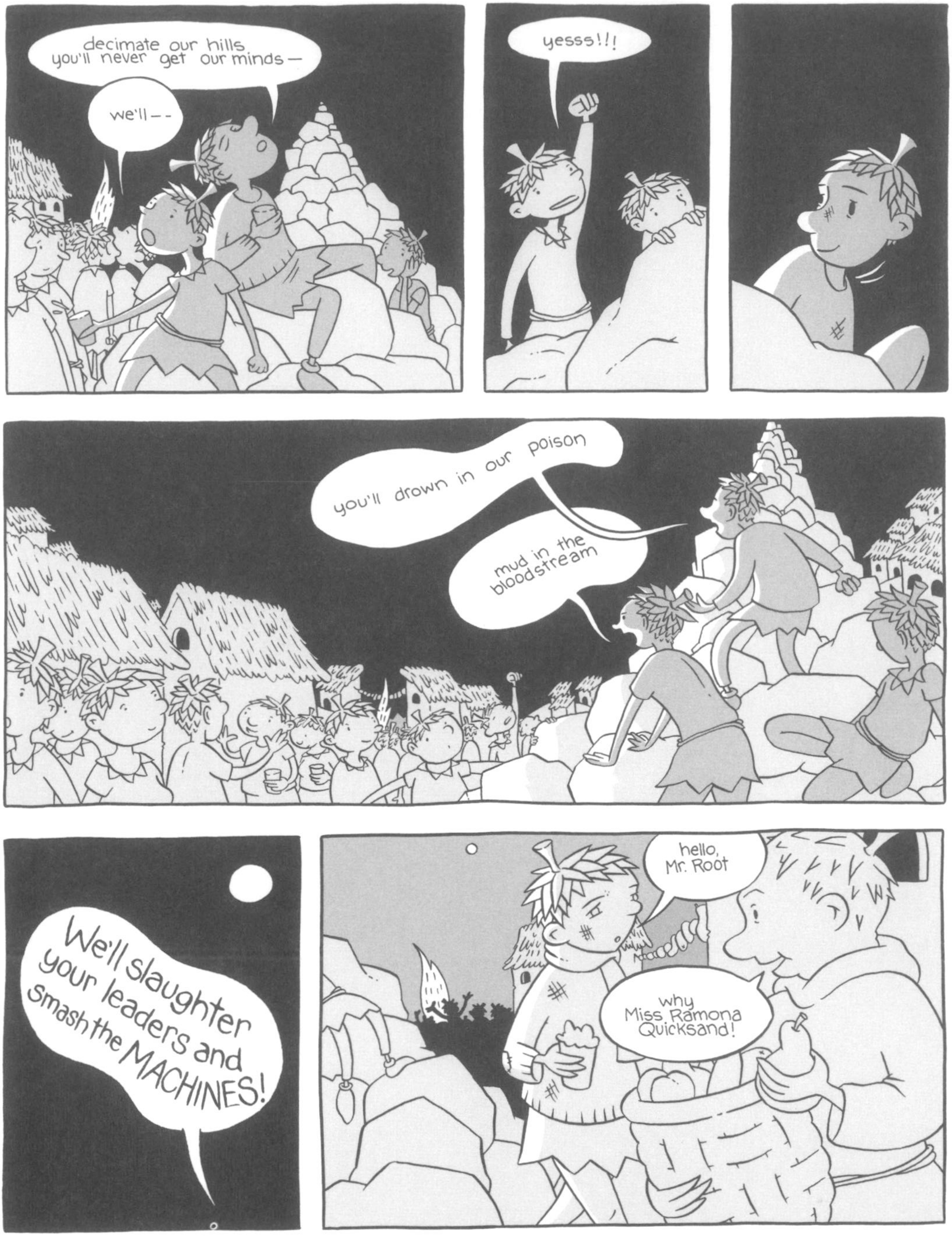
decimate our hills
you'll never get our minds—
we'll——
yesss!!!
you'll drown in our poison
mud in the bloodstream
We'll slaughter your leaders and smash the MACHINES!
hello, Mr. Root
why Miss Ramona Quicksand!

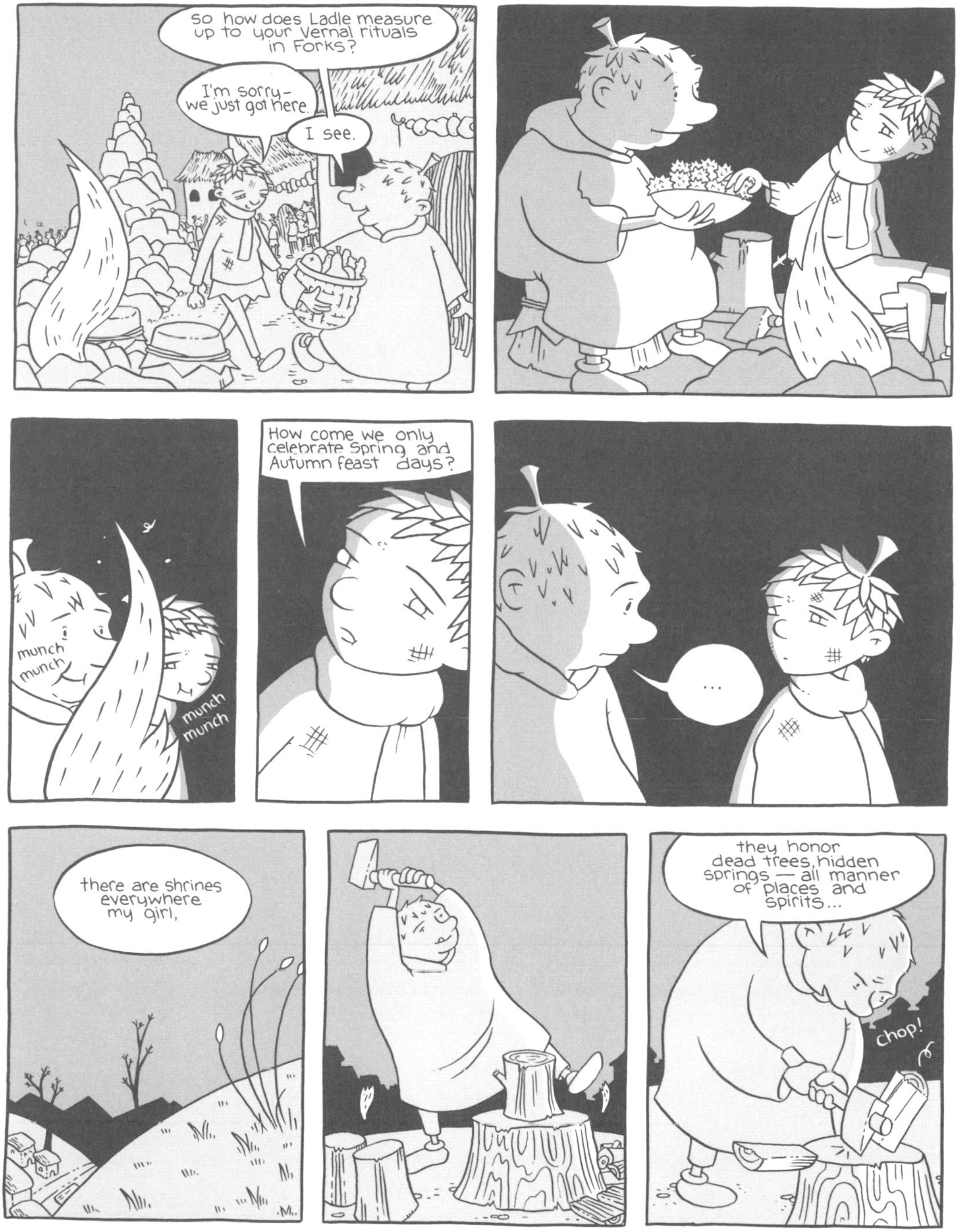
so how does Ladle measure up to your Vernal rituals in Forks?
I'm sorry- we just got here.
I see.
munch munch
munch munch
How come we only celebrate Spring and Autumn feast days?
...
there are shrines everywhere my girl,
they honor dead trees, hidden springs — all manner of places and spirits...
chop!

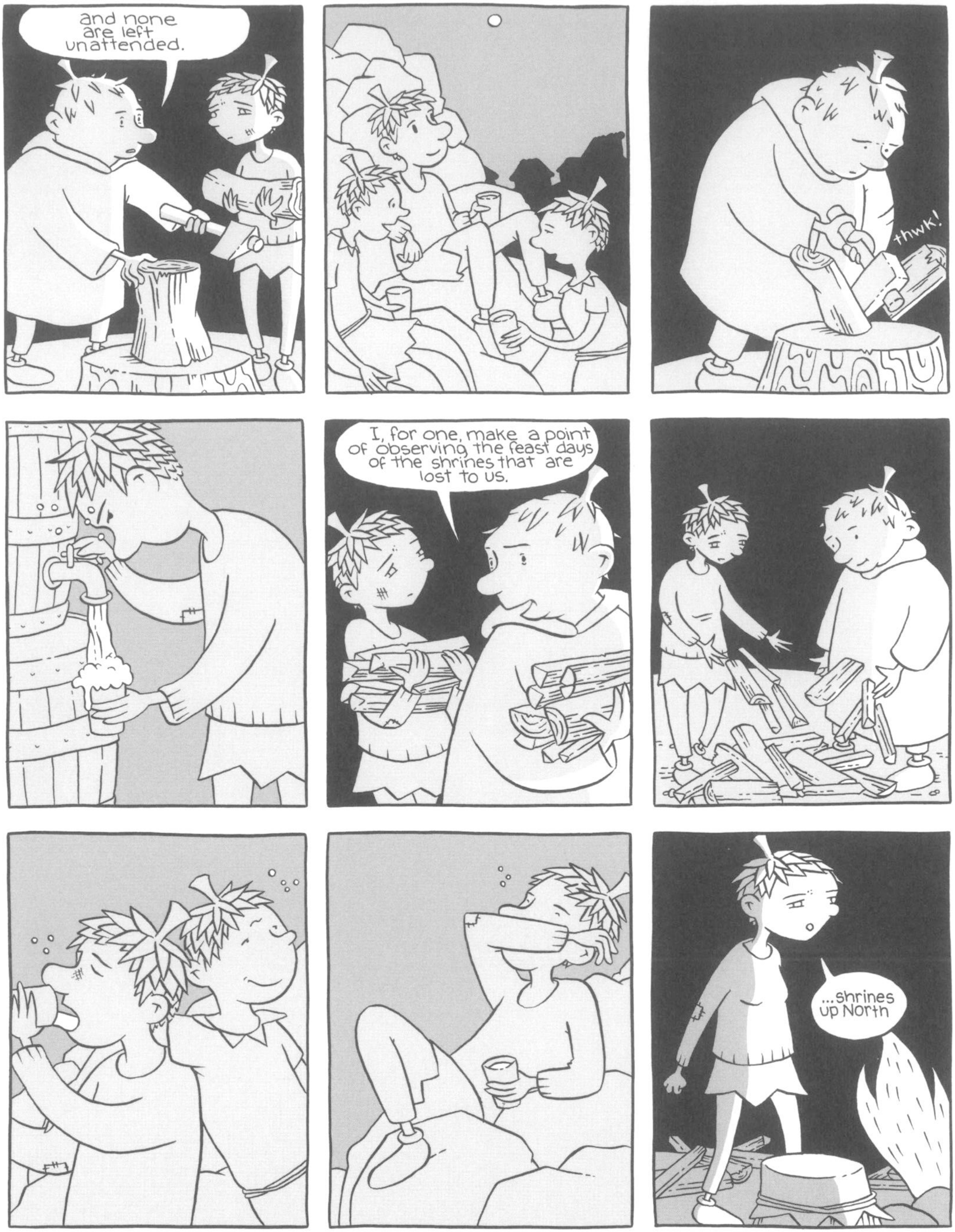
and none are left unattended.
thwk!
I, for one, make a point of observing the feast days of the shrines that are lost to us.
...shrines up North

Your family doesn't go in much for the old traditions.

no.

...

perhaps you could apprentice yourself to a shrinekeeper.

now wouldn't your mother love that!

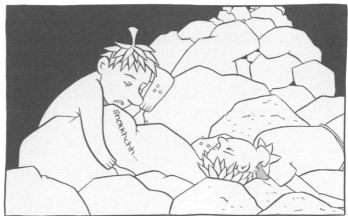

snckkhhh....

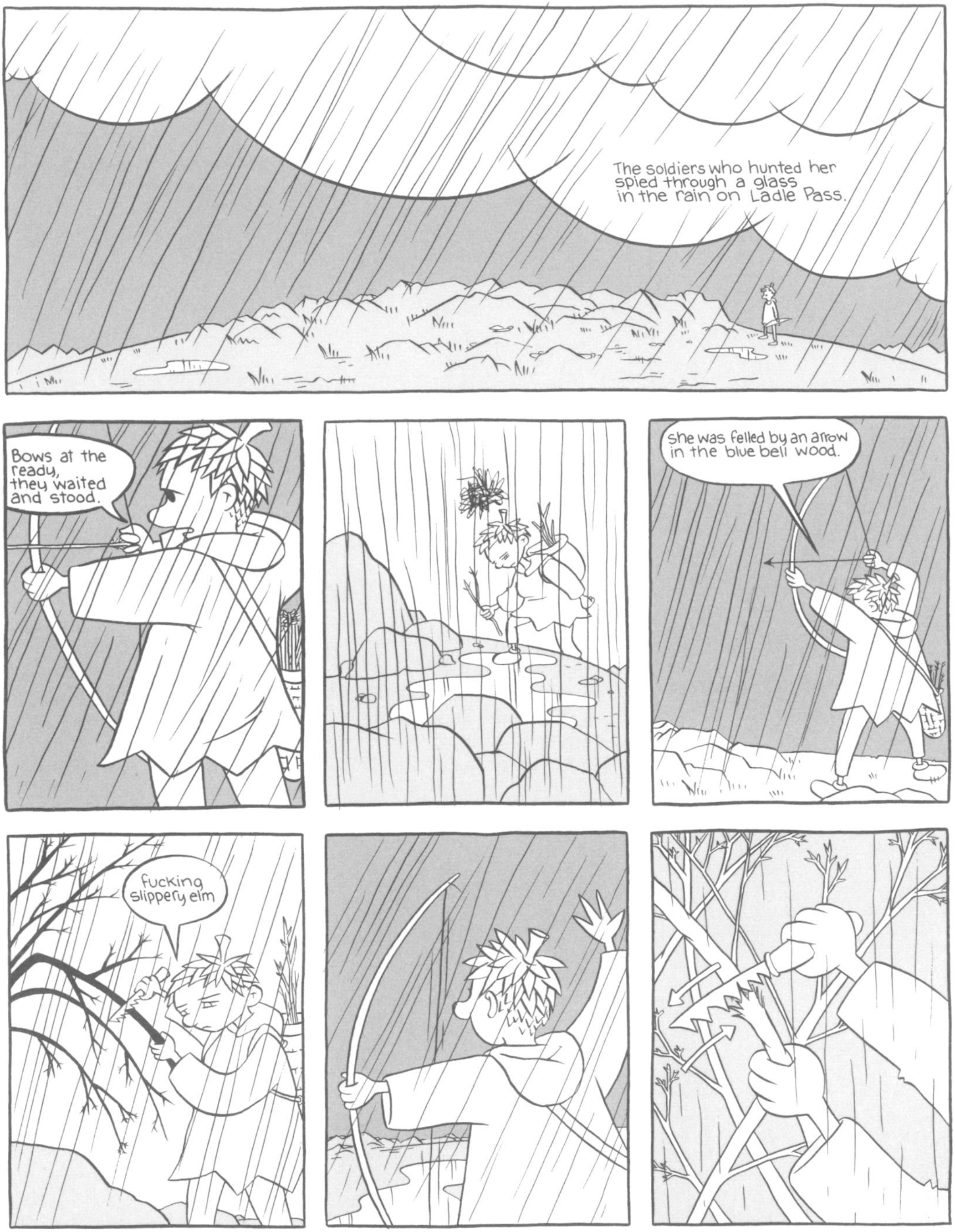
The soldiers who hunted her spied through a glass in the rain on Ladle Pass.
Bows at the ready, they waited and stood.
She was felled by an arrow in the blue bell wood.
fucking slippery elm

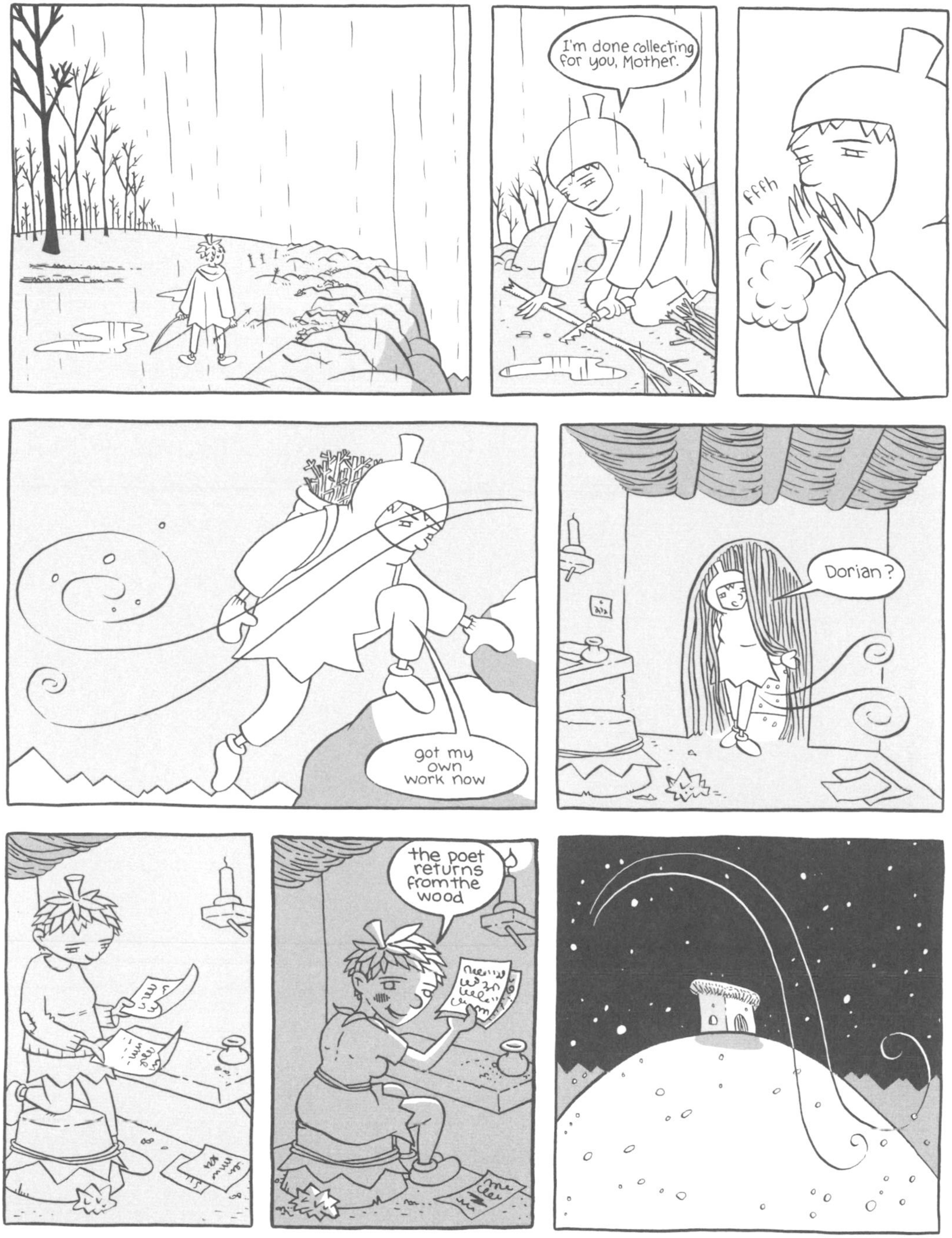

I'm done collecting for you, Mother.
ffth
got my own work now
Dorian?
the poet returns from the wood

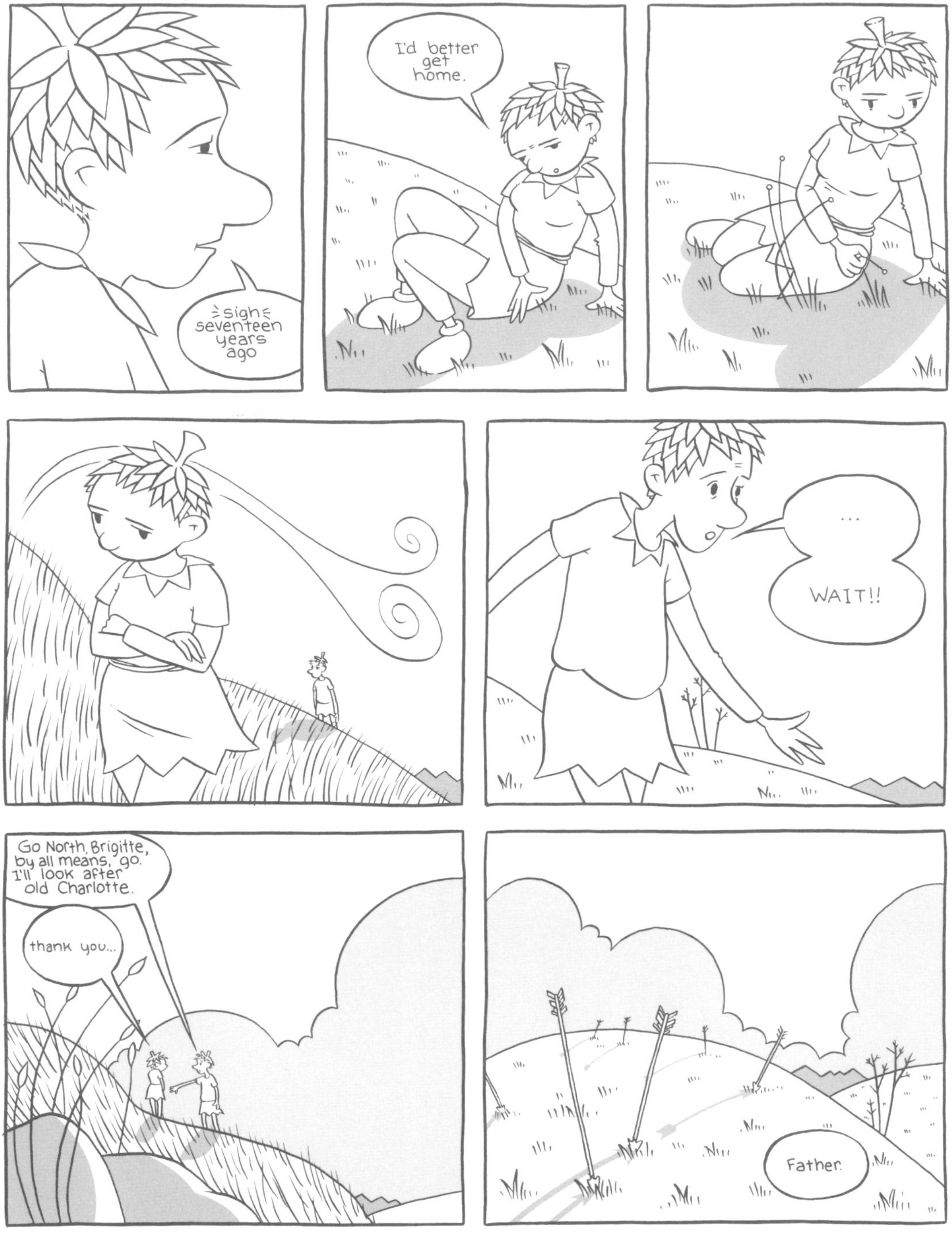

sigh
seventeen years ago
I'd better get home.
...
WAIT!!
Go North, Brigitte, by all means, go. I'll look after old Charlotte.
thank you...
Father.

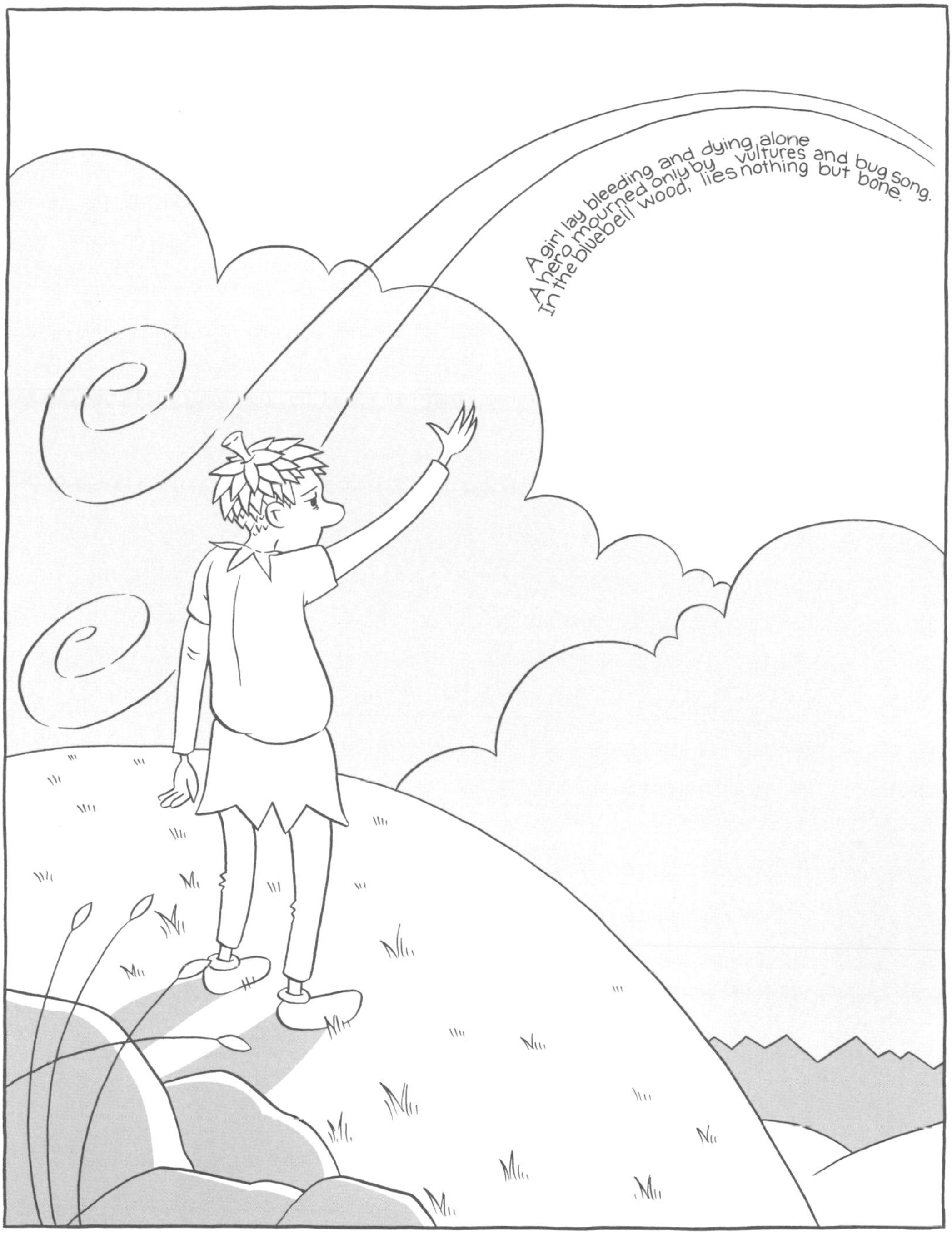
A girl lay bleeding and dying alone
A hero mourned only by vultures and bug song.
In the bluebell wood, lies nothing but bone.

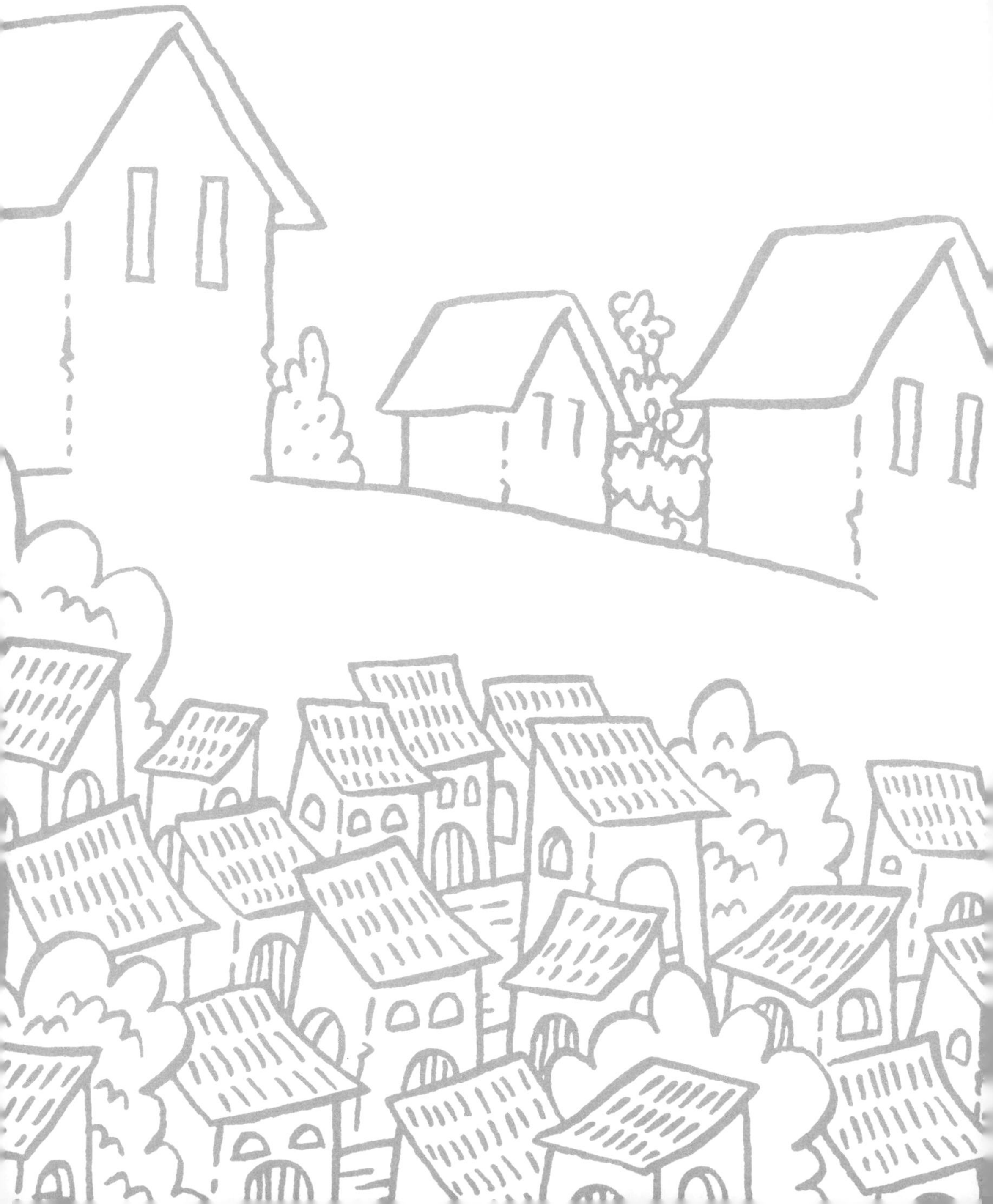

Chapter 5
ROYAL CHILD

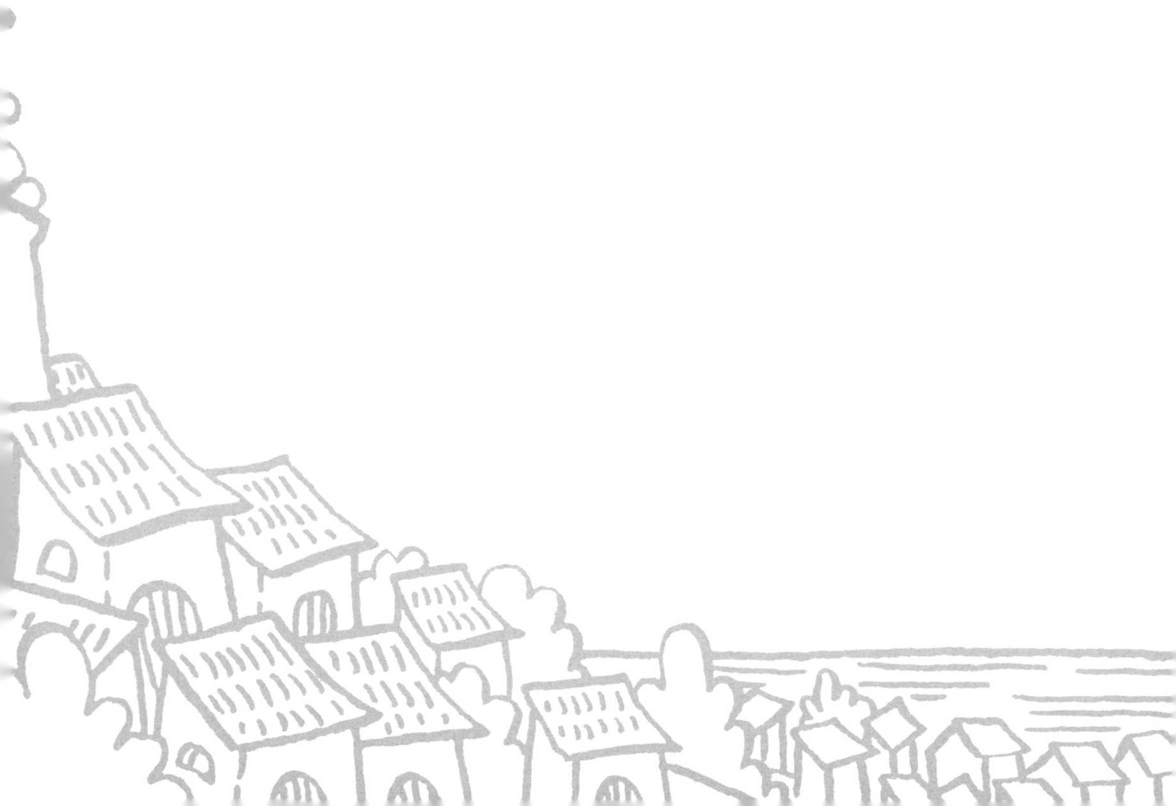

Goodbye, South.
swsss
Hello, North.
glug glug
Swsssss
Swssssss
Swssssss
Swsssss
Swssss
brrr!
chnk!
klnk!
klnk!
klnk!
Ooops!

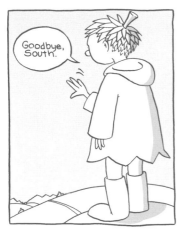

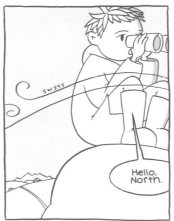

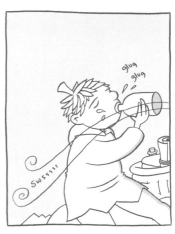

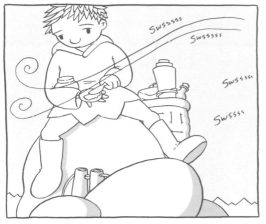

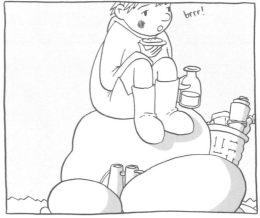

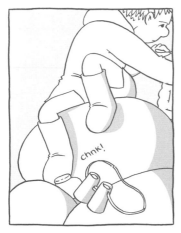

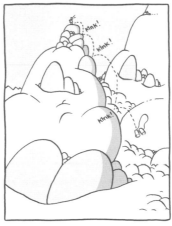

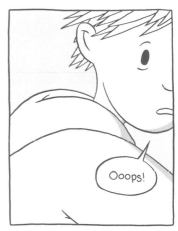

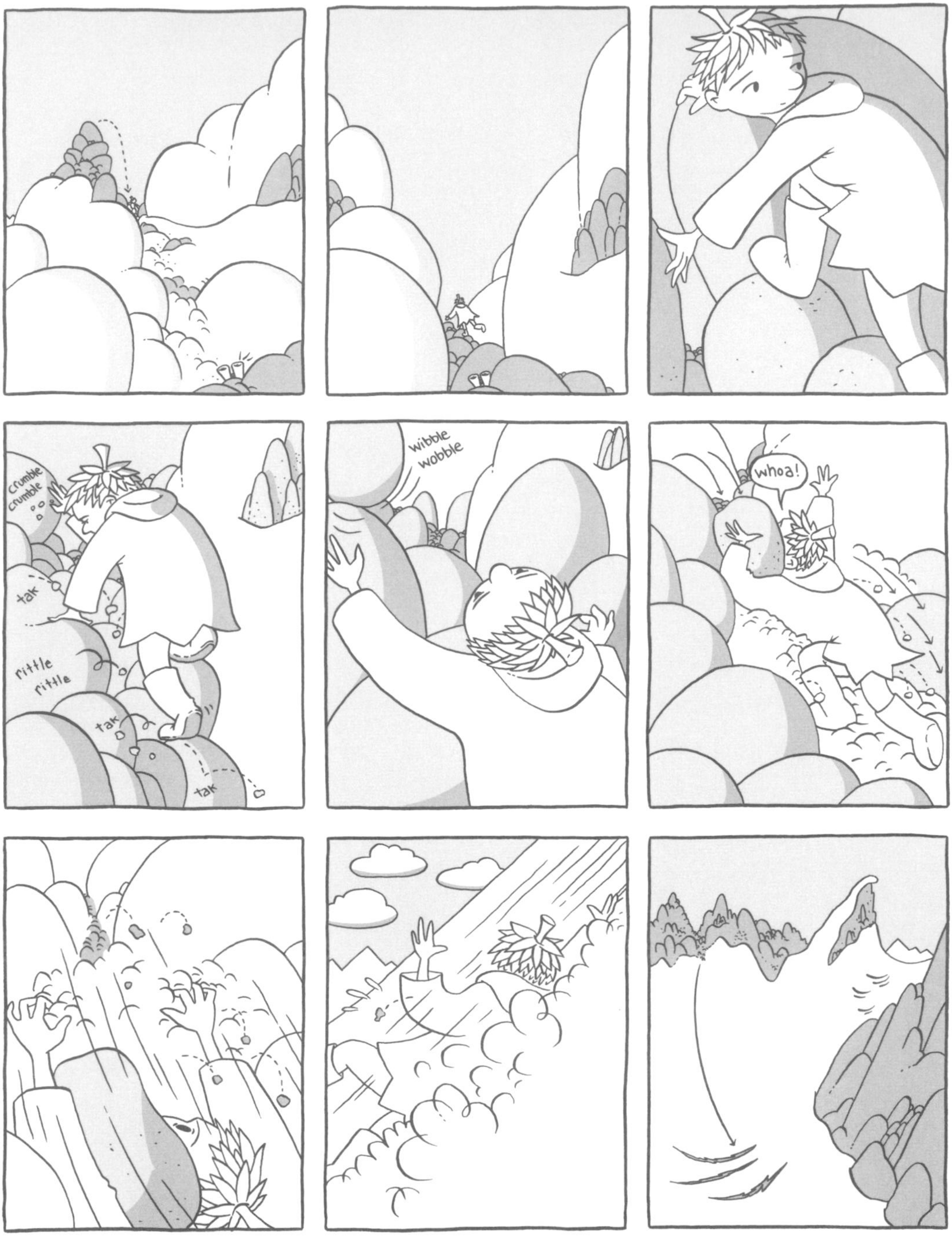
crumble
crumble
tak
rittle
rittle
tak
tak
wibble
wobble
whoa!

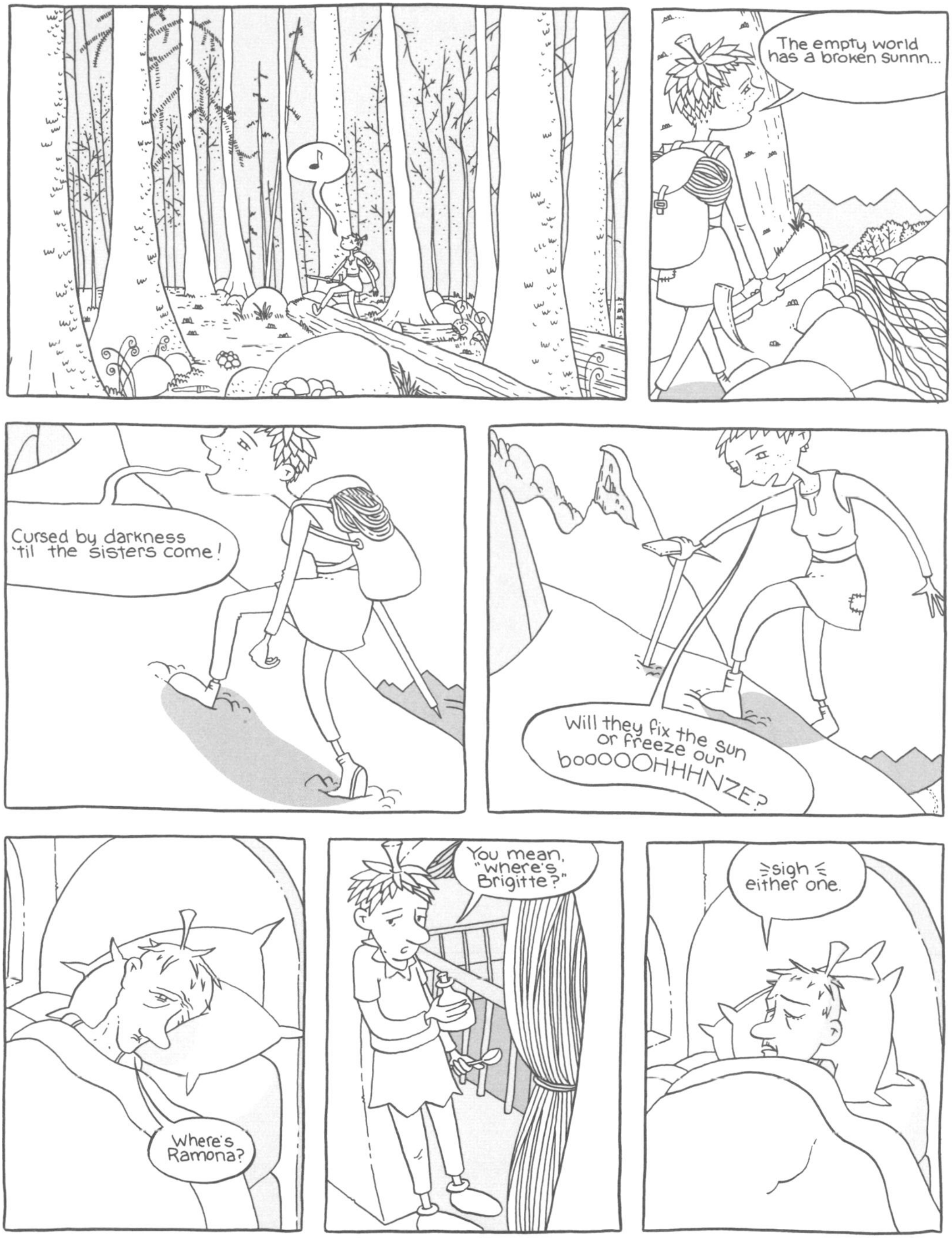
The empty world has a broken sunnn...
Cursed by darkness 'til the sisters come!
Will they fix the sun or freeze our booOOOHHHNZE?
Where's Ramona?
You mean, "where's Brigitte?"
≋sigh≋ either one.

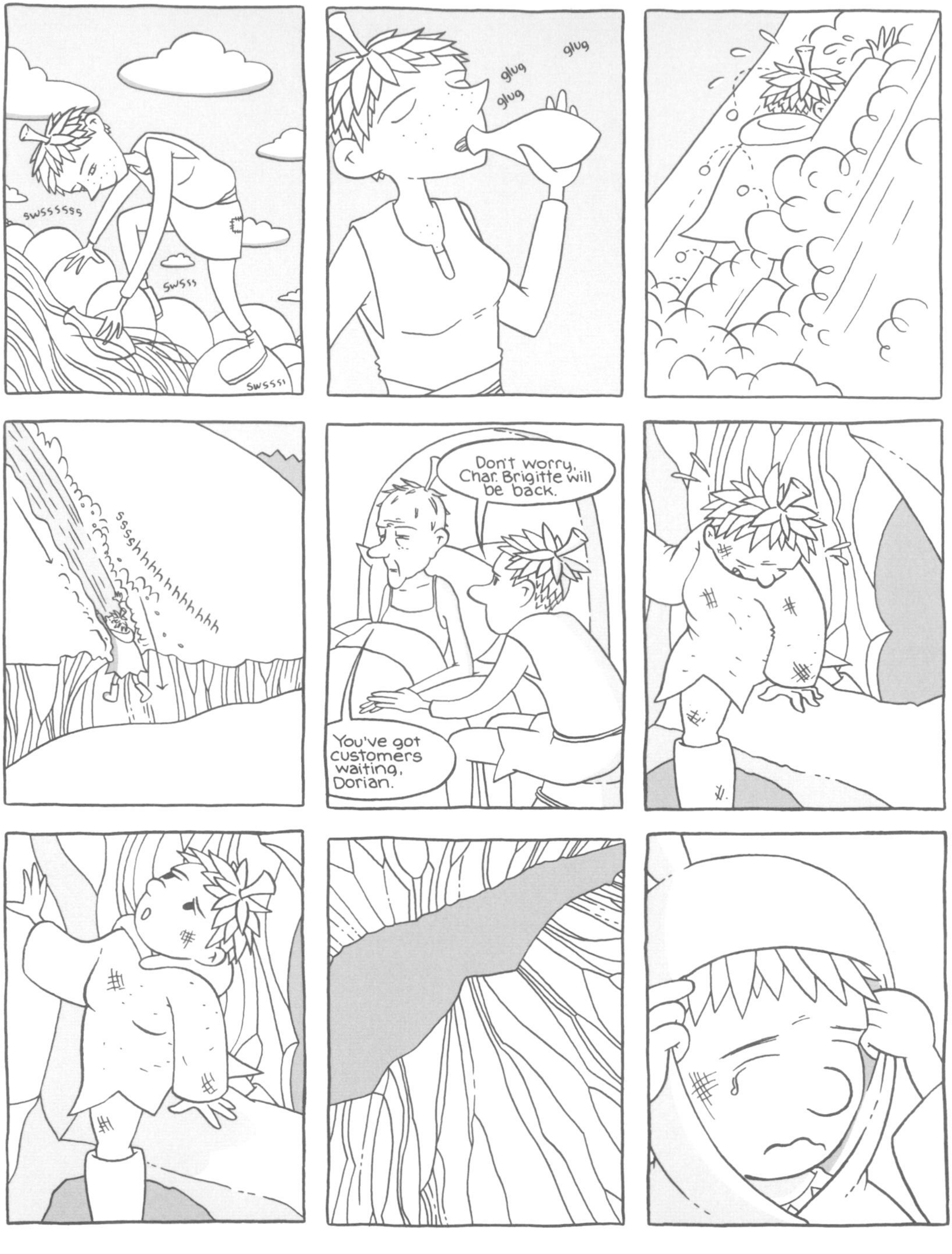
swssssss
swsss
swsssı
glug
glug
glug
ssshhhhhhhhhhhh
Don't worry, Char. Brigitte will be back.
You've got customers waiting, Dorian.

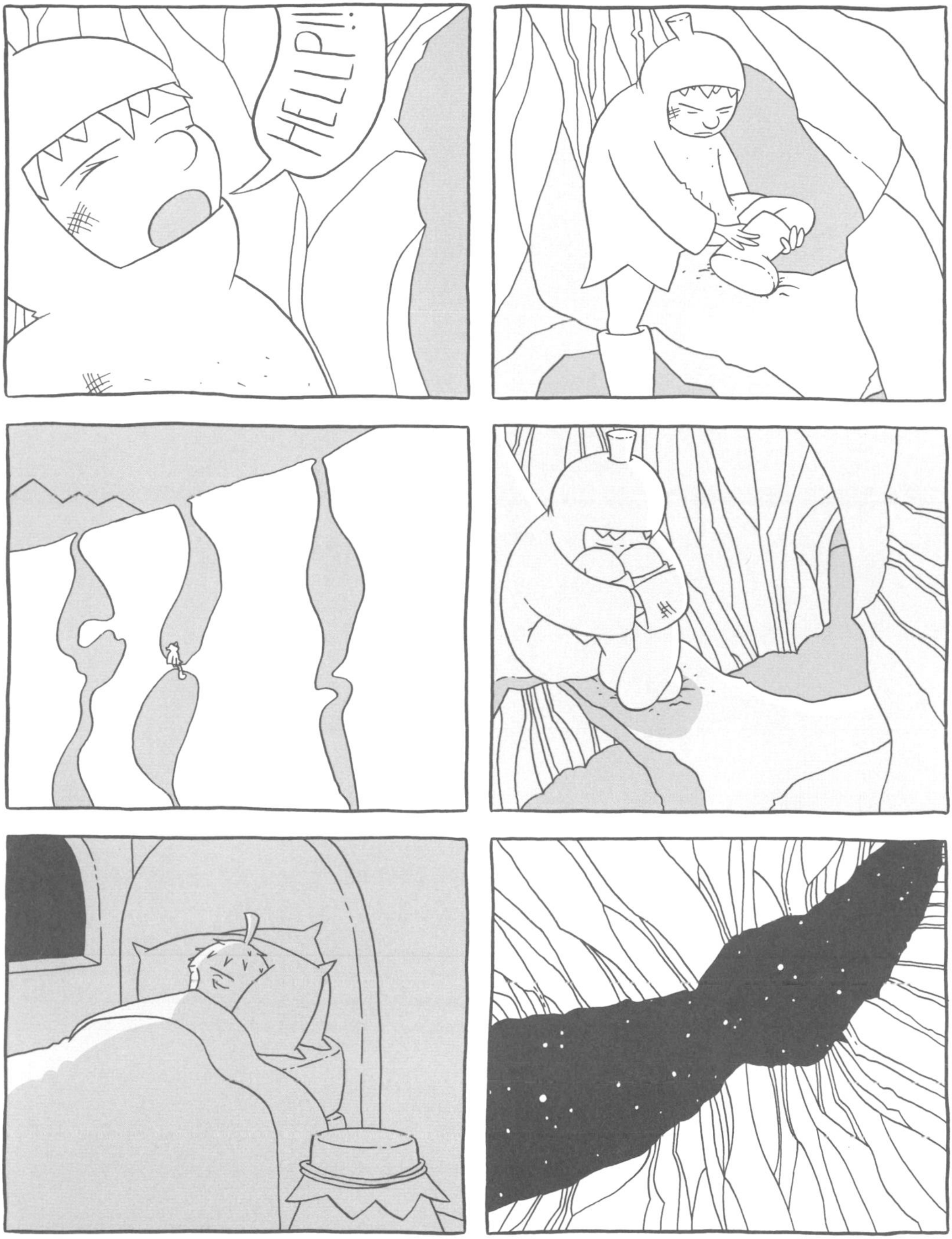
HELP!!

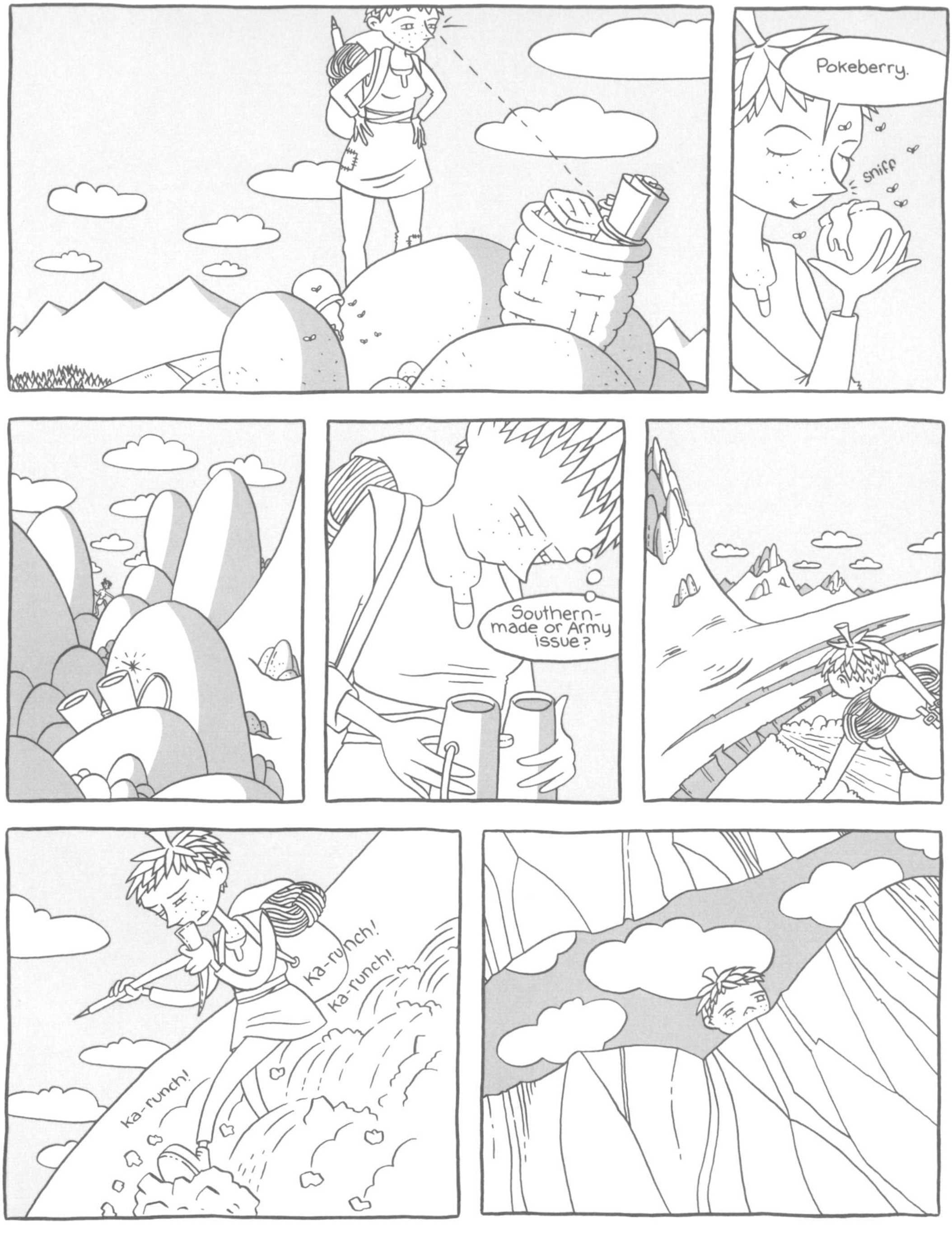
Pokeberry.
sniff
Southern-made or Army issue?
Ka-runch!
Ka-runch!
Ka-runch!

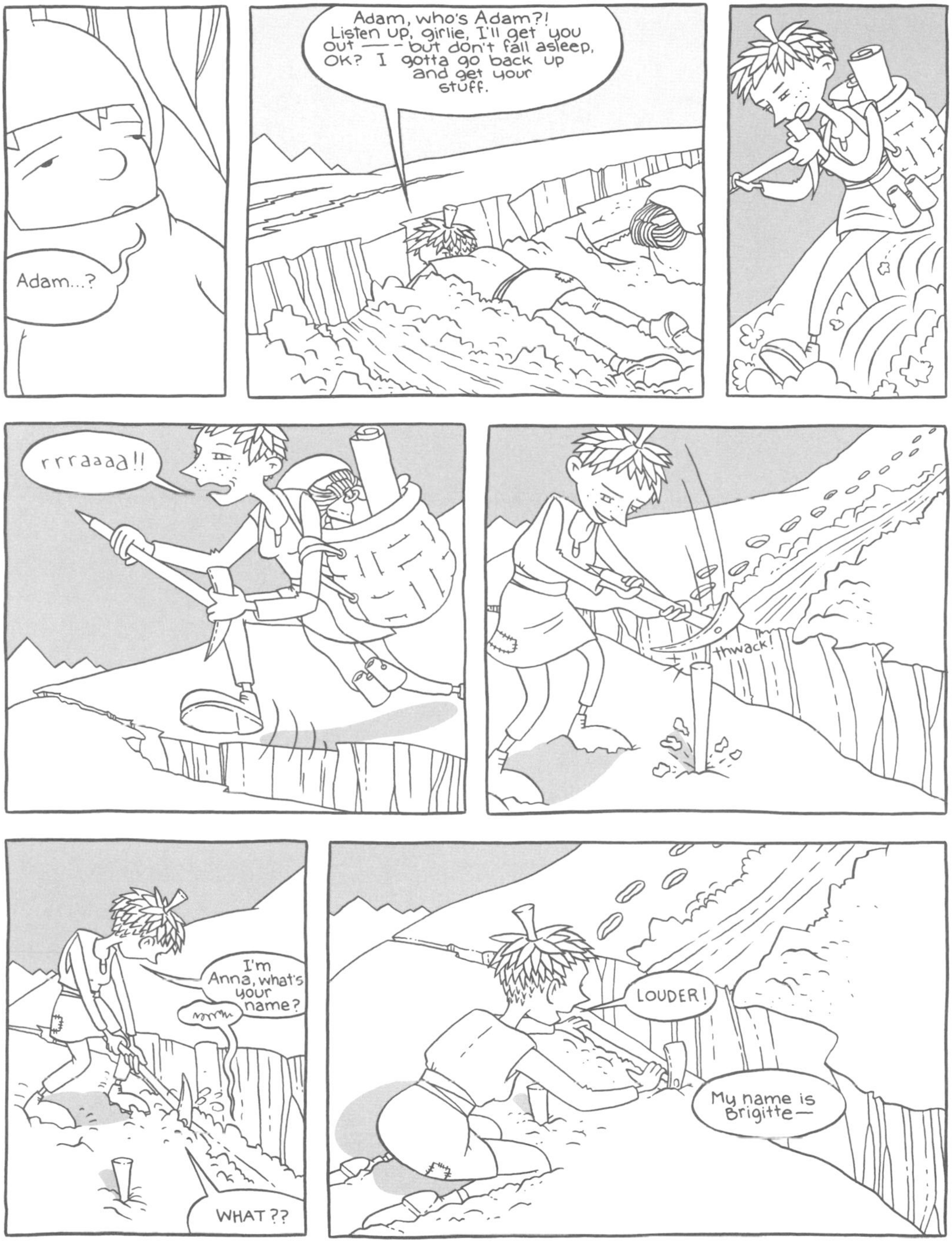

Adam...?
Adam, who's Adam?! Listen up, girlie, I'll get you out —— but don't fall asleep, OK? I gotta go back up and get your stuff.
rrraaad!!
thwack!
I'm Anna, what's your name?
WHAT??
LOUDER!
My name is Brigitte—

Brigitte. Now pay attention. Here's what's gonna happen. I'll lower down a rope with two slings, two carabiners and a pulley... are you listening?!

...the slings make a chest and seat harness. Twist each one into a figure eight—

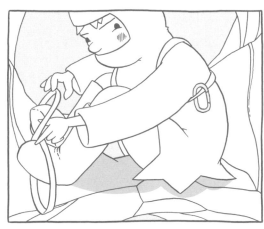

Yeah. That's right, with the "X" on your back. Arms through the loops—

oop!

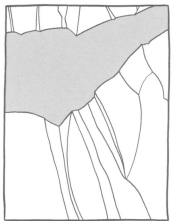

I can't do it!

164

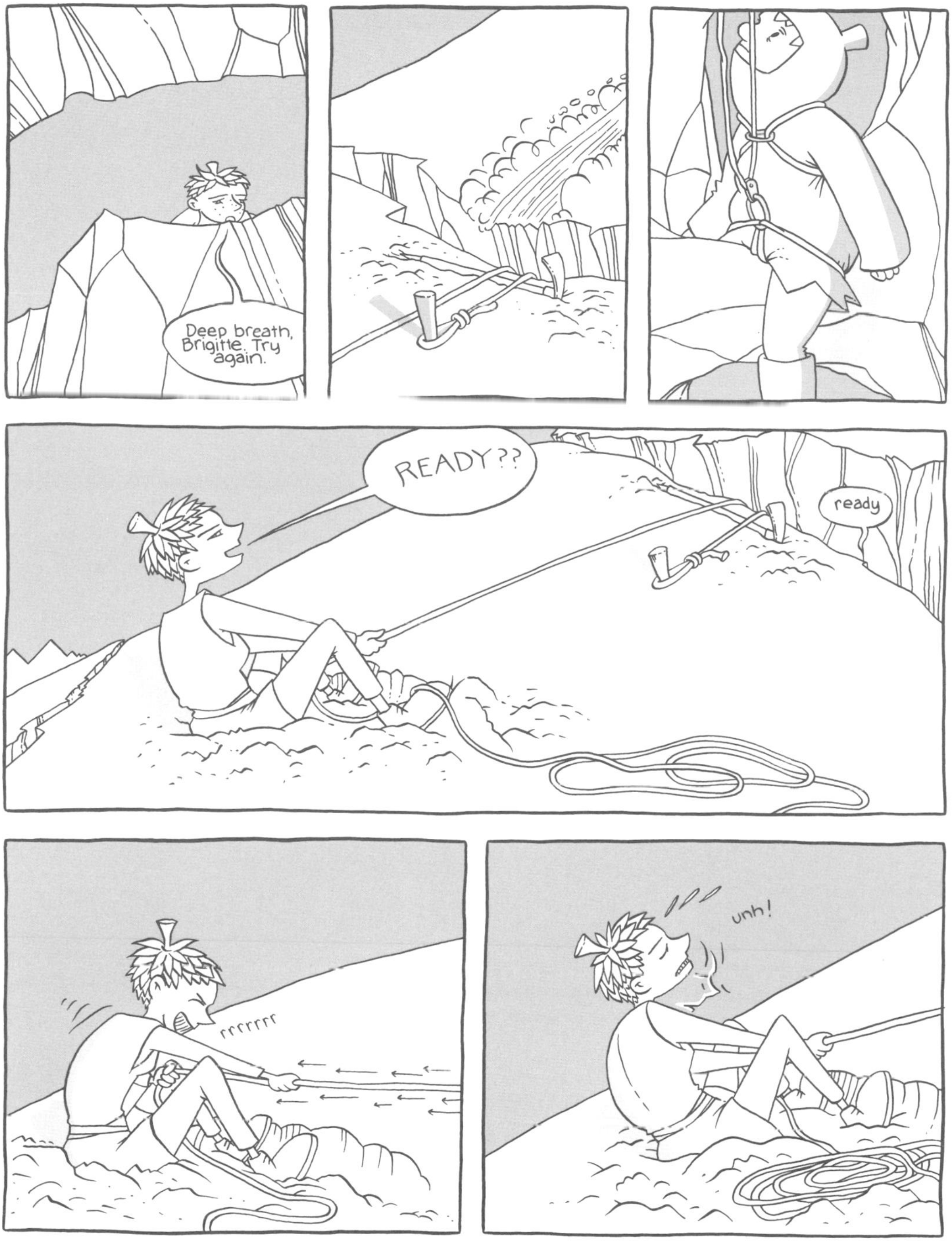
Deep breath, Brigitte. Try again.
READY??
ready
rrrrrrr
unh!

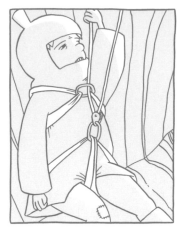

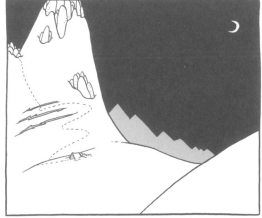

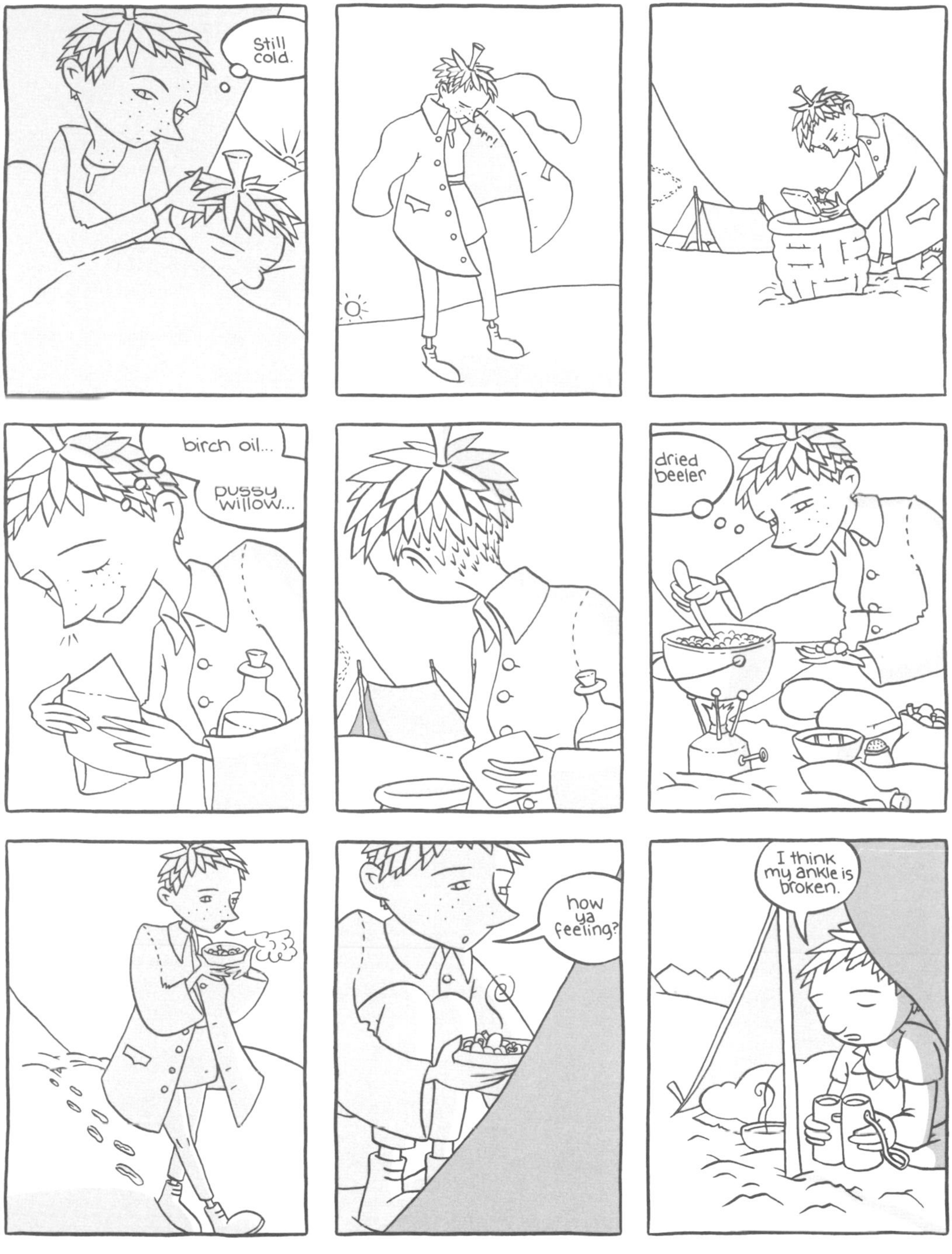

Still cold.
brr!
birch oil...
pussy willow...
dried beeler
how ya feeling?
I think my ankle is broken.

Could you make me some trillium tea? I have some in my first aid kit.

Tea? Oh right... for the swelling, right?

Owww!

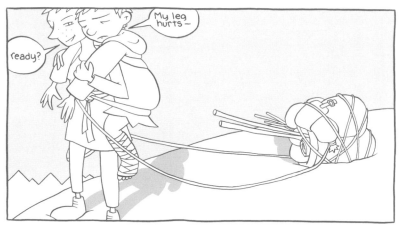

My leg hurts—

ready?

You're jouncing me!

"The empty world has a broken sun!"

"Cursed by darkness 'til the sisters come."

shh

ushh

shhh

"Will they end their feud or freeze our bones?"

North/South border

"Toss it straight up past the solstice stones."

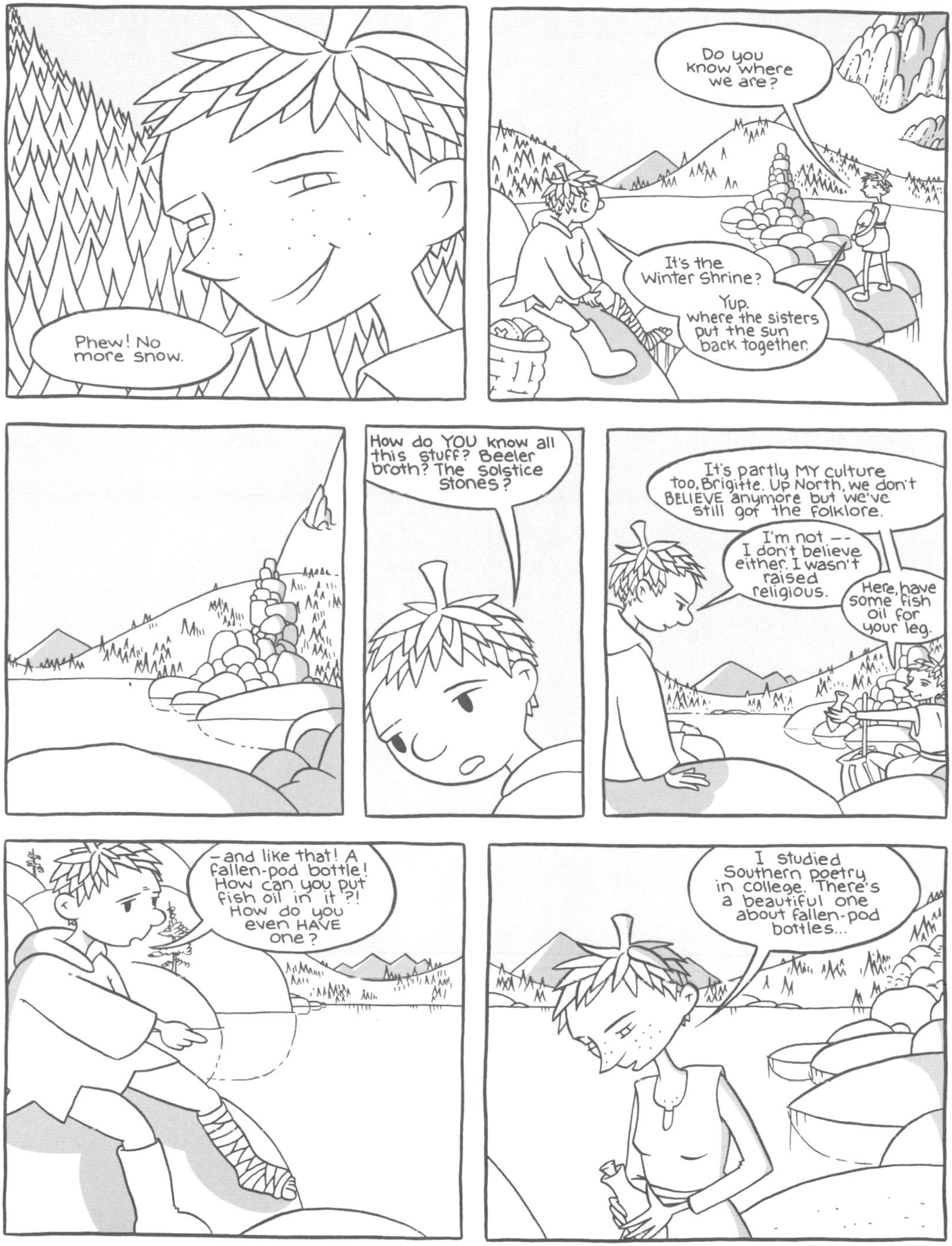
Phew! No more snow.
Do you know where we are?
It's the Winter Shrine?
Yup. where the sisters put the sun back together.
How do YOU know all this stuff? Beeler broth? The Solstice stones?
It's partly MY culture too, Brigitte. Up North, we don't BELIEVE anymore but we've still got the folklore.
I'm not -- I don't believe either. I wasn't raised religious.
Here, have some fish oil for your leg.
-and like that! A fallen-pod bottle! How can you put fish oil in it?! How do you even HAVE one?
I studied Southern poetry in college. There's a beautiful one about fallen-pod bottles...

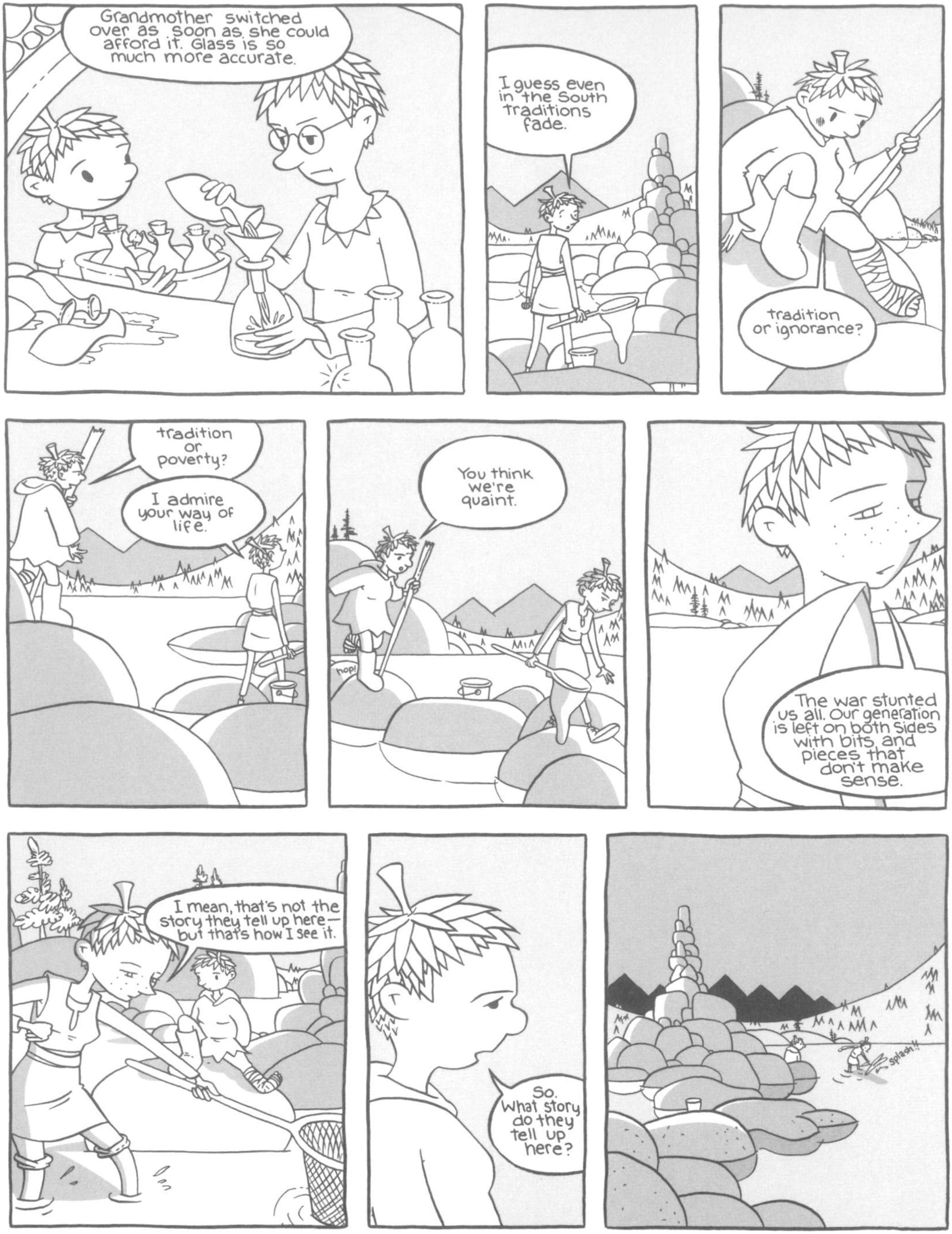
Grandmother switched over as soon as she could afford it. Glass is so much more accurate.
I guess even in the South traditions fade.
tradition or ignorance?
tradition or poverty?
I admire your way of life.
You think we're quaint.
hop!
The war stunted us all. Our generation is left on both sides with bits and pieces that don't make sense.
I mean, that's not the story they tell up here— but that's how I see it.
So. What story do they tell up here?
splash!!

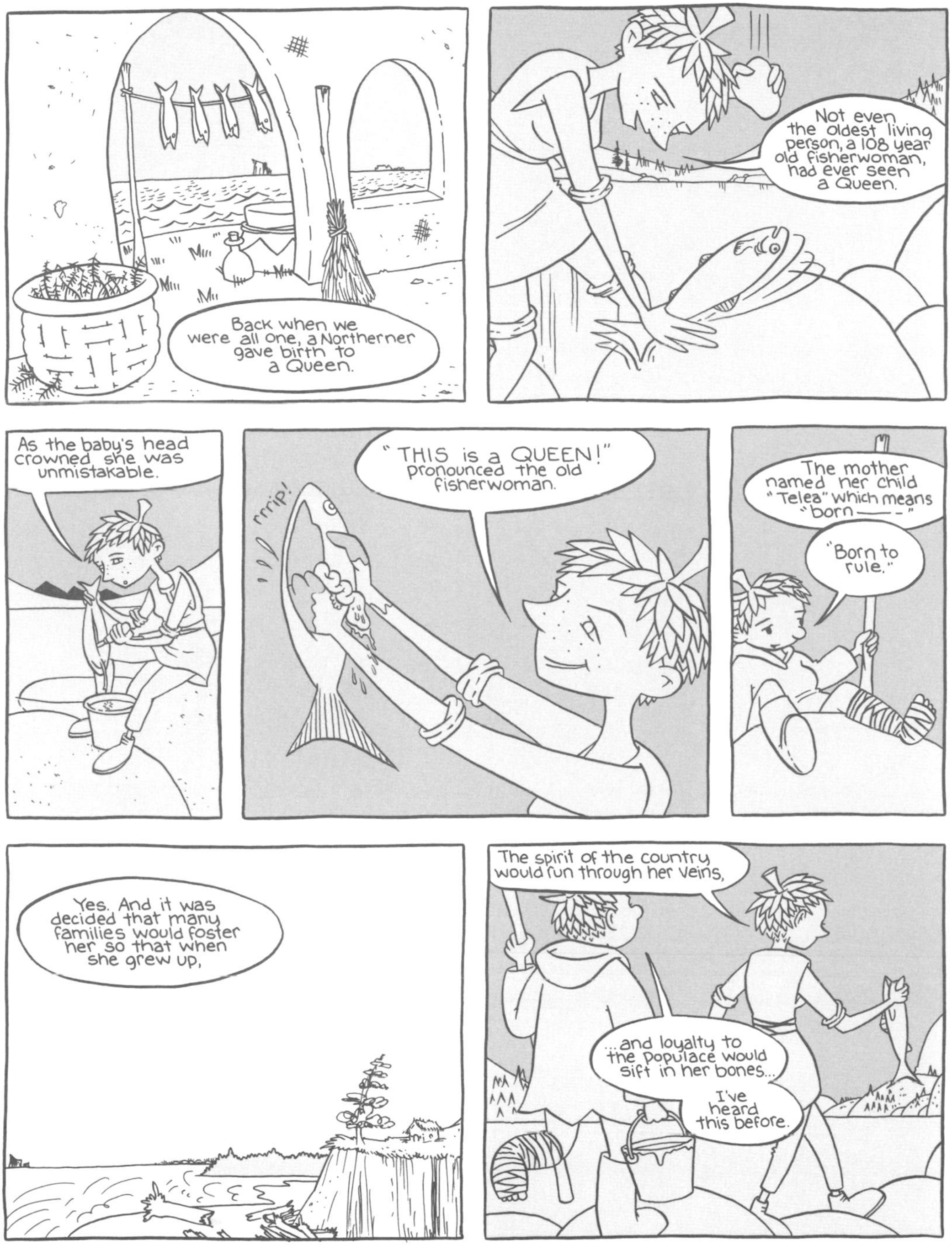

Back when we were all one, a Northerner gave birth to a Queen.
Not even the oldest living person, a 108 year old fisherwoman, had ever seen a Queen.
As the baby's head crowned she was unmistakable.
rrrip!
"THIS is a QUEEN!" pronounced the old fisherwoman.
The mother named her child "Telea" which means "born ---"
"Born to rule."
Yes. And it was decided that many families would foster her so that when she grew up,
The spirit of the country would run through her veins,
...and loyalty to the populace would sift in her bones...
I've heard this before.

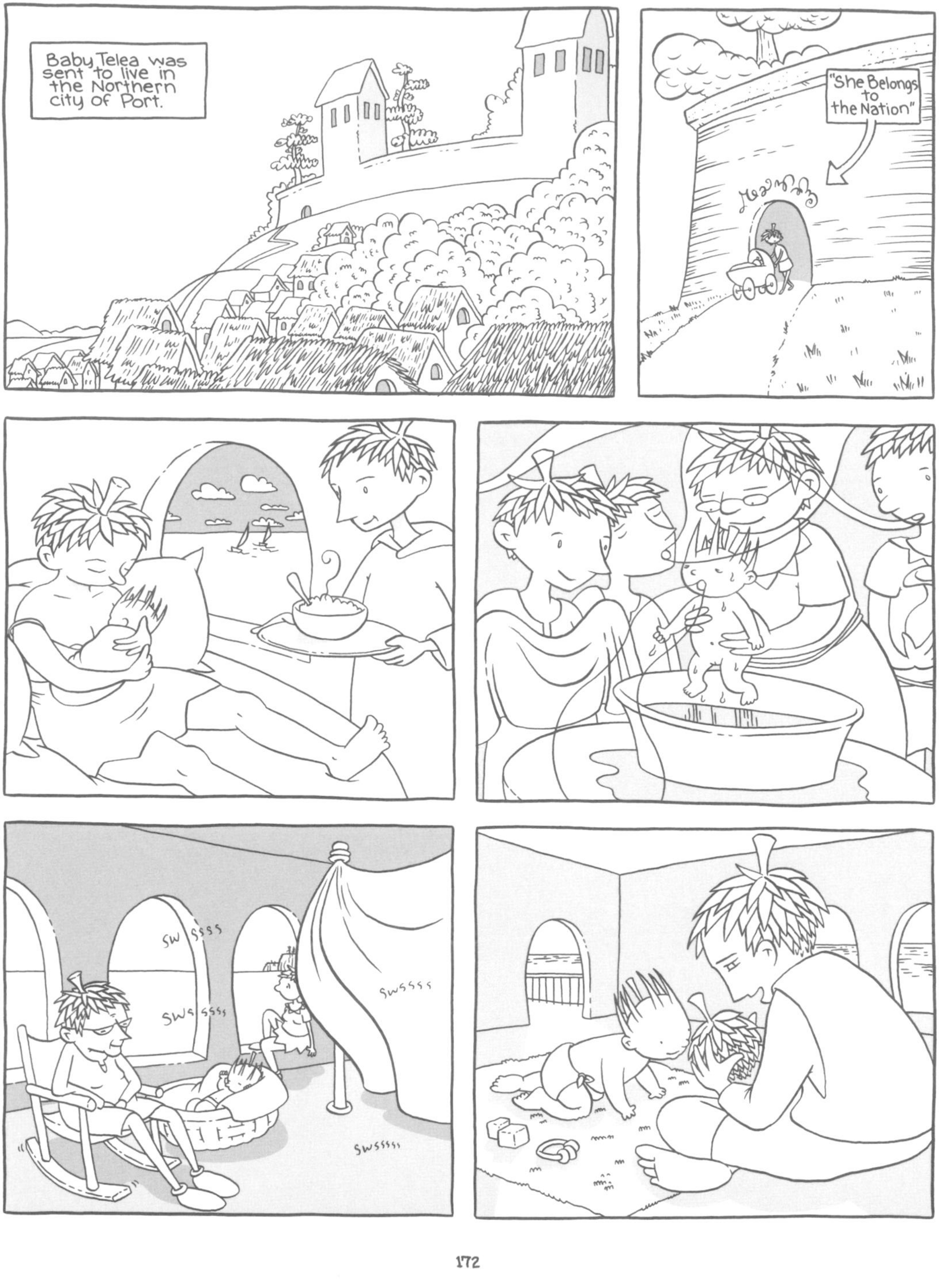
Baby Telea was sent to live in the Northern city of Port.
"She Belongs to the Nation"
SW SSSS
SWSSSS
SWS SSSS
SWSSSSS

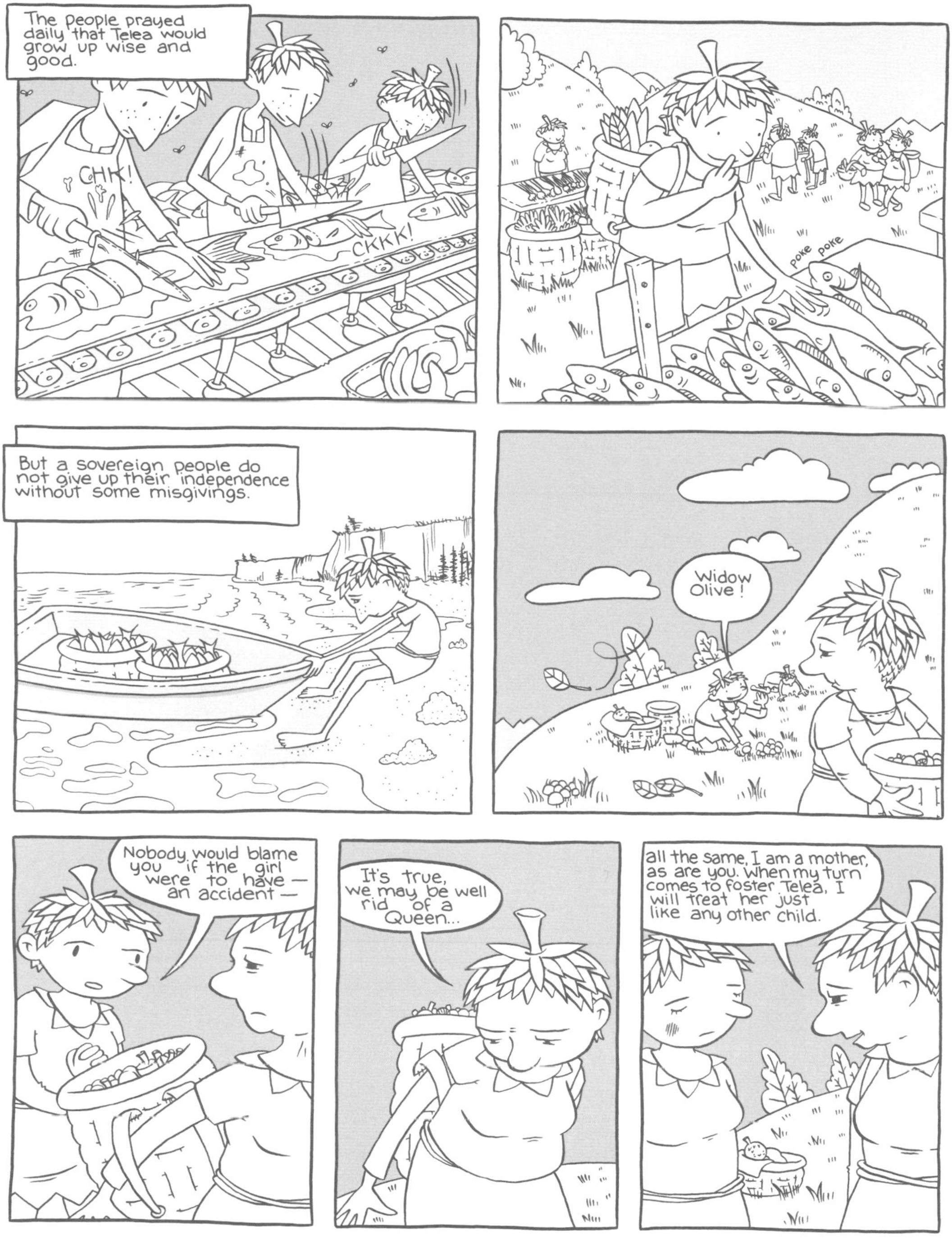
The people prayed daily that Telea would grow up wise and good.
CHK!
CKKK!
poke poke
But a sovereign people do not give up their independence without some misgivings.
Widow Olive!
Nobody would blame you if the girl were to have — an accident —
It's true, we may be well rid of a Queen...
all the same, I am a mother, as are you. When my turn comes to foster Telea, I will treat her just like any other child.

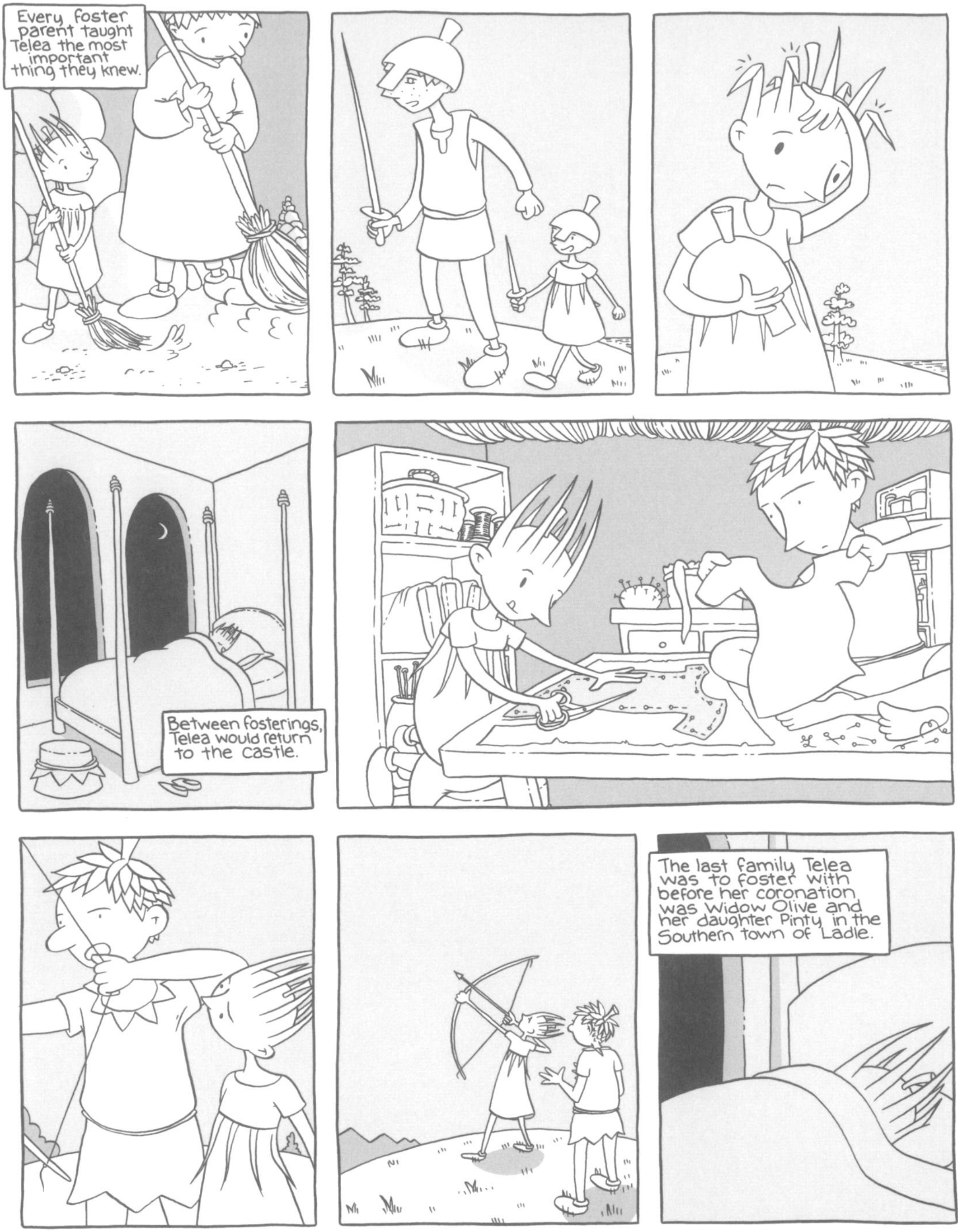
Every foster parent taught Telea the most important thing they knew.
Between fosterings, Telea would return to the castle.
The last family Telea was to foster with before her coronation was Widow Olive and her daughter Pinty in the Southern town of Ladle.

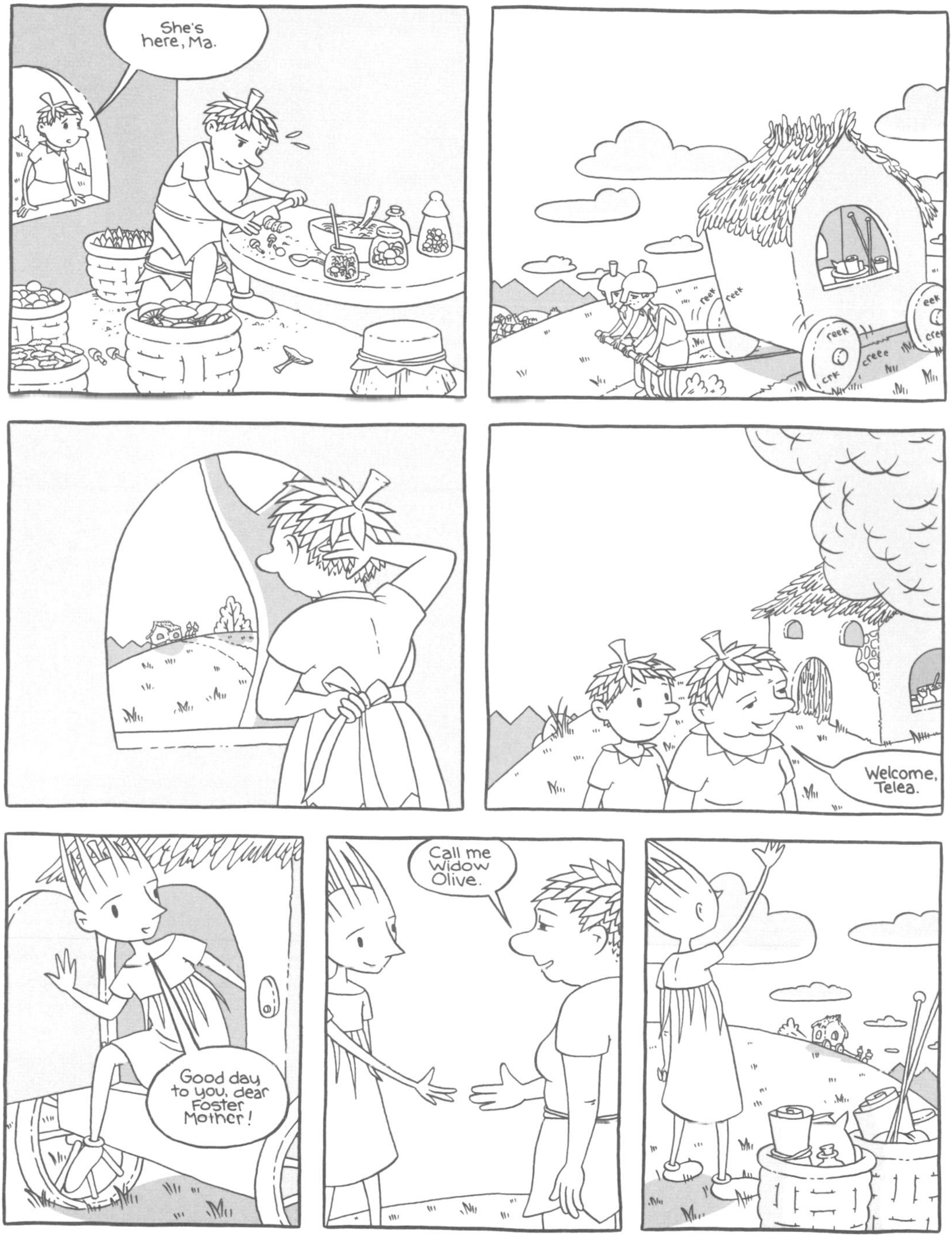
She's here, Ma.
reek
reek
eek
reek
creee
crk
cree
Welcome, Telea.
Good day to you, dear Foster Mother!
Call me Widow Olive.

tak
tak
tak

tak
tak

tak
tak

This is Golden Cap ragout— You'll learn that one — and Foghat pilaf. And Sautéed Beelers. We'll hunt for Beelers tomorrow.

tak
tak
tak

tak
tak

We dry and pickle the Beelers so we can eat them during the barren months.

... Pebbles, which are sometimes called "Fallen Stars" are for medicinal purposes only.

You must be a bit of a mountaineer to hunt the Foghat — they are an alpine species.

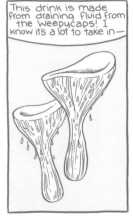

This drink is made from draining fluid from the Weepycaps! I know it's a lot to take in—

And here are some boiled potatoes to make you feel more at home.

Oh, yes, please!

—and more Beelers for you, Pinty?

Oh yes, Mama! They're delicious tonight.

How 'bout you, Telea?

n-no thank you...

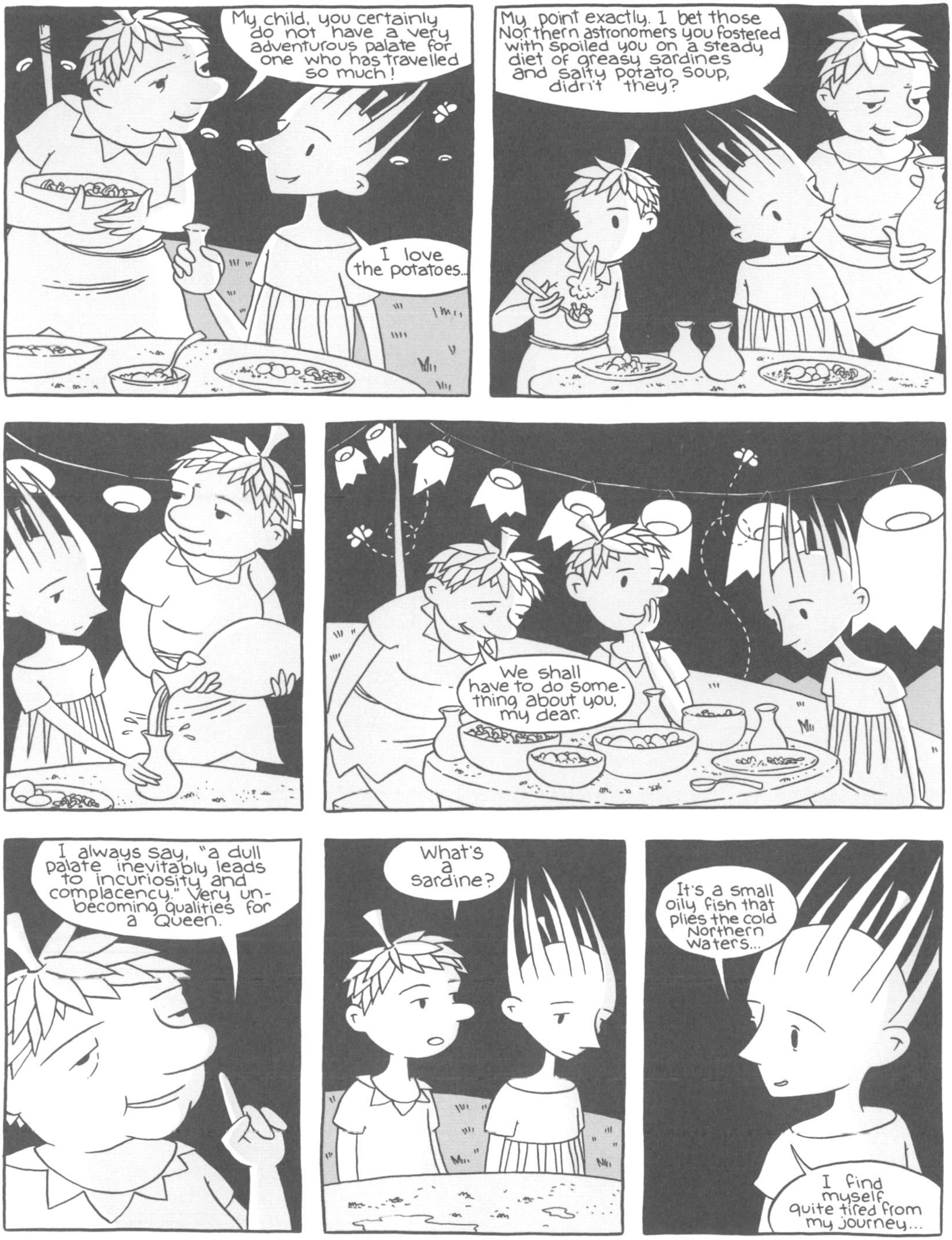
My child, you certainly do not have a very adventurous palate for one who has travelled so much!
I love the potatoes...
My point exactly. I bet those Northern astronomers you fostered with spoiled you on a steady diet of greasy sardines and salty potato soup, didn't they?
We shall have to do some-thing about you, my dear.
I always say, "a dull palate inevitably leads to incuriosity and complacency." Very un-becoming qualities for a Queen.
What's a sardine?
It's a small oily fish that plies the cold Northern waters...
I find myself quite tired from my journey...

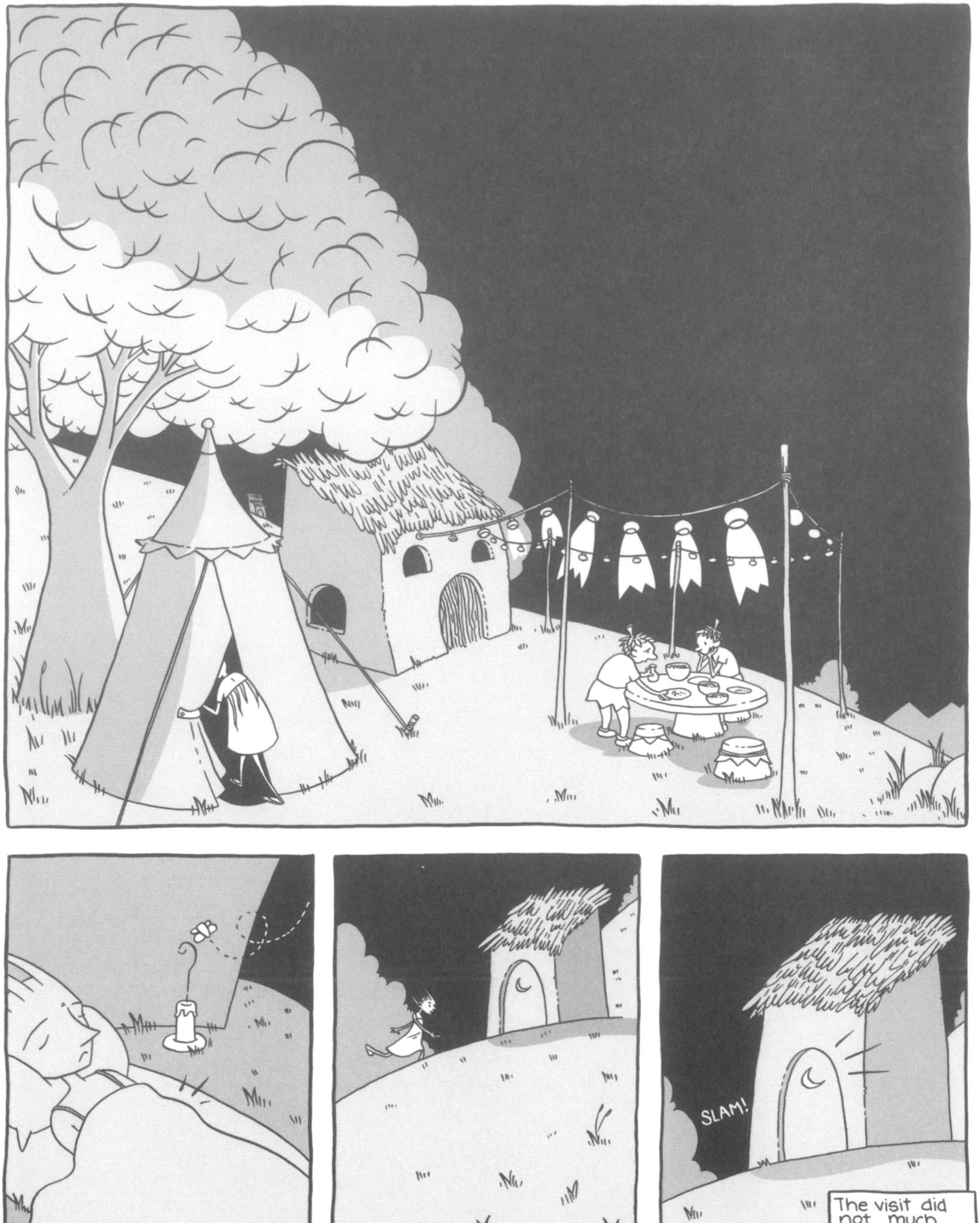
SLAM!
The visit did not much improve.

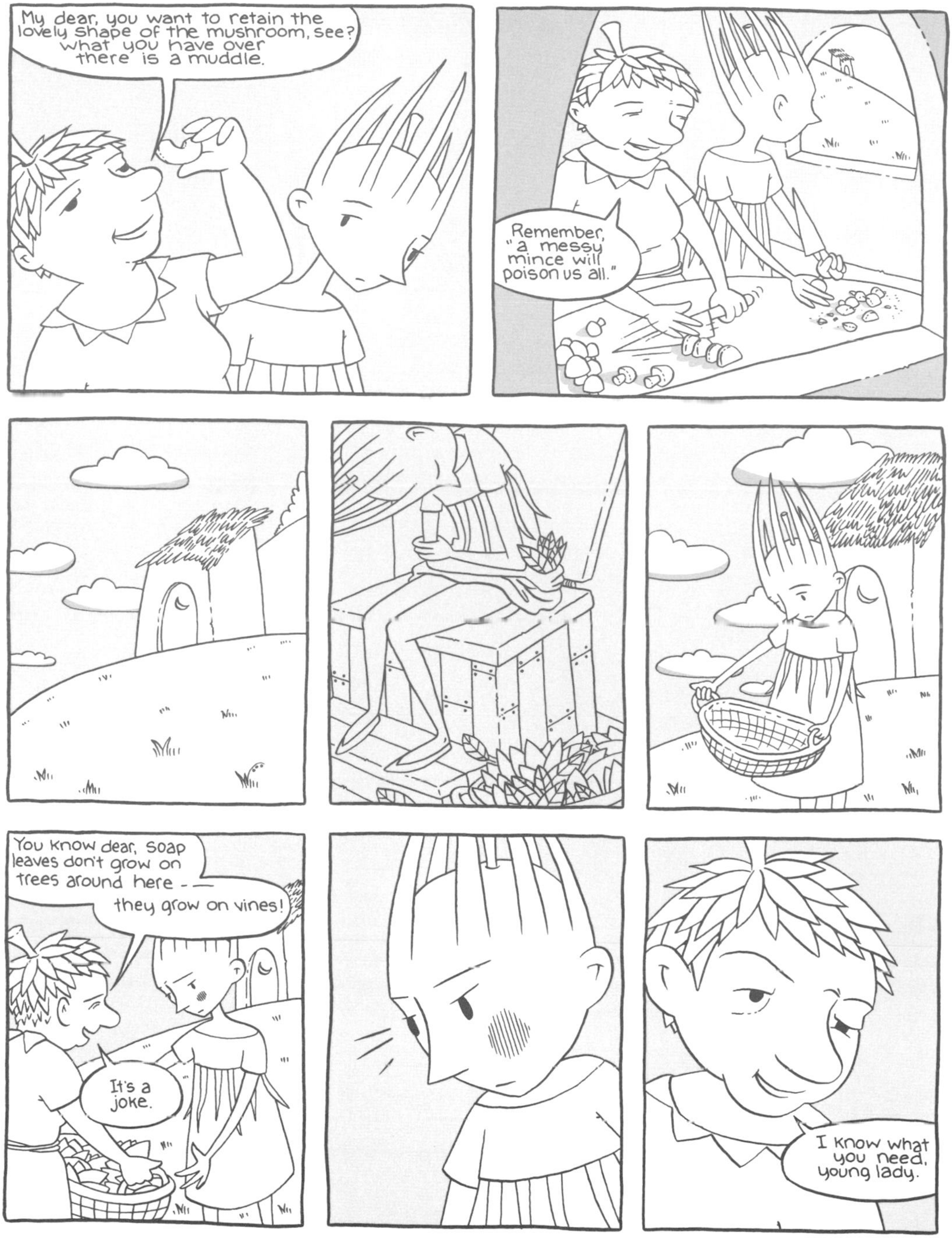
My dear, you want to retain the lovely shape of the mushroom, see? what you have over there is a muddle.
Remember, "a messy mince will poison us all."
You know dear, soap leaves don't grow on trees around here --
they grow on vines!
It's a joke.
I know what you need, young lady.

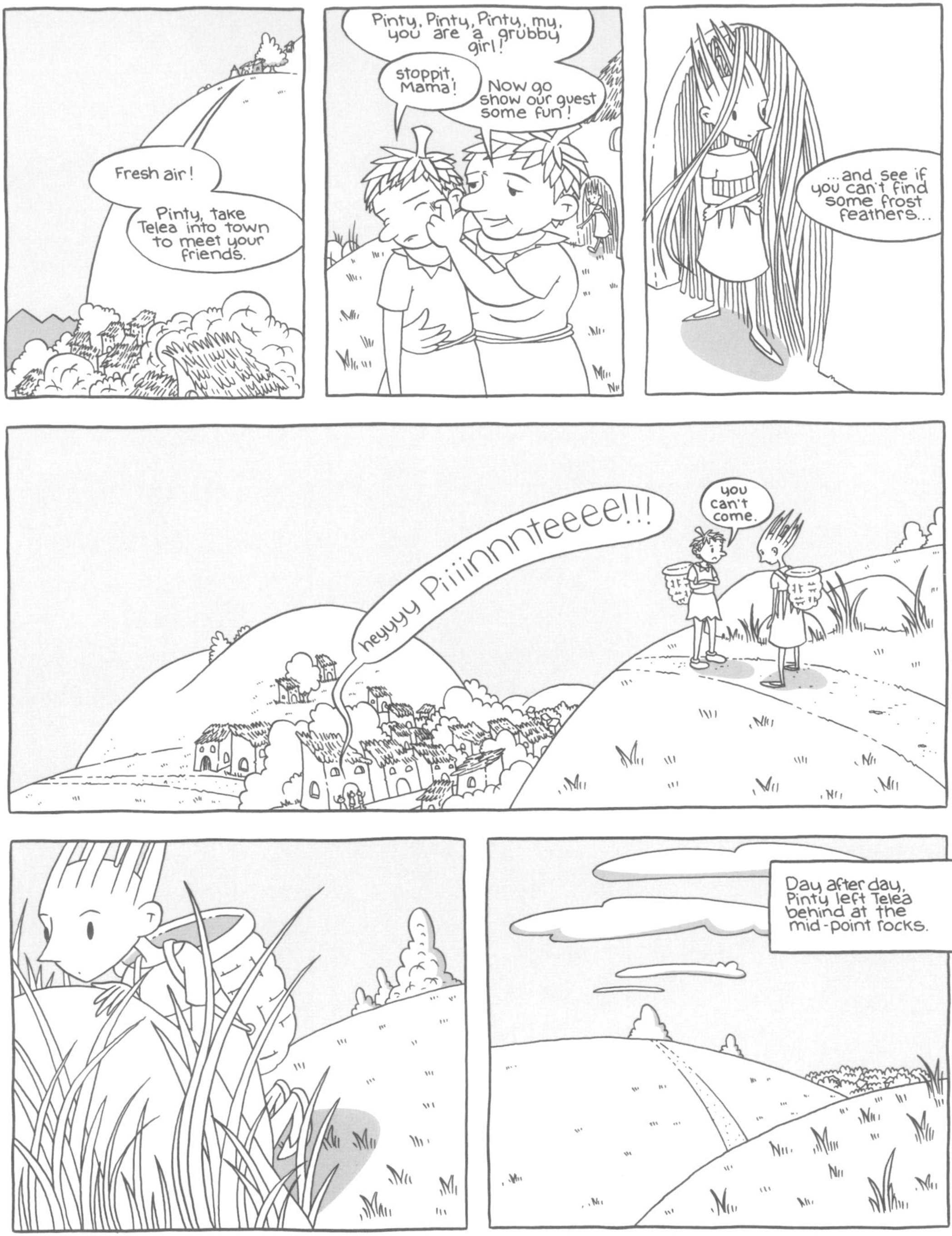

Fresh air!
Pinty, take Telea into town to meet your friends.
Pinty, Pinty, Pinty, my, you are a grubby girl!
stoppit, Mama!
Now go show our guest some fun!
...and see if you can't find some frost feathers...
heyyyy Piiiinnnteeee!!!
you can't come.
Day after day, Pinty left Telea behind at the mid-point rocks.

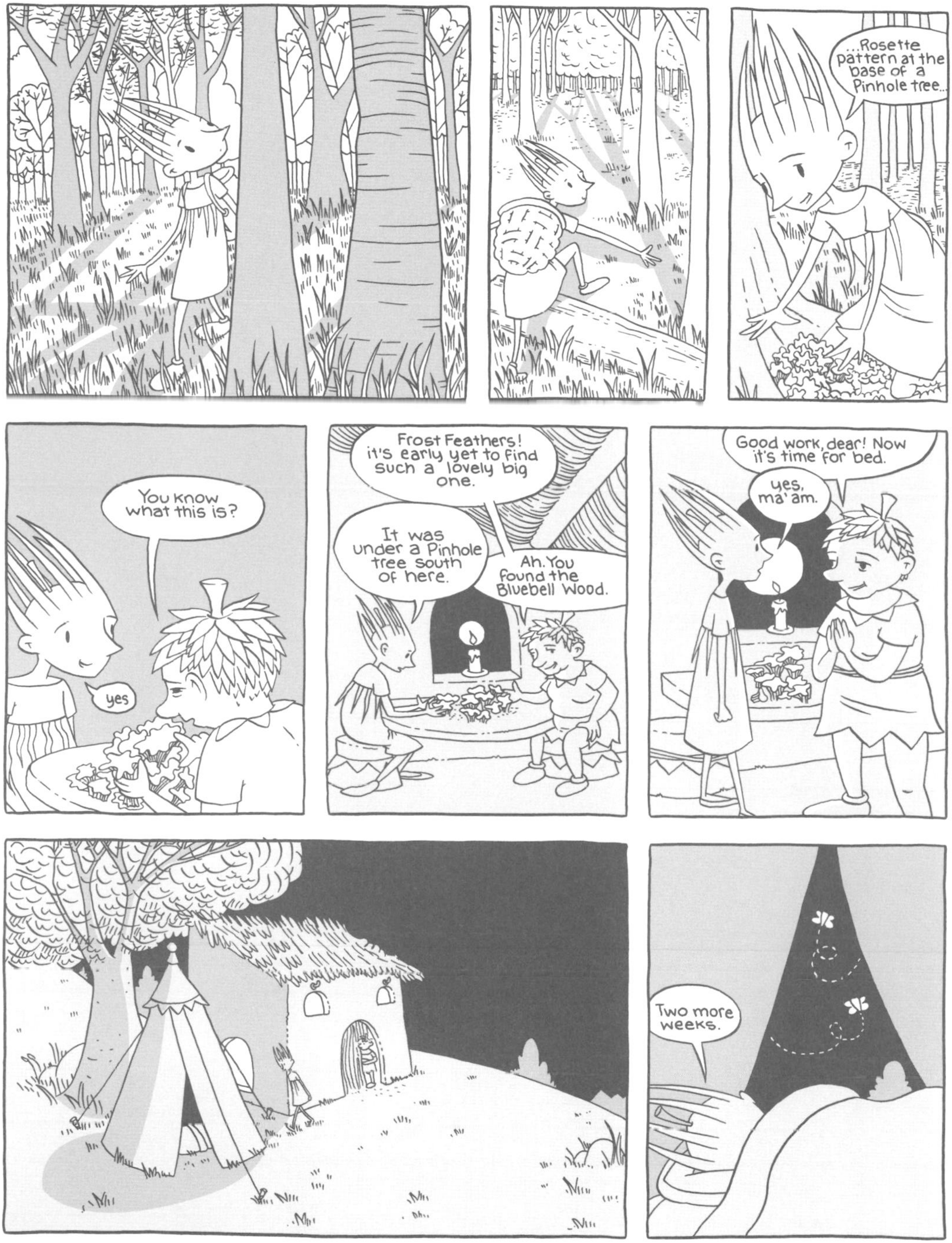
...Rosette pattern at the base of a Pinhole tree...
You know what this is?
yes
Frost Feathers! it's early yet to find such a lovely big one.
It was under a Pinhole tree south of here.
Ah. You found the Bluebell Wood.
Good work, dear! Now it's time for bed.
yes, ma'am.
Two more weeks.

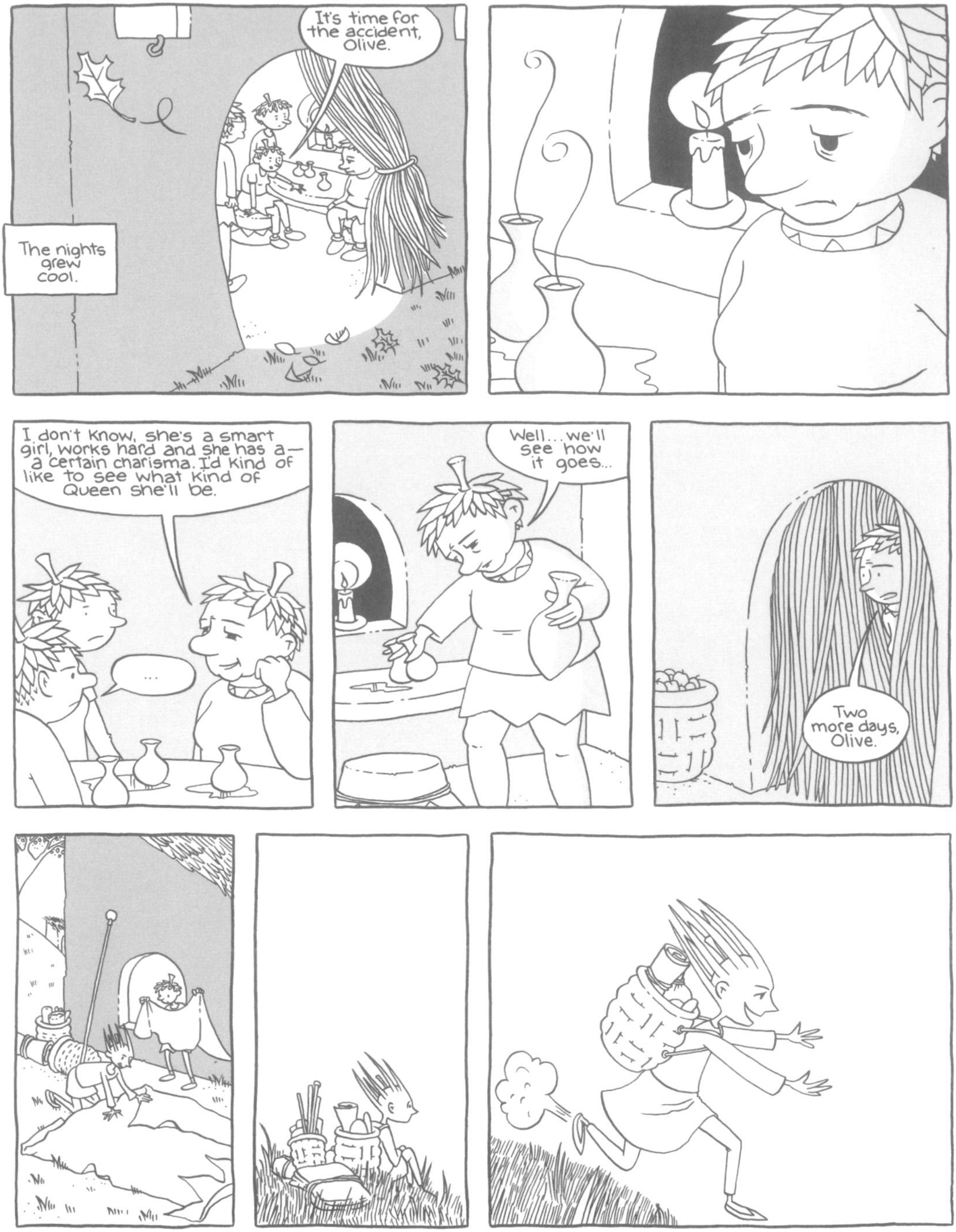
The nights grew cool.
It's time for the accident, Olive.
I don't know, she's a smart girl, works hard and she has a— a certain charisma. I'd kind of like to see what kind of Queen she'll be.
...
Well... we'll see how it goes...
Two more days, Olive.

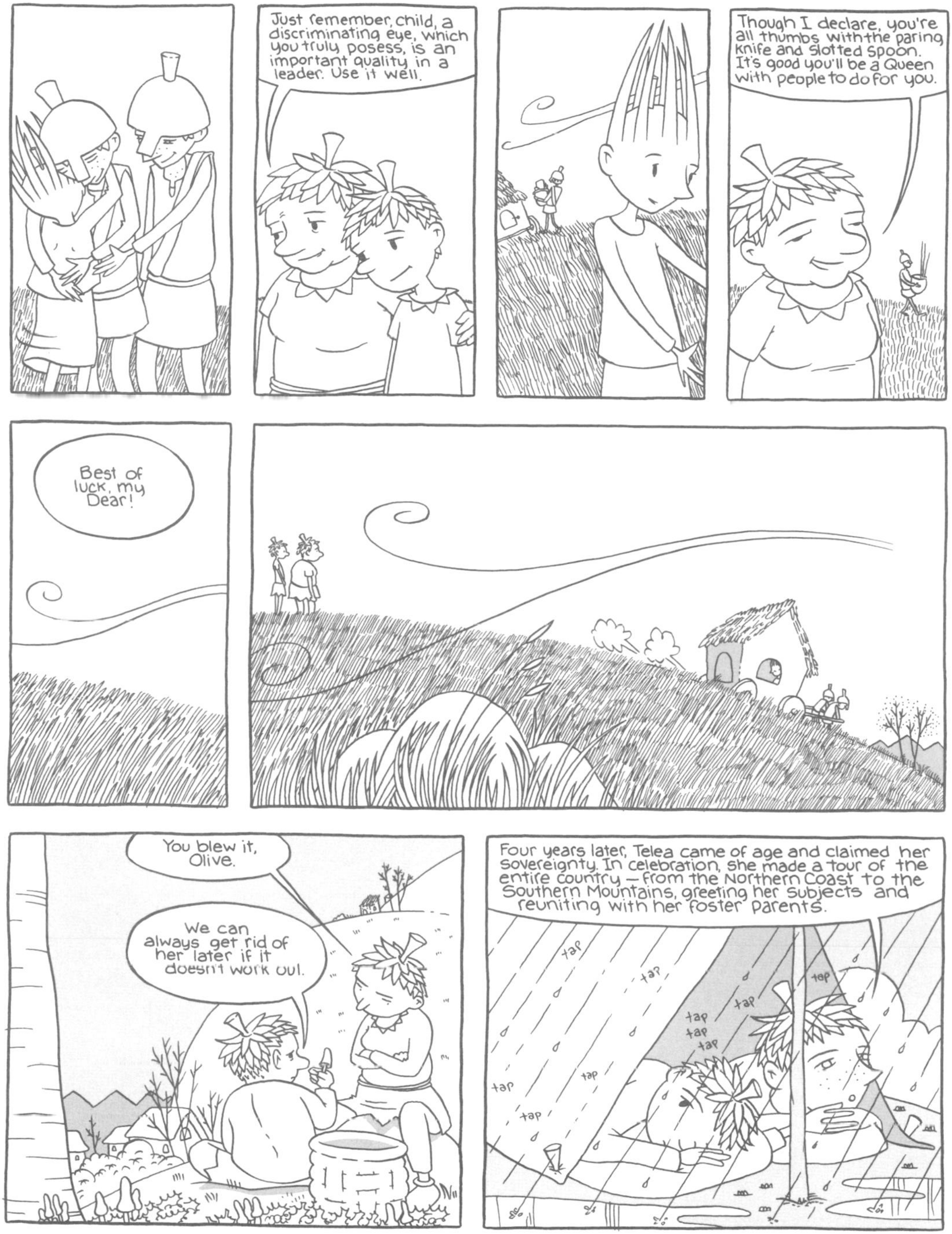

Just remember, child, a discriminating eye, which you truly posess, is an important quality in a leader. Use it well.
Though I declare, you're all thumbs with the paring knife and slotted spoon. It's good you'll be a Queen with people to do for you.
Best of luck, my Dear!
You blew it, Olive.
We can always get rid of her later if it doesn't work out.
Four years later, Telea came of age and claimed her sovereignty. In celebration, she made a tour of the entire country — from the Northern Coast to the Southern Mountains, greeting her subjects and reuniting with her foster parents.
tap
tap
tap
tap
tap
tap
tap
tap
tap

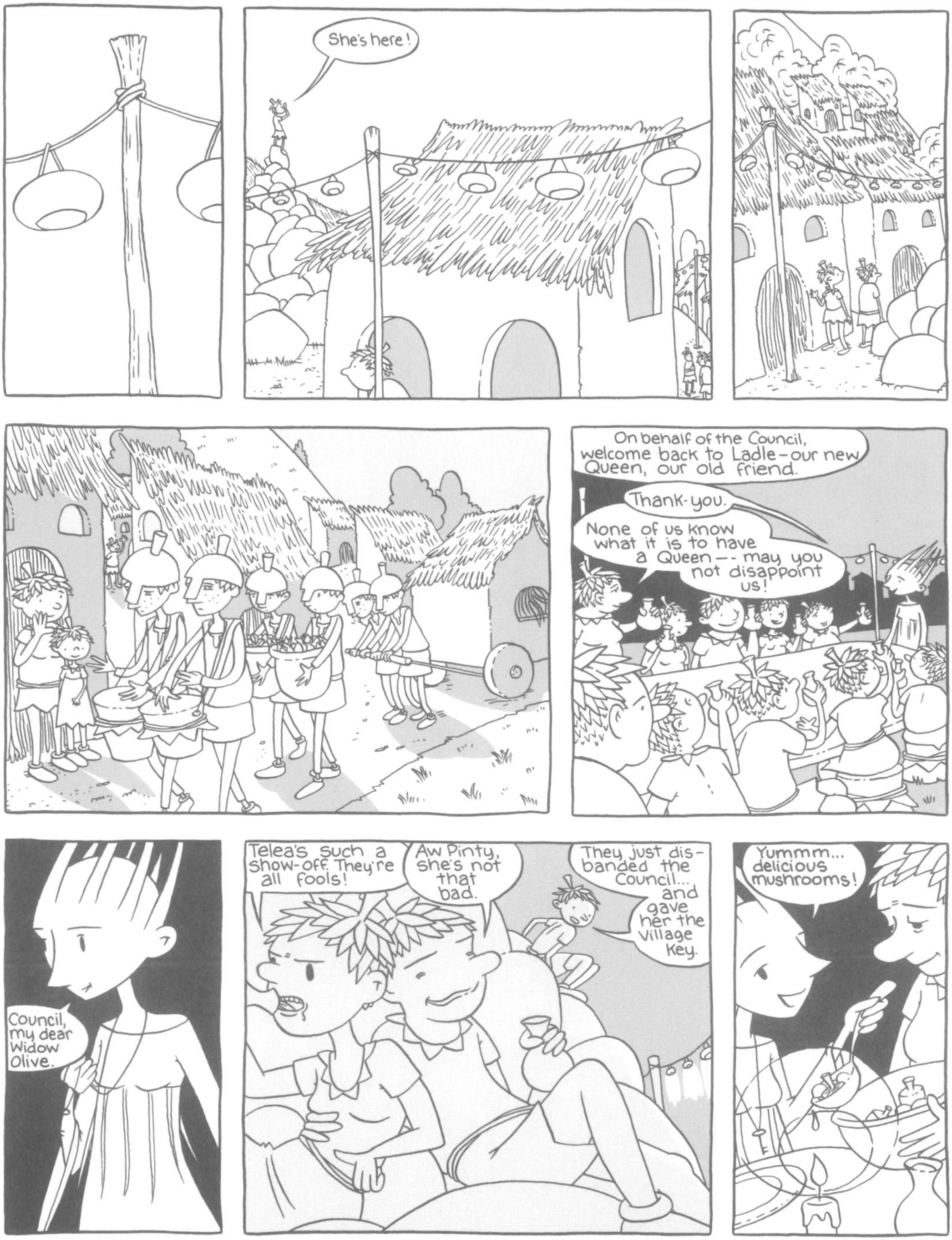

She's here!
On behalf of the Council, welcome back to Ladle–our new Queen, our old friend.
Thank-you.
None of us know what it is to have a Queen–- may you not disappoint us!
Council, my dear Widow Olive.
Telea's such a show-off. They're all fools!
Aw Pinty, she's not that bad.
They just dis-banded the Council... and gave her the Village Key.
Yummm... delicious mushrooms!

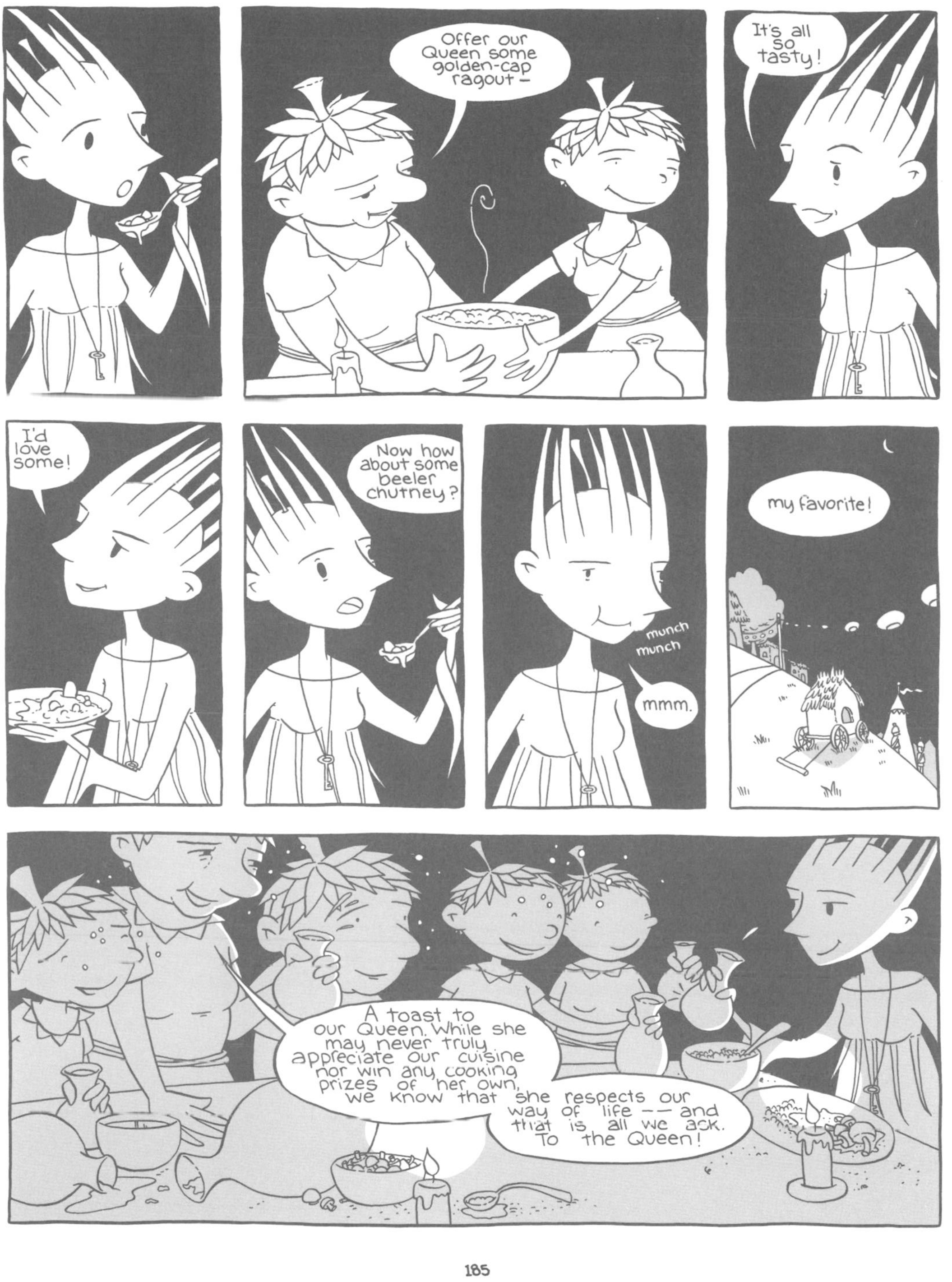
Offer our Queen some golden-cap ragout –
It's all so tasty!
I'd love some!
Now how about some beeler chutney?
munch munch
mmm.
my favorite!
A toast to our Queen. While she may never truly appreciate our cuisine nor win any cooking prizes of her own, we know that she respects our way of life -- and that is all we ask. To the Queen!

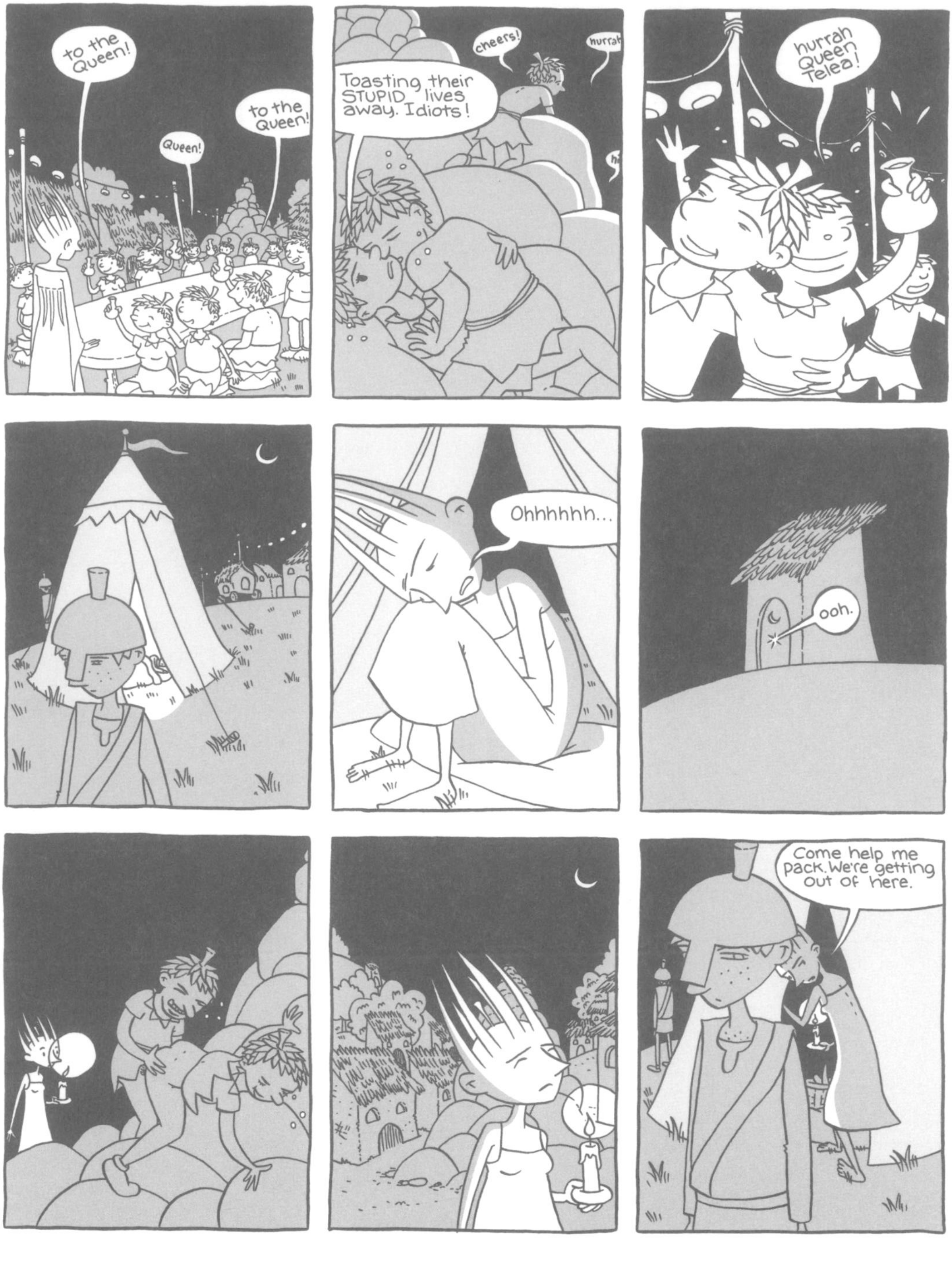
to the Queen!
Queen!
to the Queen!
Toasting their STUPID lives away. Idiots!
cheers!
hurrah
hurrah Queen Telea!
Ohhhhhh...
ooh.
Come help me pack. We're getting out of here.

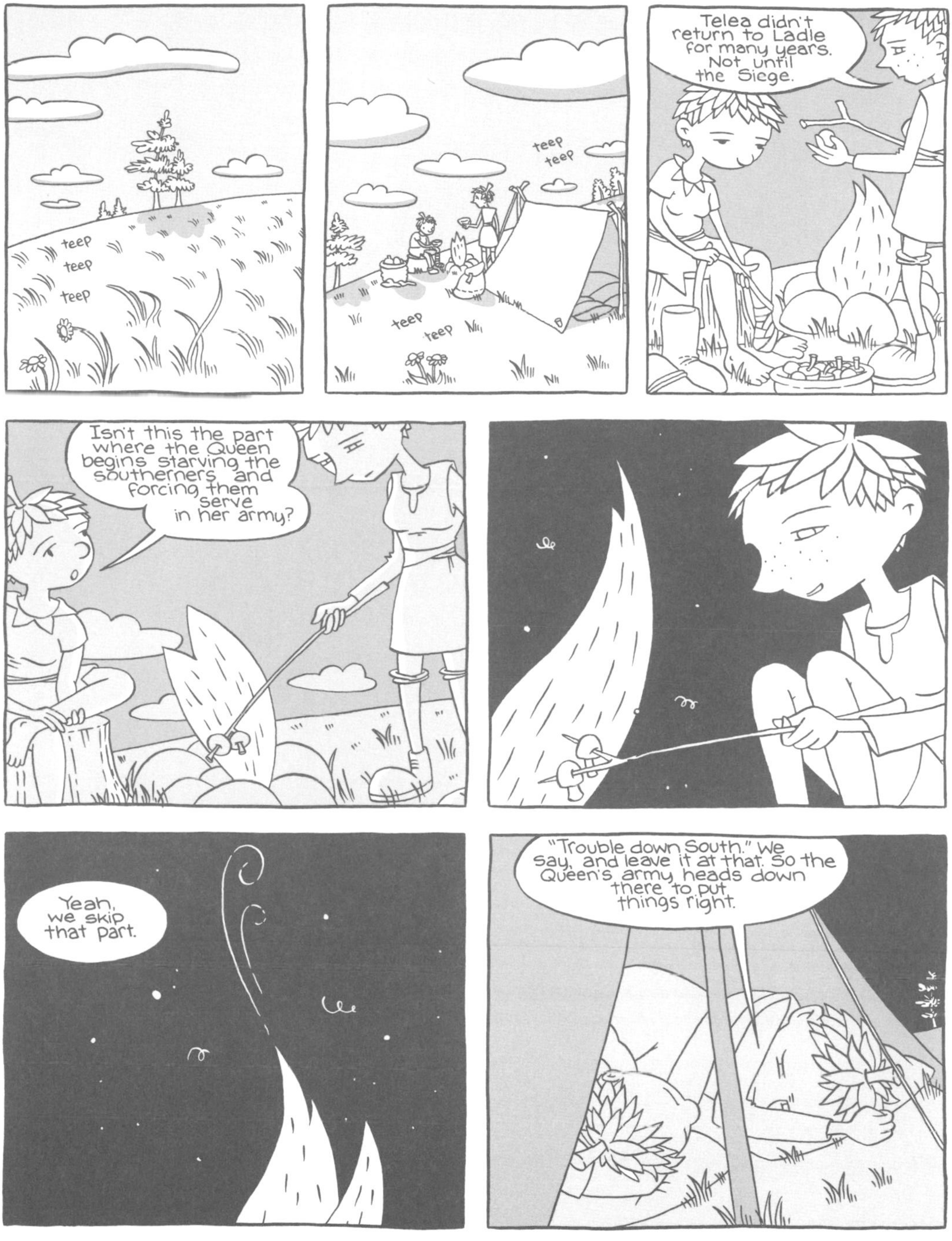
teep
teep
teep
teep
teep
teep
teep
Telea didn't return to Ladle for many years. Not until the Siege.
Isn't this the part where the Queen begins starving the southerners and forcing them serve in her army?
Yeah, we skip that part.
"Trouble down South." We say, and leave it at that. So the Queen's army heads down there to put things right.

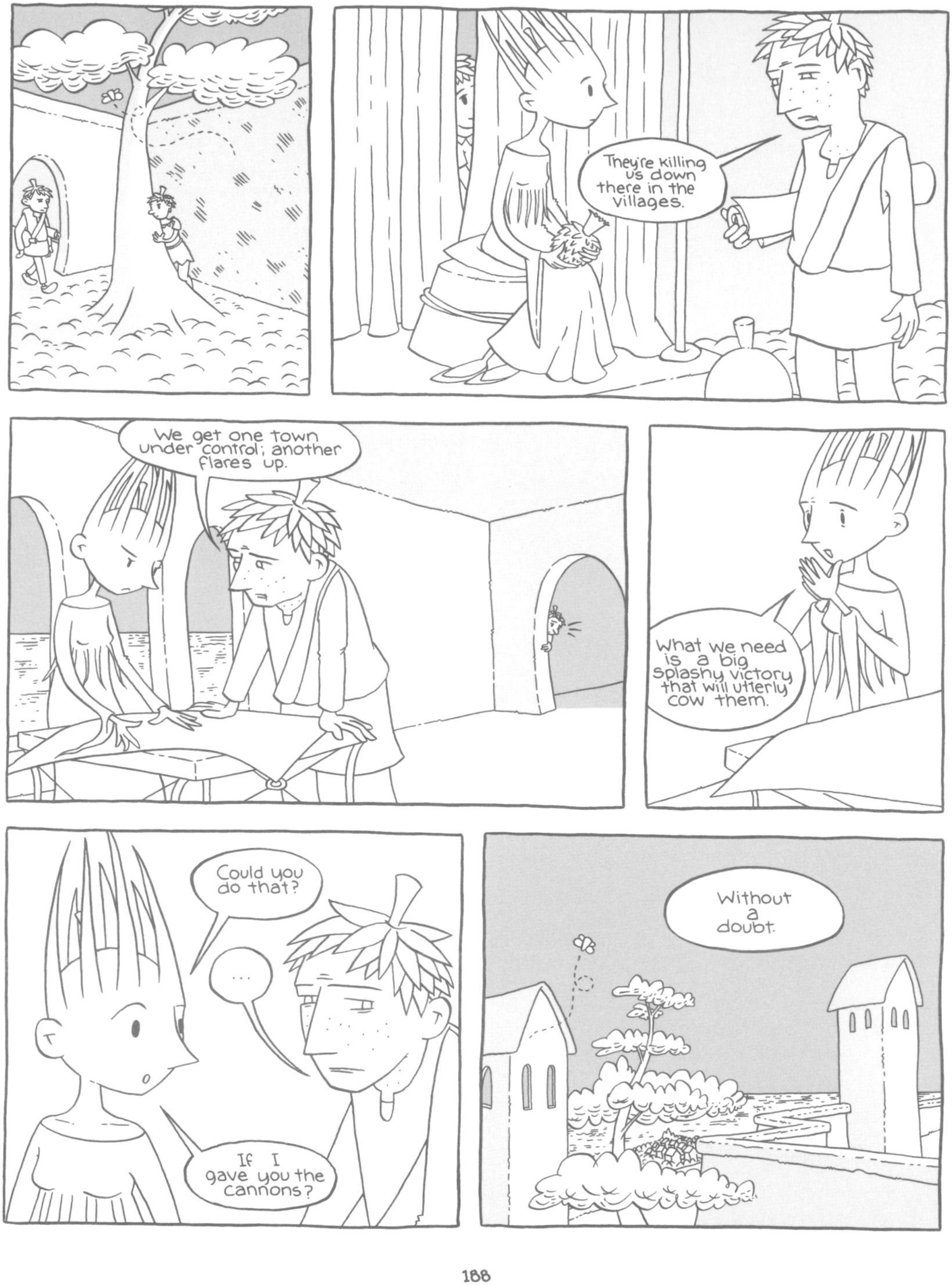
They're killing us down there in the villages.
We get one town under control; another flares up.
What we need is a big splashy victory that will utterly cow them.
Could you do that?
...
If I gave you the cannons?
Without a doubt.

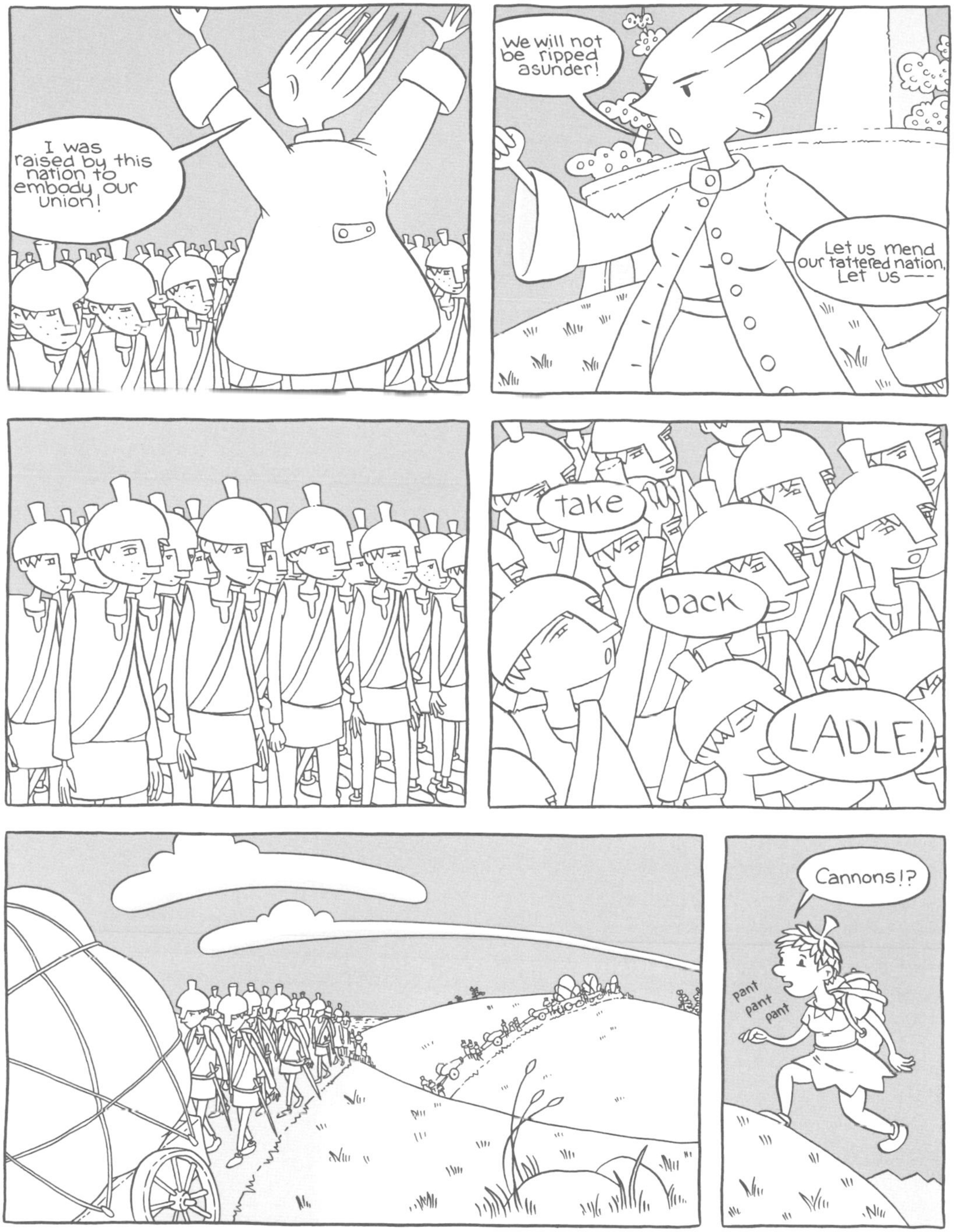
I was raised by this nation to embody our union!
We will not be ripped asunder!
Let us mend our tattered nation, Let us---
take
back
LADLE!
Cannons!?
pant pant pant

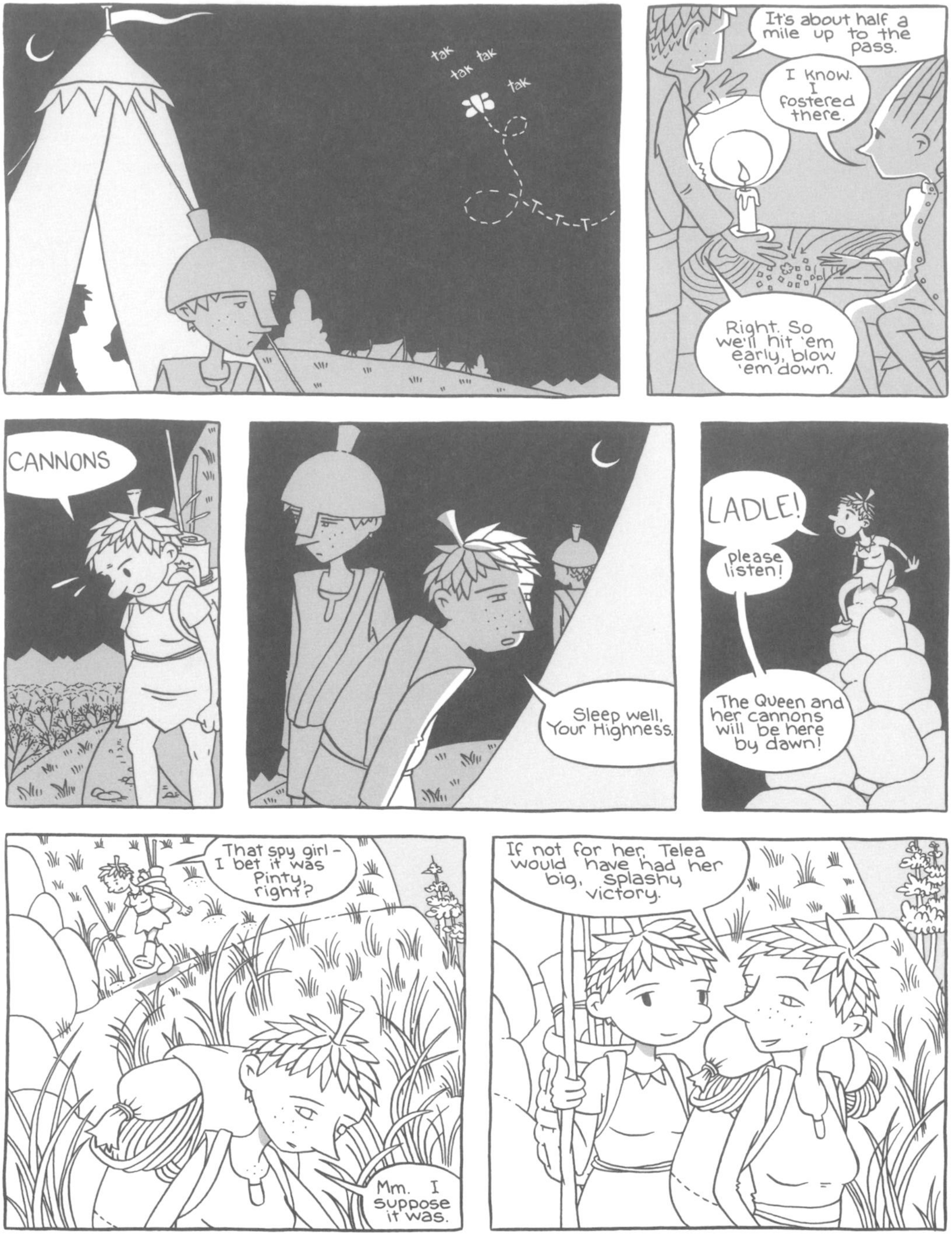
tak
tak tak
tak
-T--T--T-
It's about half a mile up to the pass.
I know. I fostered there.
Right. So we'll hit 'em early, blow 'em down.
CANNONS
Sleep well, Your Highness.
LADLE!
please listen!
The Queen and her cannons will be here by dawn!
That spy girl - I bet it was Pinty, right?
Mm. I suppose it was.
If not for her, Telea would have had her big, splashy victory.

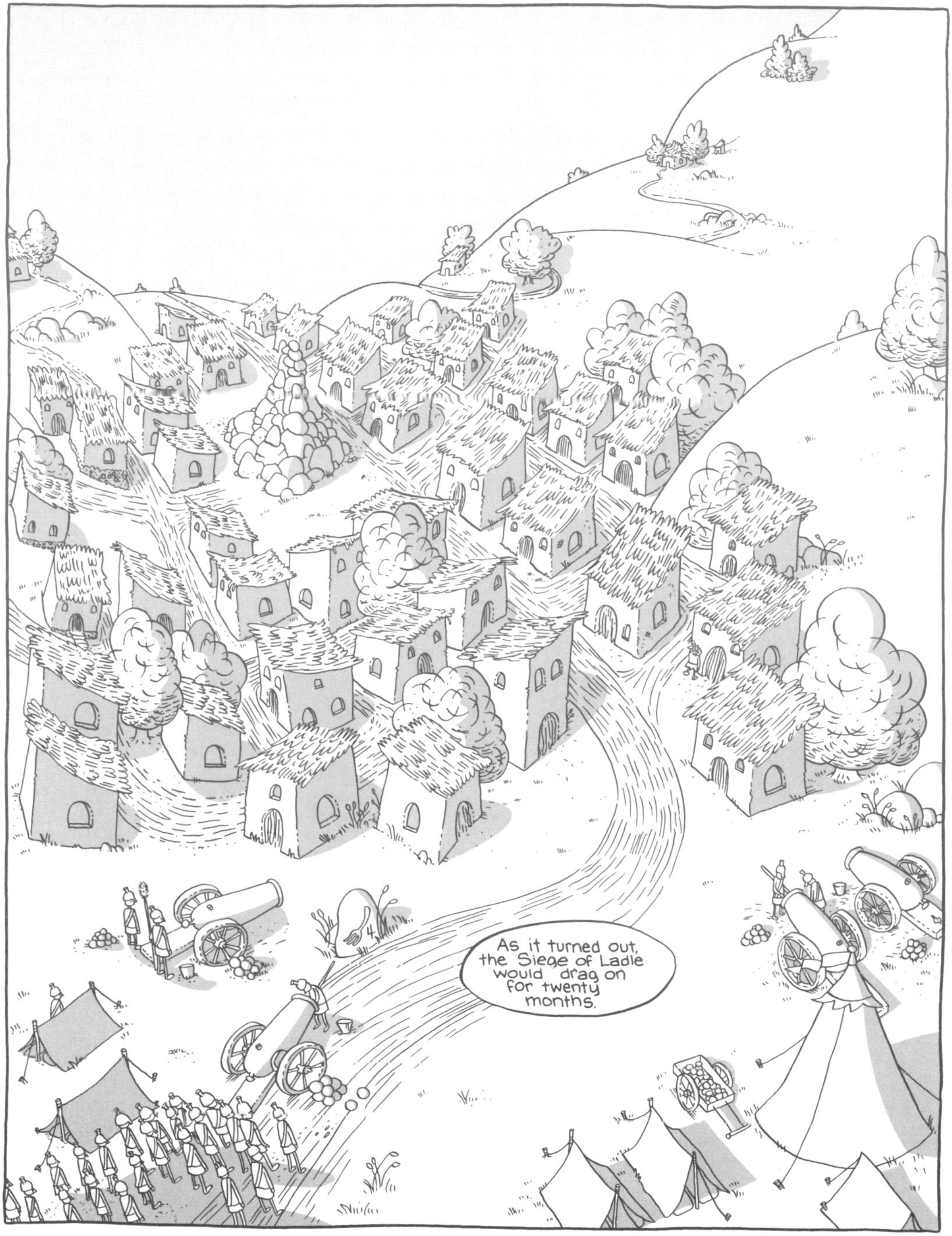
As it turned out, the Siege of Ladle would drag on for twenty months.

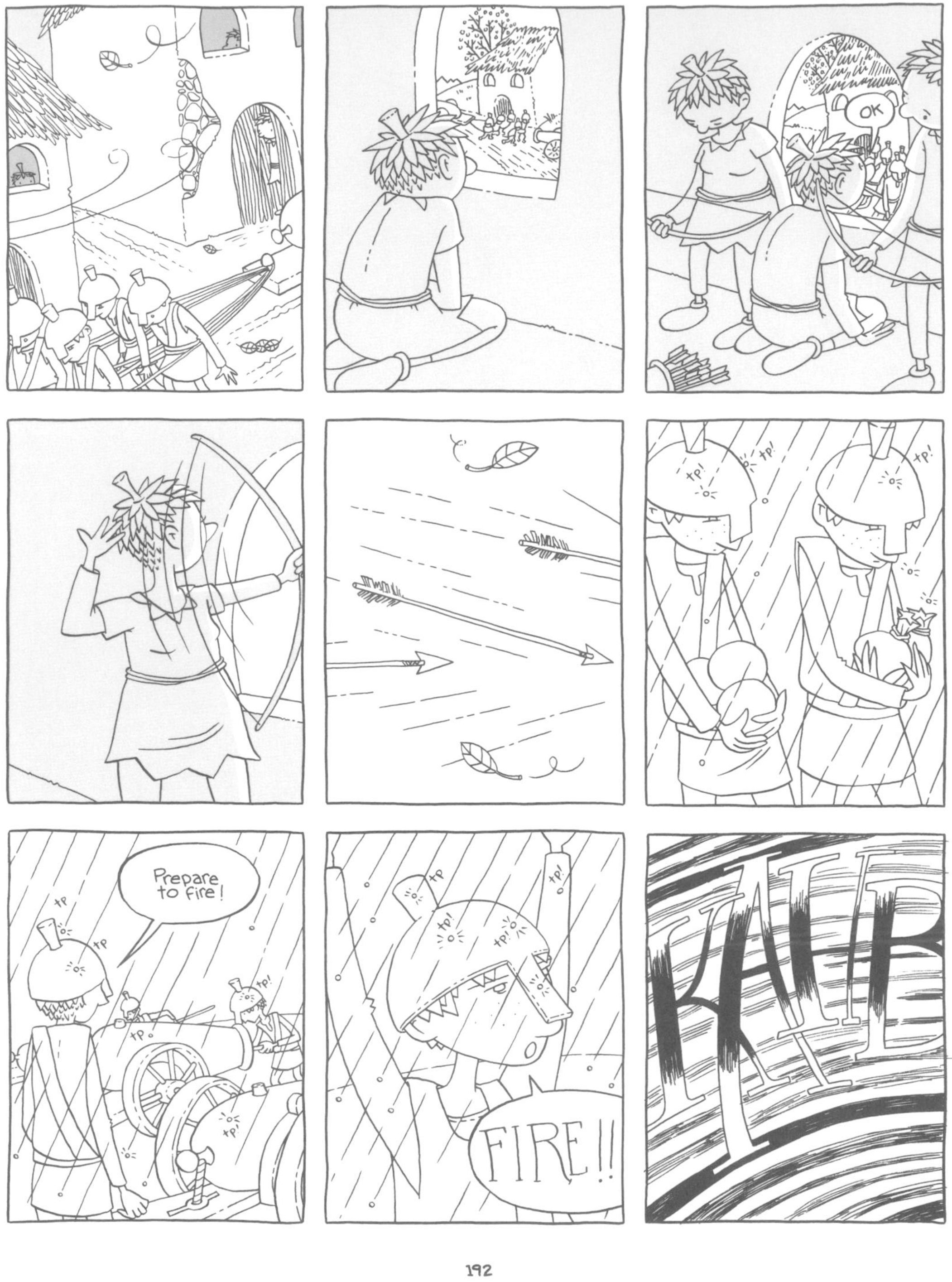
OK
tp! tp!
tp!
tp
tp
Prepare to fire!
tp!
tp
tp!
tp!
tp!
FIRE!!

BLOOM!
We smashed a few rebel nests today, but they got a couple of our guys too.
teep
teep
Big splashy victory.

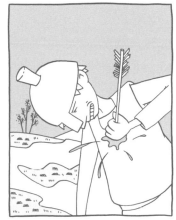

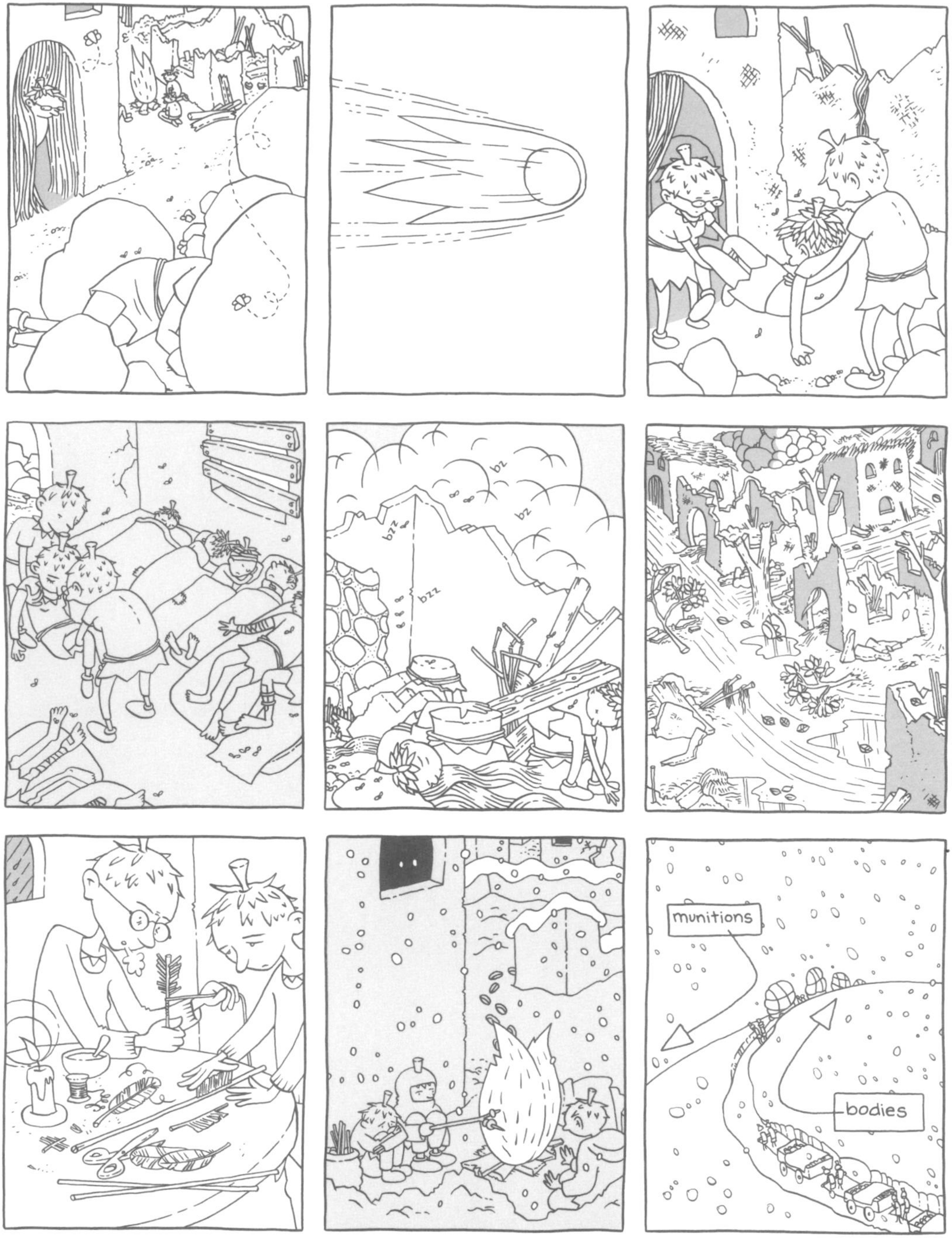
bzz
bzz
bz
bz
munitions
bodies

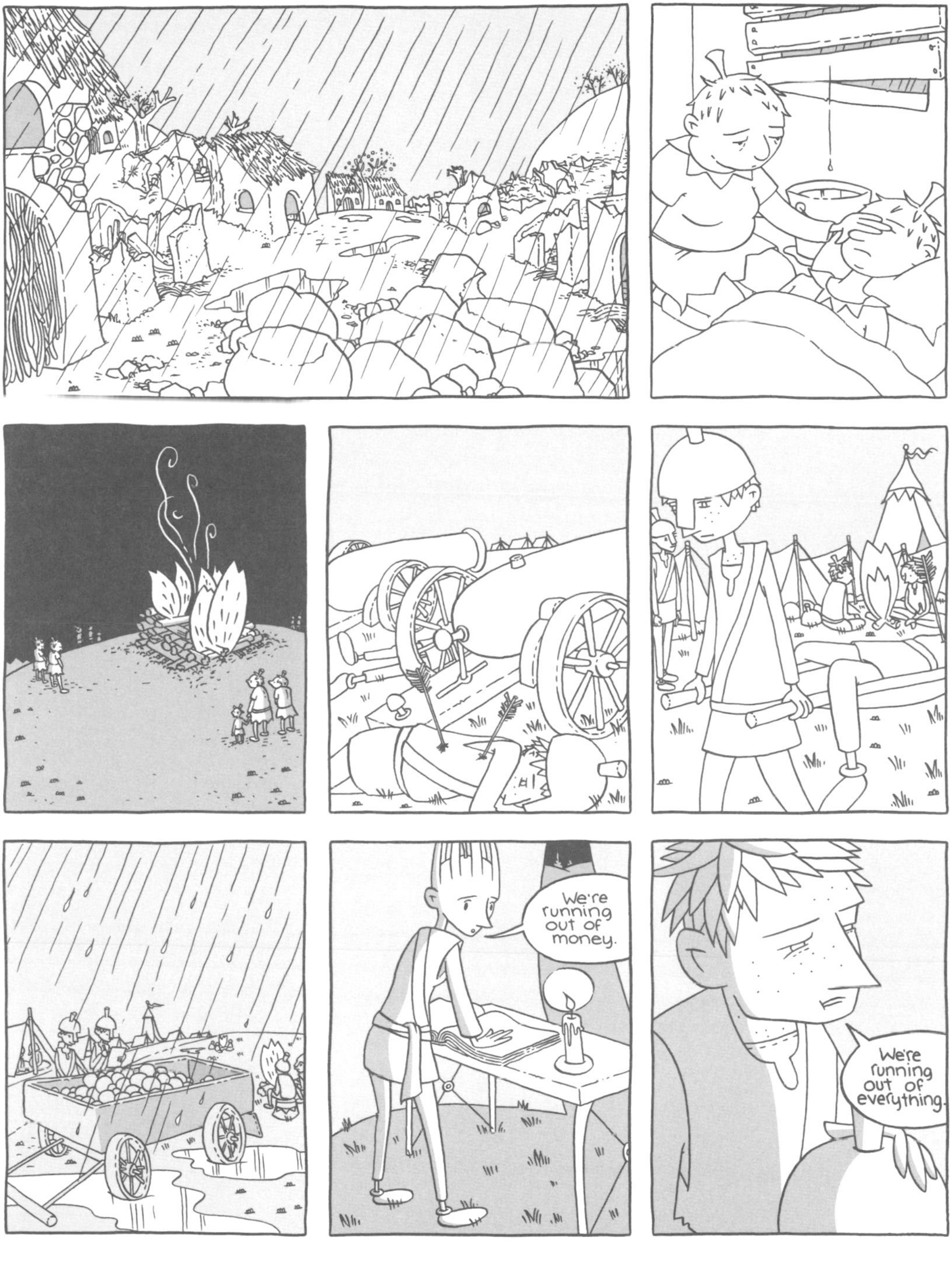
We're running out of money.
We're running out of everything.

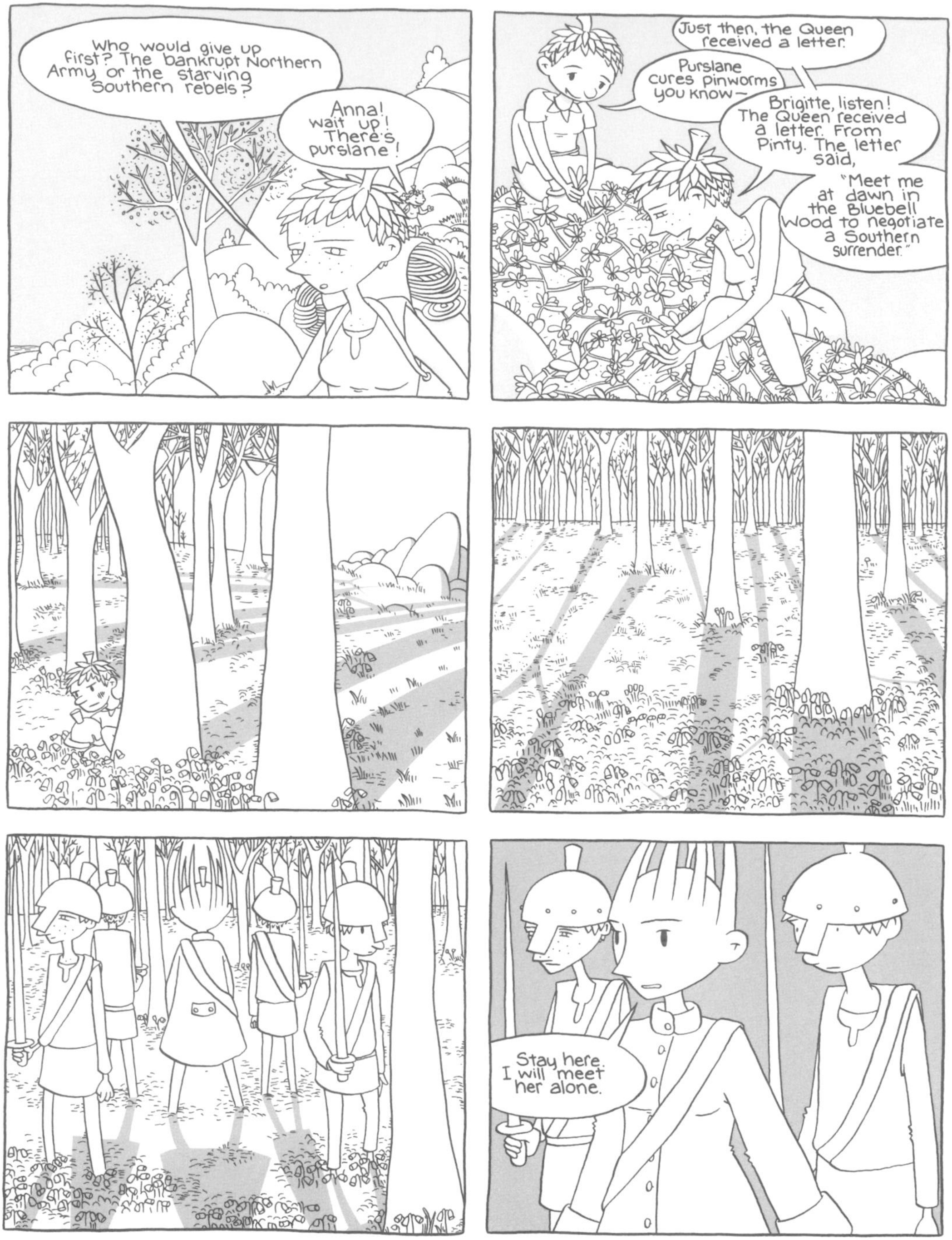

Who would give up first? The bankrupt Northern Army or the starving Southern rebels?
Anna! wait up! There's purslane!
Just then, the Queen received a letter.
Purslane cures pinworms you know—
Brigitte, listen! The Queen received a letter. From Pinty. The letter said,
"Meet me at dawn in the Bluebell Wood to negotiate a Southern surrender."
Stay here. I will meet her alone.

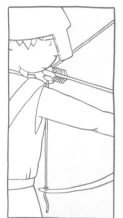

"A hero mourned only by vultures and bug song—

in the Blue Bell Wood lies nothing but bone."

So,

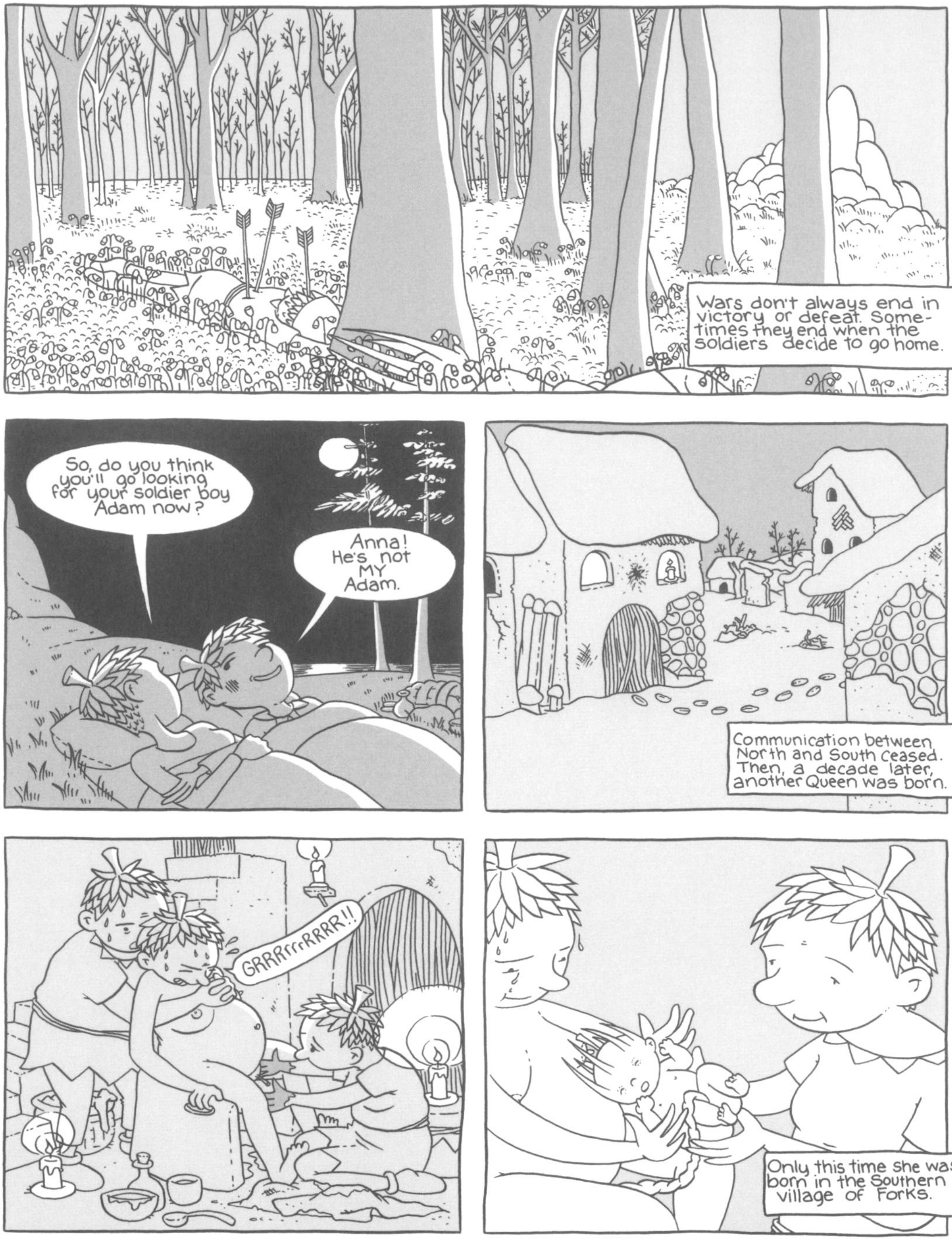
Wars don't always end in victory or defeat. Sometimes they end when the soldiers decide to go home.
So, do you think you'll go looking for your soldier boy Adam now?
Anna! He's not MY Adam.
Communication between North and South ceased. Then, a decade later, another Queen was born.
GRRRrrrRRRR!!
Only this time she was born in the Southern village of Forks.

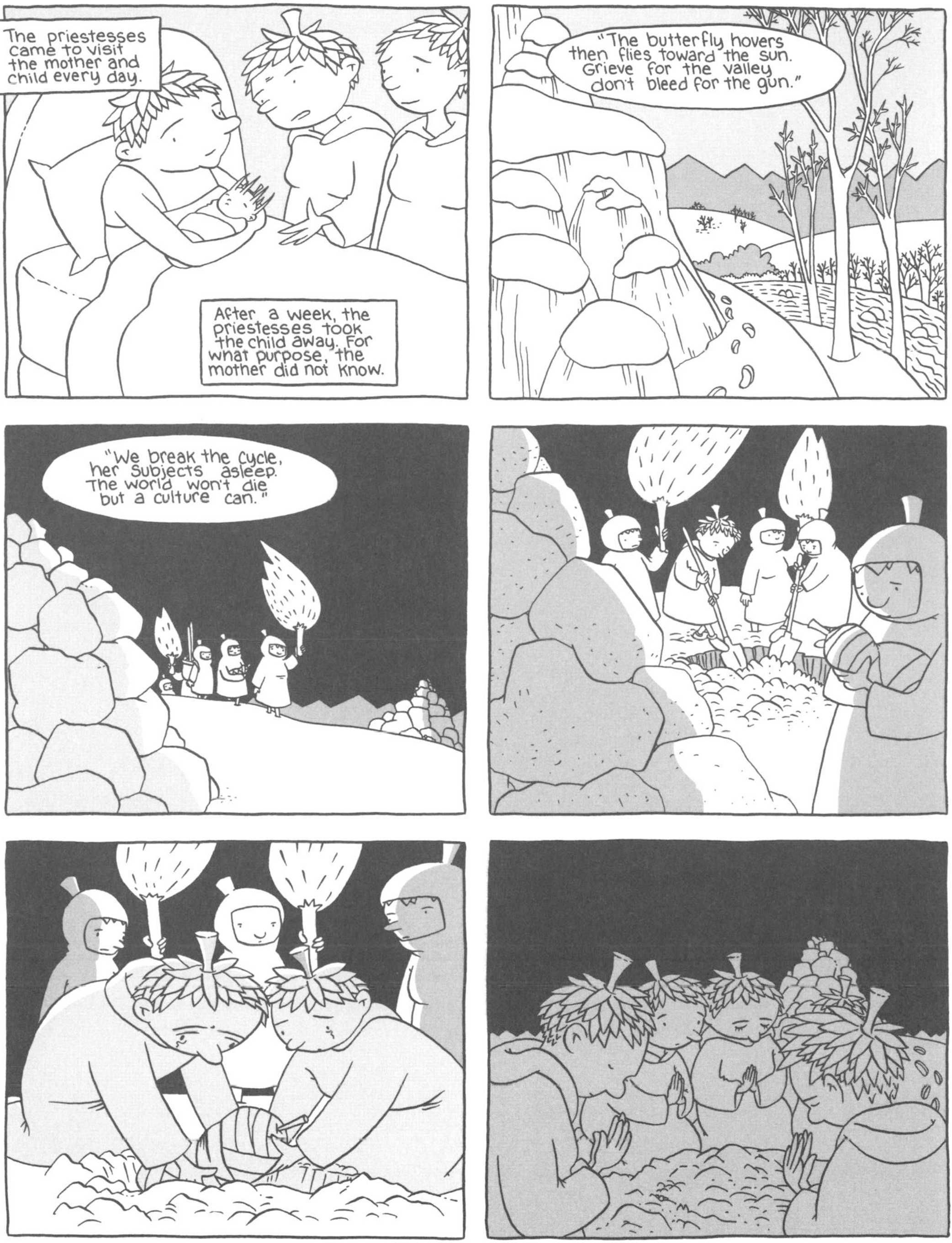
The priestesses came to visit the mother and child every day.
After a week, the priestesses took the child away. For what purpose, the mother did not know.
"The butterfly hovers then flies toward the sun. Grieve for the valley don't bleed for the gun."
"We break the cycle, her Subjects asleep. The world won't die but a culture can."

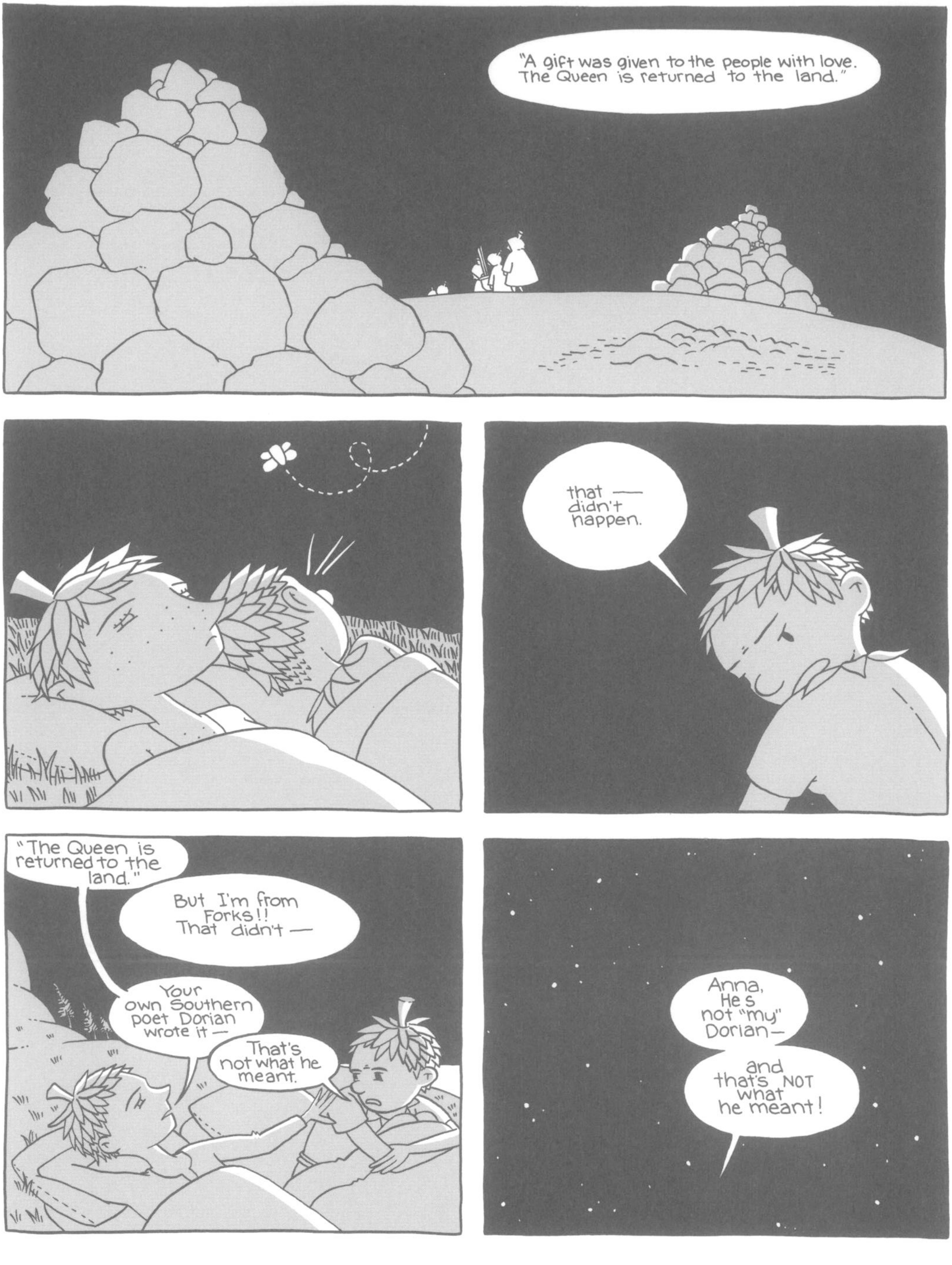
"A gift was given to the people with love. The Queen is returned to the land."
that — didn't happen.
"The Queen is returned to the land."
But I'm from Forks!! That didn't —
Your own Southern poet Dorian wrote it —
That's not what he meant.
Anna, He's not "my" Dorian —
and that's NOT what he meant!

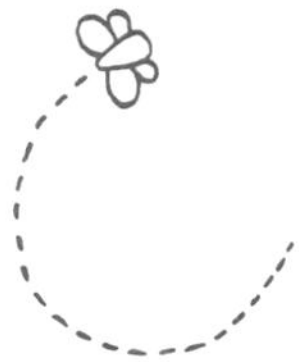

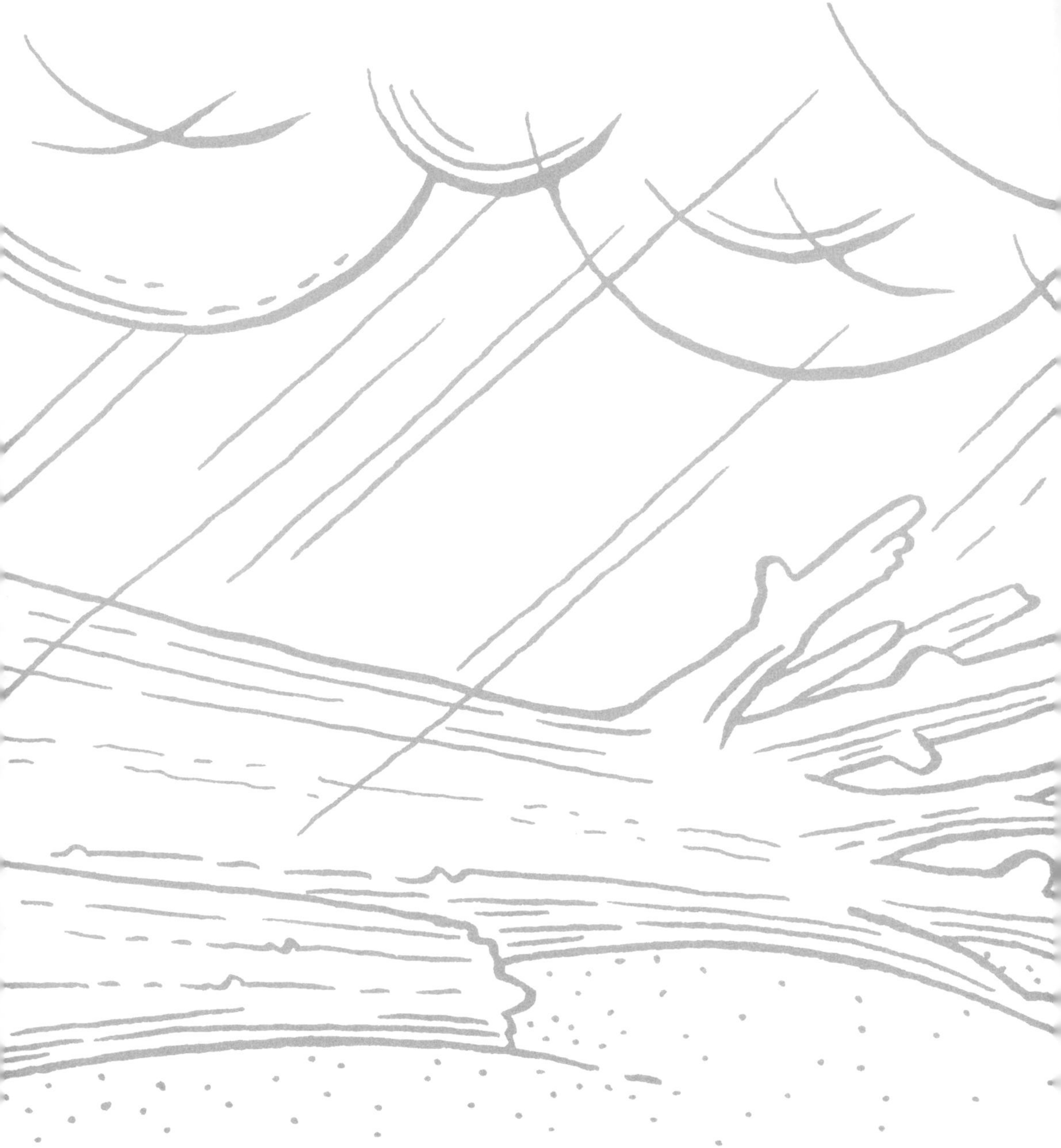

Chapter 6
SUMMER SHRINE

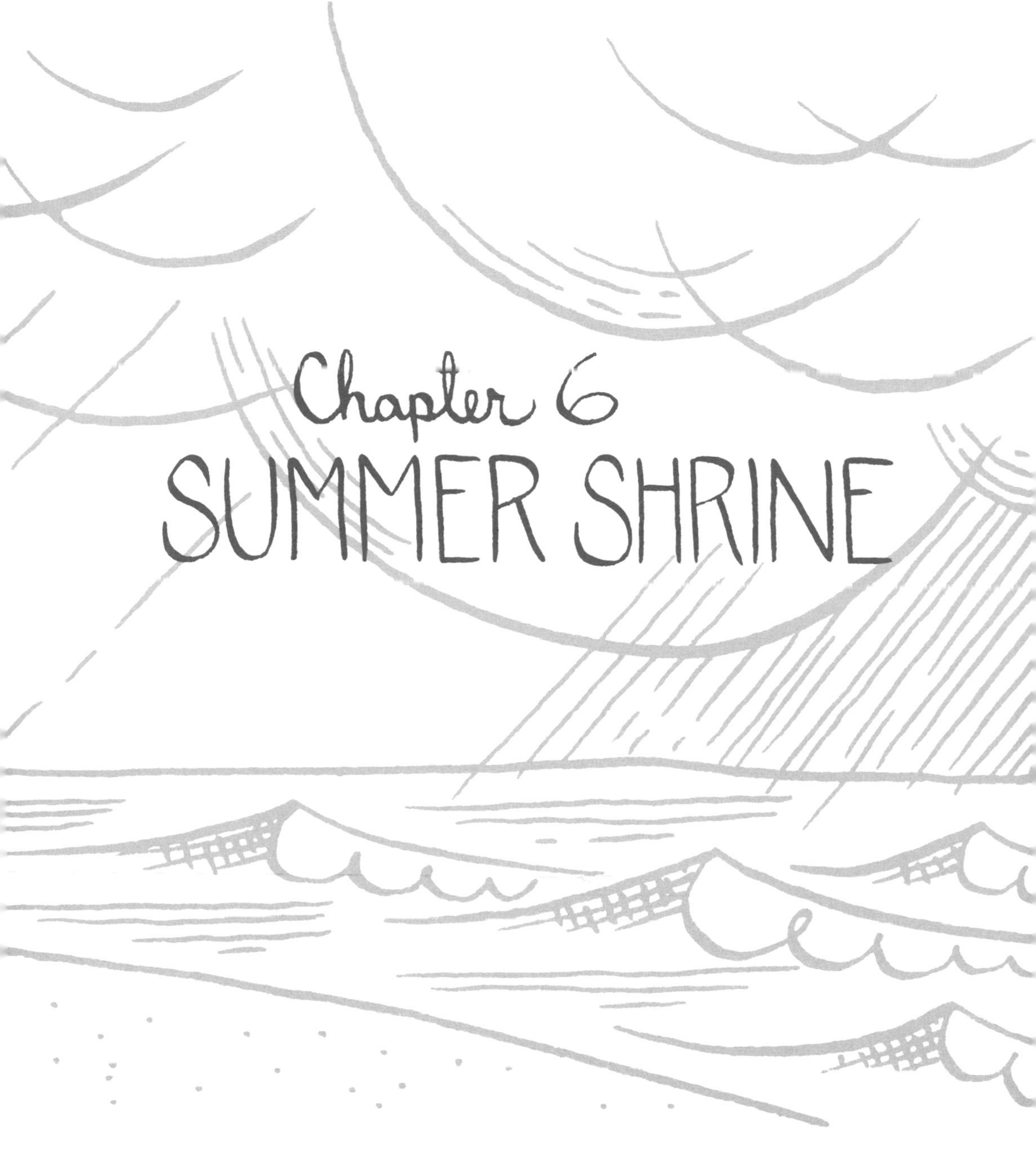

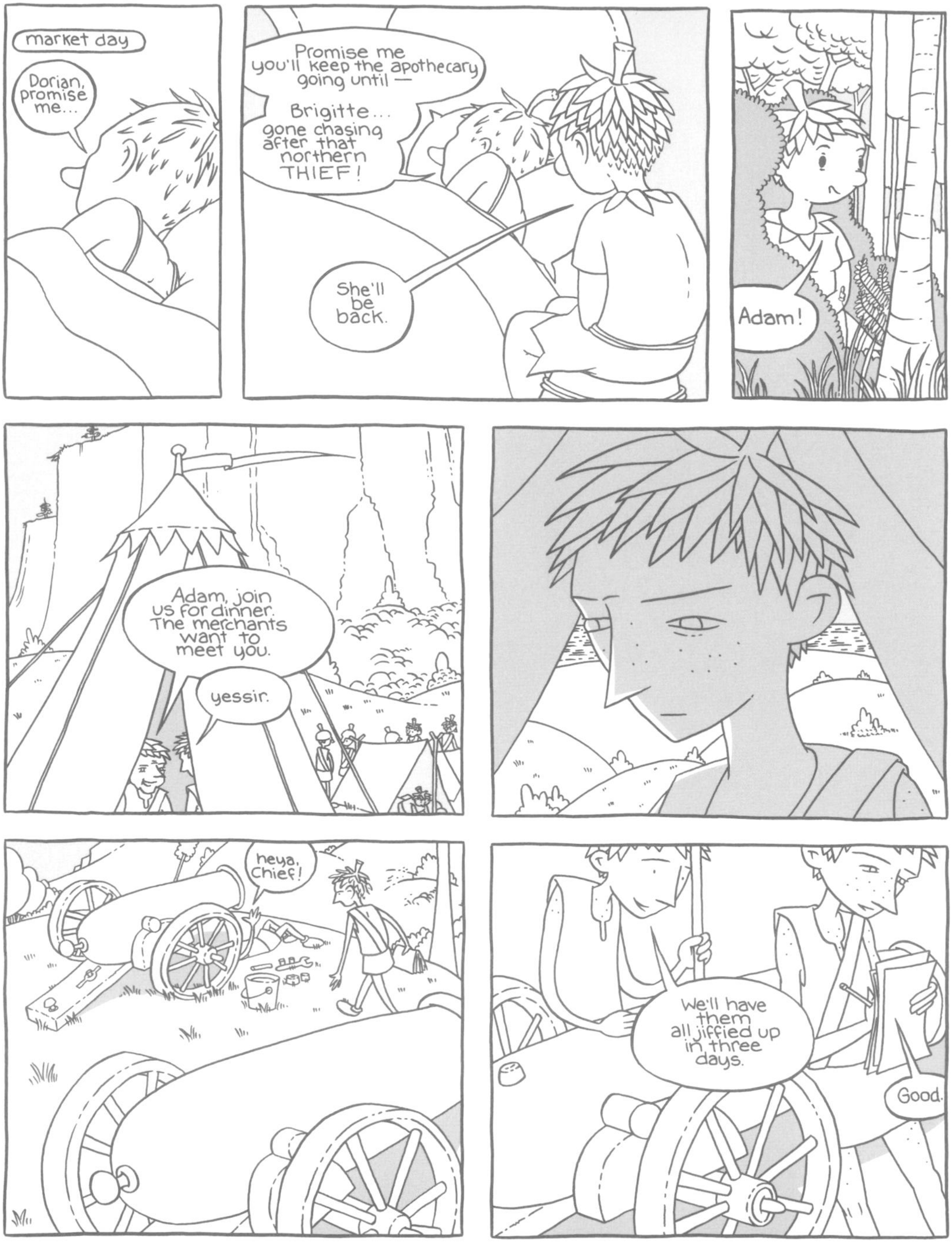
market day
Dorian, promise me...
Promise me you'll keep the apothecary going until —
Brigitte... gone chasing after that northern THIEF!
She'll be back.
Adam!
Adam, join us for dinner. The merchants want to meet you.
yessir.
heya, Chief!
We'll have them all jiffied up in three days.
Good.

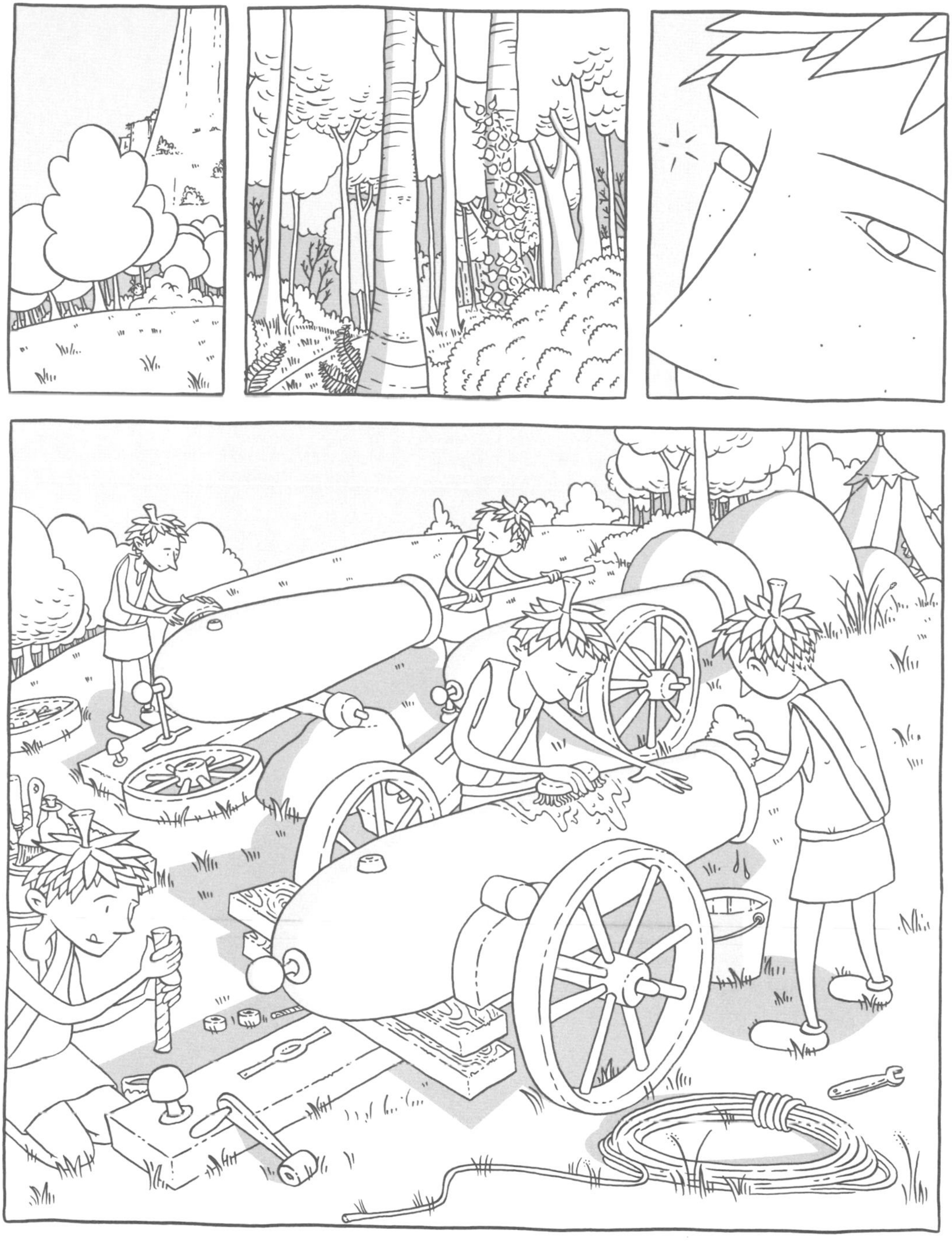

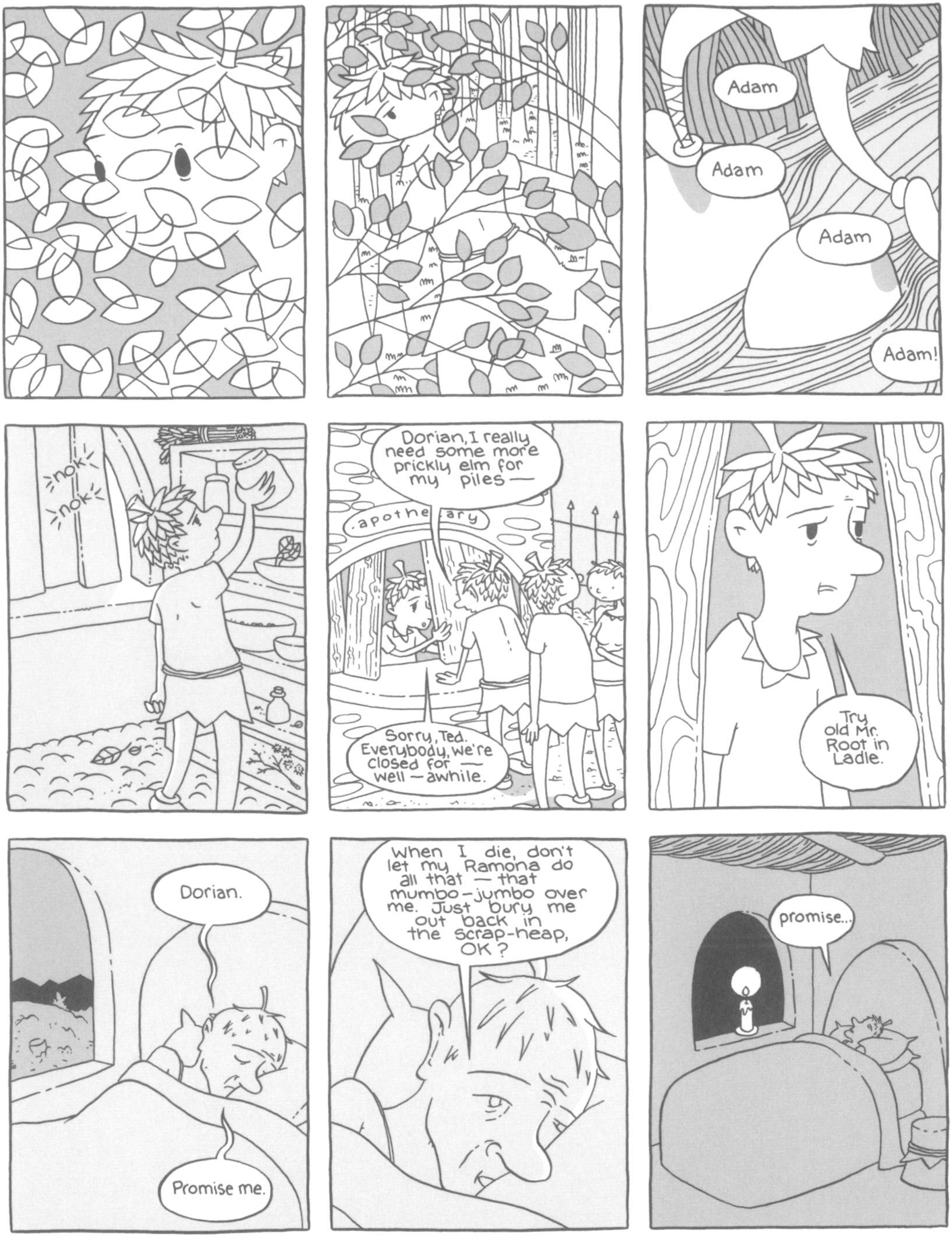
Adam
Adam
Adam
Adam!
nok
nok
Dorian, I really need some more prickly elm for my piles —
apothecary
Sorry, Ted. Everybody, we're closed for — well — awhile.
Try old Mr. Root in Ladle.
Dorian.
Promise me.
When I die, don't let my Ramona do all that — that mumbo-jumbo over me. Just bury me out back in the scrap-heap, OK?
promise...

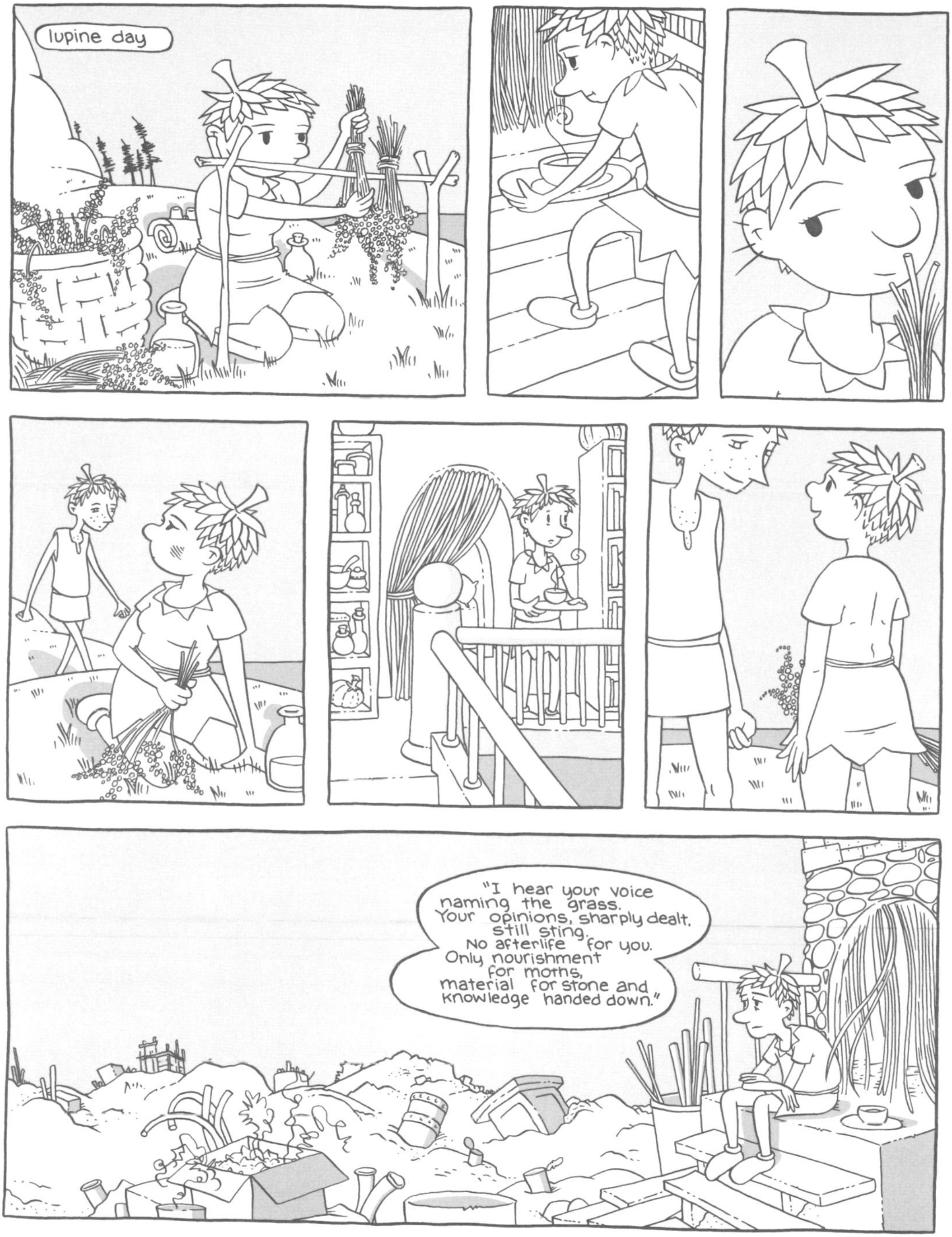
lupine day
"I hear your voice naming the grass.
Your opinions, sharply dealt, still sting.
No afterlife for you.
Only nourishment for moths,
material for stone and knowledge handed down."

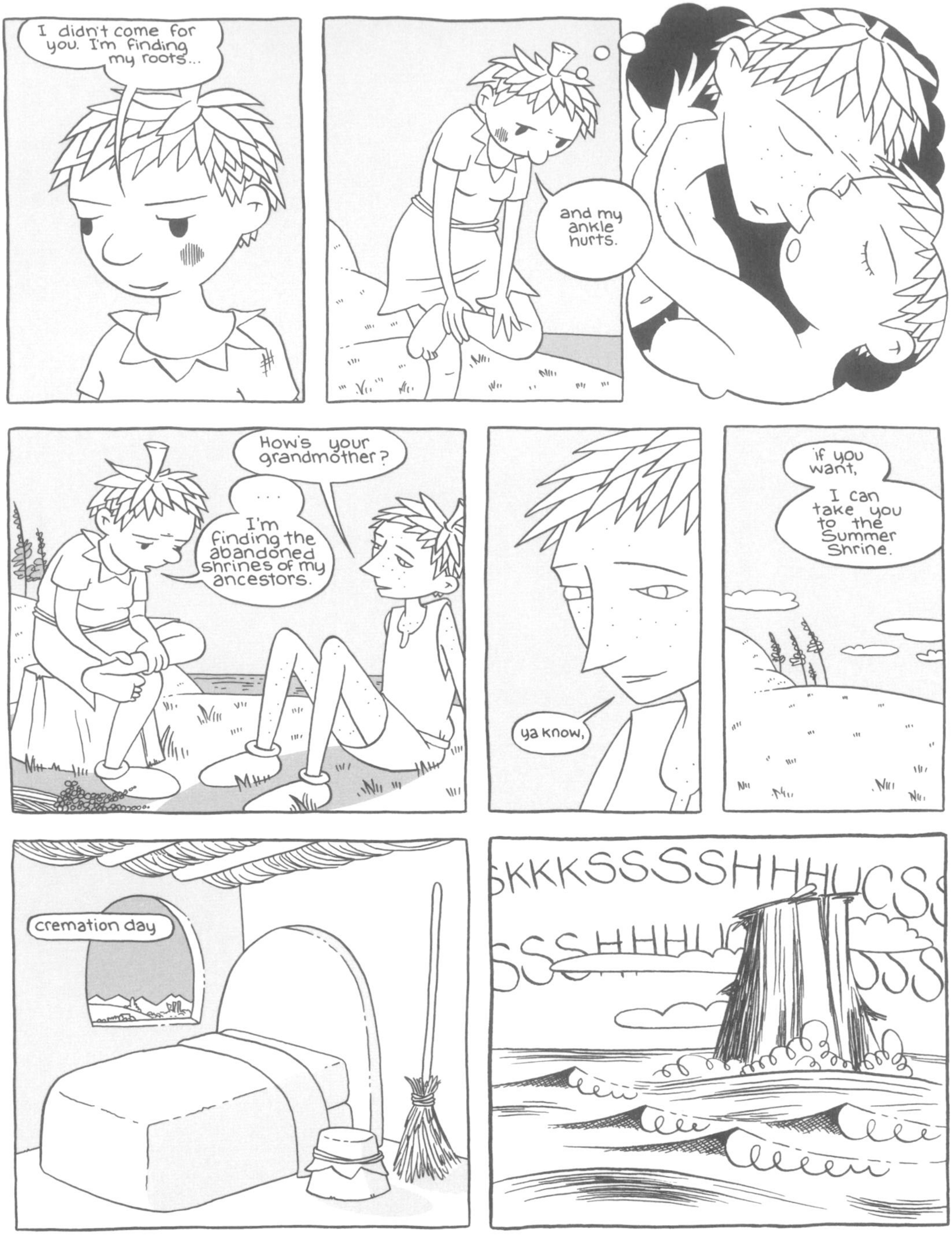
I didn't come for you. I'm finding my roots...
and my ankle hurts.
How's your grandmother?
...
I'm finding the abandoned shrines of my ancestors.
ya know,
if you want,
I can take you to the Summer Shrine.
cremation day
SKKKSSSSSHHHUCSS
SSSSHHHHU

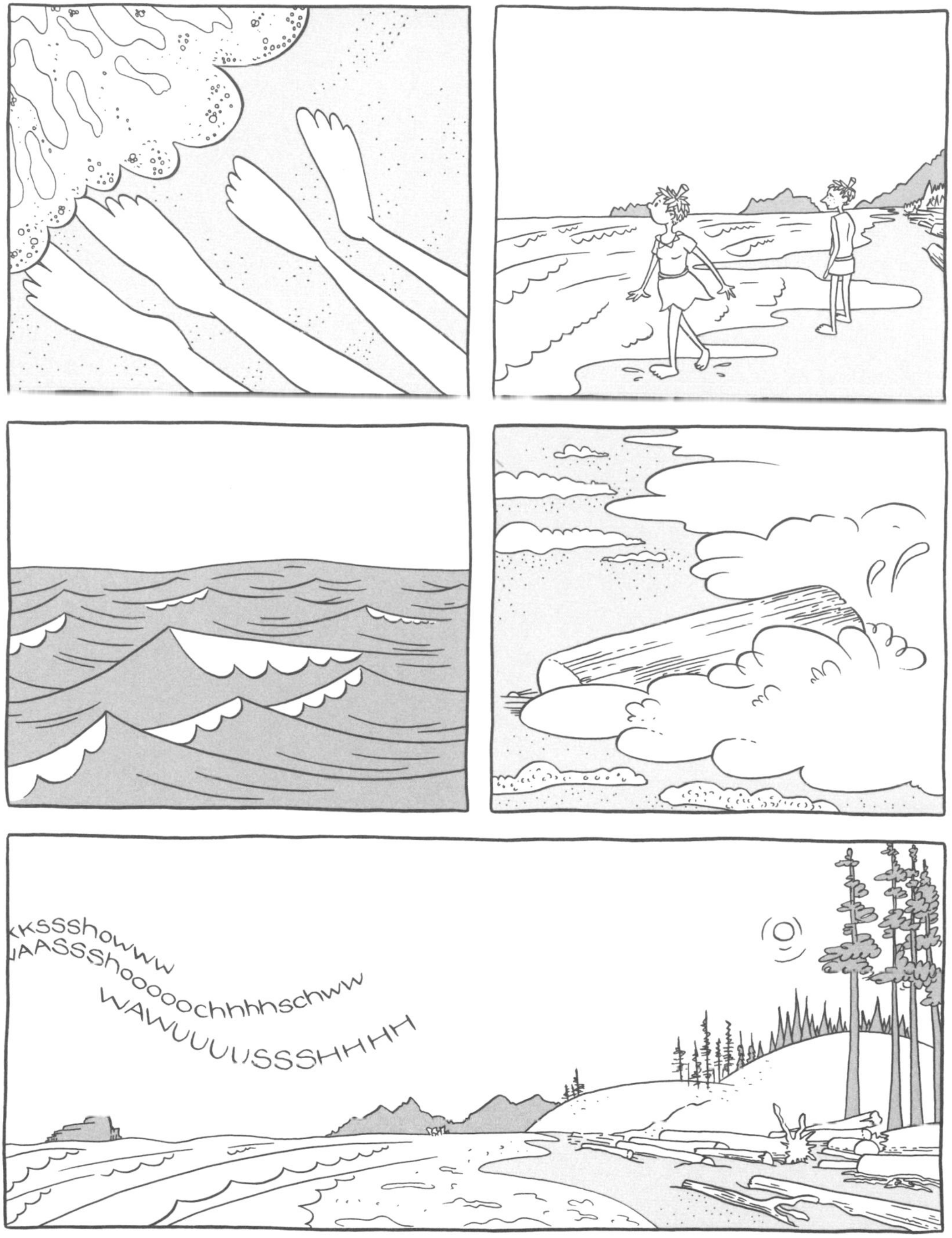
kkSSShowww
AASSShoooooochhhhschww
WAWUUUUSSSSHHHH

SSHOWWW
sssshoochh
wwuuushh

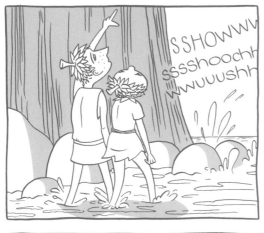

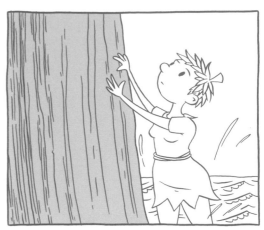

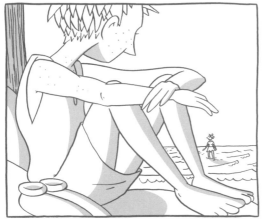

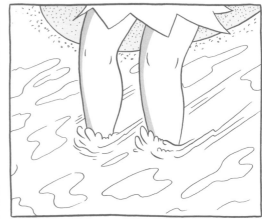

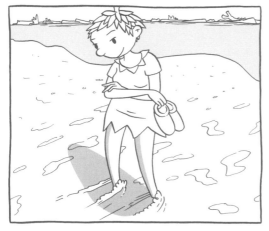

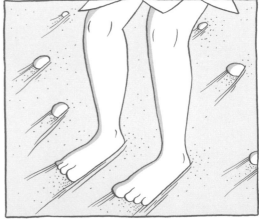

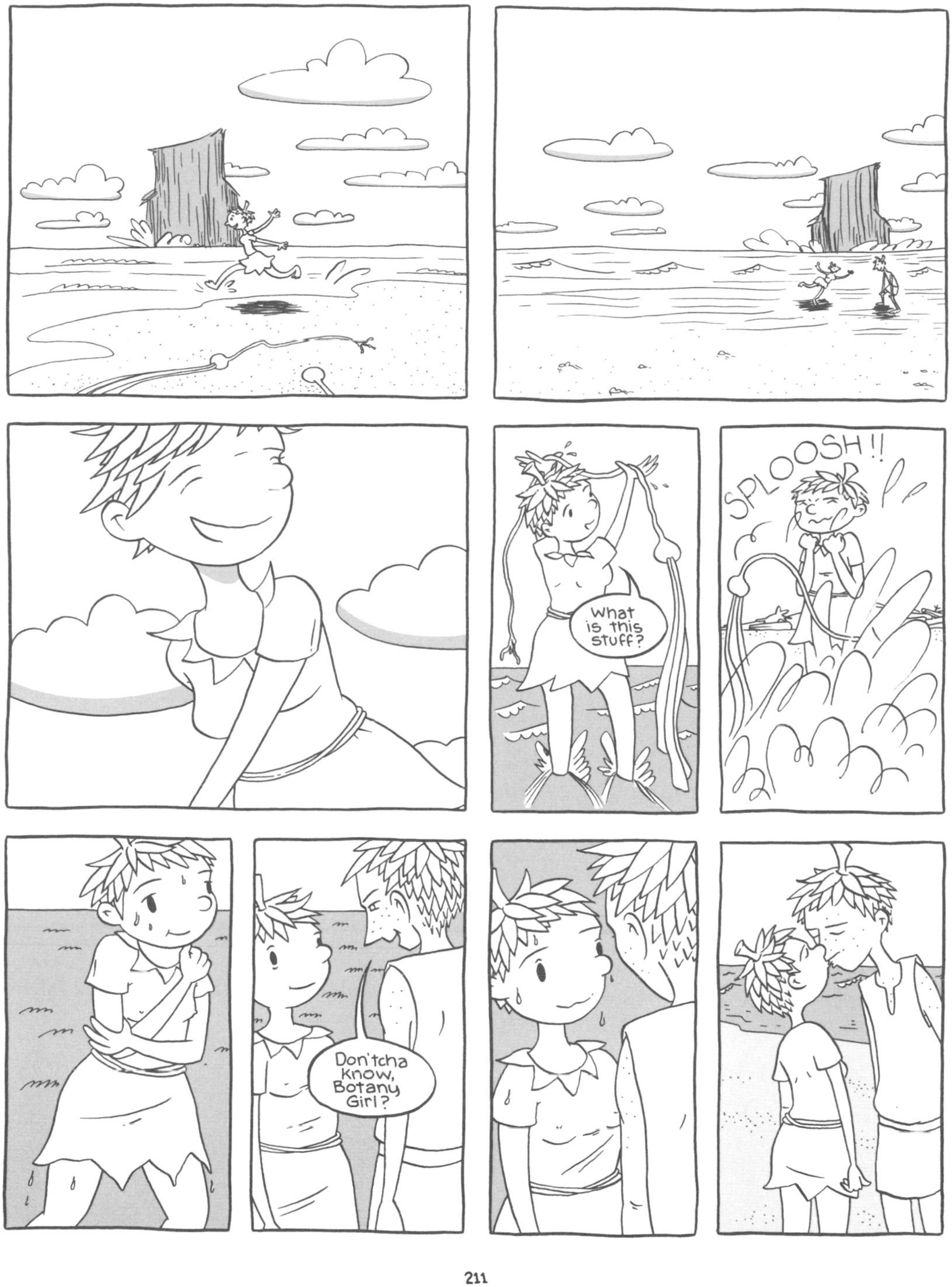
What is this stuff?
SPLOOSH!!
Don'tcha know, Botany Girl?

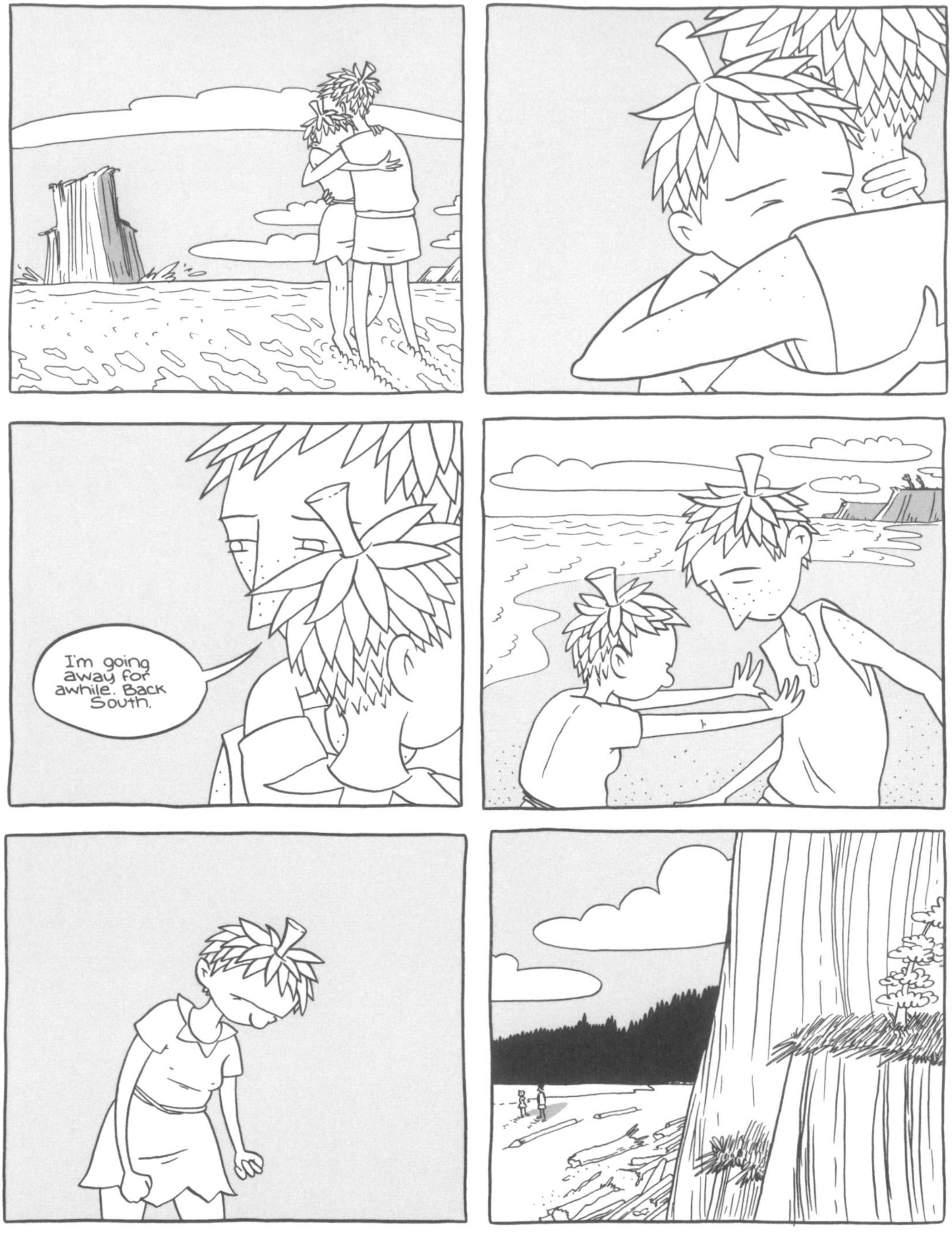
I'm going away for awhile. Back South.

Going South to smash up some towns?

Nooo... to guarantee the safety of the fish merchants—

...and the occasional display of firepower will keep prices conveniently high.

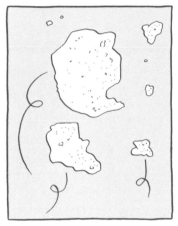

Brigitte, it's not like that — it's a security mission.

I know everything now, Adam — about the war and after and—

You can't fool me anymore with your reasonable-sounding voice.

Brigitte...

Brigitte.

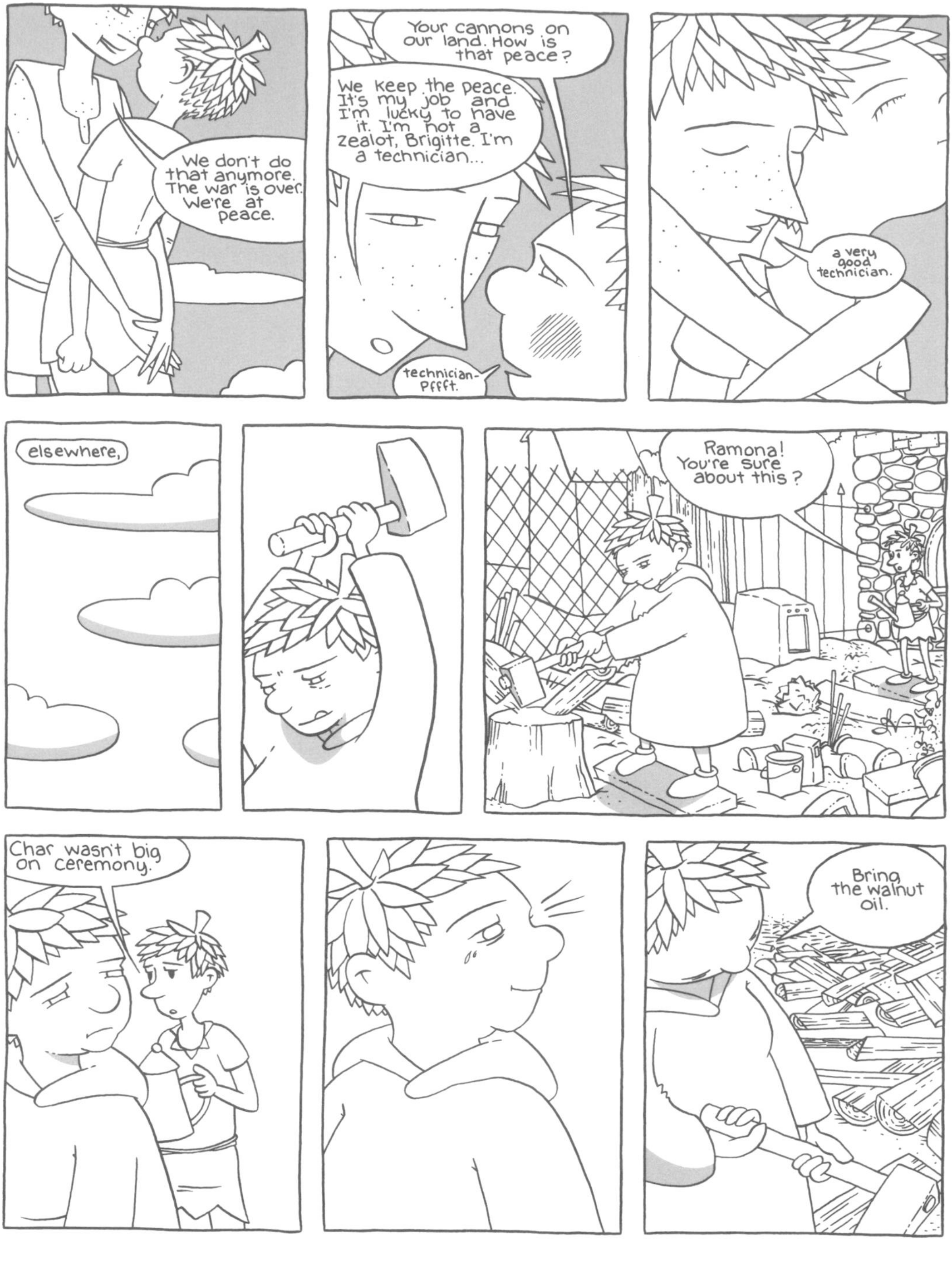
We don't do that anymore. The war is over. We're at peace.
Your cannons on our land. How is that peace?
We keep the peace. It's my job and I'm lucky to have it. I'm not a zealot, Brigitte. I'm a technician...
technician- Pffft.
a very good technician.
elsewhere,
Ramona! You're sure about this?
Char wasn't big on ceremony.
Bring the walnut oil.

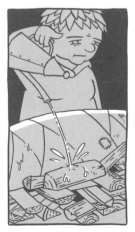

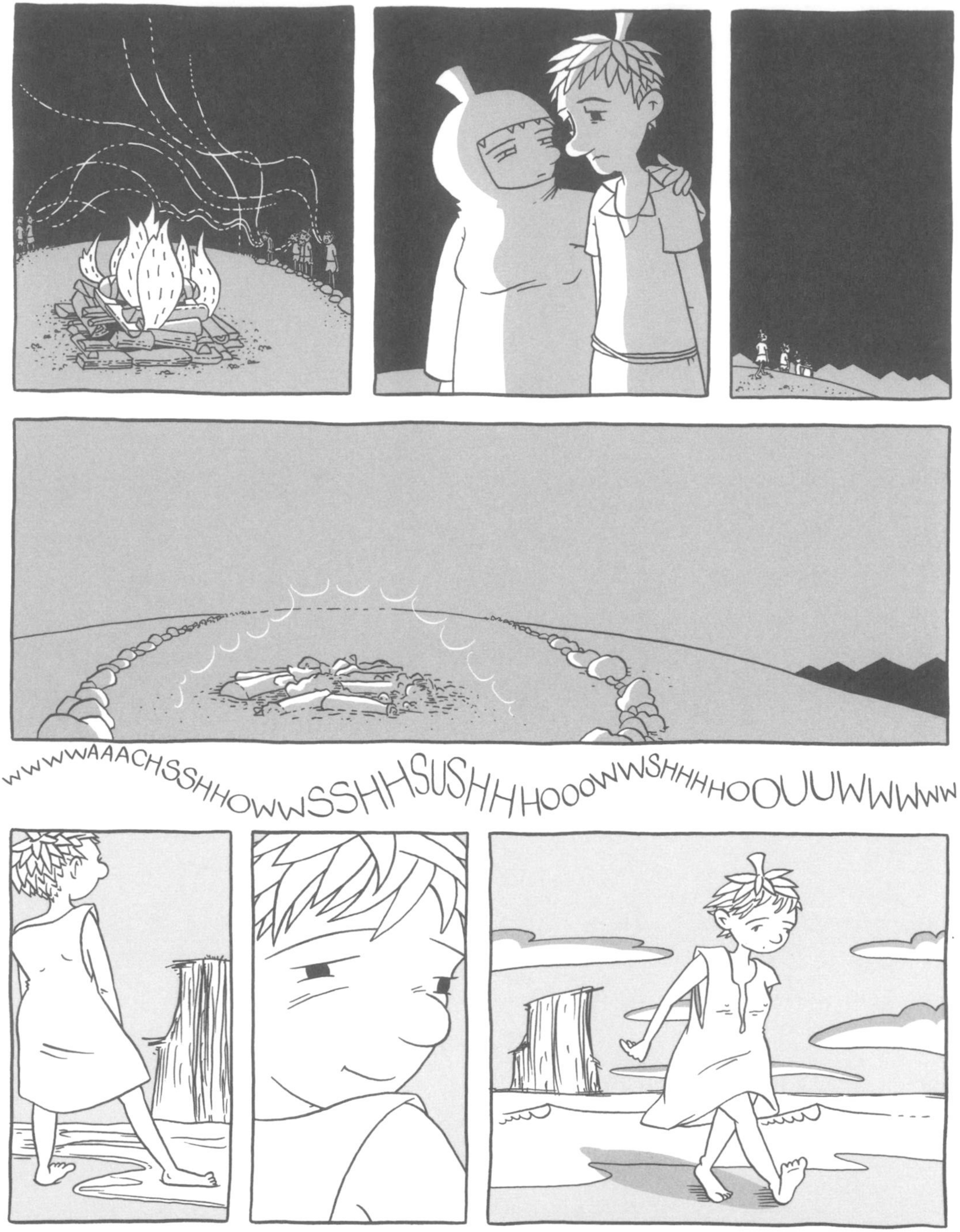
WWWWAAACHSSHHOWWSSHHSUSHHHOOOWWSHHHHOOUUWWWWW

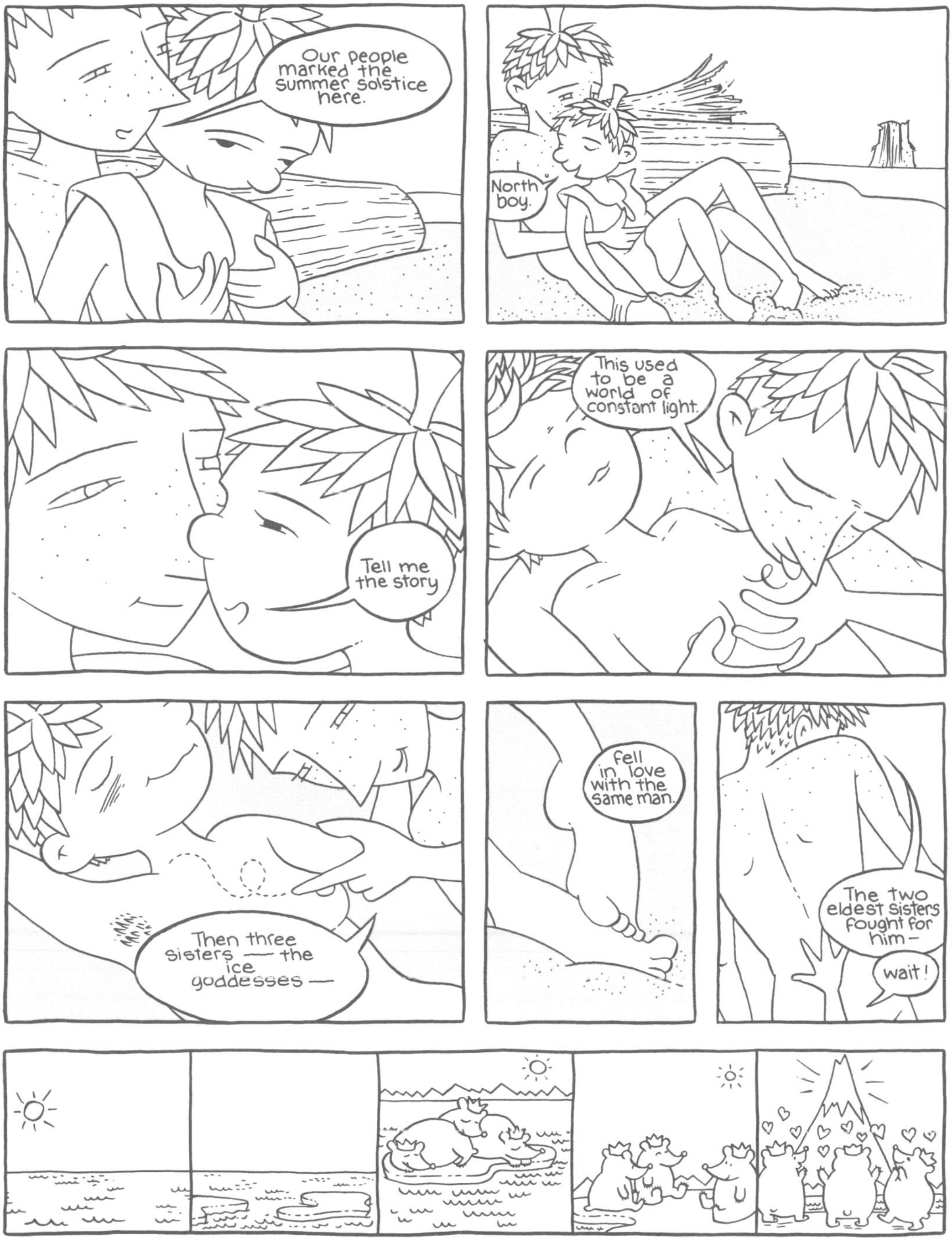
Our people marked the summer solstice here.
North boy.
Tell me the story
This used to be a world of constant light.
Then three sisters — the ice goddesses —
fell in love with the same man.
The two eldest sisters fought for him —
wait!

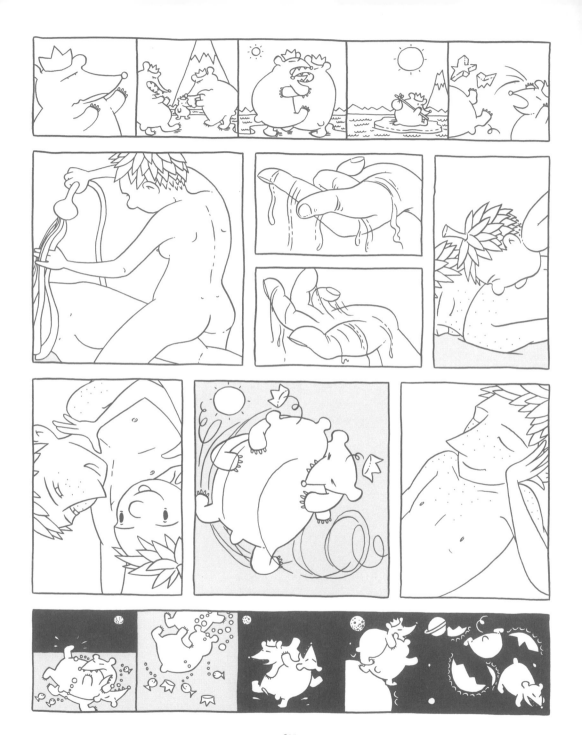

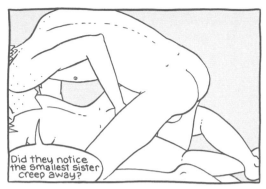

Did they notice the smallest sister creep away?

Did they notice when they broke the sun?

Which sister won?

Neither.

And the smallest sister found her man too late.

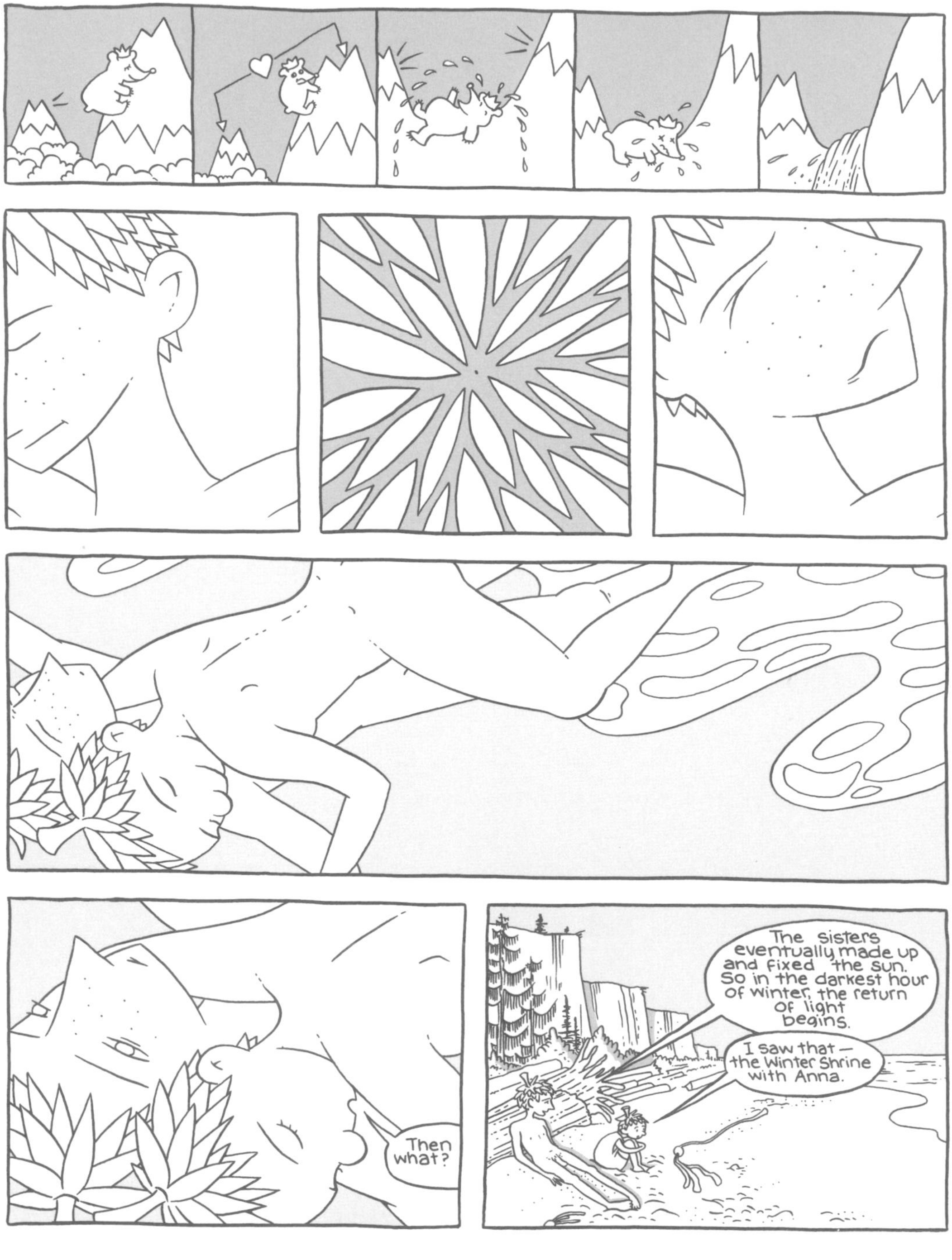
Then what?
The sisters eventually made up and fixed the sun. So in the darkest hour of winter, the return of light begins.
I saw that— the Winter Shrine with Anna.

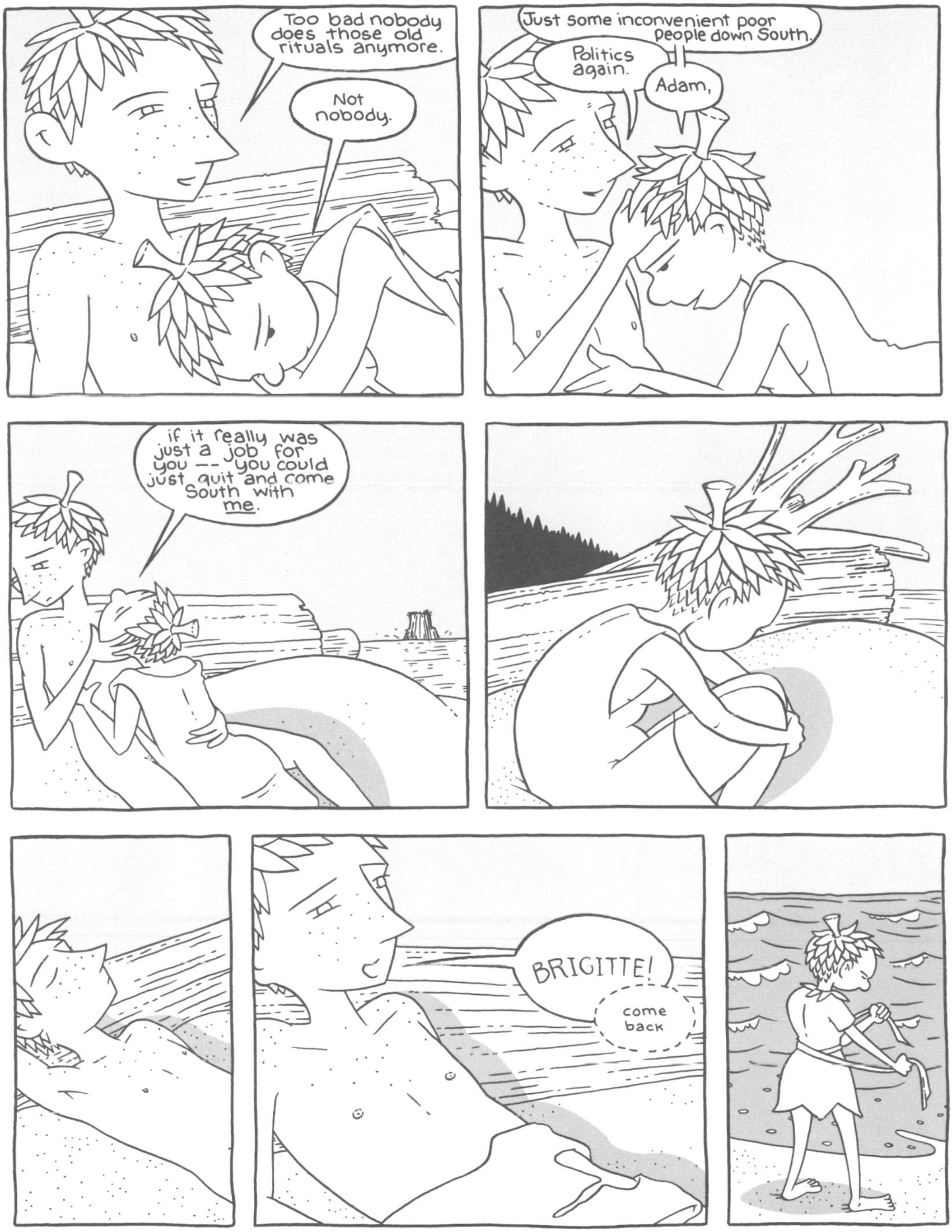
Too bad nobody does those old rituals anymore.
Not nobody.
Just some inconvenient poor people down South.
Politics again.
Adam,
if it really was just a job for you -- you could just quit and come South with me.
BRIGITTE!
come back

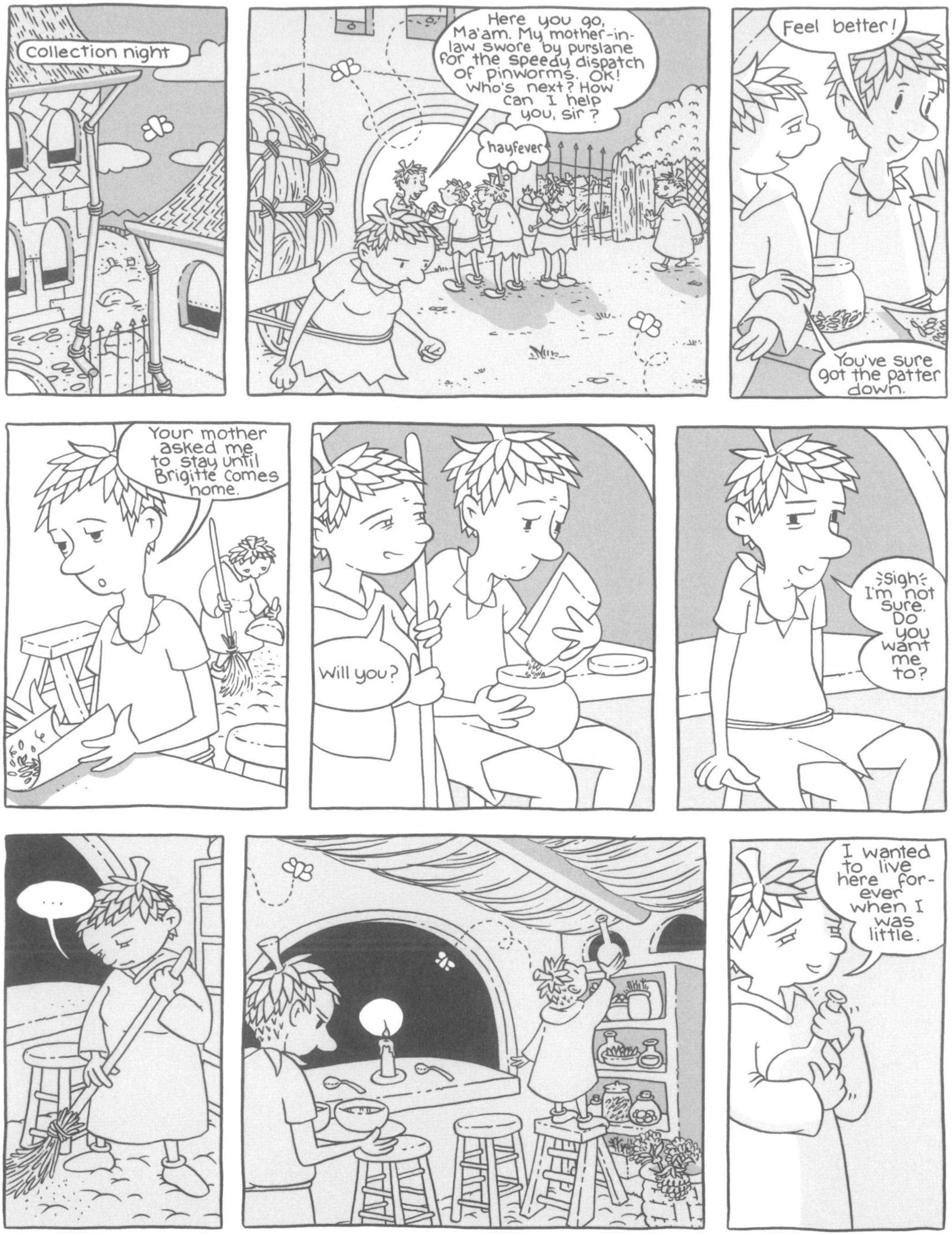
Collection night
Here you go, Ma'am. My mother-in-law swore by purslane for the speedy dispatch of pinworms. OK! Who's next? How can I help you, sir?
hayfever
Feel better!
You've sure got the patter down.
Your mother asked me to stay until Brigitte comes home.
Will you?
Sigh I'm not sure. Do you want me to?
...
I wanted to live here for-ever when I was little.

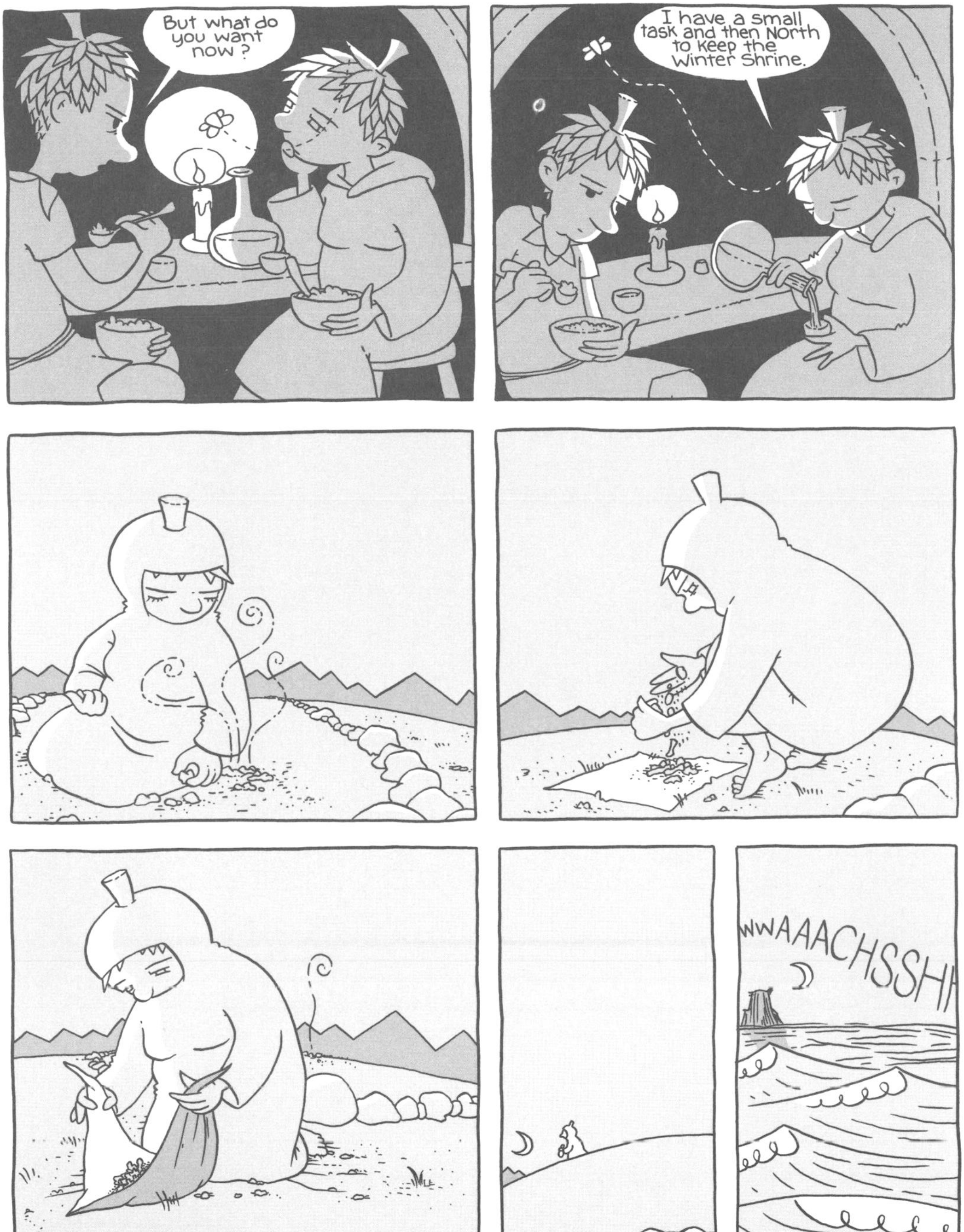
But what do you want now?
I have a small task and then North to keep the Winter Shrine.
WWAAACHSSH

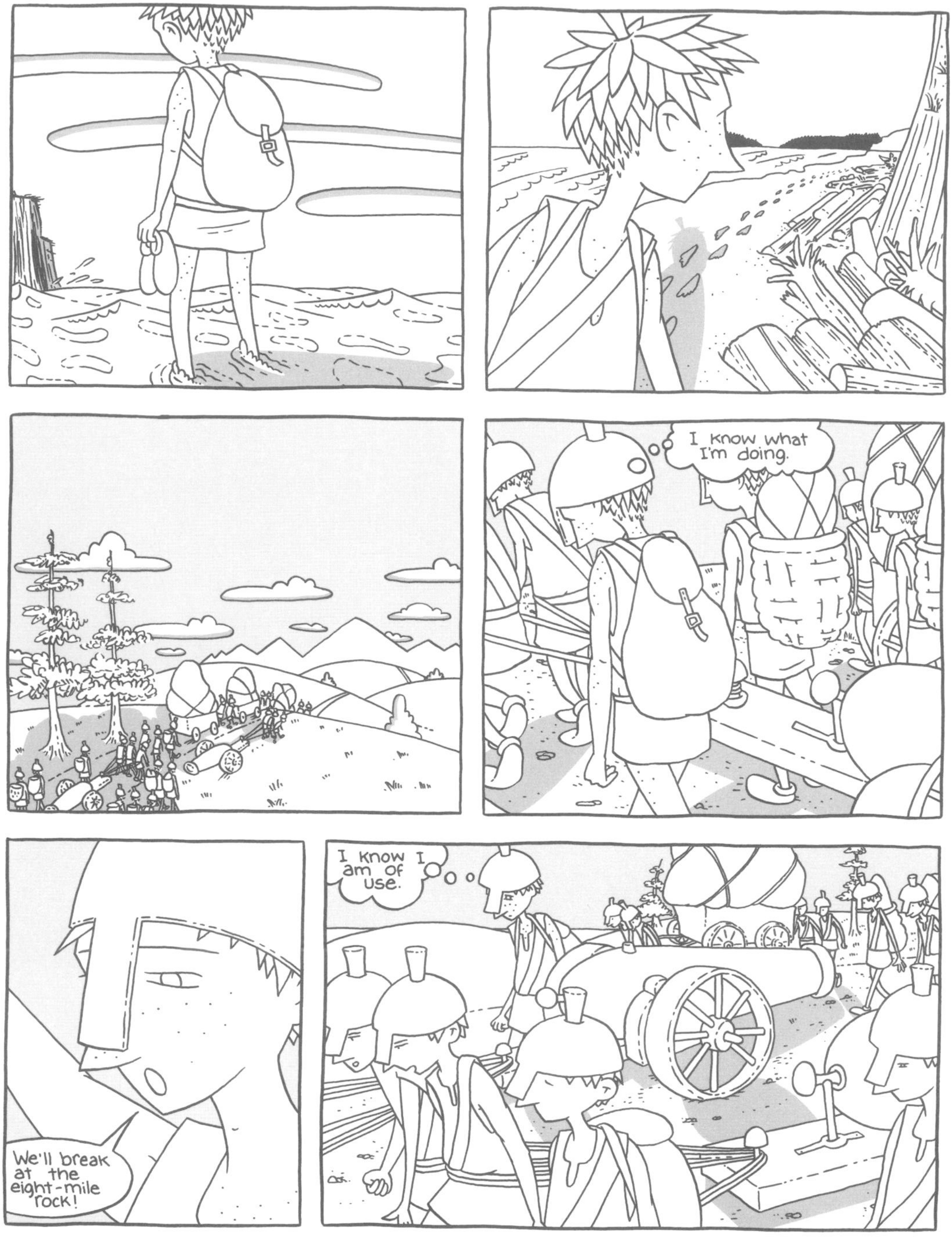
I know what I'm doing.
We'll break at the eight-mile rock!
I know I am of use.

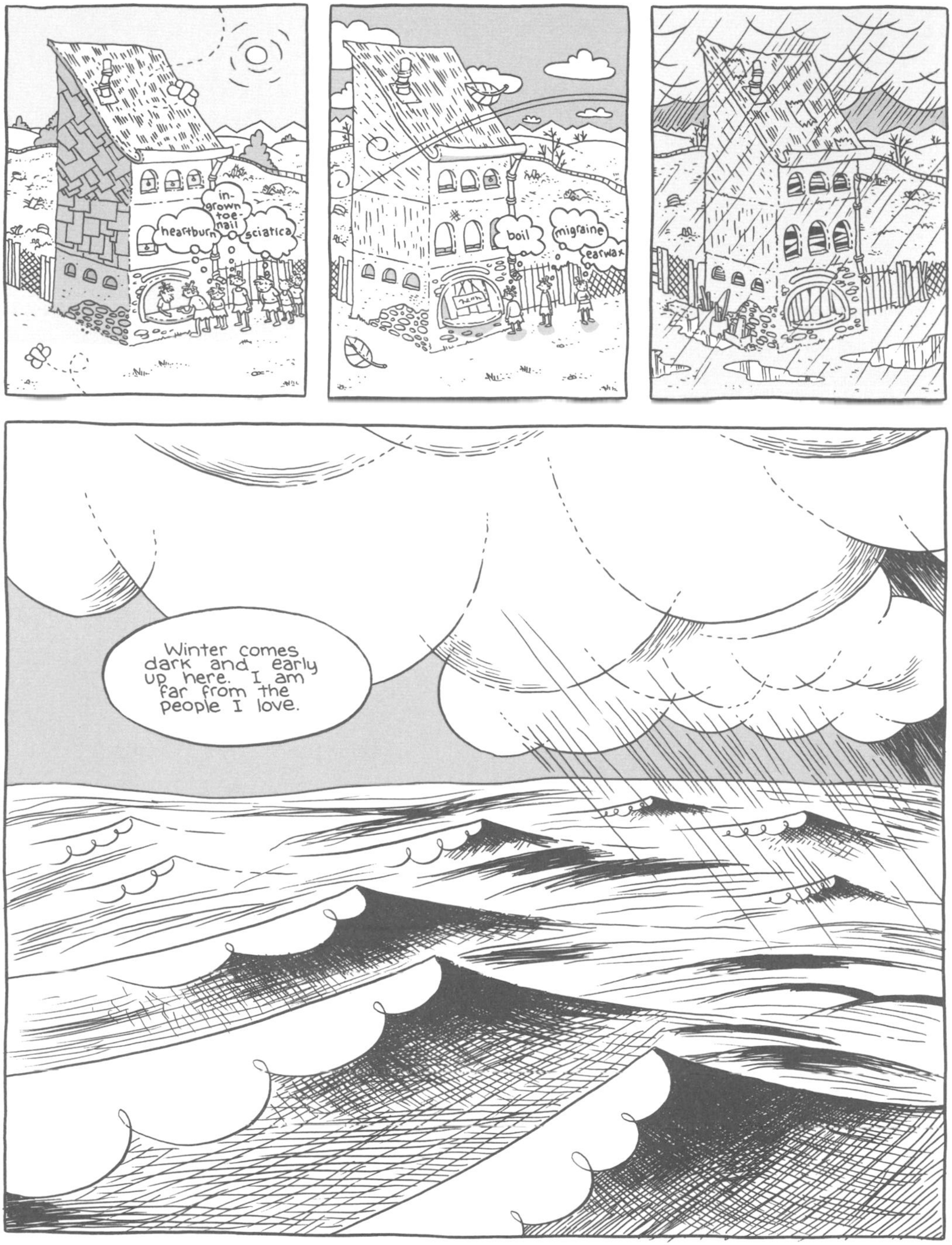
heartburn
in-grown toe-nail
sciatica
boil
migraine
earwax
Winter comes dark and early up here. I am far from the people I love.

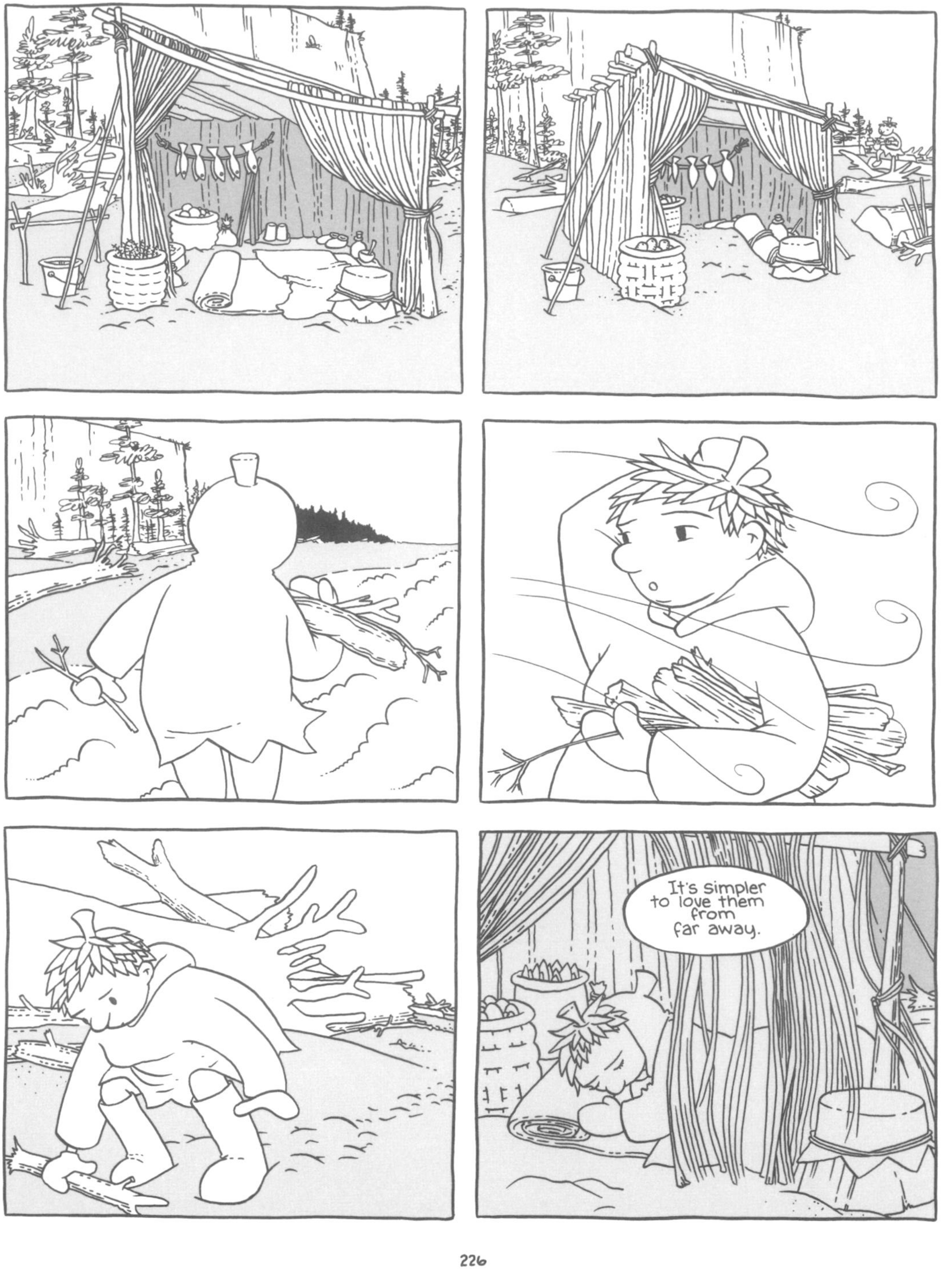
It's simpler to love them from far away.

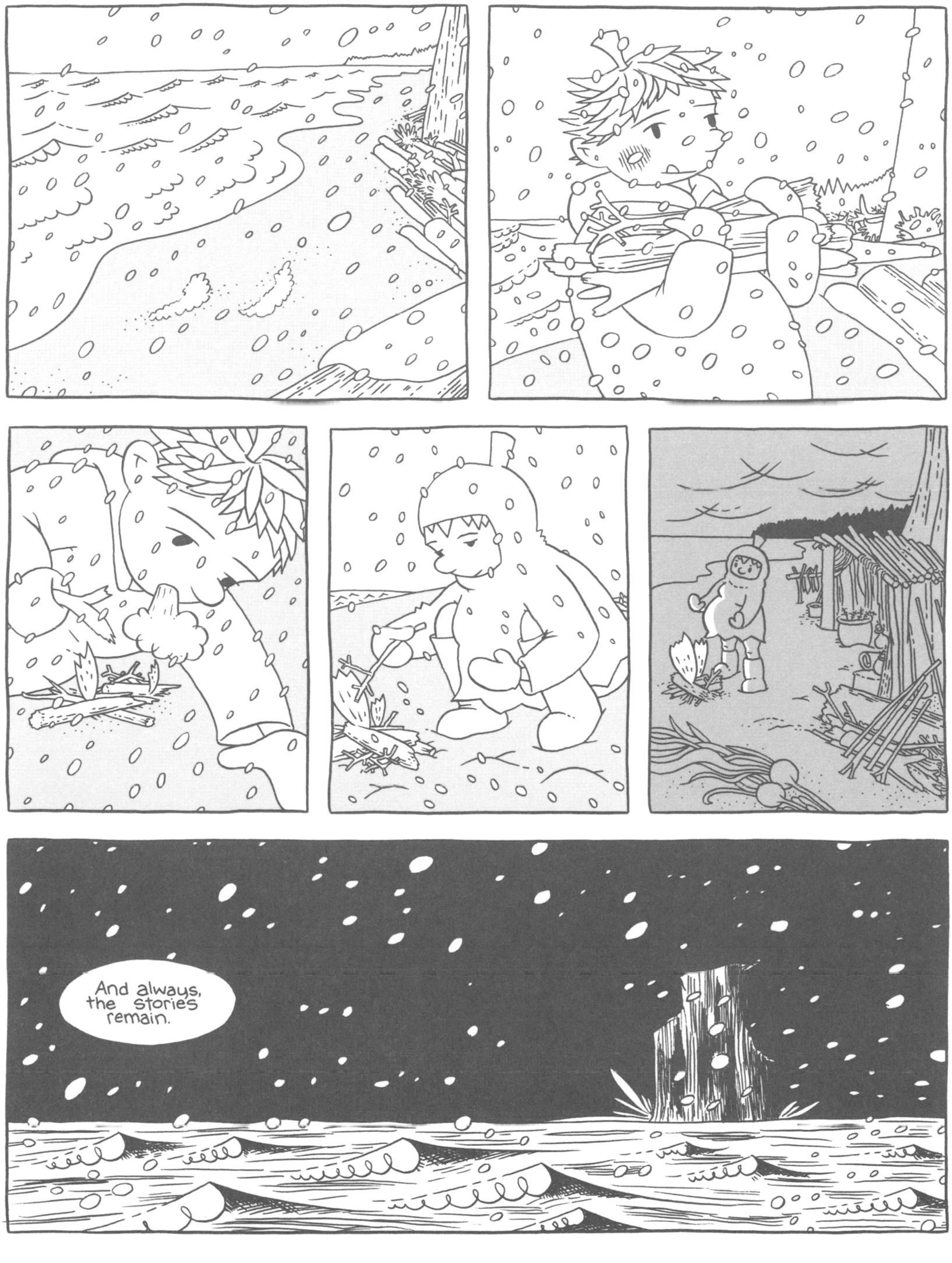
And always, the stories remain.

The
End.

Afterword

"Place" is not a character in this book. I dislike that conceit. But place did indeed turn out to be the essential idea of Artichoke Tales. While creating the places in the Artichoke world, I returned over and over, both physically and in my head to these places on planet Earth: the alpine lakes and meadows of the Cascade Range, the beaches of the Washington Coast, and the Central branch of the Brooklyn Public Library. Those three special places, long may they live. And while I'm discussing planet Earth, I want to offer the following caveat. The world I made for the Artichoke people bears a resemblance to our planet and borrows heavily from its natural history. But it is, I'm sure you realize, a fictional world, with a lot of made up stuff. The information in this book is not to be used as a resource for mushroom hunting, herbal remedies or any other non-fictional purpose!

Artichoke Tales was many years and miles in the making, spanning two centuries and the continent of North America. People from all over helped me. Thank you so much to: Jordan Crane, Tom Devlin, Randy Chang, Brooke Corey, Tim Kreider, Virginia Haedt, Ellen Lindner, Aaron Cometbus, Rob Clough, Paulo Patricio and the whole Porto gang, Myla Goldberg, Lynsey Becher, Jenny Lowery, David Chick, Kristen Chick, Mark Wheeler, Jason Lutes, Katie Kelso, Duncan Kelso, Glena Kelso, Jenny Smith and Michael Buckley. There were four books that kept me company during the making of Artichoke Tales. I offer my thanks and admiration to the authors of these books: "The Face of Battle" by John Keegan, "Honey, Mud, Maggots and Other Medical Marvels" by Robert Scott Root-Bernstein and Michele Root-Bernstein, "Mountaineering: Freedom of the Hills" by the Seattle Mountaineers Club, and "Remembering Ahanagran" by Richard White.

Thank you also to the many comics readers over the years who saw bits of this book in minicomics, on the web and in anthologies. It helped to know you were out there.

Megan Kelso
Seattle, Washington
January, 2010

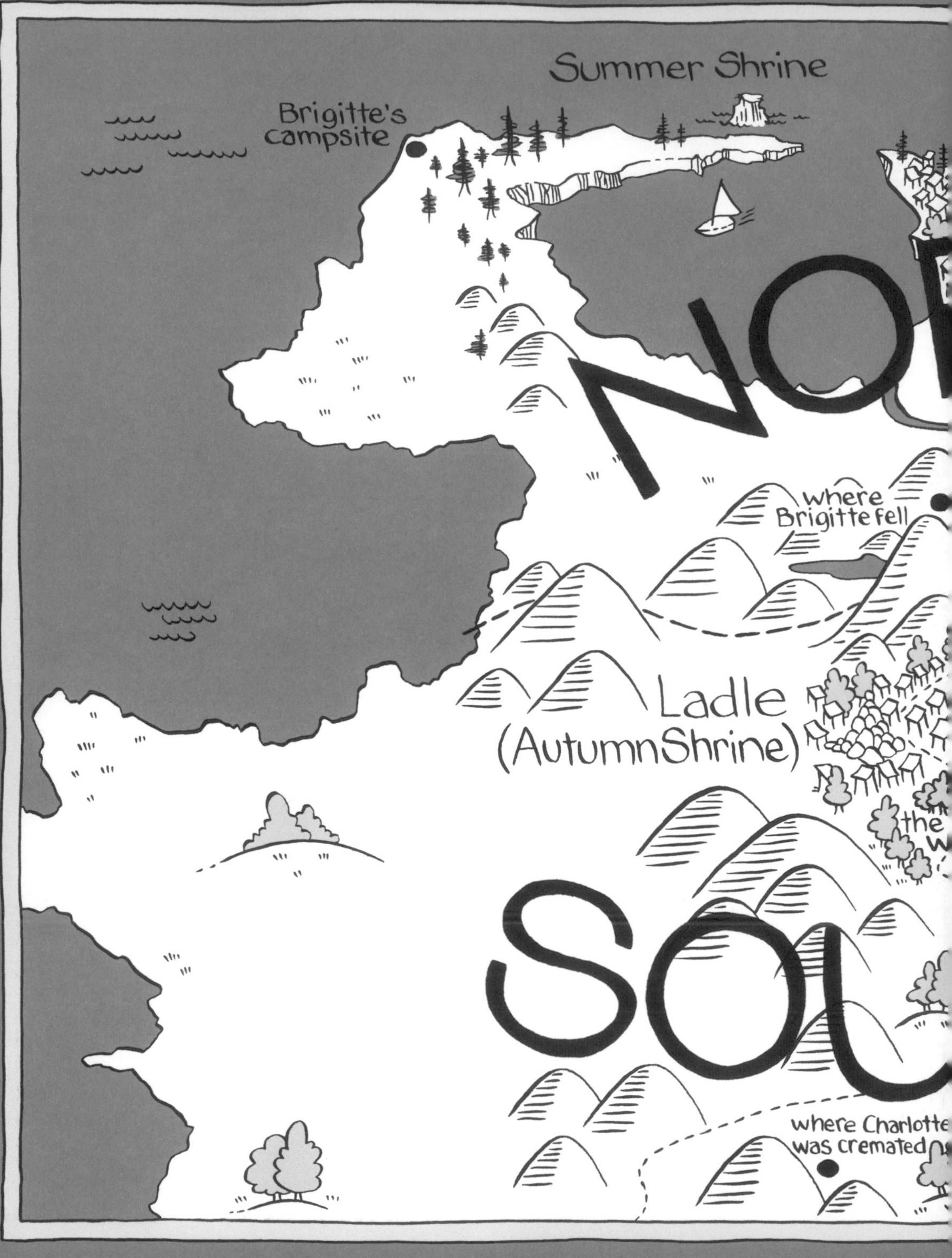
Summer Shrine
Brigitte's campsite
where Brigitte fell
Ladle (AutumnShrine)
where Charlotte was cremated